Dynamics of the Changing Global Security Order

Dynamics of the Changing Global Security Order

Emerging Trends and Key Issues in Asia

Edited by
Senthan Selvarajah, Nesrin Kenar, and
Lorenzo Fiorito

LEXINGTON BOOKS
Lanham • Boulder • New York • London

Published by Lexington Books
An imprint of The Rowman & Littlefield Publishing Group, Inc.
4501 Forbes Boulevard, Suite 200, Lanham, Maryland 20706
www.rowman.com

86-90 Paul Street, London EC2A 4NE

British Library Cataloguing in Publication Information Available

Library of Congress Cataloging-in-Publication Data Available

ISBN: 978-1-66694-913-1 (cloth)
ISBN: 978-1-66694-914-8 (electronic)

Contents

List of Figures

Acknowledgments

This book would not have been possible without the enthusiasm, support, patient, and cooperation of the chapter contributors, so we owe them many thanks. We would like to express our gratitude and appreciation to the team at Lexington Books for all their hard work, support, and expertise. We are grateful to Joseph C. Parry, Executive Acquisitions Editor (International Relations and Political Science) at Lexington Books, and Anna Debiec, Assistant Acquisitions Editor (International Relations and Political Science) at Lexington Books, for their commitment, advice, and support to complete this book project. We shall not forget to acknowledge the invaluable comments provided by anonymous reviewers, which we have taken on board.

Senthan Selvarajah, Nesrin Kenar, and Lorenzo Fiorito

The Changing Global Security Order

An Introduction

Nesrin Kenar,[1] Senthan Selvarajah,[2]
and Lorenzo Fiorito[3]

There is an inherent problem with analyzing current events: they change quickly. By the time authors have captured the essence of those experiences to create a record, evaluated that distilled reading against their framework's hypotheses, and put analysis into print, their work is—at least partly—out of date. Just as astronomers track shifts in starlight—millennia after the star itself has changed position—so observers of history must constantly and humbly acknowledge the limits of their ability to "know."

And this, in the Age of Twitter.

This book has faced that problem. From the time it was conceptually conceived to the time it went to press, at least two seismic changes to the global security order had taken place: the US military withdrawal from Afghanistan and Russia's invasion of Ukraine. Tensions with China predated both of these developments. Each of these situations, in its own way, contributes to changes in the global security order.

THE US'S WITHDRAWAL FROM AFGHANISTAN AND FREEZING OF AFGHANISTAN'S ASSETS

On August 15, 2021, Taliban fighters entered Kabul. The Afghan President went into exile (Ward, Lister, Dewan, and Mehsud, 2021). Simultaneously, the Biden administration froze $9 billion' worth of Afghanistan's Central Bank assets abroad (Mohsin, 2021). Two decades since the United States invaded Afghanistan after September 11, an era seems to have closed.

The measure of freezing Afghanistan's assets in place of military confrontation with the Taliban seems to uphold Luttwak's hypothesis (Luttwak,

1990) that economic tactics could replace military measures in some areas of security thinking. Increasingly, analysts have commented that a geoeconomic world order may have begun to take shape (Roberts, Moraes, and Ferguson, 2018). This model would involve close cooperation between states' interests and their financial and commercial sectors' behavior—including that of explicitly national actors like sovereign wealth funds and state-owned enterprises (Babic, 2021).

In other words, it is possible that while the United States proved unable to control the Taliban through "boots on the ground" in the War on Terror, it now believes it can do so more effectively through measures that invoke regulatory control over the financial and banking system, including targeted sanctions and asset freezes. This could reflect a more generalized approach to the international security order, where economic tactics achieve strategic security objectives.

Today, neither the practice of direct American military intervention nor its role as the single global hegemon of the world order can be taken for granted. Thus, the global security order that depended on its position is under challenge.

RUSSIA'S INVASION OF UKRAINE

Geoeconomics is not, however, the only pathway forward. Russia's invasion of Ukraine on February 24, 2022, has implications that stand in diametric opposition to this introduction's speculation about a geoeconomic world order.

While NATO formally remains on the sidelines, Ukraine continues to appeal for NATO involvement (Deliso, 2022). There is a credible geopolitical threat to global stability for the first time since the Cold War. Thirty-three years after the fall of the Berlin Wall, a new era may have opened: the "return of geopolitics," as Mead phrased it (Mead, 2014).

This new era, if that is what it proves to be, will be dangerous. At the time of writing (late May, 2022). It appears unlikely that Russia or Ukraine will emerge as a victor in the short term. Meanwhile, Switzerland made a nearly unheard-of exception to its neutrality policy (He, 2022; Revill, 2022), leveraging its banking sector to impose sanctions and asset freezes on Russian targets. Formerly neutral Finland and Sweden have applied to join NATO (Wright, 2022).

"We're now facing a fundamentally changed security environment in Europe," the *Washington Post* reported Swedish Prime Minister Magdalena Andersson as saying. The NATO Secretary General, Jens Stoltenberg, agreed that Finland's and Sweden's accession would be a "turning point for security" in Europe (Hudson, Morris, Bisset, and Berger, 2022). CBS reported:

> Finland's accession to NATO will cause serious damage to bilateral Russian–Finnish relations and maintenance of stability and security in the Northern European region," the [Russian] Foreign Ministry said. "Russia will be forced to take retaliatory steps, both of a military-technical and other nature, to neutralize the threats to its national security that arise from this. (CBS News, 2022)

For its part, India has taken a strident tone in support of Russia. As a UN Security Council vote on Ukraine loomed, India cited "US neo-primacy" as a factor in voting against the discussion on Ukraine (Express Tribune, 2022). In response to a question from the Norwegian foreign minister Huitfeldt, Indian foreign minister Jaishankar stated: "You talked about Ukraine. I remember less than a year ago what happened in Afghanistan, where the entire civil society was thrown under the bus by the world. We in Asia face our own sets of challenges, which often has an impact on the rules-based order." Ursula von der Leyen of the European Commission commented that the invasion of Ukraine would "deeply affect the Indo-Pacific region and the rest of the world" (Roy, 2022).

FALLOUT FROM RUSSIA'S INVASION OF UKRAINE

Back in 1997, George F. Kennan questioned the wisdom of expanding NATO. He wrote that (Kennan, 1997):

> expanding NATO would be the most fateful error of American policy in the entire post-cold-war era. Such a decision may be expected to inflame the nationalistic, anti-Western and militaristic tendencies in Russian opinion; to have an adverse effect on the development of Russian democracy; to restore the atmosphere of the cold war to East-West relations, and to impel Russian foreign policy in directions decidedly not to our liking.

In addition to his questionable motivations of upholding international law, supporting the right of self-determination, and de-Nazifying Ukraine, Russian leader Putin more accurately expressed his fear of NATO expansion to Russia's borders as his reason to invade (The Spectator, 2022). However, in the same speech announcing Russia's attack on Ukraine, he also cited countries that are now permanently destabilized or nonexistent after US or NATO intervention: Iraq, Libya, Syria, and the former Yugoslavia. Rather ominously in this context, Putin stated: "our plans do not include the occupation of Ukrainian territories."

The Russian intervention experience in Syria could provide a mooring for this statement. According to Jones (2022),

> Russian leaders wanted to stabilize Syria, which was under threat, as a strategically-important hub for Moscow in the Middle East . . . . Russian leaders assessed that the United States and its partners were attempting to overthrow Bashar al-Assad's regime and either replace it with a friendly government or leave behind a collapsed state. Russian officials were influenced by the U.S. military campaigns in the Balkans, Afghanistan, Iraq, Libya, and other countries, where they concluded that the United States had repeatedly demonstrated an ability and willingness to destabilize and even overthrow regimes.

This leads to one branch of speculation conspicuously absent from much coverage of the developing security situation. Putin's motivation may not be to annex Ukraine in full, as he did the Crimean Peninsula in 2014. Rather, it may be to create a permanently destabilized zone in the heart of Europe, from which crisis could easily spill over.

Russia's invasion of Ukraine now elicits sober considerations of the relative value of hard power—the very dynamic that the liberal international order was designed to forestall under the Bretton Woods agreement (World Trade Organization, 2022). Certainly, Western responses to Russia's invasion imply a pivot away from the geopolitical architecture that made the post-war order possible. Yet, some Indian commentators indicate nuance to the possibilities that could emerge. Talukdar (2023) writes of Indian engagement with Europe,

> Notwithstanding the Ukraine war—a development that is causing tectonic shifts in global geopolitics—New Delhi and Brussels are showing political will, determination and maturity in not letting differences over one issue disturb the tempo that is moving towards rapid formalisation of [their] partnership. [Indian Prime Minister] Modi's ongoing visit to Europe, his engagement with the continent's powerhouses in Germany and France and his attention toward Europe's Scandinavian subregions are but one dimension of the evolving multi-faceted, multi-dimensional relationship.

The Ukraine invasion indicates the post–World War II liberal international order is in serious trouble. Some are declaring it dead (Rodrik, 2022). The invasion of Ukraine, accompanied by the expansion of NATO, could be a tacit admission by all actors that this prognosis is correct.

FAILINGS OF THE PRESENT GLOBAL ORDER AND THE RISE OF CHINA

Certainly, the world order is due for a change. If, as Ikenberry argued, "the three components of liberal international order [are] *liberal democracy*, *economic interdependence*, and *international institutions*" (Ikenberry, 2011, p. 64), then each of these three pillars may be seriously compromised.

First, several *international institutions* of the liberal world order are in serious trouble. For example, even the institutional architects of post-war liberalism now question its economic underpinnings. The International Monetary Fund, one of the original Bretton Woods institutions, is among those now questioning the wisdom of neoliberalism (Ostry, 2022).

For decades, the United Nations has been all but immobile. This is partly thanks to severe budget constraints (UN Affairs, 2019) and the Security Council's structural deadlock (UN Security Council, 2017), where opposing vetoes make it near-impossible to achieve cooperation. (Indeed, President Obama's (2020) recent memoir, *A Promised Land*, included his opinion that the Security Council's paralysis had contributed to UN member states' failure to "reconstruct failing states like Somalia, or prevent an ethnic slaughter in places like Sri Lanka."

Meanwhile, in apparent response to China's use of the World Trade Organization (WTO) to its advantage—or, perhaps, due to perceptions of the multilateral organization's overreach—the United States continues to cripple the Appellate Body, the highest decision-making body of the WTO (US Trade Representative, 2020). The WTO is the successor to the post–World War II *General Agreement on Tariffs and Trade*, a crucial part of Bretton Woods' architecture for global economic integration.

Second, this challenge to liberal international institutions helps to illustrate the ongoing disruption of global *economic interdependence*. China is asserting itself as a global economic power—and as a contender for leadership of the global order. Both China and Russia have publicly proclaimed their allegiance to the concept of a "multipolar world order" in which no single hegemon emerges. Both countries have also engaged directly with the Taliban government of Afghanistan (Devonshire-Ellis, 2022).

So far, China has projected state power through the broad reach of its infrastructure financing and commercial strategy—the Belt and Road Initiative (BRI), led largely by cooperation between China's state diplomatic strategy and the interests of its state-owned enterprises (Qiong, 2017; Kirchner, 2021). China's rise has prompted a US–China trade war—initiated by President Trump (Brown and Kolb, 2022) in the name of national security interests. In the name of national security, the Biden Administration has continued parts of this policy over Chinese products like neodymium magnets (US Dept. of Commerce, 2021).

While tensions rose, neither side seemed interested in escalating this trade war into a military confrontation. In place of cooperation, however, the US Chamber of Commerce has sounded alarm bells about an economic "decoupling" between the United States and China (China Center, 2021). This feeds speculation that a "multipolar world" would see regional blocs take precedence over global economic integration.

Investment bank Morgan Stanley's research arm noted that (Morgan Stanley, 2020):

> While it's impossible to make sweeping generalizations about the realities of a broader world order, multipolarity tends to favor companies and sectors whose supply chains are not globally complex and whose products and services don't pose a threat to economic or national security. Even better positioned are companies that could become stronger regional champions, with services key to national interests and perhaps better protected from competitive pressures. Conversely, companies, industries and sectors that have globally integrated supply chains, especially those with technology and health security liabilities, could be increasingly vulnerable to multipolar trade and national or economic security policy trends.

Thus, multipolarity and economic decoupling appear to be linked; both manifest a trend away from globalization and toward regionalization. The possible multipolar world—and, by extension, the possible geoeconomic world order—contains many unforeseen configurations. However, the linkage between economic interests and national security has never been more straightforward than it is today.

Under Ikenberry's rubric, the final pillar of the liberal international order is *liberal democracy*. A state's actions on the world stage are not automatically linked to its domestic policy. But, in our view, nothing about the Trump administration's conduct demonstrated it's inner "will to power" so forcefully as the failed insurrection of January 6, 2021. It is also noteworthy that China's illiberal domestic approach underpins its ability to expand its international reach—for it does business without imposing human rights conditionalities on Belt and Road participant countries (Human Rights Watch, 2019).

Liberal democracy is under challenge from populism throughout the Western world. Even in India, the world's largest democracy, its limits have been tested. In states like China, it does not exist.

Thus, to summarize, all three pillars of the liberal international order are under attack, if not yet completely demolished. The United States is deeply introspective about its future and seems skeptical about the merits of foreign intervention. China projects power economically but seemingly has little desire to engage the United States militarily. Russia does not appear to share China's inhibition—daring NATO to act as it plunges Ukraine into potentially long-lasting turmoil. India maintains its long-standing friendship with Russia but engages in diplomacy with Europe.

The Russian invasion of Ukraine points to one route away from liberalism—the return of geopolitics. The global security order could revert into anarchy, with international relations being determined by military capabilities, threats, and the will to carry out those threats. This has been the reality of many Asian, African, and Latin American states at different points since the end of World War II; Europe and North America could experience it again.

The current American approach to Afghanistan, and trade wars between the United States and China, point to an alternative route. A geoeconomic world order could avoid the "Thucydides Trap" (Allison, 2017), the situation where a rising and declining power engages in war to determine their rank. Similarly, India exerts its influence through economic cooperation with Europe, even while it defends Russia's attack on Ukraine. A geoeconomic arrangement of global security is thus one viable candidate to replace the near-moribund liberal international order. If a global system of rules is insufficient to contain tensions between states, then economic competition could fill the role that military brinksmanship once played.

ABOUT THE CHAPTERS OF THIS BOOK

This book brings knowledge, insights, and understanding of why and how the US-led unipolar world order is shifting more in a multipolar direction under the influence of the power contests involving economic and military weaponry and the impact this transformation will have on international security and thus the challenges, crises, and risks that mankind faces.

It offers a systematic exploration of the evolving new (theoretical) positions such as geoeconomics, socioeconomic-political and cultural implications, tensions at the national, regional, and global levels, as well as debates, trends, policies, practices, and examples concerning the power and international relations praxis in the form of cutting-edge articles from scholars and experts with diverse cultural, social, and geographical backgrounds.

It is designed not only for students and teachers of Political Science and International Relations but also for all those interested in politics and current affairs wanting to know how power competition between states and relations between them condition their security in the Asian region.

The volume is divided into the following five sections:

Part I: The Rise of China and the Power Struggle in Asia

China's strategic position in the Eurasian landmass, its gigantic conventional military force, its growth as the world's second largest economic power, and its nuclear arsenal capacity have made China a major power heavily influencing the changing global security order. Knowledge about China's capabilities is essential to understand the changing dynamics of global security. Part one of this book consists of four chapters highlighting how China's rise challenges the neoliberal, post–Cold War order in several ways as it seeks to reshape its sphere of influence in Asia. The first chapter, which follows this introduction, written by *John Miglietta*, examines Central Asia in international politics and geopolitics in international relations, as well as the history of the region in modern times and its incorporation as part of the Russian Empire/Soviet Union. The region's political dynamics are discussed with emphasis on political changes in Kyrgyzstan and the civil war in Tajikistan. The foreign policies of China, Russia, and the United States, as well as mid-level power in the region, are examined. The energy sources and the environmental implications of the Soviet period are examined, focusing on the Aral Sea and nuclear testing in Kazakhstan. The second chapter, authored by *Lorenzo Fiorito*, analyzes the nexus between geoeconomics, sovereign debt, and state sovereignty through a case study of the China-Sri Lanka Colombo Port City Project. This chapter shows that the Colombo Port City project displays a hybridity between two traditionally competing frameworks: geopolitics and international economic law. The logic behind the proposed Port City thus embodies what this chapter interprets as the "geoeconomic world order." The third chapter, coauthored by *Rajib Timalsina and Indivar Paudel* analyze the announced agendas, activities, and recent initiatives of Quadrilateral Security Dialogue (QUAD), particularly aiming at unpacking the implications—economic, political, strategic and regional—of this endeavor by the major and rising world powers. This chapter places special attention on China, an influential player in South Asia, and its BRI to understand whether the agendas of QUAD are motivated at countering China and BRI or to gain the national-multilateral interest of these four nations in securing a peaceful and stable Indo-Pacific that is inclusive and resilient. Probable benefits to the nations in the region and the possibility of great power rivalry and polarization in the region are discussed to demystify what QUAD holds for South Asia. The fourth chapter by *Muamer Hirkić, examines* China's position in the Western-led order and involvement in global flows, its place in the so-called "Asian century" and the "post–American world," as well as the consequences of its actions on the neighboring countries and the US-dominated world.

Part II: The Changing Nature of Warfare and Weaponry

The use of Private Military Company (PMC) and military drones in wars, the freezing of foreign reserves, and the ever-increasing arms race between superpowers directly impact the changing global security. These realist approaches to security pose a threat to the liberal order as they treat national security as a zero-sum game. This part comprises five chapters, aiming to discuss these security issues in detail. The fifth chapter by *Ushmayo Bhattacharya* leverages Strategic culture as the prism of analysis to draw out the stagnancy of scholarship on understandings of security in the new millennium. It draws from the argument of Edward Lock, of the Second Generation of Strategic Culture theorists, which aims to problematize the taken-for-granted status that states have enjoyed in their erstwhile understandings of security and to give agency to other upcoming actors within the domain of security; namely the PMC, an enterprise that is becoming increasingly instrumental in international conflicts all over the world. The sixth chapter by *Ghazala Yasmin Jalil* focuses on the emerging US–Russia arms race, the US–China rivalry, and their implications for global security. It also discusses how the global arms races would impact regional races/competitions like India–Pakistan. The seventh chapter of *Hafssa Fakher Elabiari* brings to light the impact of military drone possession on power and risk-taking behavior in war-torn countries. Using the case study of Turkish and Emirati drones in Libya between 2019 and 2020, the chapter scrutinizes how the possession of military drones inflates a country's power and appetite for risk and erases the operational barriers linked to foreign intervention, thus creating an encouraging environment for reckless moves and clash durability. The eighth chapter, contributed by *Michael Larrick* explains how domestic issues can drive international and domestic security policy. He uses the executive order issued by the US government on February 11, 2022, to block the foreign reserves of Afghanistan's Da Afghanistan Bank (DAB) as a case study to explain this proposition. As he argues, through one lens, this announcement and following order was a continuation, if the escalation, of a long-standing US policy to leverage its position as a nexus of global finance to pursue national security interests, and through another lens, this announced a marked departure from previous exercises, expropriating another country's assets with no due process and having little pretense of legality either domestically or internationally. The ninth chapter by *Aslam Khan* examines the implications of the US withdrawal from Afghanistan on the global order, focusing on realist theory. On the one hand, this chapter argues that while jihadist elements around the world see the US's withdrawal from Afghanistan as a victory, it has provided motivation for their future endeavors, and on the other hand, it has weakened the US's position in the global order and surrendered Afghanistan to actors with whom America has fought for decades. This chapter focuses on how this withdrawal has led China and Pakistan to act on an axis and how Pakistan's alignment with the Taliban has created a setback for India.

Part III: Sociological Approaches to Conflicts and Security

The role of social factors in conditioning the changing global security order and proposing solutions to the tensions and concerns is extremely important. The three chapters included in this section focus on how win–win solution-oriented and people-centered cooperation and collaboration can address security threats and lead to peace. *Iqbal Shailo*, in the tenth chapter, advocates for an "Organic Regional Security Model" (ORSM) in the South Asian region as an alternative security framework to construct collective identity, regional solidarity, and mutual trust. A South Asian security concept would be premature if imposed or constructed by other (outsiders/super) powers. This chapter places its main emphasis on security integration approaches to put forward an argument for an ORSM in the South Asian region as an alternative security paradigm to build collective identity, regional solidarity, and mutual trust. The eleventh chapter by *Siavash Chavoshi and Mohammad Reza Saeidabadi*, opens up a nonmaterialistic interpretation of states' provocative and conflict-seeking behavior through misrecognition, ontological insecurity, and the role of historical trauma in constructing states' conflictual behavior in a Hegelian fashion. This chapter interprets state conflict-seeking behaviors by the actors' desire for recognition and ontological security through the master and slave dialectic. It embarks on a qualitative study of a single case, focusing on the Islamic Republic of Iran's foreign policy choices by mainly focusing on two historical traumas in Iran: the US/British coup of 1953 against Prime Minister Mossadegh and also the US withdrawal from the Iranian nuclear agreement formally known as the Joint Comprehensive Plan of Action (JCPOA). The twelfth chapter of *Mehmet Babacan* focuses on the political, social, economic, and other structural reasons for the ongoing crises by highlighting the current situation and conflicts of the Middle East and North Africa (MENA) region within the scope of the Arab Spring wave. Current problems of the MENA region in the context of Tunisia, Egypt, Libya, Syria, and Yemen, which were affected by the Arab Spring, and its relationship with the social and economic structure of the Middle East are also discussed in this chapter.

Part IV: Coercion, Culture, and Environment in International Relations

Beyond the proliferation of destructive weapons between countries, various coercive strategies, cultural influence on political decision-making and political behavior, and the environment as an on-traditional security issue are increasingly important factors influencing the changing global security order. Three chapters included in this part concentrate on how these three factors relate to the evolving security order. In light of the Iranian nuclear crisis, the thirteenth chapter by *Jean Yves Ndzana Ndzana*, analyzes the notion of coercion in international relations, its nature, its forms, and its different mechanisms. Further, this chapter examines the various coercive strategies adopted by the US administration to compel the Iranian republic government under Ahmadinejad to reverse its nuclear programme. The fourteenth chapter by *Tamta Tskhovrebadze*, aims to depict different approaches toward cultural policies in international relations, identify convergence and disparities, especially while yoked to the "soft power" concept, and better understand the complexity of cultural policies in different national and international contexts. This chapter suggests rethinking cultural imperialism and resistance as an increasingly acute trend for countries with strong anti-hegemonic or self-hegemonic aspirations. Its focus on contemporary issues in international relations is maintained from the glances of disparities between cultural understandings, aspirations of states toward its relevance to contemporary political behaviors, and interest-based decisions making patterns. The fifteenth chapter, authored by *Adriano Mortada*, sheds light on the importance of addressing water security, which has emerged as an essential concept that encapsulates several objectives for managing water resources. It is increasingly gaining attention throughout global debates and agendas proposed by governments and international organizations. This chapter identifies the key challenges related to water security, followed by an in-depth analysis of the main issues.

Part V: Effects of Responses to the COVID-19 Pandemic on International Order

The COVID-19 pandemic has exposed the realpolitik of global health security. Global COVID-19 vaccine diplomatic efforts have revealed several bitter truths about international relations and resonated with the changing and complex global security realities. Two chapters are included in this final section to understand what dimension the COVID-19 pandemic is creating for the changing global security order. The sixteenth chapter by *Paulina Kanarek* aims to analyze the motivations behind China's mask diplomacy by uncovering the long-term foreign policy goals in selected regions. This chapter answers the following research questions through empirical investigation: Why is Chinese mask diplomacy a success in some places and a failure in others? What factors determine its effectiveness? An in-depth analysis of the contrasting attitudes toward China in Europe and Latin America sheds light on the future of the BRI in the post–COVID-19 world. The seventeeth chapter, written by *Maheen Farhat Raza and Muhammad Ali Raza*, explores the trajectory of militant organizations in the wake of COVID-19. This chapter grounds its argument on the assertion made in the Global Terrorism Index report, which found an increase in far-right violent maneuvers when compared to other forms of violent extremism, and at the same time, attempts to elaborate on the factors that motivate far-right groups to engage in violence.

The conclusion chapter by *Lorenzo Fiorito*, *Senthan Selvarajah, and Nesrin Kenar* highlights the book's argument that the global security order is changing due to the tension between a rules-based liberal international order and a world order characterized by power contests involving economic and military weaponry and underlines how each chapter in this book supports this hypothesis.

NOTES

1. N. Kenar. Sakarya University, Sakarya, Turkey. Email: nkenar@sakarya.edu.tr
2. S. Selvarajah. Centre for Media, Human Rights and Peacebuilding, London, UK. Email: senthan.selvarajah@cmhrp.org
3. L.Fiorito. Centre for Media, Human Rights and Peacebuilding, London, UK. Email: Lorenzo.fio@protonmail.com

BIBLIOGRAPHY

Allison, G. (2017). 'The Thucydides Trap' (9 June 2017) *Foreign Policy* https://foreignpolicy.com/2017/06/09/the-thucydides-trap/ accessed 22 May 2022.

Babic, M. (2021). 'State Capital in a Geoeconomic World: Mapping State-Led Foreign Investment in the Global Political Economy' (27 October 2021) *Review of International Political Economy* https://doi.org/10.1080/09692290.2021.1993301

Brown, C. P., and Kolb, M. (2022). Trump's Trade War Timeline: An Up-to-Date Guide' (10 May) Peterson Institute for International Economics https://www.piie.com/blogs/trade-investment-policy-watch/trump-trade-war-china-date-guide accessed 22 May 2022.

CBS News. (2022). 'Russia Fumes as Finland and Sweden Push for NATO Membership' (13 May) https://www.cbsnews.com/news/finland-nato-russia-sweden-ukraine-united-states-vladimir-putin/ accessed 22 May 2022.

China Center. (2021). US Chamber of Commerce, 'Understanding US–China Decoupling: Macro Trends and Industry Impacts'. https://www.uschamber.com/assets/archived/images/024001_us_china_decoupling_report_fin.pdf accessed 22 May 2022.

Deliso, M. (2022). 'How NATO Factors into the Ukraine–Russia Conflict' (25 February) *ABC News* https://abcnews.go.com/International/nato-factors-ukraine-russia-conflict/story?id=83090926 accessed 22 May 2022.

Devonshire-Ellis, C. (2022). 'China, Russia Stand Firm in 'New, Fair, Multipolar World Order' (30 March) https://www.china-briefing.com/news/china-russia-stand-firm-in-new-fair-multipolar-world-order/ accessed 22 May 2022.

Express Tribune. (2022). 'India Sides with Russia in Ukraine Crisis, Poses Challenge to "US Neo-Primacy"' (4 February) https://tribune.com.pk/story/2341959/india

-sides-with-russia-in-ukraine-crisis-poses-challenge-to-us-neo-primacy accessed 22 May 2022.

He, L. (2022). 'Switzerland Ditches Neutrality to Sanction Russia and Putin' (1 March) *CNN Business* https://edition.cnn.com/2022/03/01/business/switzerland-sanction-russia-freeze-assets-intl-hnk/index.html accessed 22 May 2022.

Hudson, J., Morris, L., Bisset, V., and Berger, M. (2022). 'Ruling Parties in Sweden, Finland Back NATO Membership in Historic Shifts' (15 May) https://www.washingtonpost.com/world/2022/05/15/finland-nato-blinken-ukraine-turkey/ accessed 22 May 2022.

Human Rights Watch. (2019). 'China: "Belt and Road" Projects Should Respect Rights' (21 April) https://www.hrw.org/news/2019/04/21/china-belt-and-road-projects-should-respect-rights accessed 22 May 2022.

Ikenberry, J. (2011). *Liberal Leviathan: The Origins, Crisis, and Transformation of the American World Order*. Princeton University Press.

Jones, S. G. (2022). 'Chapter 2: Russian Goals and Strategy' in ed. Seth G. Jones, *Moscow's War in Syria* (Centre for Strategic and International Studies, May) https://www.csis.org/analysis/moscows-war-syria accessed 22 May 2022.

Kennan, G. F. (1997). 'A Fateful Error' (5 February) *New York Times* https://www.nytimes.com/1997/02/05/opinion/a-fateful-error.html accessed 22 February 2022.

Luttwak, E. N. (1990). 'From Geopolitics to Geoeconomics: Logic of Conflict, Grammar of Commerce' 20 *National Interest* (Summer) 17–23.

Mead, W. R. (2014). 'The Return of Geopolitics: The Revenge of the Revisionist Powers' (May/June) *Foreign Affairs* https://www.foreignaffairs.com/articles/china/2014-04-17/return-geopolitics accessed 22 May 2022.

Mohsin, S. (2021). 'U.S. Freezes Nearly $9.5 Billion Afghanistan Central Bank Assets' (17 August) *Bloomberg UK* https://www.bloomberg.com/news/articles/2021-08-17/u-s-freezes-nearly-9-5-billion-afghanistan-central-bank-assets accessed 22 May 2022.

Obama, B. (2020). *A Promised Land*. Penguin.

Ostry, J. D., Loungani, P., and Furceri, D. (2016). 'Neoliberalism: Oversold?' (June) 53(2) *Finance and Development* https://www.imf.org/external/pubs/ft/fandd/2016/06/ostry.htm accessed 22 May 2022.

Qiong, Y. (2017). 'Full Text of President Xi's Speech at Opening of B&R Forum' (15 May) *CGTN* https://news.cgtn.com/news/3d59444f33677a4d/share_p.html accessed 22 May 2022.

Revill, J. (2022). 'Analysis: Neutral Switzerland Leans Closer to NATO in Response to Russia' (16 May) https://www.reuters.com/markets/europe/neutral-switzerland-leans-closer-nato-response-russia-2022-05-15/ accessed 22 May 2022.

Roberts, A., Moraes, H. C., and Ferguson, V. (2018). 'The Geoeconomic World Order' (19 November) *Lawfare* https://www.lawfareblog.com/geoeconomic-world-order accessed 22 May 2022.

Rodrik, D. (2022). 'Ukraine Invasion Signals the Death of "Liberal" World Order. What Will Replace It?' (11 March) https://www.scmp.com/comment/opinion/article/3169923/ukraine-invasion-signals-death-liberal-world-order-what-will accessed 22 May 2022.

Roy, S. (2022). 'Jaishankar Ticks Off Europe: Ukraine a Wake-up Call to Look at Problems in Asia' (27 April) *Indian Express* https://indianexpress.com/article/india/wake-up-call-for-europe-to-also-look-at-asia-jaishankar-on-ukraine-conflict-7887995/ accessed 22 May 2022.

Stanley, M. (2020). 'Mapping the New Multipolar World Order' (19 August) https://www.morganstanley.com/ideas/coronavirus-global-geopolitics-investing accessed 22 May 2022.

Stephen Kirchner. 'A Geoeconomic Alliance: The Potential and Limits of Economic Statecraft' (30 September 2021) https://www.ussc.edu.au/analysis/a-geoeconomic-alliance-the-potential-and-limits-of-economic-statecraft accessed 22 May 2022.

Talukdar, K. (2022). 'Will Driving Strategic Convergence Beyond Differences' (4 May) First Post https://www.firstpost.com/opinion/an-assessment-of-eu-india-ties-as-modi-visits-europe-sheer-political-will-driving-strategic-convergence-beyond-differences-10629911.html accessed 28 June 2023.

The Spectator. (2022). 'Full Text: Putin's Declaration of War on Ukraine' (24 February 2022) https://www.spectator.co.uk/article/full-text-putin-s-declaration-of-war-on-ukraine accessed 22 May 2022.

UN Affairs. (2019). 'UN "Financial Crisis," Years in the Making, Guterres Tells Budget Body, Proposes Solutions' (5 June) *UN News* https://news.un.org/en/story/2019/06/1039851 accessed 22 May 2022.

UN Security Council. (2017). 'Members Warn that Persistent Deadlock Threatens Security Council's "Remaining Credibility," in Meeting on United States Air Strike Against Syria' SC/12783 (7 April) https://www.un.org/press/en/2017/sc12783.doc.htm accessed 22 May 2022.

US Dept. of Commerce. (2021). 'U.S. Department of Commerce Announces Section 232 Investigation into the Effect of Imports of Neodymium Magnets on U.S. National Security' (24 September) https://www.commerce.gov/news/press-releases/2021/09/us-department-commerce-announces-section-232-investigation-effect accessed 22 May 2022.

US Trade Representative. (2020). *Report on the Appellate Body of the World Trade Organization* (February).

Ward, C., Lister, T., Dewan, A., and Mehsud, S. (2021). 'Afghan President Ashraf Ghani Flees the Country as Taliban Forces Enter the Capital' (16 August) *CNN* https://edition.cnn.com/2021/08/15/asia/afghanistan-taliban-advances-kabul-intl/index.html accessed 22 May 2022.

World Trade Organization. 'The GATT Years: From Havana to Marrakesh' https://www.wto.org/english/thewto_e/whatis_e/tif_e/fact4_e.htm accessed 22 May 2022.

Wright, R. (2022). 'A "New Era" of NATO Expansion Deepens the Divide Between Russia and the West' (17 May) *New Yorker* https://www.newyorker.com/news/daily-comment/a-new-era-of-nato-expansion-deepens-the-divide-between-russia-and-the-west accessed 22 May 2022.

Part I

THE RISE OF CHINA AND THE POWER STRUGGLE IN ASIA

Chapter 1

Great Power Rivalry and the Politics of Central Asia

John Miglietta[1]

INTRODUCTION

This chapter discusses the geopolitics of Central Asia and the history of the region. The politics of the region are discussed with emphasis on political change in Kyrgyzstan and the civil war in Tajikistan. The foreign policies of China, Russia, and the United States, as well as mid-level powers in the region, are also examined. The significance of regional organizations such as the Commonwealth of Independent States (CIS) and the Shanghai Cooperation Organization (SCO) are discussed. The energy sources and the environmental implications of the Soviet period are examined, focusing on the Aral Sea and nuclear testing in Kazakhstan.

HISTORY OF CENTRAL ASIA

Central Asia has a long history of outside domination. In 330 BC Alexander the Great destroyed the Achaemenid Persian Empire as his army swept into Central Asia reaching as far east as Kabul and the Hindu Kush. Alexander's empire did not last long, as it was divided amongst his generals after his death. This led to a growth of Hellenistic influence in Central Asia. In 1219, the Mongols led by Genghis Khan swept through Central Asia and into the Middle East ending the Abbasid Empire. The Mongols were brutal, but they built transportation networks and efficient urban centers. In the early 1400s, Tamerlane came out of Central Asia and defeated the Ottoman Empire. In the sixteenth century, the Russians, having overthrown the Mongol yoke, began their march south and east which would eventually conclude with their occupation of Central Asia. In 1552, the Russians conquered Kazan, and in

1556 occupied Astrakhan at the mouth of the Volga River. This began a process of Russian military expeditions, military settlements, the establishment of protectorates, and the eventual dissolution of those protectorates with the establishment of direct Russian control.[2]

World War I and the Russian Revolution had a dramatic impact on this region. In the Caucuses independent republics in Armenia, Azerbaijan, and Georgia were established in May 1918. They very quickly began to fight each other after the withdrawal of German and Turkish forces at the end of World War I. After consolidating their power in Russia, the Bolsheviks reasserted control in 1920. The situation was not as threatening in Central Asia as the Bolsheviks quickly gained control by defeating the White Russian armies and various nationalist movements in the region.[3] The most serious threat to Bolshevik rule came from the Basmachi movement which began to proliferate at the end of 1920. The Basmachi resistance continued until the end of the 1920s.

THE IMPORTANCE OF CENTRAL ASIA

The disintegration of the Soviet Union in 1991 created fifteen new states overnight. In Central Asia five new states Kazakhstan, Kyrgyzstan, Tajikistan, Turkmenistan, and Uzbekistan occupying a territory of 1,542,000 square miles with a population of 56 million became independent. Central Asia is bordered by two great powers, Russia to the north and China to the east, while in the south; it borders Iran, as well as volatile Afghanistan.[4]

The geographical importance of Central Asia has been discussed for almost two centuries. It was the site of the "Great Game" in the nineteenth century. This was a quest for control by the British and Russian empires. Russia was expanding in the nineteenth century across the top of Asia and the British were in the process of consolidating their control of much of South Asia, centering on India. The British were seeking a buffer to protect India while the Russians were pushing down from North Asia. This competition for influence was in the area now known as Iran, Afghanistan, and territory lying to the north (parts of contemporary Tajikistan and Turkmenistan). Britain and France supported the Ottoman Empire in the nineteenth century to block the Russians from access to the Mediterranean. There have been various versions of the Great Game played out after World War I. The second version was the "northern tier" strategy adopted by both Britain and the United States after World War II to keep the Soviet Union away from the Persian Gulf and Western oil interests. This strategy focused on the countries of Turkey, Iran, and Pakistan and was formalized with the creation of the Baghdad Pact in 1955 later to be renamed The Central Treaty Organization (CENTO). The third version of this Great Game is currently ongoing. With the fall of the Soviet Union and the emergence of independent states in Central Asia, there is a quest for influence by the major powers Russia (to keep its influence) and China and the United States to expand theirs in the region. Regional powers Turkey and Iran are also seeking to expand their influence in this region.

The significance of geography has long been discussed as an important dynamic in international politics. In 1904, British geography H.J. Mackinder wrote his "The Geographical Pivot of History." Here he argued that whatever power controls the Heartland, which he defined as a component of the Eurasian landmass roughly corresponding to Central Asia today, would control the world.

SOVIET RULE

The Soviets divided the territories of Central Asia into various union republics, autonomous republics, and regions. The boundaries were drawn to suit Moscow as opposed to reflecting cultural or local economic factors. As a result, the republics contain minorities which have left open the possibility of ethnic-political conflict.[5] In Kazakhstan, ethnic Kazakhs compose only a small majority of the population. In Tajikistan, Uzbeks make up about 25% of the population. In the aftermath of the Iranian revolution, much of the literature devoted to Soviet Central Asia discussed the possibility of unrest and seemed to argue that this was the most vulnerable component of the Soviet empire. The Central Asian states were economically very vulnerable and dependent on Moscow. President Nazarbayev of Kazakhstan was a strong advocate of maintaining the Soviet Union. When it became apparent that the Soviet Union was disintegrating, President Nazarbayev worked to integrate the former Soviet republics into an organization that became the CIS.[6]

THE COMMONWEALTH OF INDEPENDENT STATES (CIS)

The Minsk Agreement in 1991 created the basis for the CIS. Belarus, Russia, and Ukraine signed it. Within days the five Central Asian Republics joined. The goals of the CIS are as follows:

- coordination of foreign and security policies
- establishment of a regional economic union
- distribution of the assets of the former Soviet Union
- environmental protection

- regulation of migration politics
- development of joint communications networks
- detection and punishment of organized crime.

The CIS has not been a very strong vehicle for reintegration, but it has served to keep Moscow as a player in the politics of the territories that formerly composed the Soviet Union. In the Central Asia Republics, the old communist leaders at independence remained in power by redefining themselves as nationalists. They maintained relations with Russia while at the same time cautiously opening to the West, especially the United States. The Central Asian states have authoritarian governments of varying degrees and have blocked dissent. In Kazakhstan and Turkmenistan, there was a strong cult of personality by the national leadership. All have the potential for internal conflict. Tajikistan experienced a civil war after independence. Russia sent peacekeeping forces, and the civil war ended with Islamic parties being brought into the government in a power-sharing arrangement. Uzbekistan remains the Central Asian nation that is most prone to destabilization. It has the largest population in the region, and there is a history of Islamic opposition. It also has potential conflicts with Tajikistan. About 25% of the population of Uzbekistan is ethnic Tajiks.

THE SIGNIFICANCE OF KAZAKHSTAN

Kazakhstan is the ninth largest country in the world. It is the only one of the Central Asian countries that directly borders Russia; it also has a long border with China. While Kazakhstan is a landlocked country its size and location means that all the land and transit routes connecting Eastern Europe with southern and eastern Asia go through Kazakhstan.[7] Kazakhstan cooperates with the Russian Federation on Air Defense as well as has Russian border guards policing the Kazakhstan–China border. Another important source of cooperation is the Russian (as well as American use) of Baikonur Cosmodrome in south-central Kazakhstan.

Kazakhstan produces 60% of the region's Gross Domestic Product due to its gas and oil wealth. The economic goal of President Nazarbayev was to use Kazakhstan's oil wealth to diversify economic development and turn it into a top fifty industrial power. In 2010, he launched a five-year plan to make this a reality. In December 2012, he announced at the World Economic Forum that his country was on the brink of breaking into the top fifty industrialized powers. GDP growth was 4.9% in 2012, which was a decline from previous years. The distribution of Kazakhstan's GDP for 2012 was 56.9% for services, 37.9% for energy and industrial production, and 5.2% for agriculture.

Its major exports are oil, gas, and uranium. The World Bank reported that Kazakhstan had improved its business climate but needs to curb corruption and revamp labor laws and regulations.[8] As a result of the COVID-19 pandemic, the Kazakh economy has declined. There has been a slight increase in unemployment. Poverty is rising and is projected to rise to 12.7%. GDP is anticipated to contract by 2.5%. Economic recovery is uncertain due to the pandemic and uncertainty over the global oil demand. Government debt is likely to rise to 30% of GDP. The World Bank has identified three economic areas that need reform: (1) diversity of the economy by focusing on non-raw materials and reforms in the financial sector; (2) limiting the domination of large state-owned companies and encouraging competition; and (3) strengthening public sector institutions and the fostering of legal reforms to attract investment.[9]

AMERICAN INTERESTS IN CENTRAL ASIA: AN OVERVIEW

American goals in Central Asia can be summed up as follows: increase stability, facilitate democratization, introduce free-market economics, facilitate American commercial activity in the region, encourage human rights, and control nuclear proliferation. An American goal was to ensure that these governments cooperate with the United States in maintaining international peace and security and not be replaced by radical Islamic regimes.[10] Upon their declaration of independence, the United States moved to establish relations with the Central Asian republics and provided aid. In 1992, the United States adopted the Freedom for Russia and Emerging Eurasian Democracies and Open Markets (FREEDOM) legislation to provide aid. Early on, Washington seemed to be favoring Kazakhstan. This was largely due to the old Soviet nuclear stockpiles that Kazakhstan inherited upon independence. A serious of high-level visits were exchanged from 1992 to 1995. Kazakhstan agreed to ratify the Strategic Arms Reduction Treaty and the Lisbon Protocol, in which it gave up its nuclear weapons in May 1992. By April 1995, 1,040 SS-18 missile warheads were transferred to Russia. The United States provided aid to Kazakhstan in exchange for this transfer of nuclear weapons.[11] American security interests increased in the region after the September 11th terrorist attacks. The United States had established a military presence in several Central Asian countries to support the American military presence in Afghanistan. At one time, this included about 3,000 American military personnel stationed in Kyrgyzstan and about 1,000 in Uzbekistan.[12] The United States also provided economic assistance to the region. A Central Asia–America Initiative Fund was established with a five-year budget of

$150 million. The US Export–Import Bank provided short-term loans to Turkmenistan and Uzbekistan to purchase food and medical equipment. The US Overseas Private Investment Corporation (OPIC) signed agreements with all five Central Asian states. In Kazakhstan, the OPIC provided $80 million to finance two companies exploring oil in the country.[13] Ultimately the main goal of the United States was to ensure that Russian and Iranian interests in the region were limited. The United States accomplished this by establishing an American security presence in the region, emphasizing human rights, and attempting to gain control over the region's oil supplies. The United States has backed pipeline construction projects which favor Turkey and bypassed Russia and Iran. While this was not the most economically cost-effective route Washington supported it for political and strategic reasons. The United States urged the Central Asian countries to distance themselves from Russia and Iran regarding oil production. In November 1999, Washington facilitated the agreements on constructing the Baku–Ceyhan oil pipeline. The United States had taken the lead in financing, dispute resolution, and the negotiating of commitments with the various states of the region. The significance of this pipeline is that it excludes both Russia and Iran. In turn, the local governments are receptive to American economic and political involvement as a counterweight to Russia. Many in the region viewed Washington as a more favorable economic partner than Moscow.[14] The American presence in Central Asia became more overt in the aftermath of the terrorist attacks of September 11, 2001. Military cooperation between the United States and Central Asian states expanded rapidly. Three Central Asian states (Tajikistan, Turkmenistan, and Uzbekistan) border Afghanistan. The primary focus at this point was on anti-terrorism.[15] In the aftermath of the 2003 invasion of Iraq, American policy became more broadly defined. State Department officials valued Central Asia for the following reasons:

- Security, defined as anti-terrorism, included nonproliferation of Weapons of Mass Destruction (WMD), and drug trafficking.
- Access to the region's energy resources and ensuring that they get to global markets to help promote sustainable development.
- The development of democratically oriented political systems emphasizing market-oriented reforms.[16]

AMERICAN SECURITY INTERESTS IN CENTRAL ASIA

The United States established a military presence in Central Asia shortly after the fall of the Soviet Union. In 1994, American military personnel advised Central Asian armed forces. The first of the former Soviet republics to get

American military aid was Azerbaijan in 1994. This was done through the NATO Partnership for Peace (PfP) Program. Over the next several years, under the rubric of the PfP concluded with Georgia, Kazakhstan, Kyrgyzstan, Turkmenistan, and Uzbekistan. Officers from these countries participated in peacekeeping exercises at Patrick Air Force Base in Florida in May 1996. That same year the Montana National Guard began conducting regular exchanges with Kyrgyzstan army reservists.[17]

From these humble beginnings, an extensive security relationship began to evolve. In 1997, 500 American paratroopers took part in joint exercises in Kazakhstan with the Central Asian Battalion (CENTRASBAT) of the Commonwealth of Independent States. A bilateral security agreement was concluded between the United States and Kazakhstan. This security agreement provided for additional training programs as well as transfers of nonlethal equipment.[18] The United States established a relationship with CENTRASBAT which saw elements of the 10th Mountain Division travel to Uzbekistan in September 1998. In 1999, several security agreements were concluded between Washington and Tashkent. These included having American advisors work with Uzbek border guards and military intelligence. Border security continued as in April 2000, Secretary of State Albright, on a tour of Central Asia, awarded $3 million to Kazakhstan, Uzbekistan, and Kyrgyzstan to improve their border security.[19]

The direct American military presence in the region increased dramatically after September 11, 2001. US forces gained access to a former Soviet air base at Khanabad in eastern Uzbekistan; Kyrgyzstan opened the international airport at Manas to American forces; Tajikistan offered NATO access to three abandoned Soviet airfields. Georgia and Azerbaijan allowed the United States to use their airspace. These were quickly followed up with further agreements and high-level visits. The United States and Kyrgyzstan concluded an agreement in December 2001 that allowed the United States to construct a 37-acre staging facility next to Manas airport which would include warehouses, administrative buildings, and temporary housing for 3,000 American troops. The head of CENTCOM, General Tommy Franks, toured Kyrgyzstan, Tajikistan, and Uzbekistan and promised American support against the Islamic Movement of Uzbekistan as well as other groups. The United States signed an agreement with Uzbekistan in March 2002 in which the United States would respond to external threats to the security and territorial integrity of Uzbekistan.[20]

Uzbekistan and Tajikistan are important to the American military effort in Afghanistan. Together they have 850 miles of border with Afghanistan. Bases in these states are close to the major Afghan cities of Mazar-e-Sharif (200 miles) and Kabul (300 miles). The United States quickly established a military relationship with Uzbekistan. The United States attempted to gain influence in Tajikistan by offering various incentives, including technology to monitor the border with Afghanistan. Tajikistan provided some temporary hosting for American forces operating out of bases near the Afghan border.[21]

KAZAKHSTAN'S FOREIGN POLICY

President Nazarbayev was instrumental in creating the CIS after the fall of the Soviet Union. He urged the leaders of Russia, Ukraine, and Belarus, who were in the process of forming a Slavic Union, to broaden the organization and include other non-Slavic states.[22] He had advocated for a reorganization of the CIS with an emphasis on developing crisis management strategies. Kazakhstan was instrumental in the founding a sub-regional grouping the Eurasian Economic Union, in 2014. Kazakhstan and Russia also were the primary countries that developed the Eurasian Development Bank.[23]

Two other important treaty organizations that Kazakhstan is a member of are the Collective Security Treaty Organization (CSTO) and the Shanghai Cooperation Organization(SCO). Russia dominates the CSTO and China dominates the SCO. Kazakhstan pursues its own interests while cooperating with its stronger neighbors. Kazakhstan has sought to cooperate with these countries to better position itself to emerge as a regional or a sub-regional leader.[24]

Kazakhstan has been a leader in the nonproliferation of weapons of mass destruction. In 1995, it was the first state of the former Soviet Union to give up its nuclear weapons. In September 2006, Kazakhstan was a signatory to the establishment of a Central Asian Nuclear-Weapon-Free Zone. The Central Asian states later granted the International Atomic Energy Agency the right to make inspections of the civil nuclear facilities of the member states. Kazakhstan is very active as a member of numerous anti-proliferation organizations. It is also the only Central Asian state to be a member of the Global Initiative to Combat Nuclear Terrorism. . Kazakhstan is movingahead with its plans to develop nuclear power Kazakhstan has about 20% of world-wide reserves of uranium and is actively trying to become one of the biggest exporters of nuclear fuels. Kazakhstan became affiliated with NATO through the Organization of Security and Cooperation in Europe. Kazakhstan chaired this body in 2010 and reaped a great deal of domestic and foreign policy capital as a result. Kazakhstan aided the Western military effort in Afghanistan by granting over-flight rights and logistics support.[25]

Since March 2019, the president of Kazakhstan has been Kassym Jomart Tokayev. Former President Nazarbayev still influenced state policy. He had a lifetime appointment as chair of the Security Council of Kazakhstan where he retained influence over policy and government appointments. He was removed from this position as a result of the January 2022 protests and riots in the country. President Tokayev took over the chairmanship of this body.[26]

RUSSIAN INFLUENCE IN THE REGION

Russian security interests in Central Asia stem from concern about security threats in southern Russia/North Caucasus, specifically Chechnya, Dagestan, and Ingushetia. These groups include Jamaat Shariat (the Dagestani Front of the Caucasus Emirate's Armed Forces), Yarmuk Jamaat (The armed Forces of the United Vilayat of Kabarda–Balkaria–Karachai), and Ingush Jamaat.[27]

Economically Russia is very concerned about Western countries exploiting the region's energy resources to their detriment. Russia has sought to establish a gas cartel. This has been done largely through the control of natural gas pipelines. A gas cartel led by Moscow could have several consequences. It would force the Central Asian states to deal with Moscow and prevent them from selling natural gas on the open market. This allows Moscow to exert economic and political pressure on its customers in Western Europe.[28]

Moscow wants to prevent the United States from gaining militarily in the region. Russia wants to maintain control over the Caspian Sea and is very suspicious of states looking to the west, especially the United States, for assistance in protecting their coastlines, exploration rigs, and territories from terrorism. Moscow is concerned that Western efforts to prevent proliferation and drug smuggling are excuses to justify a greater Western military presence. Russia has formed the CSTO to serve as a counterweight to NATO. Moscow took the step of beginning to demand veto power over members of the CIS having defense agreements with the West.[29] Defense Minister Sergei Ivanov stated,

> The countries of the region are members of the Collective Security Treaty Organization (CSTO). And [if the countries of the region are] making a decision about hosting new bases on their territory, they should take into account the interests of Russia and coordinate this decision with our country.[30]

An important agenda of the CSTO is to create a framework for stationing Russian forces and giving Moscow access to bases in Kyrgyzstan, Tajikistan, and Uzbekistan with thc justification of defending these countries from terrorism. Russia has advocated the development of a force to defend the Caspian Sea called CASFOR. There are fears that should this come to pass, it would be a vehicle by which Moscow incorporates the naval forces of the Caspian Sea states and put them under Russian command and control. This is part of Russian attempts to strengthen the CIS and to make its institutions more viable. Russia is also trying to limit Chinese influence via the SCO.[31]

The CSTO held its first joint peacekeeping exercise in Kazakhstan in October 2012 which simulated the insertion of peacekeeping forces to deal with ethnic conflicts and international terrorism in a Central Asian state.[32]

While most of the Central Asian states made some attempts to draw closer to the West, they did not abandon their relationships with Russia. The states of Central Asia have disagreements with each other and would like Russian support. There is concern that Uzbekistan might try to assert some form of hegemony; and therefore, a Russian presence is necessary. Several of the Central Asian countries directly border China. While most of the Central Asian states are members of the SCO, they are suspicious of China's intentions.[33]

In response to American base rights in Central Asia in the aftermath of September 11th, Russia also increased its military forces in the region. Russia obtained an agreement from Kyrgyzstan in 2002, giving Moscow control of the Kant base. This and access to a military base in Dushanbe, Tajikistan allowed the Russians to provide air coverage to most of Central Asia. Russia also permanently deployed more than 10,000 troops on the Tajikistan–Afghanistan border. This was justified to contain threats of terrorism coming out of Afghanistan, as well as the prevention of drug smuggling.[34]

The collapse of the Soviet Union caught most of the world by surprise. Many of the emerging states were not ready for independence. Moscow had an advantage over these states economically, politically, and militarily. It was able to use the CIS to maintain its influence in most of the areas of the former Soviet Union. This was significant for security and economic reasons, as well as to protect Russian populations outside the Russian Federation. The CIS provided the political legitimacy for intervention and peacekeeping forces in the civil war in Tajikistan. The Collective Security Treaty Organization (CSTO) was a security alliance set up through the framework of the CIS in 1992. This was partly a result of the unraveling political situation in Tajikistan that led to civil war. Russia sent peacekeeping troops to Tajikistan through a multilateral agreement between the two countries. The CSTO was paralyzed by internal disagreements and suspicion of Russian motivations. It has never fully been utilized as a security arrangement, and several countries (Uzbekistan, Azerbaijan, and Georgia) left the treaty by the end of the 1990s.[35]

Tajikistan is the smallest in land area but has the third largest population of the Central Asian Republics. The country was racked by a civil war shortly after independence. Between 1991 and 1993, 500,000 people were left homeless. There were 7 billion in damages. In 2000, Tajikistan was rated among the twenty poorest countries in the world. A peace agreement was concluded in 1997, which legalized opposition parties for the 1999 election. While Tajikistan remains the poorest country in Central Asia, the poverty rate fell from 83% in 2000 to 27.4% in 2018. Economic growth for this period has averaged 7%. However, job creation has not kept pace with population growth.[36]

POLITICAL CHANGE IN KYRGYZSTAN

Kyrgyzstan has seen the most political change in the Central Asian states. Its first president at independence was Askar Akayev, who was president until 2005. He was forced out of power in 2005, and the new President Bakiyev agreed in 2006 to limit his powers in a new constitution. Later that year, the government resigned. Azim Isabekov became prime minister in 2007 in a short-lived government. The moderate opposition leader Almaz Atabayev became Prime Minister. Kyrgyzstan has been a source of great power rivalry between the United States and Russia over access to military bases. In 2009, President Bakiyev closed the Manas base to the United States in response to 2 billion in loans from Russia. Later that year, however, he signed a new agreement with the United States for the use of the base in which America agreed to triple the rent for its use. In 2020, parliamentary elections were annulled after opposition protests and allegations of vote rigging. President Jeenbekov resigned after appointing a prime minister acceptable to the opposition. While there have been frequent changes in government in Kyrgyzstan the opposition has been able to press their demands, and popular protests have led to some political change.

CHINA'S INTEREST IN CENTRAL ASIA: A BRIEF OVERVIEW

China shares borders with Kazakhstan, Kyrgyzstan, and Tajikistan. During the Soviet period, these borders were in dispute, and there were several military clashes.[37] China is interested in having stable borders, as well as having access to the oil and natural gas of the region. China sees Central Asia as emerging as an important region, but as it becomes more significant, it can lead to greater challenges to China's hold over Xinjiang.[38] The region is also central to the Chinese BRI unveiled in 2013, which is a massive expenditure to develop infrastructure and develop trade routes to many different parts of the world. Central Asia is an essential conduit for Chinese goods to Western markets.

The SCO was formed in April 1996 when the presidents of China, Kazakhstan, Kyrgyzstan, Russia, and Tajikistan signed an agreement in Shanghai pledging the demilitarization of their respective borders. Part of this agreement was that they would each not harbor ethnic separatists in their respective territories. This was very important, especially to China, as they were concerned about Uighur separatism in the Xinjiang Autonomous Province. The following year China and Russia agreed to demilitarize their 4,000-mile border. In 2001, the organization was expanded with the admission of Uzbekistan and an agreement to establish anti-terrorism policies by establishing a center to combat terrorism. There was a further agreement (Shanghai Convention) on joint action against terrorism and regional separatism. This was viewed as Russia and China attempting to enlist the support of regional nations against threats to their territories.[39] The SCO has allowed Central Asian states to balance off Russia with China. Balancing off China's need for markets and energy resources with Russia's eagerness to reassert influence over a traditional sphere of influence. The Central Asian states look upon the SCO as a tool to guarantee their political survival.[40]

China is building up this group as it is expanding trade, economics, and energy, as well as security partnerships in the region. Step one was to build the group, the first multilateral group China started on its own. Step two: expand it to discussions of trade, economics, and energy. Step three: begin discussions on more substantive security partnerships. The SCO has gone so far as to conduct its own joint military maneuvers in China's Xinjiang Autonomous Region.[41]

China is in the process of shifting its military focus by adding fully mechanized units that can be integrated with specialized units such as armor, logistics, and support. China is rapidly shifting its focus from a defensive force to a military with power projection capabilities that can achieve political and strategic objectives. China has put itself in a position where it can be a leader in any multi-force operation sanctioned by the SCO.[42]

China has been especially active in cultivating economic relations with Kazakhstan. Beijing has acquired major interests in Kazakh oil and gas fields. The Chinese National Petroleum Company purchased a 60% stake in the Zhanazol and Kekiyak fields. It also acquired a majority stake in Kazakh gas fields in the Aktyubinsk region. China formed a joint partnership with Kazakhstan to build a $4 billion coal-fired power plant at Ekibastuz. In addition to Kazakhstan, China is interested in purchasing hydroelectric power from Kyrgyzstan as well as natural gas from Turkmenistan.[43] The centerpiece of China's energy infrastructure in Central Asia is the trans-Kazakh pipeline. This is a 1,900-mile project that was completed in 2006. It connected Atasu in central Kazakhstan to the Xinjiang region of Western China. This pipeline had an initial capacity of 146.6 million barrels per year and connected with another pipeline to the Caspian Sea. In 2005, the Chinese National Petroleum Company purchased PetroKazakhstan, which gave it ownership of refineries and exploration rights for a dozen oilfields. While there are some concerns between the two countries, such as water rights and the treatment of ethnic Kazaks in Xinjiang, there are areas of common ground. In addition to economics, the government of Kazakhstan is very concerned that potential Uighur unrest in Xinjiang could spill over the border and affect the Uighur population residing in Kazakhstan.[44]

China is hoping to import 20 million tons of oil from Central Asia once its various pipeline projects are completed.[45] This has allowed Kazakhstan to be less dependent on oil exports to Russia while not actively confronting or bandwagoning with Moscow.[46] Many Central Asian leaders view China as a model of how to maintain political stability in a time of economic transition.[47]

THE SIGNIFICANCE OF XINJIANG FOR CHINA'S SECURITY INTERESTS IN THE REGION

Xinjiang is significant geo-strategically as, in addition to possessing a great deal of natural resources, it shares international borders with Mongolia, Russia, Kazakhstan, Kyrgyzstan, Tajikistan, Afghanistan, Pakistan, and Indian-controlled Kashmir.[48] China's strategic goal in Central Asia is to counter what Beijing sees as the three main threats coming out of Central Asia. These are separatism, terrorism, and religious extremism. China is especially concerned regarding the province of Xinjiang. China has and continues to build pipelines bringing oil and natural gas from Central Asia to China. Many of these go through Xinjiang.[49] The major strategic threat to China is instability among the Uighurs in Xinjiang. There is concern that Uighur separatists can use instability in the region to launch attacks on China from one or more Central Asian countries. China is suspicious of Western attempts to establish a presence in the region which could interfere with this.[50] China is concerned about the Uighur diaspora in Central Asia. There are about 500,000 Uighurs scattered across Central Asia outside of China. Over 200,000 are in Kazakhstan. China believed that Uighur nationalism was getting support from Kazakhstan and Kyrgyzstan as well as the Taliban in Afghanistan. It was China's security concerns that drove it to establish the SCO. Subsequent negotiations led to territorial concessions from Kazakhstan and more substantial territorial concessions from Kyrgyzstan.[51]

China has experienced a growing degree of ethnic conflict with its Uighur population in the last several years. Xinjiang is resource-rich, and it encompasses one-sixth of the country. Deadly riots occurred in 2009 and 2011. China has been encouraging immigration to Xinjiang of Han Chinese to change the population dynamics of the region. The population of Muslim Uighurs fell below 50%.[52] China views potential Uighur nationalism in Central Asia as a threat. Diplomatically Beijing has pressured Central Asian states to deport Uighur political refugees back to China and not to protest Chinese actions in Xinjiang.

Beijing has sought to integrate the region more firmly into China by settling large numbers of Han Chinese in Xinjiang. The treatment of the Uighurs has led to increasing global protests. Beijing's goal is that rapid development and contact with the center will break the traditional bonds of community and change the cultural and ethnic identifications of the Muslim non-Chinese population. In 2000, China established the Go West Campaign to economically develop the province. This area is a corridor of Chinese trade with Central Asia as well as with other markets. About one-third of the trade through the area is actively controlled by the state-run Xinjiang Production and Construction Corporation.[53]

IRAN AND CENTRAL ASIA

Since 1995, Iran has pursued a more moderate policy toward the Middle East and the Persian Gulf. Tehran has recognized the security considerations of the Persian Gulf sheikdoms as well as grudgingly acknowledged the permanent American military presence in the region. This led Tehran to look toward the emerging states of Central Asia to cultivate political, economic, and, eventually, security relationships. The legacy of the Iran–Iraq war has contributed to a shifting of Iranian economic activity toward the northeastern part of the country.[54]

Due to economic sanctions, Tehran does not have the technology and hard currency to offer the Central Asian Republics. Iran's trade and pipelines must go through several countries. Iran's most significant bilateral relationship in the region is with Turkmenistan. Iran supports Turkmenistan's policy of distancing itself from the CIS. Iran has a significant Turkmen population, and it is the only Central Asian state that it borders.[55] Tehran's relations with Kazakhstan are improving. The two nations have begun some oil deals which have allowed landlocked Kazakhstan to ship oil across the Caspian Sea to Iran, utilizing the Iranian oil facility at Kharg Island in the Persian Gulf.[56] A major issue between the two countries is the delineation of the Caspian Sea borders. Iran has the most tension with Uzbekistan. Tashkent cooperated with American sanctions against Iran. It is also the Central Asian country that is most vulnerable to an Islamic insurgency, which it blames Iran for supporting.[57]

The state Iran has the most in common with is Tajikistan, which is the only Central Asian state that has a Persian-dominated culture. Iran's early interference in the Tajik civil war has left a legacy that is still trying to be repaired.[58] This led to Russian intervention in Tajikistan. As a result, Dushanbe and

Moscow have a very strong relationship. Tehran was opposed to the Taliban in Afghanistan and supported the Northern Alliance.[59] Iran has been moving toward greater cooperation with Russia, especially in the Caspian Sea region. In addition to political cooperation, Tehran and Moscow have sought cooperation over the pipeline and oil transfer agreements. While the route through Iran is the most economical, it faces political opposition from the United States. This led to a rivalry between Russia, the United States, and the EU, which Iran is seeking to capitalize on.[60]

Tehran has the demographics and potential resources to assert itself in the region. Culturally Iran has a strong civil society, an ancient culture, and a strong national identity. Iran once physically controlled many parts of Central Asia. Iran, by and large, is a strategically secure state with no apparent regional threats. These advantages, however, are outweighed by Iran's weaknesses. Part of the problem for Iran is the country's revolutionary legacy. There is a great deal of suspicion due to Iran's revolutionary legacy. Initially, Iran gave outward support to Islamic groups in Uzbekistan. Iran's revolutionary legacy alienates the United States, which is emerging as the major outside power in Central Asia.[61] In the 1990s, it appeared that a new version of the "Great Game" was going to be established, pitting secular pro-Western Turkey versus Islamic revolutionary Iran. This never materialized largely because Turkey and Iran did not have the resources to effectively wage this struggle. The leaders of the Central Asian countries wanted to assert their independence and were suspicious of the intentions of Ankara and Tehran.[62]

Iran's potential for spreading Islamic militancy in the region proved to be overstated. Demographically, the majority of Central Asians are Turkic in culture and follow the Sunni tradition of Islam. As a result, the most effective missionary efforts on the part of Islamic radicals have come from Turkey and Saudi Arabia. However, Tehran is still trying to overcome the perception of spreading Islamic militancy in part because of its efforts in aiding Islamic groups in Tajikistan and Uzbekistan. Tehran did end up cooperating with Moscow in securing an agreement in 1997, which ended the civil war in Tajikistan and led to a power-sharing arrangement between secular and Islamic groups.[63]

In conclusion, Iran is finding it extremely difficult to cultivate substantive relations with Central Asia. Iran has adopted a policy of cooperation with the Russian Federation. In part, this was to balance off the perceived threat coming from the United States. Tehran views support for Russia as the best alternative to thwarting the expansion of American influence in the region. This support for Russia led to growing military and scientific cooperation. Tehran has purchased arms from Moscow, and Russia has been supportive of Iran's nuclear program. These contributed to tensions with Washington.[64]

ENVIRONMENTAL ISSUES IN CENTRAL ASIA

A major legacy of the Soviet period for Central Asia is the problems caused by Moscow's attempt to develop the region, as well as the legacy of its military infrastructure and nuclear testing. One of the major environmental disasters on the planet is the Aral Sea on the border of Kazakhstan and Uzbekistan. In the early 1900s, it was the fourth largest inland lake in the world. It was vital to the region for fishing and significant in preserving the water and soil quality of the region. The sea is fed by the Syr Darya and Amur Darya rivers. In 1918, the new Bolshevik government decided to divert water from the rivers for irrigation. The goal was to grow cotton in Central Asia. Irrigated land areas in Uzbekistan and Turkmenistan increased from 6.4 to 15.9 million acres. In two decades, the diversion of the rivers led to the shrinking of the Aral Sea, causing an environmental disaster. The drying up of the sea led to dust storms which spread toxins (chemicals and pesticides that had run off into the rivers and emptied into the Sea). This caused numerous health problems for the local population. The government of Kazakhstan, in partnership with the World Bank, built a dam to keep the waters of the northern part of the Aral Sea from draining into the larger southern Aral Sea. This has stopped the shrinking of the northern Aral Sea, and there is some environmental improvement. The southern Aral Sea has not improved and is still shrinking.[65]

Another major issue that the region, specifically Kazakhstan, must deal with is the legacy of Soviet nuclear testing. Moscow conducted 456 tests between 1949 and 1989 at the Semipalatinsk test site in northeast Kazakhstan. After the fall of the Soviet Union, the site was neglected. Nuclear material, including plutonium, was left unprotected at the site. America, Russia, and Kazakhstan cooperated in cleaning up the site and safely storing the nuclear materials. This was completed in 2012. Kazakhstan is still dealing with the health effects of prolonged nuclear testing. There are higher rates of different types of cancers. Semipalatinsk was the site of the signing of a Central Asian Nuclear Weapons Free Zone by Kazakhstan, Kyrgyzstan, Tajikistan, Turkmenistan, and Uzbekistan on September 8, 2006, the fifteenth anniversary of the closing of the site.

CONCLUSION

Central Asia is an important region globally because of its geography and natural resources. It is also a zone of great power competition between great and middle powers. The states of Central Asia have emerged as authoritarian states in varying degrees. Kyrgyzstan is the country that has experienced the most political change. Popular protests have been effective in changing governments. Kazakhstan has been the most successful in developing a relationship with the West. Since its independence Kazakhstan has been affiliated with NATO and the Organization for Security and Cooperation in Europe (OSCE). The Central Asian countries still maintain a relationship with Russia as they have economic and security interests in common. There are Russian populations in the Central Asian countries, so Moscow will always have an interest in this region. China also has economic and security interests in the region. The United States was drawn into the region because of the conflict in Afghanistan and wanting to block Iranian influence in the region.

NOTES

1. J.Miglietta, Tennessee State University, Nashville, USA. Email: jmiglietta@tnstate.edu
2. Dekmejian, R.H. and H.H. Simonian, Troubled Waters: The Geopolitics of the Caspian Region, I.B. Tauris, 2001, p. 10.
3. Dekmejian and Simonian, 2001, p. 12.
4. Cohen, S.B. Geopolitics: The Geography of International Relations, New York: Rowman and Littlefield Publishers, Inc., 2009. p. 243.
5. Dekmejian and Simonian, p. 12–13.
6. Olcott, M.B. Kazakhstan: Unfulfilled Promise, Washington, D.C.: Carnegie Endowment for International Peace, 2002, p. 25.
7. Hanks, R.R. "'Multi-vector politics' and Kazakhstan's emerging role as a geostrategic player in Central Asia," Journal of Balkan and Near Eastern Studies, Volume II, No. 3, September 2009, p. 258.
8. Nichol, J. "Kazakhstan: Recent Developments and U.S. Interests," Congressional Research Service, Washington, D.C.: July 22, 2013, p. 13–15.
9. World Bank, Kazakhstan Overview, worldbank.org/en/country/Kazakhstan/overview
10. Aras, B. The New Geopolitics of Eurasia and Turkey's Position, London: Frank Cass Publishers, 2002, p. 69.
11. Aras, 2002, p. 70, 75.
12. Maynes, C.W. "American Discovers Central Asia," Foreign Affairs, Volume 82, No.2, March/April 2003, p. 122.
13. Aras, 2002, p. 74.
14. Blank, S. "The United States and Central Asia," in Roy Allison and Lena Jonson Eds., Central Asian Security: The New International Context, Washington D.C.: Brookings Institutions, 2001, p. 132–133.
15. Wishnick, E. "Russia, China, and the United States in Central Asia: Prospects for Great Power Competition and Cooperation in the Shadow of the Georgian Crisis," Strategic Studies Institute, U.S. Army War College, February 2009, p. 5.
16. Wishnick, 2009, p. 5.

17. Lawson, F.H. "Political Economy, Geopolitics, and the Expanding US Military Presence in the Persian Gulf and Central Asia," Critique: Middle Eastern Studies, Vol. 13, No. 1, Spring 2004, p. 11–12.
18. Lawson, 2004, p. 12.
19. Lawson, 2004, p. 12–13.
20. Lawson, 2004, p. 14.
21. Goldstein, L. "Beyond the Steppe: Projecting Power into the New Central Asia," Journal of Slavic Military Studies, Vol. 17, 2004, p. 195.
22. Goldstein, 2004, p. 195.
23. Hanks, 2009, p. 125.
24. Schmitz, A. "The Political Economy of Kazakh Foreign Policy," in Institutional Reform in Central Asia, Ed. Joachim Ahrens and Herman W. Hoen, N.Y.: Routledge, 2013, p. 114–115.
25. Schmitz, 2013, p. 117–118.
26. Gotev, Georgi, "Kazakh president removes ex-leader Nazarbayev from post amid unrest," EURACTIV.com with Reuters, Jan. 28, 2022. https://www.euractiv.com/section/central-asia/news/kazakh-president-removes-ex-leader-nazarbayev-from-post-amid-unrest/.
27. Ariel Cohen, "Russia's Counterinsurgency in North Caucasus: Performance and Consequences," U.S. Army War College, Strategic Studies Institute, 2014.
28. Blank, S. "U.S. Interests in Central Asia and Their Challenges," Strategic Studies Institute, U.S. Army War College, 2007, p. 6–7.
29. Blank, 2007, p. 23–24.
30. Blank, 2007, p. 8.
31. Blank, 2007, p. 7–10.
32. German, T. "Russia and the Caspian Sea: Projecting Power or Competing for Influence?" United States Army War College, Strategic Studies Institution, 2015, p. 58–59.
33. Zhenghong, Z. "Regional Security in Central Asia and Russia After 9/11," Far Eastern Affairs, Vol. 33, No. 1, 2005, p. 24.
34. Allison, 2004, p. 468.
35. Hanks, R.R. Global Security Watch Central Asia, Santa Barbara, CA: ABC-CLIO Inc., 2010, (Hanks, p. 121).
36. World Bank, Tajikistan, https://www.worldbank.org/en/country/tajikistan.
37. Bluth, C. US Foreign Policy in the Caucasus and Central Asia: Politics, Energy and Security, New York: I.B. Tauris, 2014, p. 57.
38. Hyer, E. "China's Policy Towards Uighur Nationalism," Journal of Muslim Minority Affairs, Vol. 26, No. 1, April 2006, p. 82.
39. Nichol, 2008, p. 54.
40. Freire, M.F., "Russian Policy in Central Asia: Supporting, Balancing, Coercing, or Imposing?" Asian Perspective, Vol. 33, No. 2, 2009, p. 138.
41. Ramo, J.C. The Beijing Consensus,
London: The Foreign Policy Centre, 2004, p. 52–53.
42. Weitz, R. "China's Military Goals, Policy, Doctrine, And Capabilities in Central Asia" in Stephen Blank ed., Central Asia After 2014. U.S. Army War College, Strategic Studies Institute, November 2013, p. 81–82.

43. Bluth, 2014, p. 59.
44. Nichol, J. 2008, p. 55–56.
45. Bluth, 2014, p. 60.
46. Freire, 2009, p. 143.
47. Goldstein, 2004, p. 193.
48. Cunningham, C. "Counterterrorism in Xinjiang: The ETIM, China, and The Uyghurs," International Journal on World Peace, Vol. 29, No. 3, September 2012, p. 16.
49. Panda, J.P. "Beijing's Perspective on Expansion of the Shanghai Cooperation Organization: India, South Asia, and the Spectrum of Opportunities in China's Open Approach," Asian Perspectives, Vol. 36, 2012, p. 518.
50. Weitz, 2013, p. 82–83.
51. Bluth, 2014, p. 57–58.
52. Weitz, 2013, p. 84.
53. Cooley, A. Great Games, Local Rules: The New Great Power Contest in Central Asia, New York: Oxford University Press, 2014, p. 75–77.
54. Efegil, E., and Stone, L. "Iran's Interest in Central Asia: A Contemporary Assessment," Central Asian Survey, Vol. 20, No. 3, September 2001, p. 353–354.
55. Mesbahi, M. "Iran and Central Asia: paradigm and policy," Central Asian Survey, Vol. 23, No. 2, June 2004, p. 123.
56. Nichol, 2008, p. 56.
57. Efegil and Stone, 2001, p. 356.
58. Efegil and Stone, p. 357–358.
59. Herzig, E. "Iran and Central Asia," in Roy Allison and Lena Jonson Eds., Central Asian Security: The New International Context, Washington D.C.: Brookings Institutions, 2001, p. 190.
60. Shirazi, H.A. "Russian and Iranian national interests and their policies in the Caspian geopolitical region," in Sally N. Cummings, Ed., Oil, Transition and Security in Central Asia, New York: Routledge Curzon, 2003, p. 244.
61. Dannreuther, R. "Bridging the Gulf? Iran, Central Asia and the Persian Gulf," The Review of International Affairs, Vol. 2, No. 4 Summer 2003, p. 32–33.
62. Dannreuther, 2003, p. 38–39.
63. Dannreuther, 2003, p. 39–40.
64. Dannreuther, 2003, p. 40–41.
65. World Resources Institute, "Disappearance of the Aral Sea" wri.org/blog/2008/05/disappearance-aral-sea.

BIBLIOGRAPHY

Allison, R. "Regionalism, Regional Structures and Security Management in Central Asia," *International Affairs*, Vol. 80, No. 3, 2004, 463–483.

Aras, B. *The New Geopolitics of Eurasia and Turkey's Position*, London: Frank Cass Publishers, 2002.

Blank, S. "The United States and Central Asia," in Roy Allison and Lena Jonson Eds., *Central Asian Security: The New International Context*, Washington, DC: Brookings Institutions, 2001, 171–198.

Blank, S. "U.S. Interests in Central Asia and Their Challenges," Strategic Studies Institute, U.S. Army War College, 2007.

Bluth, C. *US Foreign Policy in the Caucasus and Central Asia: Politics, Energy and Security*, New York: I.B. Tauris, 2014.

Cohen, A. "Russia's Counterinsurgency in North Caucasus: Performance and Consequences," U.S., Army War College, Strategic Studies Institute, 2014.

Cohen, S.B. *Geopolitics: The Geography of International Relations*, New York: Rowman and Littlefield Publishers, Inc., 2009.

Cooley, A. *Great Games, Local Rules: The New Great Power Contest in Central Asia*, New York: Oxford University Press, 2014.

Cunningham, C. "Counterterrorism in Xinjiang: The ETIM, China, and the Uyghurs," *International Journal on World Peace*, Vol. 29, No. 3, September 2012, 16.

Dannreuther, R. "Bridging the Gulf? Iran, Central Asia and the Persian Gulf," *The Review of International Affairs*, Vol. 2, No. 4, Summer 2003, 32–46.

Dekmejian, R.H., and H.H. Simonian. *Troubled Waters: The Geopolitics of the Caspian Region*, I.B. Tauris, 2001.

Efegil, E., and Stone, L. "Iran's Interest in Central Asia: A Contemporary Assessment," *Central Asian Survey*, Vol. 20, No. 3, September 2001, 353–365.

Freire, M.F., "Russian Policy in Central Asia: Supporting, Balancing, Coercing, or Imposing?," *Asian Perspective*, Vol. 33, No. 2, 2009, 125–149.

German, T. "Russia and the Caspian Sea: Projecting Power or Competing for Influence?," United States Army War College, Strategic Studies Institution, 2015.

Goldstein, L. "Beyond the Steppe: Projecting Power into the New Central Asia," *Journal of Slavic Military Studies*, Vol. 17, 2004, 183–213.

Gotev, Georgi, "Kazakh President Removes Ex-Leader Nazarbayev from Post Amid Unrest," EURACTIV.com with Reuters, January 28, 2022. https://www.euractiv.com/section/central-asia/news/kazakh-president-removes-ex-leader-nazarbayev-from-post-amid-unrest/.

Hanks, R.R. *Global Security Watch Central Asia*, Santa Barbara: ABC-CLIO Inc., 2010.

Hanks, R.R. "'Multi-Vector Politics' and Kazakhstan's Emerging Role as a Geo-Strategic Player in Central Asia," *Journal of Balkan and Near Eastern Studies*, Vol. II, No. 3, September 2009, 257–267.

Herzig, E. "Iran and Central Asia," in Roy Allison and Lena Jonson Eds., *Central Asian Security: The New International Context*, Washington, DC: Brookings Institutions, 2001, 171–198.

Hyer, E. "China's Policy Towards Uighur Nationalism," *Journal of Muslim Minority Affairs*, Vol. 26, No. 1, April 2006, 75–86.

Lawson, F.H. "Political Economy, Geopolitics, and the Expanding US Military Presence in the Persian Gulf and Central Asia," *Critique: Middle Eastern Studies*, Vol. 13, No. 1, Spring 2004, 7–31.

Mackinder, H.J. "The Geographical Pivot of History," *Royal Geographical Society*, Vol. 23, No. #4, April 1904, Reprinted in The Geographical Journal, Vol. 170, No. 1, December 2004, 298–321.

Maynes, C.W. "America Discovers Central Asia," *Foreign Affairs*, Vol. 82, No. 2, March/April 2003, 120–132.

Mesbahi, M. "Iran and Central Asia: Paradigm and Policy," *Central Asian Survey*, Vol. 23, No. 2, June 2004, 109–139.

Nichol, J. *Central Asia: Security, Internal Affairs and U.S. Interests*, New York: Novinka Books, 2008.

Nichol, J. "Kazakhstan: Recent Developments and U.S. Interests," Congressional Research Service, Washington, DC, July 22, 2013.

Olcott, M.B. *Kazakhstan: Unfulfilled Promise*, Washington, DC: Carnegie Endowment for International Peace, 2002.

Panda, J.P. "Beijing's Perspective on Expansion of the Shanghai Cooperation Organization: India, South Asia, and the Spectrum of Opportunities in China's Open Approach," *Asian Perspectives*, Vol. 36, 2012, 493–530.

Ramo, J.C. *The Beijing Consensus*, London: The Foreign Policy Centre, 2004.

Schmitz, A. "The Political Economy of Kazakh Foreign Policy," in Joachim Ahrens and Herman W. Hoen Eds., *Institutional Reform in Central Asia*, New York: Routledge, 2013, 111–128.

Shirazi, H.A. "Russian and Iranian National Interests and Their Policies in the Caspian Geopolitical Region," in Sally N. Cummings, Ed., *Oil, Transition and Security in Central Asia*, New York: Routledge Curzon, 2003.

Weitz, R. "China's Military Goals, Policy, Doctrine, and Capabilities in Central Asia," in Stephen Blank Ed., Central Asia After 2014. U.S. Army War College, Strategic Studies Institute, November 2013.

Wishnick, E. "Russia, China, and the United States in Central Asia: Prospects for Great Power Competition and Cooperation in the Shadow of the Georgian Crisis," Strategic Studies Institute, U.S. Army War College, February 2009.

World Bank. "Kazakhstan Overview," worldbank.org/en/country/Kazakhstan/overview.

World Bank. "Tajikistan," https://www.worldbank.org/en/country/tajikistan.

World Resources Institute. "Disappearance of the Aral Sea," wri.org/blog/2008/05/disappearance-aral-sea.

Zhenghong, Z. "Regional Security in Central Asia and Russia After 9/11," *Far Eastern Affairs*, Vol. 33, No. 1, 2005, 21–28.

Chapter 2

China's Geoeconomic Strategy and Sri Lanka's International Commercial Dispute Resolution Centre

Lorenzo Fiorito[1]

INTRODUCTION

Overview

Could Port City Colombo's International Commercial Dispute Resolution Centre (ICDRC) allow China to project extraterritorial influence over commercial disputes in the Indo-Pacific region? This chapter hypothesizes a gradual, but currently ongoing shift—from a liberal international order, toward geoeconomics—in the dominant global paradigm of international relations. In this analysis, one way to project influence extraterritorially is to repurpose traditional mechanisms of international law (including international commercial law) to accommodate state interests. The Port City Special Economic Zone's in-house commercial arbitration mechanism, the ICDRC, might allow China to geoeconomically project influence over commercial disputes in the Indo-Pacific.

Much has been made of the potential security risks—for example, to India—if China were to use Sri Lanka's commercial ports for naval purposes (Patrick, 2016). While the Chinese government strategically adopts a military posture on occasion (Washington Post Editorial Board, 2021), this chapter's reading of current trends indicates that its preferred methods are geoeconomic. This shifts the paradigm of security: where one usually thinks of troops, tanks, and aircraft, the geoeconomic lens instead highlights financial instruments, investments, and debt-for-equity (or debt-for-territory [BBC, 2011]) swaps.

A state's influence over commercial transactions can affect other countries' security—in such areas as energy independence, food security, or access to essential consumer goods. In its strategic location on the Indian Ocean shipping route that connects Asia with Africa, the Middle East, and Europe, Port City Colombo could provide a potential "choke point" in global commerce, similar in strategic importance to the Suez Canal.

The following paragraphs of this Introduction will now define the term "geoeconomics."

What Is Geoeconomic Strategy?

In his announcement of the Belt and Road Initiative (BRI), China's President Xi described merchants along the ancient Silk Road as having "won their place in history not as conquerors with warships, guns or swords. Rather, they are remembered as friendly emissaries . . ." He stressed that this was applicable to the BRI: "we should build the Belt and Road into a road for peace. The ancient silk routes thrived in times of peace, but lost vigour in times of war. The pursuit of the Belt and Road Initiative requires a peaceful and stable environment" (Embassy of China in the UK, 2017).

In its bid to lead the world order, China may wish to avoid a costly arms race (Zhongping, 2021). Arguing for China's participation in strategic arms limitation with the United States and Russia, Zhao (2020) notes:

> over the previous years of material abundance, high levels of confidence within the Chinese expert community and the general public about China's long-term capability to out-invest and outcompete its main rivals in defense [*sic*] capabilities were widespread. It is uncertain how quickly the new economic realities today will change people's perceptions, but rational decision-makers need to be cool-headed and far-sighted about the economic implications for China's defense [*sic*] policy. They need to think about and prepare for a future in which they would have much fewer resources to invest in military modernizations than before.

As a rising power—presently militarily outmatched by its rival—China does not seem to want to beat the United States at its own game. Rather, it appears to have chosen the economic terrain: and in so doing, to slowly shift the logic by which states succeed or fail in the international order (Beeson, 2018). This speculation is supported by Chinese Foreign Minister Wang Yi's statement in 2015: 'The "Belt and Road" initiative . . . is a product of inclusive cooperation, not a tool of geopolitics, and must not be viewed with the outdated Cold War mentality' (China Foreign Affairs Ministry, 2015).

As the Cold War ended, Luttwak (1990) aptly described geoeconomics as an emergent trend in which the "methods of commerce are displacing military methods." He identified a process that, while employing the "grammar of commerce," follows the "logic of conflict." Domosh (2013) argues that geoeconomic thinking was an essential complement to traditional early-twentieth-century geopolitics, as the rising American power began to compete with the then-hegemon, Great Britain. In this context, she provides a concise definition of geoeconomics: a "strategy of the expansion of power—commercial dominance without direct political control" of one state over another.

Nevertheless, the international landscape has changed since the United States' use of geoeconomics in the early twentieth century. Today, there exist several multilateral institutions and structures of international economic law, bequeathed by the post–World War II Bretton Woods system. This chapter understands states' preference for "soft power" (Nye, 1990) over "hard power," in the geoeconomic paradigm, to mean that the state relies on commercial mechanisms and interests—rather than the traditional security apparatus—to project its influence.

Csurgai (2017) shows that geoeconomics entails cooperation between the state and its private sector to mutually advance their shared interests. He furthermore indicates that geoeconomics could replace the liberal (or neoliberal) paradigm of international relations.

> The existence of state–industry co-operation challenges the neo-liberal perspective. There has been no diminution of the importance of the state, but a transformation of its strategic role in order to adapt to a new power reality of the twenty-first century in which commercial, financial, technological and cultural factors play an increasing role. *The objective of this "Strategic State" is to create the conditions for establishing a successful geoeconomic disposition that can create synergy between the private sector and government agencies.* (Emphasis added)

Compare Csurgai's close identification of the state and its market sector, in geoeconomic thinking, with President Xi's statement as he launched the BRI:

> Finance is the lifeblood of modern economy. . . .We should establish a stable and sustainable financial safeguard system that keeps risks under control, create new models of investment and financing, *encourage greater cooperation between government and private capital* and build a diversified financing system and a multi-tiered capital market. We should also develop inclusive finance and improve financial services networks. (Embassy of China in the UK, 2017; emphasis added)

For a nonmarket economy to expand—particularly, that of a rising power which suffers from a military disadvantage—geoeconomic strategy becomes *systemically* necessary. In China's case, the predominance of state-owned enterprises (SOEs), both within the national economy and in contracts along the BRI, requires this interrelation of state and commercial interests. While governments of free-market economies may decide (whether for better or worse) to leave the private sector to its own devices, by contrast, China's state-owned industries can only enjoy commercial growth in international markets if the state adopts a geoeconomic strategic outlook. Hence, China has initiated the BRI.

Corresponding with the rise of China, geoeconomic analysis appears to be resurgent, as scholars search for analytical tools that effectively explain current trends in international relations. As Roberts, Moraes, and Ferguson (2018) write:

> We appear to be entering into a new geoeconomic world order, characterized by great power rivalry between the United States and China and the clear use of economic tools to achieve strategic goals. This increased convergence of economic and security thinking and strategies is likely to lead to a *significant restructuring of the laws and institutions that govern international trade and investment.* (Emphasis added)

This chapter agrees with their assessment: the future of world order may prove to be geoeconomic. Since geoeconomic tactics appear to be more cost-efficient than expensive investments in traditional security arrangements, they could provide a niche of strategic advantage to those who adopt them. Furthermore, if geoeconomics implies a greater collaboration between the state and its commercial sector, then it follows logically that the state should attempt to reshape the "laws and institutions that govern international trade and investment" in ways that benefit its own firms.

When commercial entities engage in cross-border transactions and trade, they operate within a framework of treaties and international organizations that govern the flow of trade and investment. States are the relevant actors at the level of treaties and international organizations. A geoeconomic "Strategic State" would attempt to subvert, alter, or paralyze these mechanisms in favor of its domestic firms. The paragraphs that follow make up a case study and illustrate that an attempted shift from a rules-based international order to a geoeconomic order has already begun to take place at the World Trade Organization (WTO).

The Geoeconomic Character of Competition between the United States and China: The WTO as a Case Study

President Obama, whose "pivot to Asia" strategy intended to contain China through the (now-moribund) Trans-Pacific Partnership, writes about the United States' longstanding trade grievances with China in his recent memoir (Obama, 2020). He says:

> China kept evading, bending, or breaking just about every agreed-upon rule of international commerce during its "peaceful rise." For years, it had used state

> subsidies, as well as currency manipulation and trade dumping, to artificially depress the price of its exports and undercut manufacturing operations in the United States . . . China wasn't going to change its trading practices without firm pressure from my administration; I just had to make sure we didn't start a trade war that tipped the world into a depression.

Obama's expression, "trade war," expresses the concept of geoeconomics precisely. His successor, President Trump, took a stridently geoeconomic approach to the United States' foreign economic relations throughout his administration. Trump Tweeted: "Trade wars are good, and easy to win" (Franck, 2018).

In March 2018, the United States invoked Article XXI of the GATT (General Agreement on Tariffs and Trade), the WTO's national-security exception, to apply its Section 232 tariffs on imports of aluminum and steel at the WTO level. China characterized the move as an example of banned, protectionist, "safeguard measures although it's [*sic*] in the name of national security. We believe the measures taken by the United States are not consistent with its obligations under the relevant provisions of the GATT 1994 and Safeguards Agreement" (WTO, 2018).

The ensuing trade war expanded to tariffs on at least $360 billion worth of Chinese goods, to which China responded with tariffs on $110 billion worth of US goods (Mullen, 2021). The Biden Administration has continued Trump's trade policies—including that of paralyzing the WTO's Appellate Body (Baschuk, 2021). Under President Biden, not only do many Trump-era tariffs remain in place on Chinese goods (Bartash, 2020), but the Biden administration appears prepared to investigate whether new Section 232 tariffs, invoking national security, may be necessary on imports of neodymium magnets (White House, 2021). In the area of international trade, then, US–China relations appear to have assumed an ongoing geoeconomic character.

Thus, the case study of US–China trade relations, taken together with China's actions in the BRI, provides evidence to support this chapter's underpinning hypothesis: that a geoeconomic world order may be emerging to replace the post–World War II liberal international order. Under these circumstances, institutions overseeing economic legal relationships can be repurposed to serve geoeconomic ends. One such circumstance is through the state's invocation of its domestic public policy.

The ICDRC might be an example of a forum that speaks in the grammar of commerce, but whose arbitral decisions could entail security effects. As Müllerson (2014) writes, "Competing visions of the world also create competing interpretations of international law and it's [*sic*] à la carte application—bending and choosing whatever pleases one's taste or best suits one's vision of the world." Geoeconomics, in its bid to remake the international order, promises to blur the distinction between geopolitics and international law—including international commercial law.

Methodology and Structure

This chapter uses a qualitative research methodology—drawing on academic literature, news articles, thinktank reports, and books by authors in relevant fields—to demonstrate that the Port City Colombo's ICDRC could be used to further China's geoeconomic interests over commercial disputes in the Indo-Pacific.

The geoeconomic paradigm is a relevant contender to replace the post–World War II international order. It can combine interstate economic competition with traditional security processes. Because it requires a close degree of coordination between the state and its commercial sector, based on shared objectives and interests, geoeconomic strategy sometimes requires the state to repurpose existing legal mechanisms that oversee international commercial relations.

This chapter will explore the economic relationships between China and Sri Lanka that made the Port City Special Economic Zone possible. It appears that China converted Sri Lanka's need to meet foreign exchange obligations (Nadkarni, 2021; Xinhua, 2021) into a 99-year lease, a land reclamation deal, and a potential international commercial hub (Francis, 2021) that serves Chinese interests in the Indo-Pacific.

This chapter will then explain three ways that the ICDRC's arbitration mechanism could be repurposed to facilitate Chinese geoeconomic influence over commercial disputes in the Indo-Pacific. First, the Chinese SOE that owns Port City could exert undue influence over the composition of the ICDRC's pool of preferred arbitrators. Second, the arbitration mechanism itself could facilitate illicit commercial transactions—for example, evading sanctions or laundering money—without appropriate safeguards. Finally, a losing commercial party at the ICDRC could challenge an unfavorable arbitral award on the grounds of Sri Lankan "public policy."

If Port City Colombo proves to succeed, its very existence would provide concrete evidence that the old liberal international order may be giving way to a more complex, dynamic, geoeconomic world order.

PORT CITY COLOMBO: THE RESULT OF A CONFLUENCE BETWEEN CHINA'S BRI GEOECONOMIC STRATEGY AND SRI LANKA'S FOREIGN DEBT OBLIGATIONS

The "Chinese Debt-Trap"

Much has been made of whether China uses "debt-trap diplomacy"—in which Sri Lanka would be "Exhibit A" (Chellaney, 2017)—or whether, instead, China simply provides preferential credit terms to developing countries (Brautigam, 2020). Chellaney's term, the "Chinese debt trap," hypothesizes that China intentionally loans money to states that it knows cannot repay these funds, as a strategy to ultimately peddle influence in those countries. Since China's subjective intentions are difficult to prove, it is more productive to examine the outcomes of these transactions.

Nadkarni (2021) writes: "While often characterised as a debt swap, the funds from the [Port City] lease were used to boost foreign currency reserves, not to restructure debt to China." Such a characterization, while accurate, focuses on detail at the expense of a broader picture. Financial obligations can provide underlying context for currency swaps.

Sri Lanka appears wary of an IMF bailout deal (Ondaatjie, 2021a). (Indeed, at the time of writing, discussion of the issue in Sri Lanka's cabinet has resulted in stalemate [EconomyNext, 2021].) Sri Lanka's bilateral debt to China includes sovereign currency-swap facilities (Karunatilake and Pal, 2021), and direct loans from state-owned policy banks like the China Development Bank (Srinivasan, 2021). Port City Colombo is wholly owned by an SOE: the China Harbour Engineering Company (CHEC), whose parent company is the China Communications & Construction Company (CHEC Port City Colombo, 2021).

These Chinese actors' behaviors need not have been intentionally coordinated: given the overarching direction that the BRI sets, they may all simply operate with a similar mindset toward Sri Lanka. Nevertheless, geoeconomic strategy may imply a strong level of coordination between the Chinese state and its commercial SOEs. In turn, as a heavily indebted, IMF-averse state, Sri Lanka's needs coincide well with China's strategic ambitions in the Indo-Pacific.

A revenue stream that Sri Lanka uses to shore up foreign currency reserves, like the Port City lease, therefore need not formally be tied to a debt instrument or credit facility. It may, nevertheless, imply a correlation in which Sri Lanka is more open to persuasion by Chinese diplomacy. The question remains: Why did Sri Lanka become so vulnerable to China's geoeconomic strategy? Why did it need to take on so much debt? To answer these questions, this chapter turns briefly to Sri Lanka's history of conflict.

Sri Lanka's Debt and China's BRI

Sri Lanka fought a brutal war with armed actors representing the de facto state of Tamil Eelam (The Economist, 2007; Baruah, 2003) between 1983 and 2009. The conflict's legacy in the form of debt to the IMF continues to this day. This context shows the objective logic of Port City: China has "agreed" to help repay Sri Lanka's IMF debt, together with some bond debt—denominated in foreign currencies—in exchange for a claim over the financial and strategic benefits that Port City may bring it in the Indo-Pacific.

A US Senate Foreign Relations Committee report (2009) clarified, months after the war ended, the blow that the war delivered to the state's finances.

> The [Government of Sri Lanka]'s budget suffered from the high cost of fighting the war. Expensive purchases of war-related equipment and ammunition, often on longer term contracts and using up valuable foreign reserves, coupled with a drop in exports due to the global economic downturn, pushed Sri Lanka to request a $2.6 billion standby arrangement from the IMF in early 2009 which was approved in July. . . . Longer term contracts with foreign suppliers of military equipment, particularly China, continue to weigh heavily on the budget. . . . [M]ilitary and civilian officials stressed to staff that the bulk of the requested increase of about 15 percent in the defense budget is due primarily to the [Government]'s need to pay down military debts incurred during the final stages of the war.

Standby arrangements (SBAs) administered by the IMF, such as the one granted to Sri Lanka in July 2009, are considered non-concessional loans (IMF, 2021a). The term "non-concessional" means that the loan is not offered on preferential terms, but rather according to a standard lending program.

The IMF's reserves are taken from member countries' dues, or "quotas" (IMF, 2021b). These reserves are held in the form of a non-currency asset known as the Special Drawing Right (SDR). According to the IMF: "The value of the SDR is based on a basket of five currencies—the U.S. dollar, the euro, the Chinese renminbi, the Japanese yen, and the British pound sterling" (2021c). Each currency is assigned a weight against the SDR. Borrowing countries may take out loans denominated in SDR, or in one of the five basket currencies, or in another currency. Depending on the terms of the loan, they may repay in the same currency, or in SDR (IMF Legal Department, 2019). (Repaying in SDR means paying back the loan with some combination of the five currencies in the basket, as the value of each is weighted against the SDR.)

Thus, repaying IMF loans requires that Sri Lanka should hold enough of the required currency in its foreign exchange reserves, at the time of maturity. As of February 2021, Sri Lanka owes 942.24 million in SDR outstanding to the IMF (2021d). This figure does not include interest (which is calculated separately). According to the IMF, this is one of Sri Lanka's several external government debt obligations:

> China's outstanding official loans to the Sri Lankan central government amount to approximately US$3 billion based on end-2018 data or 9 percent of external central government debt, compared to 13 percent by the Asian Development Bank, 10 percent by Japan, and 10 percent by the World Bank. (IMF Asia and Pacific Department, 2019)

In a footnote, the report hastens to add: "China's loans to the Sri Lankan public sector, including SOEs, are around US$5 billion (15% of external debt)."

To maintain its balance of payments amid all this instability, Sri Lanka has also raised billions of dollars in sovereign bond debt from private lenders, which tend to have relatively long maturity periods and can therefore buy time for a sovereign. Facing a pinch, Sri Lanka's Central Bank used its foreign exchange reserves to repay bond debt coming to maturity in July 2021 (Ondaatjie, 2021b). These amounted to $1 billion in sovereign bonds coming due, just as Moody's placed Sri Lanka under review for a potential creditworthiness downgrade (Sri Lanka Ministry of Finance, 2021).

Chinese state media quotes Governor of the Central Bank of Sri Lanka, W. D. Lakshman, as saying, the "newly enacted legislative framework for the Port City Colombo project will help raise non-debt foreign exchange inflows for Sri Lanka" (Xinhua, 2021). By "non-debt foreign exchange inflows," Lakshman quite logically means that those revenues raised from CHEC's Port City lease do not have to be repaid. However, those same "non-debt inflows" could then be turned around to refinance Sri Lankan debt, owed in foreign currencies.

Port City Colombo may not correspond point-for-point with the purest concept of the "Chinese debt-trap." It certainly does appear that Sri Lanka's debt has placed it in a compromising position toward China. That position has given China a great deal of influence over Sri Lanka; and some of that influence could, in the future, be projected through Port City's ICDRC.

POTENTIAL GEOECONOMIC USES OF PORT CITY COLOMBO'S ICDRC

Geoeconomics and International Commercial Arbitration

The Introduction's example of geoeconomic competition at the WTO shows effectively that ostensibly neutral legal forums and instruments can be leveraged to serve geoeconomic purposes. Csurgai's identification of the way that geoeconomics requires a close relationship between the state and its commercial sector—even more relevant in China's nonmarket economy—indicates that China's controlling influence over the Port City could therefore make international dispute resolution at its ICDRC a geoeconomic issue as well.

International commercial arbitration is traditionally seen as a private legal system that exists separately from any state's judiciary, and that allows nationally neutral resolution of disputes over cross-border contracts. This system is the sole recourse for commercial disputes with the Port City Commission in the Special Economic Zone.

In 2020, the Sri Lankan Ministry of Justice, Human Rights, and Legal Reforms announced that it would be reviving the defunct Sri Lanka National Arbitration Centre (SLNAC). The Ministry's secretary, J. J. Rathnasiri, noted that "Sri Lanka should have its own international arbitration centre, especially to solve the issues that might arise from the Port City" (Thavapalakumar, 2020).

Dabarera and Vimanga (2021) note, however, that "constant political instability in the country and the failure of the judiciary to uphold [the] rule of law [have] . . . acted as hindrances to propel Sri Lanka as a global hub for International Arbitration." They assert that the "current International Arbitration Centre in Sri Lanka, despite being based upon the UNCITRAL model law of Arbitration, has ultimately failed in winning over the confidence of the public and investors due to the arbitration proceedings dragging too long (as long as three years in certain instances)."

Dabarera and Vimanga's concern about the rule of law in Sri Lanka is telling. In 2013, then-President Mahinda Rajapaksa (brother of the current President Gotabaya Rajapaksa) dismissed Sri Lanka's Supreme Court Chief Justice, Shirani Bandaranayake (BBC, 2013). It touched off a global perception that Sri Lanka's judiciary lacked independence from the country's executive branch. This could be the reason that CHEC Port City Colombo has insisted on the mandatory use of arbitration to settle disputes.

In the situation that this chapter describes above—where Sri Lanka is subject to a high degree of Chinese influence through BRI debt—its lack of judicial independence has larger ramifications. A geoeconomic strategy toward international commercial law would leverage the state's existing position within the arbitration system.

This chapter will show that geoeconomic features are already present within the Port City Commission Bill's mandatory referral of all disputes to the ICDRC. It will identify three means through which China's geoeconomic strategy in Port City Colombo could influence the way the ICDRC functions. First, it explains how international arbitration functions.

International Commercial Arbitration: A Brief Overview

State Authority Underpins the System of International Commercial Arbitration

International arbitration was developed as an alternative to national courts for cross-border contractual disputes. Continental scholars, notably Emmanuel Gaillard (2007), have leaned toward the interpretation that commercial law (*lex mercatoria*) has developed such a degree of independence that it produces its own legal authority, without the state. Others, such as British judge Lord Mustill (1988), have taken the opposing view: that the *lex mercatoria* has not yet overcome its reliance on the national legislative authority.

This chapter takes the latter perspective. True, commercial arbitration ran parallel to the national legal order several hundred years ago; and more recently, economic globalization appeared for some time to reduce the role of the state in the commercial arbitral legal order (Michaels, 2008). Nevertheless, the institutions that provide international arbitration services today derive their authority from national Arbitration Acts.

Furthermore, arbitral awards (the name for arbitrators' decisions) are recognized and enforceable in a worldwide system that is ratified by states: under the New York Convention of 1958 (more formally known as the *United Nations Convention on the Recognition and Enforcement of Foreign Arbitral Awards*). The New York Convention has 168 signatories, or "Contracting States." Again, this rather sweeping power of the international arbitration system derives from a state-led process of treaty ratification.

Some Traditional Features of International Commercial Arbitration

Having demonstrated that states do hold an essential role in how the *lex mercatoria* is administered, this section now examines some features of international arbitration that could become relevant to any geoeconomic strategy. These are: neutrality of the arbitration process, arbitrator impartiality, and the finality of awards as understood through the lens of party autonomy. This section explains each concept below.

When a foreign company signs a contract to conduct business in another company's home state, that contract would traditionally be subject to domestic law. Consequently, the foreign investor would be subject to a potentially biased judiciary. This is known as the problem of "neutrality," and it is the primary reason that the arbitration system was developed as an alternative to national courts in commercial dealings.

Neutrality through Party Autonomy

Traditionally, international arbitration resolves the problem of neutrality in a few different ways. One of these is through "party autonomy": the parties are not forced to do anything that they do not freely agree to do, if a dispute arises. Importantly, then, the parties are free to choose their own arbitrators. They traditionally choose arbitrators that are of different nationalities to either of them. Thus, neither party formally has the political advantage of a biased domestic judiciary.

Arbitrator Impartiality

Another feature of traditional arbitration is impartiality. The arbitrators must declare any conflicts of interest, and if the conflict is serious enough, they may not arbitrate the case. (This depends on the rules of ethics that apply to a given arbitration and/or arbitrator). Problems could arise, as shown below, if the arbitrators do not declare conflicts of interest—or, if such conflicts are integrally built into the arbitral institution.

Procedural Set-Asides

In general, neither the winner nor the loser can challenge the award (known as the "finality" of awards), except to identify very serious errors of procedure. However, during such procedural challenges, the problem of neutrality may sometimes reassert itself. A losing party will refer these procedural challenges to the "seat of arbitration": to a national judiciary that applies its domestic Arbitration Act.

In accordance with party autonomy, the parties may agree to set their "seat of arbitration" in any jurisdiction in the world. However, more often, the parties do not name the seat; and it then defaults to the physical jurisdiction where the arbitral forum is located. As the ICDRC is in Sri Lanka, Sri Lanka is the default seat of arbitration for cases that come to the ICDRC.

This section now turns to identify three problems that arise from the way the ICDRC is constituted. These problems present the potential for geoeconomic uses of the international arbitration procedure.

Problem 1: Potential Limits to the Impartiality of the ICDRC's Arbitrator Pool

First is the problem of arbitrator impartiality. This has two dimensions. First, the Port City Commission Bill imposes mandatory arbitration. Second, CHEC Port City Colombo—a Chinese SOE—administers the physical location where the ICDRC will stand.

Parties who want to do business through the Port City Special Economic Zone *must* include an arbitration clause that names the ICDRC as the forum for dispute resolution in their commercial contracts. Article 32 of the Port City Commission Bill reads (Gazette of the Democratic Socialist Republic of Sri Lanka, 2021):

> The Commission shall enter into an agreement with every authorized person . . . in relation to the investment to be engaged in within the Area of Authority of the Colombo Port City. *Every such agreement shall include a provision whereby the parties agree to the resolution of any dispute arising therefrom, by way of arbitration in terms of Part XIII* of this Act. (Emphasis added)

Part XIII of the Bill establishes the ICDRC. Article 62(2) of Part XIII reads (Gazette of the Democratic Socialist Republic of Sri Lanka, 2021):

> Any dispute that may arise, within the Area of Authority of the Colombo Port City, between—(a) the Commission and an authorised person or an employee of an authorised person where relevant; and (b) the Commission and a resident or an occupier, provided that there exists in relation thereto, an agreement or other legally binding document as between the Commission and such resident or occupier, *shall be resolved by way of arbitration conducted by the International Commercial Dispute Resolution Centre.* (Emphasis added)

Thus, commercial parties who invest in Port City are tied to the ICDRC—by order of the Sri Lankan legislature. In the case of a dispute, the parties must use institutional rules and procedures prescribed by the ICDRC. It appears that both parties may still choose any arbitrator they wish—but more often, because the disputes are being heard at the ICDRC, they would choose from among the ICRDC's preferred list of arbitrators. The Port City Commission Bill's Article 32 approaches arbitration by *restricting* party autonomy.

In turn, the ICDRC will sit on territory directly administered by CHEC Port City Colombo, a Chinese SOE. It is possible that, in certain circumstances, CHEC Port City Colombo, and its parent company, the CHEC, could exert undue influence over the arbitrators available for a case of high interest. In cases covered by Articles 32 and 62, which could potentially be most cases, there is no alternative to the ICDRC. This could grant an unfair advantage to any Chinese SOEs who are party to commercial arbitrations that the ICDRC hosts. Alluding to similar situations, Sharma (2014) writes:

> Where impartiality and independence of the arbitrators is equated with direct relation to or bias towards one of the parties, neutrality is related to the nationality of the arbitrator. In international sphere, the "appearance of neutrality" is considered equally important, meaning an arbitrator is neutral if his nationality is different from that of the parties. Nationality generally is not an issue if the parties have agreed to appoint an arbitrator of the same nationality as that of one of the parties, but it has a different impact when national courts act as the appointing authority.

Importantly, then, a conflict of interest appears integrally built into the ICDRC system. Without clear rules on how arbitrators are selected, this conflict of interest would favor a geoeconomic strategy—where a Chinese SOE pre-influences the outcome of an arbitration, by restricting the arbitrator pool to candidates it understands to be pliable.

The only avenue for a procedural challenge to the ICDRC's decisions is, in the bulk of cases, to go to the Sri Lankan judiciary—which is seen to lack independence from the national executive. Sri Lanka, in turn, is vulnerable to influence from China through its current relationship of economic dependence. The potential exists for a geoeconomic strategy, in the selection of arbitrators, to influence the outcome of commercial arbitrations at the ICDRC.

Problem 2: The Geoeconomic Potential to Use ICDRC Arbitration for Money Laundering Or to Evade Sanctions

It is unclear what safeguards are in place to prevent abuse of the ICDRC's arbitration mechanisms by facilitating illicit transfers of money. Arbitration practitioners have identified the risk that a commercial dispute could be manufactured between two parties who could not normally transfer funds between each other legally—for instance, via a shell company acting on one party's behalf. Such a contrived dispute would enable money-laundering or help one of the parties to evade sanctions.

In the case of Port City, where at least one company operating in the Special Economic Zone appears to be on the United States' sanctions list, the ICDRC's dispute resolution forum may contain the potential for such abuse. Former United States Ambassador Alaina Teplitz is quoted as saying, "the United States does have one of the companies working on the Port City Development on our sanctions list so doing business with that company may not be something that's advisable" (The Island, 2021). CHEC Port City Colombo contests this allegation.

Nevertheless, the ICDRC could provide a way around such sanctions. Nacimiento, Hertel, and Gayer (2017) point to three such situations.

> The confidentiality of arbitration, which finds [its] basis in the parties' agreement, can provide an ideal environment to conceal and disguise the origin of money. An arbitral award—issued in terms that enshrine a settlement between the parties—might be seen as the perfect means to legitimize money flows.

There are three main scenarios in which a potential money laundering concern may emerge in an arbitration. In the first instance, a party to the arbitration may raise questions regarding money laundering itself, potentially as a defence in the proceedings. Second, the arbitral tribunal may become suspicious regarding the legitimacy of the dispute or the purported transaction underlying that dispute. This may in turn raise questions about whether the whole purpose of the arbitration proceedings is to launder money. Third, and this could coincide with the second scenario where the entire arbitration is fabricated, the arbitration may be financed by illegal activities: for example, the security for costs is paid by laundered money. In all three scenarios the arbitral tribunal could itself become—at least to some extent—an unwilling participant in the money laundering process.

If dispute resolution at Port City follows geoeconomic logic, there might be no way to prevent suspect transactions—which would otherwise raise international alarms—from flowing through Port City. If either China or Sri Lanka were to influence their firms to use arbitration in ways that facilitate geoeconomic strategic objectives, the ICDRC could facilitate the process. Such a scenario would challenge the rationale for an International Arbitration Centre at Port City as such. It remains to be seen what safeguards the ICDRC will implement to forestall negative outcomes like this one.

Problem 3: The Sri Lankan Arbitration Act's Public Policy Carveout

A primary example of Sri Lanka's notoriously illiberal approach to trade and investment is its "public policy carveout." Article 32(1)(b)(vi) of the Sri Lankan Arbitration Act reads: "An arbitral award made in an arbitration held in Sri Lanka may be set aside by the High Court . . . where the High Court finds that . . . the arbitral award conflicts with the public policy of Sri Lanka." This phrase contains the strongest possible potential for the geoeconomic use of the ICDRC's arbitration procedures.

As seen above, procedural challenges to ICDRC awards will generally be referred to the Sri Lankan courts, since Sri Lanka is its default seat of arbitration. As also previously noted, the Sri Lankan judiciary has been subject to tactics that raise the question of its independence from the executive branch. If the judiciary believes that an arbitral award conflicts with Sri Lankan state policy, it may set that award aside.

Such a set-aside would have global effects—quite literally. As seen previously, one of the strongest advantages of international arbitration is that arbitral awards are enforceable in 168 countries worldwide, under the New York Convention. Article III of the Convention reads, in part, "Each Contracting State shall recognize arbitral awards as binding and enforce them in accordance with the rules of procedure of the territory where the award is relied upon."

However, the public policy carveout in Article 32 of Sri Lanka's Arbitration Act gives the New York Convention's Article III the reverse effect. If the Sri Lankan judiciary holds that an ICDRC award—otherwise perfectly sound—runs contrary to the public policy of Sri Lanka, that set-aside takes priority in all 168 countries. For foreign recognition and enforcement of awards can only take place "*in accordance with the rules of procedure of the territory where the award is relied upon.*" Article V(2)(b) of the New York Convention expressly permits this: "Recognition and enforcement of the award may be refused, at the request of the party against whom it is invoked only if that party furnishes to the competent authority where the recognition and enforcement is sought, proof that: . . . The recognition or enforcement of the award would be contrary to the public policy of that country."

Participation in China's BRI is a central feature of Sri Lanka's state policy—particularly in the case of Port City Colombo. Any ICDRC award that conflicts with Sri Lanka's public policy may be set aside by the Sri Lankan judiciary—potentially, under the influence of the executive branch.

This is no idle speculation. Rodrigo (2021) points to an extensive history of "suspicious," "hawkish," and "interventionist" Sri Lankan judicial attitudes toward dispute settlement via arbitration. Nevertheless, Sri Lanka's High Court found, in its 2014 decision reviewing the arbitral award in *Mahawaduge Priyanga Lakshitha Prasad Perera v China National Technical Imports & Export Corporation*, that the "principle of minimal judicial interference in the arbitral process is fundamentally important to the efficacy of the arbitral process so that the arbitral process does not get affected by judicial review of arbitral rulings unless it is statutorily permitted by the Arbitration Act." Rodrigo describes the *China National* decision as "striking" and a "radical break with the past." It remains to be seen whether the old ways, or the new, will prevail among Sri Lanka's judiciary when dealing with arbitral awards.

In spite of the *China National* High Court decision, the potential remains: a commercial arbitral award, implicitly unfavorable to Chinese business interests, might still be found legally inimical to Sri Lanka's national interests. This fact could provide grounds for the Sri Lankan courts to set aside that award on the grounds of public policy. Such a set-aside in the Sri Lankan courts would make that award internationally unenforceable.

CONCLUSION

This chapter has examined Port City Colombo's potential through a geoeconomic lens. Geoeconomics, in Luttwak's phrase, uses the "grammar of commerce, but the logic of conflict." The Introduction demonstrated that geoeconomics is a candidate to replace the liberal international order, and that this paradigm has already begun to characterize the trade relationship between the United States and China. It showed that China's BRI, of which Port City forms a part, appears to follow a geoeconomic logic.

While China's subjective intention was unnecessary for its relationship with Sri Lanka to follow a geoeconomic logic, this chapter leaned toward Chellaney's explanation that China created a debt trap to project its influence in Sri Lanka for strategic reasons. Port City offers a potential "choke point" for international trade routes (much like the Suez Canal), which could potentially affect areas like energy independence, food security, and access to basic consumer goods.

This chapter explained a few of the founding principles of the system of international commercial arbitration system, including independence from the national judiciary. It then identified potential issues that could arise during ICDRC proceedings: lack of arbitrator impartiality, compromised integrity of the dispute resolution process, and Sri Lanka's public policy carveout.

Unless these problems are resolved, more established free-market commercial entities might choose to avoid conducting business through the Port City Commission. As the Sri Lankan legislation that enables the ICDRC is presently constituted, Port City's business would more likely rely on Chinese shippers and their subsidiaries; and, perhaps to some degree, on less independent firms from other countries.

This chapter points to the ICDRC as an example of how China's existing geoeconomic strategy, the BRI, could take shape soon. China has a clientelist credit relationship with Sri Lanka. Its potential uses of Port City Colombo to project influence through several channels simultaneously—such as credit facilities, shipping lanes, and commercial dispute resolution—may pose a challenge to liberal paradigms of world order.

NOTE

1. L. Fiorito. Centre for Media, Human Rights and Peacebuilding, UK. Email: Lorenzo.fio@protonmail.com

BIBLIOGRAPHY

Bartash, J. (2020) Biden to Keep Trump Tariffs on China as Leverage Against 'Abusive' Trade Practices. *MarketWatch*, 2 December, https://www.marketwatch.com/story/biden-may-tone-down-war-of-words-with-china-but-trump-tariffs-not-going-away-soon-11605132400, accessed 10 August 2021.

Baruah, A. (2003) 'LTTE has Set Up De Facto State'. *The Hindu*, 12 April, https://www.thehindu.com/todays-paper/ltte-has-set-up-de-facto-state/article27755923.ece, accessed 16 January 2022.

Baschuk, B. (2021) Biden Picks Up Where Trump Left Off in Hard-Line Stances at WTO. *Bloomberg*, 22 February, https://www.bloomberg.com/news/articles/2021-02-22/biden-picks-up-where-trump-left-off-in-hard-line-stances-at-wto, accessed 10 August 2021.

BBC. (2011) Tajikistan Cedes Land to China. 13 January, https://www.bbc.co.uk/news/world-asia-pacific-12180567, accessed 22 July 2021.

BBC. (2013) Sri Lanka President Sacks Chief Justice Bandaranayake. 13 January, https://www.bbc.co.uk/news/world-21002642, accessed 23 July 2021.

Beeson, M. (2018) Geoeconomics with Chinese Characteristics: The BRI and China's Evolving Grand Strategy. Taylor and Francis Online, 3 September, https://doi.org/10.1080/20954816.2018.1498988

Brautigam, D. (2020) A Critical Look at Chinese 'Debt-Trap Diplomacy': The Rise of a Meme. *Area Development and Policy* 5(1): 1–14.

CHEC Port City Colombo (Pvt.) Ltd. (2021) Frequently Asked Questions: Company Background, 2021, accessed 21 July 2021.

Chellaney, B. (2017) China's Debt Trap Diplomacy. *Project Syndicate*, 23 January, https://www.project-syndicate.org/commentary/china-one-belt-one-road-loans-debt-by-brahma-chellaney-2017-01, accessed 21 July 2021.

Csurgai, G. (2017) The Increasing Importance of Geoeconomics in Power Rivalries in the Twenty-First Century. *Geopolitics* 23(1): 38–46.

Dabarera, H. and Vimanga, K.D. (2021) Are We Getting the Colombo Port City Financial Centre Right? *Daily News*, 18 May, http://www.dailynews.lk/2021/05/18/business/249522/are-we-getting-colombo-port-city-financial-centre-right, accessed 23 July 2021.

Domosh, M. (2013) Geoeconomic Imaginations and Economic Geography in the Early Twentieth Century. *Annals of the Association of American Geographers* 103(4): 944–966.

The Economist (2007) Briefing: A War Strange As Fiction. *The Economist*, 7 June, https://www.economist.com/briefing/2007/06/07/a-war-strange-as-fiction, accessed 10 August 2021.

EconomyNext (2021) Sri Lanka Cabinet Debates IMF Bailout for Second Week. *EconomyNext*, 21 December, https://economynext.com/sri-lanka-cabinet-debates-imf-bailout-for-second-week-88992/, accessed 16 January 2022.

Embassy of China in the UK (2017). Work Together to Build the Silk Road Economic Belt and the 21st Century Maritime Silk Road. Speech by H.E. Xi Jinping, 14 May, http://www.chinese-embassy.org.uk/eng/zgyw/t1465819.htm, accessed 21 July 2021.

Franck, T. (2018) Trump Doubles Down: 'Trade Wars are Good, and Easy to Win'. *CNBC*, 2 March, https://www.cnbc.com/2018/03/02/trump-trade-wars-are-good-and-easy-to-win.html, accessed 10 August 2021.

Francis, K. (2021) Sri Lankan Court: China-Built Port Board Needs Public Assent. *AP*, 19 May, https://apnews.com/article/china-health-coronavirus-pandemic-business-f7c2c5145ee845a87f80015a21a7eb86, accessed 21 July 2021.

Gaillard, E. (2007) Souveraineté et autonomie: réflexions sur les representations de l'arbitrage international. *Journal du droit international* 4(October–December 2007): 1163–1173.

Gazette of the Democratic Socialist Republic of Sri Lanka. (2021) Colombo Port City Commission Bill. 19 March, https://www.parliament.lk/uploads/bills/gbills/gazette/english/6218.pdf, accessed 13 August 2021.

Haviland, C. (2013) Remembering Sri Lanka's Black July. *BBC*, 23 July, https://www.bbc.co.uk/news/world-asia-23402727, accessed 21 July 2021.

International Trade Administration, United States Department of Commerce. (2021) Foreign Retaliations Timeline. https://www.trade.gov/feature-article/foreign-retaliations-timeline, accessed 10 August 2021.
International Monetary Fund. (2021a) IMF Stand-By Arrangement (SBA). 18 May, https://www.imf.org/en/About/Factsheets/Sheets/2016/08/01/20/33/Stand-By-Arrangement, accessed 22 July 2021.
International Monetary Fund. (2021b) Where the IMF Gets Its Money. 26 April, https://www.imf.org/en/About/Factsheets/Where-the-IMF-Gets-Its-Money, accessed 22 July 2021.
International Monetary Fund. (2021c) Special Drawing Rights (SDR). 18 February, https://www.imf.org/en/About/Factsheets/Sheets/2016/08/01/14/51/Special-Drawing-Right-SDR, accessed 22 July 2021.
International Monetary Fund. (2021d) Sri Lanka. https://www.imf.org/en/Countries/LKA, accessed 22 July 2021.
International Monetary Fund Asia and Pacific Department. (2019) Sri Lanka: Fifth Review Under the Extended Arrangement Under the Extended Fund Facility, Request for Waivers of Nonobservance of Performance Criteria, Extension of the Arrangement and Rephasing of Purchases-Press Release; Staff Report and Statement by the Executive Director for Sri Lanka. https://www.imf.org/en/Publications/CR/Issues/2019/05/15/Sri-Lanka-Fifth-Review-Under-the-Extended-Arrangement-Under-the-Extended-Fund-Facility-46900, accessed 22 July 2021.
International Monetary Fund Legal Department. (2019) Selected Decisions and Selected Documents of the IMF, Fortieth Issue – Use of SDRs in Loans: Article XIX, Section 2.
Special Drawing Rights: Additional Uses. 30 April, https://www.imf.org/external/SelectedDecisions/Description.aspx?decision=6001-(79/1)%20S, accessed 22 July 2021.
The Island. (2021) US Ambassador's Remarks on CHEC Port City: Investor Sets the Record Straight. 5 August, https://island.lk/us-ambassadors-remarks-on-chec-port-city-investor-sets-the-record-straight/, accessed 13 August 2021.
Karunatilake, W. and Pal, A. (2021) China Approves $1.5 Billion Currency Swap with Sri Lanka. *Reuters*, 10 March, https://www.reuters.com/article/us-sri-lanka-economy-china-idUSKBN2B21UL, accessed 21 July 2021.
Luttwak, E. (1990) From Geopolitics to Geoeconomics: Logic of Conflict, Grammar of Commerce. *National Interest* 20: 17–23.
Michaels, R.C. (2008) The True Lex Mercatoria: Law Beyond the State. Indiana Journal of Global Legal Studies, Duke Law School Legal Studies Research Paper No. 220. August, http://ssrn.com/abstract=1259979, accessed 14 August 2021.
Ministry of Foreign Affairs of the People's Republic of China. (2015) Foreign Minister Wang Yi Meets the Press. 8 March, https://www.fmprc.gov.cn/mfa_eng/zxxx_662805/t1243662.shtml, accessed 12 August 2021.
Moody's Investor's Service. (2021) Rating Action: Moody's Places Sri Lanka's Caa1 Rating Under Review for Downgrade. 19 July, https://www.moodys.com/research/Moodys-places-Sri-Lankas-Caa1-rating-under-review-for-downgrade--PR_450080, accessed 21 July 2021.

Mullen, A. (2021) US-China Relations: Is There Still a Trade War Under Joe Biden's Presidency? *South China Morning Post*, 23 May, https://www.scmp.com/economy/global-economy/article/3134191/us-china-relations-there-still-trade-war-under-joe-bidens, accessed 10 August 2021.

Müllerson, R. (2014) Geopolitics Dressed in the Language of Law and Morals. *Eurozine*, 19 November, https://www.eurozine.com/geopolitics-dressed-in-the-language-of-law-and-morals/#, accessed 12 August 2021.

Mustill, M. (1988) The New Lex Mercatoria: The First Twenty-Five Years. Arbitration International: 86–119, https://www.trans-lex.org/126900, accessed 14 August 2021.

Nacimiento, P., Hertel, T. and Gayer, C. (2017) Arbitration and Money Laundering: What are the Obligations Placed on Counsel and Arbitrators and What Risks Do They Face? *Kluwer Arbitration Blog*, 10 November, http://arbitrationblog.kluwerarbitration.com/2017/11/10/arbitration-money-laundering/, accessed 23 July 2021.

Nadkarni, S. (2021) Sri Lanka Passes Controversial Port City Bill. *Seatrade Maritime News*, 25 May, https://www.seatrade-maritime.com/ports-logistics/sri-lanka-passes-controversial-port-city-bill, accessed 21 July 2021.

Nye, J.S. (1990) Soft Power. *Foreign Policy* 80(Autumn): 153–171.

Obama, B. (2020) *A Promised Land*. New York: Penguin Random House, 474–476.

Ondaatjie, A. (2021a) China in $1.5 Billion Swap Deal as Sri Lanka Seeks to Shun IMF. *Bloomberg*, 22 March, https://www.bloomberg.com/news/articles/2021-03-22/china-in-1-5-billion-swap-deal-as-sri-lanka-seeks-to-shun-imf, accessed 21 July 2021.

Ondaatjie, A. (2021b) Sri Lanka to Use Forex Reserves to Repay $1 Billion Debt in July. *Bloomberg Quint*, 8 July, https://www.bloombergquint.com/onweb/sri-lanka-keeps-rate-on-hold-as-focus-shifts-to-debt-repayment, accessed 22 July 2021.

Patrick, A. (2016) Revival of Colombo Port City Project: Implications for India. *National Maritime Foundation*, 27 October, https://maritimeindia.org/revival-of-colombo-port-city-project-implications-for-india/, accessed 22 July 2021.

Roberts, A., Moraes, H.C. and Ferguson, V. (2018) The Geoeconomic World Order. *Lawfare Blog*, https://www.lawfareblog.com/geoeconomic-world-order, accessed 30 July 2021.

Rodrigo, A. (2021) Sri Lanka. *Global Arbitration Review*, 7 July, https://globalarbitrationreview.com/review/the-asia-pacific-arbitration-review/2022/article/sri-lanka, accessed 16 January 2022.

Sharma, S. (2014) Neutrality v. Nationality. *Kluwer Arbitration Blog*, 8 April, http://arbitrationblog.kluwerarbitration.com/2014/04/08/neutrality-v-nationality/, accessed 23 July 2021.

Sri Lanka Ministry of Finance. (2021) Statement by Moody's Investor's Service is Ill-Timed, Ill-Judged, and Hence Unacceptable. 19 July, https://www.treasury.gov.lk/news/article/48, accessed 22 July 2021.

Sri Lanka National Arbitration Centre. (1995) Arbitration Act No. 11 of 1995. 30 June, https://www.slnarbcentre.com/pdf/ARBITRATION-ACT.pdf, accessed 13 August 2021.

Srinivasan, M. (2021) China Extends $500 Million Loan to Lanka. *The Hindu*, 12 April, https://www.thehindu.com/news/international/china-extends-500-million-loan-to-lanka/article34305277.ece, accessed 21 July 2021.

Thavapalakumar, M. No More Trips to Singapore for Arbitration. *The Morning*, 15 March, https://www.themorning.lk/no-more-trips-to-singapore-for-arbitration/, accessed 22 July 2021.

United Nations Treaty Collection. Chapter XXII: Commercial Arbitration and Mediation. 1. Convention on the Recognition and Enforcement of Foreign Arbitral Awards. New York, 10 June 1958. https://treaties.un.org/Pages/ViewDetails.aspx?src=IND&mtdsg_no=XXII-1&chapter=22&clang=_en, accessed 13 August 2021.

US Senate Foreign Relations Committee Report (2009). Sri Lanka: Recharting U.S. Strategy After the War. [Senate Prints 111–36] [From the U.S. Government Publishing Office]. 111th Congress S. Prt. 1st Session Committee Print 111–36 https://www.govinfo.gov/content/pkg/CPRT-111SPRT53866/html/CPRT-111SPRT53866.htm, accessed 28 June 2023.

Washington Post Editorial Board. (2021) Opinion: China's Xi Promises the World 'Heads Bashed Bloody'. He Should Be Taken Seriously. 5 July, https://www.washingtonpost.com/opinions/2021/07/05/chinas-xi-promises-world-heads-bashed-bloody-he-should-be-taken-seriously/, accessed 22 July 2021.

White House. (2021) Building Resilient Supply Chains, Revitalizing American Manufacturing, and Fostering Broad-Based Growth. June, https://www.whitehouse.gov/wp-content/uploads/2021/06/100-day-supply-chain-review-report.pdf, accessed 10 August 2021.

World Trade Organization. (2018) Immediate Notification Under Article 12.5 of the Agreement on Safeguards to the Council for Trade in Goods of Proposed Suspension of Concessions and Other Obligations Referred to in Article 8.2 of the Agreement on Safeguards—China. 29 March, https://docs.wto.org/dol2fe/Pages/FE_Search/FE_S_S009-DP.aspx?language=E&CatalogueIdList=244292,244291,244237,236486,235988,231386,61766,62577,46843,96880&CurrentCatalogueIdIndex=2&FullTextHash=&HasEnglishRecord=True&HasFrenchRecord=True&HasSpanishRecord=True, accessed 10 August 2021.

Xinhua. (2021) Port City Colombo Project to Help Raise Non-Debt Forex Inflows for Sri Lanka: Central Bank Governor. *Xinhua*, 28 June, http://www.xinhuanet.com/english/asiapacific/2021-06/28/c_1310032751.htm, accessed 10 August 2021.

Zhao, T. The Case for China's Participation in Trilateral Arms Control. In Ulrich Kühn (ed.), Trilateral Arms Control? Perspectives from Washington, Moscow, and Beijing. IFSH Research Report #002, Institute for Peace Research and Security Policy at the University of Hamburg, p. 75.

Zhongping, S. (2021) Why Washington Intends to Stir Up Asia Arms Race? *Global Times*, 21 July, https://www.globaltimes.cn/page/202107/1229292.shtml, accessed 12 August 2021.

Chapter 3

Implications of Quadrilateral Security Dialogue (QUAD) on South Asia

Rajib Timalsina[1] and Indivar Paudel[2]

INTRODUCTION

Under an urgent backdrop of the 2004 Indian Ocean tsunami, an informal grouping of India, Japan, Australia, and the United States was formed as an impromptu response to address the devastating polls of this cataclysmic disaster. Bringing in nations from completely different geographies, this form of response marked the beginning of a newer form of diplomacy in the Indo-Pacific region. After multiple phases of evolution along with almost a decade of hiatus, this informal grouping has culminated into a Quadrilateral Security Dialogue or simply QUAD (Le Thu, 2019). India, Japan, Australia, and the United States, now each either a major or rising world power in the twenty-first century, have come once again come together, revitalizing QUAD and joining hands in this initiative which aims to support a free, open, secure and prosperous Indo-Pacific region and the world (The White House, 2022). Each of these four countries has its own peculiar geopolitical and geoeconomic development as well as each of these nations has and is seeking an increasingly significant role in the Indo-Pacific region and on the global level. This changed context of the twenty-first century world order has played the role of catalyst for increased prioritization of QUAD. This grouping, however, still lacks or prefers to operate without much formal institutional aspects, which could be to dissuade the impression of a formal security alliance or a coalition that QUAD might generate or is speculated across certain quarters.

The revitalization of QUAD since 2017 seems to have been further energized by the two recent summits, a virtual summit in 2021 and an in-person summit of leaders from all four nations in 2022. With this increased attention to QUAD by all four members, the grouping, and the Indo-Pacific region itself have generated much attention and some criticism as well, from the other major/rising world powers. Nations like the United Kingdom, and France and regional organizations like the European Union have also shifted their strategic focus to the Indo-Pacific region, and the effects that the rise of QUAD will have on them, which presents a clear understanding of the increasing effects that the dynamics in Indo-Pacific will have on Europe's prosperity and security (Mohan, 2020). All these new geopolitical development in the Indo-Pacific region demands a careful observation of what the new form of security grouping of major powers entail for South Asia and the nations in this region.

Thus, this book chapter focuses on analyzing the implications of the Quadrilateral Security Dialogue (QUAD) on South Asia—which largely falls under the Indo-Pacific region and demands a careful observation of what this new grouping "QUAD" entails for South Asia and the nations in this region. Methodologically, this write-up is an outcome of an exploratory, descriptive research design. The data were extracted through extensive secondary content analysis through the eclectic approach. All the available library resources related to the keywords and themes were collected. Using axiological coding, the information was categorized into broad themes. Then information directly linked to the Quadrilateral Security Dialogue (QUAD) and South Asia was sampled and interpreted to convert into this book chapter.

This book chapter is organized into six sections. This section intends to give an overview of the overall chapter. The second section explores the role of India as a QUAD member in South Asia. The third section includes an analysis of relations between China, South Asia, and the QUAD grouping. In the fourth section, opportunities and challenges for South Asian nations are discussed. Then, another section answers how QUAD plans to operate and achieve its goals in South Asia. The final section concludes the book chapter with reflections from the authors.

ROLE OF INDIA AS QUAD MEMBER IN SOUTH ASIA

India, the only nation in QUAD from South Asia, is an influential actor within South Asia and within QUAD because of its rising economy, traditional influence in South Asia, and unique foreign policy. Though India is a key stakeholder of QUAD, this nation shares a distinct relationship with the other three QUAD members. For instance, the other three members condemned the 2022 invasion of Ukraine by Russia, whereas India maintains a distinct and rather beneficial relationship with Russia neither condemning Russia nor joining the West in its sanctions against Russia (Jacob, 2022).

In the gradually unveiling greater reaching out by QUAD to the South Asian nations, how India balances its role, positioning, and stance in this reaching out remains a crucial factor for South Asia. Traditionally India has been the dominant actor in the South Asia region and still prefers to maintain its dominance in the region (Lahiry, 2013). India further has been wary of extra-regional powers getting involved in the region. So, how India balances the attempt and interest of greater attention by three other QUAD nations in the region looms large in understanding the effects QUAD nations, including India, will have in South Asia. The British Empire created structural links between America, India, and Australia (Raghavan, 2018: 3). At the present time, all these three nations have their own priorities and abilities. When it comes to the case of QUAD, this is a grouping of three former British colonies and Japan. In such context, a crucial question comes, will India be willing to accept increased activities and engagement by other members of QUAD in South Asia or will greater engagement by QUAD in South Asia be only through India, citing it as the only member from South Asia? This question looms large and remains highly consequential.

Oftentimes, India and Pakistan, the two comparably larger nations in the region have gained much attention when it comes to South Asia. "In the wake of the India–Pakistan war of 1971, the United States had to grapple with two further developments in the region that would eventually predominate over traditional concerns of the Cold War—(i) the competitive pursuits of a nuclear weapon by India and Pakistan in South Asia and (ii) the rise of Islamist politics in Pakistan and Afghanistan in the 1970s (Raghavan, 2018: xix)."

India for centuries has been the regional hegemon in South Asia owing this to its geographical history, culture, tradition, and even religion (Khan, 2008; Hultquist & Adhikari, 2022). This dominant position of India in South Asia however, at times, has been taken to portray India as big brother power in the region which at times riles up the population of other South Asian nations against Indian activities in the region (Sharma, 2020). At such times, often South Asian nations have sought to increase their cooperation and strengthen their relationship with China, basically as a hedge against India (Senanayake, 2020). Nepal, Bangladesh, Sri Lanka, and even Pakistan have been carefully balancing, at times hedging, and their relationship with both India and China. These points out a sense of displeasure among other South Asian nations when India plays a heavy hand in the region.

In this scenario, if through the strengthening of QUAD grouping and its obvious specialized attention on South Asia, India is to be further dominant in the region, it might draw a backlash in many of the nations as have been in the past. If QUAD nations increase their attention, it could be greater opportunities, but if in the name of QUAD, it results in just the further consolidating of Indian dominance in the region, this can lead to an unsought result, of which other QUAD members might be less aware of. So, even in the face of the more influential role that India will have in the rise of QUAD, India must be careful to maintain its stature as a key regional player while not playing a heavy-handed role or a role of "big brother," "trying to micromanage" other nations like has been in the past on certain instances across multiple nations of the region.

CHINA, SOUTH ASIA, AND USA, ALONG WITH QUAD GROUPING

"Until now, China has never been a naval power with its large land mass, multiple borders, and short sea routes to trading partners, it did not need to be, and it was rarely ideologically expansive (Marshall, 2016: 36)." It was always a land power, with many land and many people—now nearly 1.4 billion. In the nineteenth and twentieth centuries, the imperial powers arrived in China, the Europeans, the British, and the Japanese among them. A few outside observers thought the post-war years (post-1945) might bring liberal democracy to China (Marshall, 2016). When the communist emerged victorious in 1949, Mao centralized power to an extent never seen in previous dynasties in China. Mao's successors tried to turn the long march to communist victory into an economic march toward prosperity. Since Chinese leader Deng Xiaoping coined the term "Socialism with Chinese Characteristics," China was becoming a major trading power and a rising military giant. Marshall (2016) writes, "by the end of 1990s, China had regained Hong Kong and Macau from the British and Portuguese respectively, and could look around its borders, assess its security and plan ahead for its great move out into the world.

If we look at the southwest part of China, the border with Laos is hilly jungle terrain, difficult for traders to cross- and even more complicated for the military (Marshall, 2017). The jungle hills become mountains until, at the western extreme, they begin to merge into the Himalayas. The Himalayas run the length of the Chinese-South Asian border, a nature's version of the Great Wall of China. Very little trade has moved between China and India over the centuries, and that is unlikely to change soon (Marshall, 2017: 45). Though South Asia is adjacent to China, the United States is one of the largest trade partners of China. The United States is an equally important trade and commerce partner for India and other South Asian nations. China is slowly becoming another important trade partner for some of the South Asian Nations.

This is not the first time the US looking to the East. Indian subcontinent and China were two important geographies for Americans after their independence in the late eighteenth century. "The War of Independence left the American economy in tatters: markets were disrupted, inflation unloosed, and debt piled up (Raghavan, 2018: 4)." Against this backdrop, the North American traders started looking East in the late eighteenth century right after their independence. Raghavan (2018) writes the 400-ton vessel manned by a crew of forty had departed from Philadelphia in March 1784 and arrived Pondicherry on December 26, 1784. The ship was the first United States vessel to touch India (South Asia). In the same year, the first United States ship, the *Empress of China*, reached Canton. Even though, there was a prohibition of direct trade from the British for Americans and their little knowledge about the link between coastal and inland trade in South Asia, in 1788, commerce of the United States was accorded the most favored nation's treatment in India and the US federal government established a consular service in 1790 in Calcutta (Raghavan, 2018: 6). Srinath Raghavan (2018) writes the import from India increased from $0.5 million in 1795–1796 to $3.4 million in 1803–1804, and imports from China went up during the same period from $0.3 million to $1.6 million. China and South Asia were the main trade partners for the early foundation of the American economy. The economic interdependence is still important between China– United States and United States –South Asia. Other than that when Westerners talk about Tibet, the Chinese find it deeply irritating, not dangerous, not subversive—just irritating (Marshall, 2017). When QUAD group members raise the issue of human rights, the Chinese leaders see it not through the prism of human rights but that of geopolitical security and can believe that the Westerners are trying to undermine their security (Marshall, 2017: 46). So, Chinese leaders have seen QUAD grouping as other efforts to undermine the Chinese security by the Westerners taking the support from Japan and India.

Speculations have been rife that the recent strengthening of QUAD is to particularly tackle and contain the rise of China and its economy on a global level and its assertiveness in the region (Pan, 2018). Rosa Luxemburg (1940) wrote, "history has the fine habit of always producing along with any real social need whereas," where Jamie Susskind (2018) says, "The social need is clear: to protect people from servitude . . . to keep the power of the supercharged state in check." In terms of Susskind (2018), China has been termed one of the supercharged states of our time along with others. When looked at from the perspective of China, South Asia is a highly important region to keep the power of China in check in the near future, mainly because Afghanistan, Pakistan, India, Nepal, and Bhutan from South Asia directly share a border and large share of their market with China. In addition, most nations from South Asia view China as a primary export market for their products, and already nations like Bangladesh, Sri Lanka, and Maldives share a large portion of their trade and commerce with China, which is a major economic power rapidly translating its growing global economic prowess into the influence in the Indo-Pacific region.

Although formally refuted by QUAD leaders, on the QUAD platform, as not being against others but for democracy and rules-based-order in the Indo-Pacific region, China is and will remain a major actor and factor in this region, which is taken into consideration by each of the QUAD nations and other nations in their activities in South Asia (Pandey, 2022).

Scholars like Tanvi Madan (2021) consider South Asia as a venue of ensuing competitive prism, where the India–China rivalry and US–China rivalry take place. This more likely gets reflected and is manifested in the operations of these nations in South Asia whether it is under the banner of QUAD or the Belt and Road Initiative (BRI).

Unlike other QUAD members, India, however, might be pursuing a soft-balancing strategy to restrain China through "limited alignments and formal ententes" (Paul, 2018).

QUAD, however, is not limited to security agenda. A broader agenda of QUAD encompasses further issues, including development, vaccines, critical technology, climate change, maritime security, and navigation. Also, this broader agenda has been speculated to be to counter the BRI of China.

China's engagement with nations in South Asia is not limited to cooperation on military or security aspects alone but largely is expanding across infrastructures, development, trade, and economic ties. So, the broadening of the QUAD's agendas, including providing COVID vaccines to nations in the region, can also be looked at from the perspective of reaching out to nations across all important issues, which obviously would be providing an alternative to the networks within BRI projects.

So, whatever be the underlying goal of QUAD, there obviously will be greater attention and reaching out to the South Asian nations through this grouping and across a wider range of issues.

Comparably lesser prioritized states of South Asia—Afghanistan, Bangladesh, Bhutan, Maldives, Nepal, and Sri Lanka—each have a peculiar and, in recent times, an expanding relationship with China, especially in economic and trade relationships. Further, some of these nations like Maldives, Nepal, and Sri Lanka have an economy largely reliant on tourism and Chinese tourists in recent decades have been a valuable and growing source for each (Pal, 2021). Similarly, increased infrastructure investments in ports, airports, and roads have been observed as part of BRI projects in these nations, along with Chinese investments in technology and telecommunications in some of these nations.

While these showcase the greater investment opportunities from China at the hands of South Asian nations, recently some of these nations have been wary of immediately accepting Chinese investments. The case of Hambantota port in Sri Lanka, initially the construction of which was touted as an alluring example of benefits offered by Chinese investment, later had to be leased to Chinese management for ninety-nine years as a result of Sri Lanka's inability to pay back debts, has turned into a prime factor for the decision-makers of other South Asian nations. The dangers of debt burdens beyond the capacities of their economies and, eventually, the debt trap has turned much less eager in accepting Chinese investments without a detailed analysis of every probable scenario (Pal, 2021). Similarly, the rhetoric against the Chinese telecommunications industry and it's expanding investment in other nations, particularly against Huawei by the United States, on the grounds of concerns the compromised security, has also generated some level of concerns within the decision-makers in South Asian nations on whether to accept the much-needed technological investments including upgradation of crucial technologies like 5G or not.

Recently, the COVID pandemic and its possible containment have been the top priority for almost all nations. The vaccines against this coronavirus, which offer quick and most effective known protection, have been prepared and administered by economically and technologically leading nations like the United States and China. Regardless of these vaccines being beyond their present capability to develop or even having enough funds to buy and get to buy the vaccines, these truly life-saving vaccines are of crucial importance even for the South Asian people. Nations like China and India provided these life-saving vaccines to other South Asian nations.

Even in supplying vaccines during the pandemic, China and India sought to outpace one another (Singh et al., 2022). China heavily invested in supplying these vaccines along with other medical essentials to nations around the world, including in South Asia, which often has been called "vaccine diplomacy." India also has been stretching its hand in supplying vaccines and other medical essentials to other South Asian nations, which probably, will be more reenergized with the announcement made at the 2022 QUAD summit to supply more than 1 billion vaccines worldwide (Reuters, 2022). This move by QUAD has also been interpreted by many to be a direct attempt to counter China's vaccine diplomacy.

OPPORTUNITIES AND CHALLENGES FOR SOUTH ASIAN NATIONS

The increased opportunities for the nations in South Asia across multiple platforms and a broader range of issues for their development and the South Asia region in general for being a democratic, free, open, and rule-based order paints a rosy picture for the region. Additionally, this comes with the recently rising opportunities of increased cooperation, assistance, investments, and particularly trade relationships offered by China under its BRI, which could mean greater choices for the South Asian nations.

In all this new scenario, the QUAD nations and the investments they are willing to make in South Asia can offer a much-need alternative to the South Asian nations. The availability of alternatives will provide South Asian nations greater leverage to choose the projects and investments that better suit the circumstances of their nation and peculiar need at hand, from all those offerings, by looking at the terms, conditions, and probably some preconditions that might come attached with each such investment.

Whatever the motives of different kinds of a grouping of nations, developing nations at the receiving end gain several opportunities. For example, the life-saving vaccines getting within reach of people in need from nations like Nepal which neither has the technological nor an economic ability to either develop or sufficiently buy such vaccines but with support from nations like India, China, and the United States has been able to recently administer more than 47 million doses, which translates to almost about 80% of its population, shows the kind of greater benefits nations which otherwise could have been neglected receive after the increased attention from major/rising world powers toward South Asia (World Health Organization, 2022). The same is the case, more or less, in other South Asian nations as well, while the percentage of the immunized population varies.

On the technological front, the United States has been vehemently criticizing. It has even lodged a case against Chinese technology and telecommunication devices on the grounds of national security in the United States. It has asked many of its allies and other friendly nations to refrain from using them in the crucial technology infrastructures of their nation (Ovide, 2021). While some argue that this move by the United States is motivated by countering the rise of China in technology and maintaining US competitiveness, the US cites it as a compromise to its national security (Congressional Research Service, 2022).

Through the further strengthening of QUAD, if the South Asian nations, lagging comparably behind in terms of technological advancement, get a choice to access and utilize technology from the leading technological powerhouses like the United States, China, and Japan in an incentivized manner, it could be a hugely rewarding scenario for South Asia in general. This greater technological support from technologically advanced nations could open up a multitude of further possibilities for the South Asian people and whose spillover effects have the potential to transform many aspects of the society itself, ranging from expanded economic to educational opportunities.

On the challenge side, the ideological and cultural differences will be one big issue. South Asia has the majority of people who are Muslim. "For more than two generations, al-Qaeda has successfully peddled the view that the West is engaged in a "war against Islam" with the active connivance of client rulers in capitals around the Muslim world (Soufan, 2017: 296)." This opinion is by no means confined to a handful of extremists. On the contrary, millions of Muslims worldwide believe that the West is deliberately suppressing their religion and stifling political change to keep repressive secular governments in power. Indeed, the involvement of QUAD countries in Arab countries has fueled the narratives (Soufan, 2017).

However, will the South Asian nations be able to cooperate with and utilize assistance, support, and investments and maintain cordial relationships with all the partners? Or will the nations be forced to choose cooperation, assistance, and support from either QUAD nations or China?

Suppose the South Asian nations have to eventually pick sides, whether to further cooperate with QUAD nations or with China. In that case, this will be greatly disastrous not just for the individual nations but for the South Asia region. In that case, it will be the seed that could sow divisions and even rivalry and enmity among the region's nations.

HOW QUAD PLANS TO OPERATE AND ACHIEVE ITS GOALS IN SOUTH ASIA?

All the QUAD members—India, Japan, Australia, and the United States—have friendly bilateral relationships and are diplomatically engaged with (most) nations in South Asia. Each of these four members has a unique and peculiar relationship with each of the South Asian nations, with its strong points and fault lines. So, how will the workings and diplomatic overtures of these nations change after the strengthening of QUAD a question?

Will the nations continue to individually, on a national level, increase attention and further cooperation and engagement with the South Asian nations, or will they, after the strengthening of QUAD, attempt to increase cooperation with South Asian nations through this grouping?

The lack of formal institutional mechanisms and structures of QUAD seems to point out that the four members, although through a coordinated and streamlined manner, will choose to operate and engage individuals on a national level with other nations. Australia, recently, through its new South Asia Regional Infrastructure Connectivity Initiative, announced $25 million for building regional economic connectivity with South Asia (Minister for Foreign Affairs, 2019). India and Japan, for decades, have been major contributors to infrastructure investments in the South Asian region. Similarly, the United States has largely increased its attention on countries across South Asia—unlike being limited to Afghanistan and Pakistan as in the past—attempting to strengthen its foothold and, most importantly, prevent the region from slipping into China's orbit (Mohan, 2022). Srinath Raghavan (2018), in his book *The Most Dangerous Place* claims that India, Pakistan, and Afghanistan were of greatest interest and concern to Americans over this long period.

The major concern for all the nations of South Asia is their economic development, and this bolstering of QUAD grouping, with its attention on South Asia, could bring in much-needed investments, assistance, and support in the economic development of the nations. Further, as mentioned before, the investments had already started coming in from China, especially for infrastructure development and greater economic ties with nations in South Asia. With the increased attention of QUAD on this region, greater investments by powerful economies will most likely pour into the region. India remains far weaker than other QUAD nations regarding economic development in terms of GDP/per capita (Beckley, 2018). So, this can be a positive implication of strengthening QUAD for South Asia from the economic growth and development perspective.

This perceived positive implication, in no time, might turn into a double-edged sword if, ultimately, nations have to choose or side with either one of the powers, QUAD members, or China, rather than getting to choose the best from all the partners willing to support. So, a high probability exists of turning South Asia into a contested region with a great power rivalry and enmity among nations polarizing across two blocs.

Further, there will be spillover effects in other South Asian nations of increased economic development of India, the only nation in QUAD from South Asia, resulting from stronger ties with the other three QUAD members, who are the major and powerful economies. However, as these powerful and/or rising economic giants and the cooperation between them increase, this might turn QUAD into, or at least create an impression of itself as, an elite network where the focus lies in increasing benefits—on multiple levels—among the four QUAD members. The other South Asian nations, with comparably smaller economies, might feel and be further neglected as second or third-tier nations.

One of the stated goals of QUAD is maritime security, and this could ensure secure connectivity to South Asian nations along the Indian Ocean with greater trade and economic opportunities. The United States and Japan have always paid greater attention to the Pacific and Indian Ocean maintaining its strategic presence in these sea lanes. The influence and naval capabilities that Australia holds in the Indian Ocean cannot be neglected as well (Lee, 2018). Indian External Affairs Minister S. Jaishankar (2020) delineates the greater importance that nations along the Indian Ocean Rim will have and a greater engagement that India will seek in cooperation with and assistance to these nations to be a key part of the Indian foreign policy in coming years. At the same time, the greater infrastructure investments from China, like sea ports and air ports, seem to be focused on nations along the Indian Ocean, particularly Bangladesh, Maldives, and Sri Lanka (US Institute of Peace, 2020). This showcases the greater significance of sea lanes and maritime security in the globalized world order of today, where each major power seems to be seeking ways to consolidate its presence in the vital sea lanes. What is expected by the four QUAD nations, and also China, from the South Asian nations about such broader opportunities they seek to open up in the region? The first rule in economics is that there is no such thing as a free lunch.

Taking the instances of the Rajapaksa family from Sri Lanka (Abi-Habib, 2018) and Abdullah Yameen from Maldives (Mundy & Hille, 2019), it's often argued that Chinese investments are focused on attempting to strengthen the political regimes that seem to be more amenable to Chinese interests.

Likewise, the QUAD nations would naturally have their self-interest in this greater prioritization toward the Indo-Pacific region. The economic rise of China and the resulting rise in China's international clout has been speculated as the major concern for these four QUAD nations coming together. But each nation surely has its peculiar interest in this initiative apart from their joint interest at checking and balancing China's growth.

From the perspective of South Asia and most nations in the region lagging in its development goals, the most important benefit of this increased attention that the region has received would be knowledge spillover. The promise of increased investment in the region, which intends to cover many aspects such as infrastructure, critical technologies, and even tackling climate change, means the knowledge, skills, technology, and other resources from advanced economies of QUAD members would be utilized in many South Asian nations. The immediate visible benefits from each of these investments in improving human lives in South Asia are apparent. In the long run, apart from these immediate benefits, the spillover effects of each such investment would be much large in these nations.

How each development project—including the knowledge, skills, and technology used in the project—translates into people in that specific community in particular and the country in general, getting acquainted with and learning these very skills and technology would be a cumulative advantage for the nation, holds the greatest seed of empowerment. This means the initiatives of QUAD, as outlined in the 2022 summit, could translate not just into the immediate benefits of access to vaccines and awareness about climate change but also to greater know-how in these nations in developing vaccines—in case of future emergencies, in developing and implementing creative techniques and technologies to address climate change, and in coming up with locally developed tools/technologies to address local/national problems. This accumulation of knowledge would spill over to not just the select few sectors but across many sectors and on multiple levels in the South Asian nations ranging from greater innovation to societal upliftment.

Equally important is the question of the sustainability of QUAD. Will these four nations be willing to cooperate for a longer period based on common interests and priorities? Will the QUAD members be able to align their national interest and audience in line with their initiatives on a multilateral level? How effective will this grouping be in projecting a common interest in the face of international issues like the Russo-Ukrainian War of 2022? How will the geographical complexity of four nations from four different spatial regions be turned into an advantage rather than a disadvantage? Will QUAD survive in case of any nation backing out of this grouping—that is, not repeating the fate of the Trans-Pacific Partnership (TPP)? All these and many more questions will arise in the near future when QUAD moves into or attempts to move toward action from just the rhetoric and promises in its recent infancy.

CONCLUSION

When looking at economic growth and development from the perspective, not considering the other strategic calculations, the QUAD grouping, based on the interests and objectives outlined by the four nations, looks promising for the South Asian nations. These South Asian nations, while reaping the benefits, mostly in the human development, technology, and economic front, could get the best and most out of QUAD if they are careful to cushion the blunt strategic calculations QUAD nations individually or jointly might have, even if it be implicit. QUAD, in this light, holds the promise of catalyzing South Asia's economic and human development and the possibility of turning it into a contested and polarized region. Reaping benefits while cushioning the rivalry, polarization, and contestation in South Asia largely depends on the individual nations' diplomatic skills and national integrity—which could be amplified through a unified regional voice—and on the outlook India envisions for South Asia.

South Asian nations, thus, will be very keenly observing the development and rise of QUAD as it remains to be clear what the ultimate goal of this grouping is, whether it is limited to the ones outlined in the recent summits, and most importantly, how does QUAD plan to achieve these goals. After all, the process through which QUAD seeks to achieve its goal will be of more relevance to South Asian nations as it might bring greater opportunities and choices at the same time, even in the form of increased leverage in dealing with either QUAD nations or China, or further dominance of India in the region, or even having to ultimately choose between and side with either QUAD or China, which might be a form of cold war or at least a form of great power rivalry between QUAD nations and China, turning Indo Pacific in general and South Asia in particular to a heated and contested area.

NOTES

1. R. Timalsina. Tribhuvan University, Kirtipur, Nepal. Email: rajib.timalsina@dcpds.tu.edu.np

2. I. Paudel. Tribhuvan University, Kirtipur, Nepal. Email: indivarcp@gmail.com

BIBLIOGRAPHY

Abi-Habib, M. (June 25, 2018). How China Got Sri Lanka to Cough Up a Port. *The New York Times*. Retrieved from https://www.nytimes.com/2018/06/25/world/asia/china-sri-lanka-port.html

Beckley, M. (2018). *Unrivaled: Why America Will Remain the World's Sole Superpower.* Cornell University Press, pp. 16–18.

Congressional Research Service (January 5, 2022). U.S. Restrictions on Huawei Technologies: National Security, Foreign Policy and Economic Interests. Retrieved from https://www.everycrsreport.com/files/2022-01-05_R47012_65c5c54827b8fef912a19079f10e144b3b88d009.pdf

Hultquist, P. & Adhikari, P. (2022). *Hegemonic Instability? India's Himalayan Hegemony in Theoretical and Historical Perspectives.* Retrieved from https://digitalrepository.unm.edu/cgi/viewcontent.cgi?article=1091&context=nsc_research

Jacob, H. (February 28, 2022). The Anatomy of India's Ukraine Dilemma. *The Hindu.* Retrieved from https://www.thehindu.com/opinion/lead/the-anatomy-of-indias-ukraine-dilemma/article65090424.ece?homepage=true

Jaishankar, S. (2020). *The Indian Way: Strategies for an Uncertain World.* New Delhi: Harper Collins Publisher India.

Khan, B. (2008). India and the Making of a Hegemon. *AQ: Australian Quarterly*, 80(1), 29–40. Retrieved from http://www.jstor.org/stable/20638532

Lahiry, S. (2013). India's Relationship with Its South Asian Neighbours: Contemporary Trends. *World Affairs: The Journal of International Issues*, 17(4), 70–79. Retrieved from https://www.jstor.org/stable/48505095

Le Thu, H. (Ed.). (2019). Quad 2.0: New Perspectives for the Revived Concept: Views from the Strategist. Australian Strategic Policy Institute. Retrieved from http://www.jstor.org/stable/resrep23015

Lee, L. (November 8, 2018). India Has Most to Lose If It Doesn't Embrace the Quad. Retrieved from https://www.aspistrategist.org.au/india-has-the-most-to-lose-if-it-doesnt-embrace-the-quad

Luxemberg, R. (1940). *The Russian Revolution.* New York: Workers Age Publishers.

Madan, T. (2021). *Major Power Rivalry in South Asia*. Council on Foreign Relations. Retrieved from https://media.carnegie.org/filer_public/56/c5/56c57819-4328-4ea8-a69d-71396f48e6ce/dpmadanoct21_final_for_cms.pdf

Marshall, T. (2016). *Prisoners of Geography*. London: Elliot and Thomson Limited.

Minister for Foreign Affairs. (January 9, 2019). *Australia Invests in South Asian Connectivity*. Retrieved from https://www.foreignminister.gov.au/minister/marise-payne/media-release/australia-invests-south-asian-connectivity

Mohan, C. R. (April 6, 2022). Across South Asia, U.S. and India Push Back Against China. *Foreign Policy*. Retrieved from https://foreignpolicy.com/2022/04/06/us-india-china-sri-lanka-south-asia-geopolitics/

Mohan, G. (2020). *Europe in the Indo-Pacific: A Case for More Coordination with Quad Countries*. German Marshall Fund of the United States. Retrieved from http://www.jstor.org/stable/resrep21235

Mundy, S. & Hille, K. (February 10, 2019). The Maldives Counts the Costs of Its Debts to China. *Financial Times*. Retrieved from https://www.ft.com/content/c8da1c8a-2a19-11e9-88a4-c32129756dd8

Ovide, S. (November 4, 2021). The Strange Saga of Huawei. *The New York Times*. Retrieved from https://www.nytimes.com/2021/11/02/technology/huawei-us-policy.html

Pan, C. (2018). Qualms about the Quad: Getting China Wrong. *The Center of Gravity Series*. Australian National University Strategic and Defense Studies Center. Retrieved from https://bellschool.anu.edu.au/sites/default/files/uploads/2018-03/cog_39_web_-_debating_the_quad.pdf

Pal, D. (2021). *China's Influence in South Asia: Vulnerabilities and Resilience in Four Countries*. Carnegie Endowment for International Peace. Retrieved from https://carnegieendowment.org/files/202110-Pal_SouthAsiaChina_final1.pdf

Pandey, V. (May 24, 2022). Quad: The China Factor at the Heart of the Summit. *BBC*. Retrieved from https://www.bbc.com/news/world-asia-india-61547082

Paul, T. V. (2018). *Restraining Great Powers: Soft Balancing from Empires to the Global Era*. Yale University Press, p. 26.

Raghavan, S. (2018). *The Most Dangerous Place: A History of the United States in South Asia*. New Delhi: Penguin Random House India.

Reuters. (February 11, 2022). Quad-Supported Vaccine Roll-Out to Begin in First Half. *Reuters*. Retrieved from https://www.reuters.com/business/healthcare-pharmaceuticals/quad-supported-vaccine-roll-out-begin-first-half-2022-02-11/

Senanayake, D. P. H. (2020). Understanding the Dragon's Entry to South Asia: Revisiting the Regional Security Complex Theory. *Torun International Studies*, 1(13), 73–91. Retrieved from https://doi.org/10.12775/TIS.2020.006

Sharma, V. (August 20, 2020). India's Lack of Respect for Its South Asian Neighbours Is Now Mutual. *The Wire*. Retrieved from https://thewire.in/diplomacy/india-south-asia-neighbours-foreign-policy-respect

Singh, B., Singh, S., Singh, B. & Chattu, V. K. (2022). India's Neighbourhood Vaccine Diplomacy During COVID-19 Pandemic: Humanitarian and Geopolitical Perspectives. *Journal of Asian and African Studies*. Retrieved from https://doi.org/10.1177/00219096221079310

Soufan, A. (2017). *Anatomy of Terror*. New York: W. W. Norton & Company.

Susskind, J. (2018). *Future Politics*. Oxford: Oxford University Press.

The White House. (May 24, 2022). Quad Joint Leaders' Statement. Retrieved from https://www.whitehouse.gov/briefing-room/statements-releases/2022/05/24/quad-joint-leaders-statement/

US Institute of Peace. (2020). China–Smaller South Asian States Relations. In *China's Influence on Conflict Dynamics in South Asia* (pp. 39–43). US Institute of Peace. Retrieved from http://www.jstor.org/stable/resrep27534.9

World Health Organization. (2022). Nepal. Retrieved from https://covid19.who.int/region/searo/country/np

Chapter 4

China's Position in the Global Order

Challenging the US Supremacy in the Twenty-First Century

Muamer Hirkić[1]

INTRODUCTION

As it is well-known, China's rise is currently a major topic in the field of international relations. Furthermore, China's growth is also central to the very concept of multipolarity in the twenty-first century, especially in regions where either dominant regional power or a global hegemon is present. After the so-called "Century of Humiliation" that represents a national, foreign-orchestrated subjugation in the period between 1839 and 1949, China entered the new millennium as one of the world's rising powers. The main reason for this is the notable economic development that resulted in the establishment of projects such as the Belt and Road Initiative (BRI). In this sense, the Chinese government adopted the traditional American idea of "going westward for prosperity," while President Xi Jinping asserted that the "Chinese Dream" could revitalize the nation. This kind of wordplay and ambitious objectives show Chinese aspirations to become a fully developed nation, and thus leave room for many to expect inevitable, long-term rivalry with the United States.

This chapter reveals whether Chinese actions in its immediate neighborhood are aimed at reaffirming the idea that China is a regional hegemon, and whether China currently represents a serious challenge to the US dominated world. Moreover, the chapter takes into consideration some of the widely accepted definitions of the term "superpower" and attempts to situate the two countries in that context. The analysis has shown that, although the United States has lost its status of the so-called "hyperpower," China is currently still a rising power that exercises the superpower politics in some areas, mostly through its economy and technology. However, the lack of soft and hard power projection prevents China from acquiring the full-scale status of a superpower, which does not exclude the possibility of gaining such status in the future.

The rest of this chapter is organized as follows. The first section gives a brief justification of the methodology, provides a theoretical foundation, and offers a literature review in order to elucidate the logic behind the selection of particular works and authors. The second section discusses ideas of the post-American world and Asian century while taking into consideration both US and China-centered views on the matter. The third section reveals the possibility of the so-called Thucydides Trap, soft-balancing strategies, and China's presence in traditionally Western-led institutions, and thus emphasizes the future challenge that China could face in order to preserve its position and status. The fourth section explores the case of the South China Sea, which represents both the source of China's strength in the region and the source of animosity toward China's leadership. The fifth section reviews the assertiveness of China in the twenty-first century, enlists some of the cases of exhibited global governance, and puts forward the idea of China using traditional American concepts in its global strategies. Lastly, the final section concludes with some of the principal ideas and considerations derived from the comprehensive analysis.

THEORETICAL CONSIDERATIONS AND LITERATURE USED

When we try to answer the question "What makes one country a superpower?," it is possible to single out three generally accepted characteristics, which most authors point out as the most relevant: (i) economy/wealth; (ii) military and the ability to project hard power; and (iii) cultural/ideological influence or something that we refer to as "the story" (Beckley, 2018). Therefore, it is possible to realize that there is no official definition of what a superpower is. That is why a definition relies very much on individual and group perceptions—meaning that the role of the soft power or "the story" of the country gains an increasing importance. Therefore, if we return to the original definition of the political scientist William T. R. Fox, who was one of the first authors to use and coin the term "superpower," we can note that his definition was rounded as "great power plus great mobility of power," with the remark that mobility does not necessarily have to be geographical in nature (Fox, 1980). The importance of not only possessing power but also having an opportunity for mobility or wider projection has been emphasized by other authors such as Dreyer, who argues that a superpower must be able to project its power, soft and hard, globally. (Dreyer, 2007). Therefore, all three previously mentioned characteristics, together with the emphasis on the mobility of power, will be considered in the analysis in the following sections.

This chapter, which is descriptive in its nature, presents some of the most significant studies, ideas, and discoveries written on the subject of US–Sino relations over the past two decades. The chapter rests on primary and secondary sources such as books, scientific papers, reports, political analyses, communique, and articles from various news outlets and thus attempts to contribute to the discussion of whether China is an actor with regional or global outreach. The advantage of this approach is hidden in the possibility to analyze the current state of affairs critically and objectively, in accordance with a number of ideas that, throughout the years, occupied an important place in both academia and media. Subsequently, it is possible to critically evaluate such suggestions while considering a range of events and occurrences that confirmed or disregarded them. The works of prominent authors were selected on the basis of their relevance for the Sino–US studies, as well as on the basis of the possibility of contextualization of the selected theoretical considerations. Some of the studies in the chapter include: Allison, *The Thucydides Trap: Are the US and China Headed for War?* (The Atlantic, 2015); Zakaria, *Say hello to a post-America world* (Washington Post, 2017); Christensen, *The Advantages of an Assertive China* (Foreign Affairs, 2011); Ikenberry, *The Rise of China and the Future of the West* (Foreign Affairs, 2008); Khanna, *The Future Is Asian: Commerce, Conflict, and Culture in the 21st Century* (Simon and Schuster, 2019); Mearsheimer, *The Gathering Storm: China's Challenge to US Power in Asia* (The Chinese Journal of International Politics, 2010); Blanton and Kegley, *World Politics Trend and Transformation* (Cengage Learning, 2016); and Beckley, *Unrivaled: Why America Will Remain the World's Sole Superpower* (Cornell University Press, 2018).

POST-AMERICAN WORLD

After the collapse of the Soviet Union, the United States remained a dominant force and was at the height of its unipolar moment. However, the accelerated development of countries such as China, India, and Brazil has made global power distribution more inclined toward multipolarity. This inspired authors such as Fareed Zakaria, who studied this phenomenon and concluded that "it is not the decline of America but rather the rise of the rest," where accelerated globalization led to the appearance of new actors who seek their interests. Several decades ago, America was the leader or "hyperpower" in most fields, had the most modern infrastructure, the largest companies, and the largest film industry. Now, that primacy is in many ways taken by other countries such as China, India, Singapore, and the United Arab Emirates (Zakaria, 2017). Nonetheless, China's growth is presented as a new occurrence, but it is often forgotten that China was the leading economy in eighteen of the past twenty centuries. In that sense, this phenomenon could be observed more as a "comeback of China" than "the rise of China." The majority of modern-day culture is Euro and US-centric, meaning that it is hard to imagine a world where the economic power gravity is situated in Asia. However, with the rapid progression of many Asian countries, this has now become a reality. Parag Khanna believes that the twenty-first century is the Asian century, asserting that "China is one of the most important features of this system, but it is not the only feature" (Araya, 2019). The phrase "China-led Asia" is thus no more acceptable to most Asians than the notion of a "US-led West" is to Europeans (Khanna, 2019). Moreover, Khanna argues that after the nineteenth century belonged to Europeans and the twentieth to the United States, the era of Western hegemony has irretrievably passed. Additionally, he notes that the United States will need to remain active in the region if it wants to retain primacy, and that it could be desirable to consider forming a partnership on China-led projects such as the BRI. However, the US leadership was particularly skeptical of the China-dominated global order for many years.

In the first years of the twenty-first century, after Bush's "War on Terror" and the doctrine of the so-called "preemptive strikes" were announced, the entire focus of the world public switched to the Middle East—signifying a move that will remain the main source of animosity toward the US foreign policy in the new millennium. However, in Obama's second term in office, there was a turning point in a foreign policy known as the "Pivot to Pacific." The balance of global power shifted significantly to the East, and one of the fundamental reasons for this, in addition to China's growth, was the strategic importance of the South China Sea. Later, the Trump administration pursued a more aggressive approach, starting a "war on tariffs" aimed at strengthening the American economy. China's leadership began taking advantage of Trump's rhetoric and foreign policy right from the start, announcing that it was happy to play the role of the chief promoter of trade and investment around the world, cutting deals with countries from Latin America to Africa to Central Asia (Zakaria, 2017).

THUCYDIDES TRAP, SOFT-BALANCING STRATEGIES, AND CONTROL THROUGH WESTERN INSTITUTIONS

China has played a smart game so far, basing the entire foreign policy philosophy and narrative on the Five Principles of Peaceful Coexistence from 1954 and becoming the main contributor to the UN peacekeeping missions over the years. This helped in building the image of a nonviolent state which only wants to keep its own integrity and not interfere in the affairs of other nations. However, pervasive hostilities could emerge between any pair of challengers for dominance. For instance, Blanton and Kegley argue that competition could escalate between the globe's two major contenders for supremacy, the United States and China, if the United States practices containment to try to prevent China's rise or if China threatens US security interests (Blanton and Kegley, 2016). So far, the most important point of divergence between the two countries has been the question of Taiwan—particularly following the Russian invasion of Ukraine and China's repeated threats to use force (Dominguez, 2023).

Harvard Professor Graham T. Allison has been exploring this phenomenon and eventually, he coined the term "Thucydides trap," which is based on a historical example of the conflict between Athens and Sparta. The foundation of the theory is set by the Greek philosopher Thucydides, who spoke about the impossibility of avoiding the Peloponnesian War. When a rising power is threatening to displace a ruling power, standard crises that would otherwise be contained, like the assassination of an archduke in 1914, can initiate a cascade of reactions that, in turn, produce outcomes none of the parties would otherwise have chosen (Allison, 2015). Moreover, he cites sixteen cases when a rising power has challenged the dominant power over the past 500 years, where twelve cases resulted in war. During his term, Barack Obama noted that he does not believe in the existence of this trap and that the United States must be the responsible actor on the international stage. Even Chinese President Xi Jinping talked about the possibility of falling into the Thucydides trap and warned great powers—stating that anyone who attempts to bully China "will get their heads bashed" (Reuters, 2021).

The pivotal thesis in Allison's theory is that the ascent of a state can cause fear. Furthermore, fears will lead to a clash of strategic interests, and strategic interests are a factor that leads to open conflict. The change in the balance of power between China and the United States affects their perception of national interests, and the dynamics of the growth of these factors contribute to the possibility of war escalation. Currently, it is not in China's interest to confront the United States directly but rather to challenge them through soft-balancing strategies—implying that both countries need to maintain strong economic ties because of market access. On the one hand, China's soft balancing strategy has been achieved through the promotion of multilateral institutions that exclude the United States, while on the other hand, China continuously strengthens bilateral relations with countries that currently have weak ties or desire to distance themselves from the United States (Gill,

2010). Thus, three major pillars of China's soft balancing strategy include the BRI, the Silk Road Fund, and the Asian Infrastructure Investment Bank (AIIB), which suggests that China has managed to directly challenge the dominance of traditional Western and US-led institutions such as the IMF and the World Bank. The strategic logic behind it is to maintain a stable external environment for China to concentrate on economic growth and accumulate comprehensive national power without provoking a vigorous US response (Wang, 2006). China has recently introduced a trio of ideological frameworks, including the Global Civilization Initiative, the Global Security Initiative, and the Global Development Initiative. Despite being short on content, they emphasize the importance of sovereignty and diverse development paths (Palmer, 2023).

On the other hand, John Ikenberry, a professor at Princeton University, believes that real power, and therefore the future of the balance of power, lies in the institutions established by the West, such as the World Trade Organization (WTO). Furthermore, he claims that the American decline in relative power would open the doors of the Western world to China—and China is well-aware that modernization could not happen without integration into the global capitalist system. Essentially, the continued growth of the Asian giant is inevitable, and its place in a system that has traditionally favored the United States has also become inevitable, meaning that China will learn how to prosper in such an institutional framework. Ikenberry argues that if the United States wants to preserve this leadership, Washington must work to strengthen the rules and institutions that underpin that order—making it even easier to join and harder to overturn. The US grand strategy should be built around the motto "The road to the East runs through the West" (Ikenberry, 2008). In this way, the entire system would continue to revolve around the West, and the United States would be able to control other competitors through institutions and maintain its supremacy even after its relative power has declined. In the past, the integration of China into Western institutions had to go hand in hand with comprehensive economic reforms. Primarily, this refers to Deng Xiaoping's era, where economic liberalization was reminiscent of Mikhail Gorbachev's reforms in the Soviet Union (Lynch, 2012). However, one of the main differences was that in China, "perestroika" was carried out without "glasnost." Namely, Chinese leadership kept the authoritarian style of leading the country, while Gorbachev allowed for greater political freedom and thus produced a division within the Communist Party nomenclature. Any form of liberalization, whether accompanied or unaccompanied by political freedoms, remains a challenge to China's future and the role that the country could play in international affairs.

CASE OF SOUTH CHINA SEA—THE SOURCE OF POWER OR ANIMOSITY?

The South China Sea is one of the most disputed places on Earth. In China, it is known as "South Sea"; in the Philippines, the government began using the name "West Philippine Sea," while Indonesia refers to the northern border of its Exclusive Economic Zone (EEZ) as the "North Natuna Sea." This resource-rich corner of the world is disputed between six states—China, Taiwan, Brunei, Vietnam, Malaysia, and the Philippines. Essentially, most of the above-mentioned states claim one part of the South China Sea, while China claims all of it (Council on Foreign Relations, 2020).

In this pivotal strategic location, there are hundreds of islands, mostly uninhabited. The massive shipping passage hosts one-third of all global maritime trade, and lucrative fisheries are crucial for the food security of millions in Southeast Asia. It is estimated that 80% of the Chinese energy imports pass through the South China Sea, and 11 billion barrels of oil are yet to be discovered along the margins of it (Asia Maritime Transparency Initiative, 2019). Additionally, it is believed that vast reserves of natural gas lie beneath the sea. Stuart-Fox argues that South China Sea resources can contribute significantly to China's economic development; their distance from the Chinese mainland will stimulate China's naval capability to defend its territory; and this naval power projection, plus the islands' strategic position will translate into strategic advantage vis-à-vis Southeast Asia (Stuart-Fox, 2003). In the past decade, China has emerged as an assertive regional power in the Asia–Pacific with forceful A2/AD capabilities, using advanced ballistic and cruise missiles in conjunction with air and maritime defense systems to deter US military operations in the region (Missle Defense Advocacy Alliance, 2018). Furthermore, with these capabilities, the People's Liberation Army (PLA) attempts to limit the freedom of movement of the US Army within the disputed area.

China has actively built seaports, naval bases, and airstrips on the Spratly Islands since 2013. The Spratly Islands are not only important for its abundant natural resources, such as fisheries, but also for its geography, since they lie at the heart of the South China Sea, and whoever owns them can extend their EEZ. Militarization was also carried out at the Woody and the Paracel Islands, where fighter jets and missiles were delivered and stationed. In order to protect its interests, China began to use the so-called "cabbage strategy" where its warships surround the islands "in layers" and thus cut them off from the rest of the world (Ariffin, 2018). The best-known case of the construction of artificial islands is the Fiery Cross Reef, which was converted into an island in 2014, having around 200 PLA soldiers stationed in the base. Nonetheless, it is assumed that this number has increased significantly since then (Rapp-Hooper, 2015). The construction of man-made islands with military facilities, as well as the assertive actions in the region, were condemned on numerous occasions by its neighbors and all the major global actors (Al Jazeera, 2021). At the same time, China gained significant leverage for establishing facts on the ground and it is highly unlikely that any claimants to the South China Sea will be able to realize any of their territorial claims.

Before-mentioned states began to claim islands in the 1970s, and all of them use 200 miles EEZ to determine the border except China. In contrast to others, China argues that they have had a historical claim to the South China Sea from the time of naval expeditions. For this purpose, they use the Nine-Dash Line, which encompasses 90% of the entire space. Nine-Dash Line represents a separation line used by China and Taiwan in the twentieth century to justify their claims on the South China Sea (South China Morning Post, 2016). However, the EEZ can only be claimed up to 200 nautical miles (NM) from the coast of a country. The area around which all countries have disputes includes the Spratly Islands, the Paracel Islands, the Pratas Islands, the Scarborough Shoal, and the Macclesfield Bank. In January 2013, the Philippines brought the dispute with China over the South China Sea to international arbitration under the United Nations Convention on the Law of the Sea (Lingjie, 2015). Although China refused to participate in the arbitral proceedings, the Permanent Court of Arbitration in 2016 ruled that there is no historical evidence that China has a "historical right" to this sea. The case was initiated by the Philippines and, according to Annex VII to the 1982 United Nations Convention on the Law of the Sea, the Court found that China has no right to control resources and waters within Nine-Dash Line and to invade the Philippines' rightful territory in the South China Sea. However, China declined to accept the court's decision, and shortly after, Chinese officials invited Philippine President Rodrigo Duterte to visit and discuss a potential package of Chinese investments for the Philippines.

For years, China has been reluctant to pursue a multilateral solution to the Spratly's problem, but the ASEAN countries have also failed to resolve their own overlapping claims (Stuart-Fox, 2003). Likewise, Mazza believes that Southeast Asian claimants to maritime territory in the South China Sea have disputes with one another, not solely with China; competitive impulses among the Association of Southeast Asian Nations (ASEAN)states drive military procurement, and cross-border militant activities raise tensions between governments (Mazza, 2018). In 2002, ASEAN signed a nonbinding DOC (Declaration of Conduct of Parties in the South China Sea) with China, which was regarded as a milestone within ASEAN (Buszynski, 2003). Furthermore, in 2011, the countries involved in the dispute over the EEZ pledged to help resolve it. Although the issue of oil and gas drilling remained unresolved, it was decided to respect marine environmental protection, scientific research, the safety of navigation and communication, search and rescue, and combating transnational crime (DOC, 2012). This step is described as an important step forward in general relations between China and ASEAN countries. Later, the same parties engaged in a new set of talks with the vision of producing a new Code of Conduct (COC). A single draft of the COC was first put forth in August 2018, with an agreement reached in November 2018 by China and ASEAN to finalize the COC within three years, starting from 2019 (The Diplomat, 2019).

This region has also recorded a significant US presence since the Obama administration. For instance, Barack Obama used the 2015 Asia-Pacific Economic Cooperation (APEC) forum to send a strong message to China over the South China Sea dispute. Namely, Obama pledged $250 million in military contributions to several Asian nations to support their efforts to stand up to China (Shear, 2015). Elizabeth C. Economy, Director for Asia Studies at the Council on Foreign Relations, believes that Obama played the APEC card in order to keep China in the liberal international order, where agreements on issues such as the extension of visas, establishment of rules for maritime and air encounters in the western Pacific and pledging to do more on climate change could be seen as the overall win for the United States (Economy, 2014). The United States increased its presence in the region through freedom of navigation operations (FONOPs) at the beginning of 2018. Their ships regularly patrol the South China Sea and protect the interests of partners in Southeast Asia. Likewise, Japan sold military ships to Vietnam and the Philippines in order to counter Chinese domination in the region. Given the humiliation of the previous loss of territory to European powers and Japan, not to mention Taiwan, this is a highly sensitive issue with domestic political implications (Stuart-Fox, 2003). Most recently, Joe Biden reaffirmed the US support for the Philippines and their rights in the South China Sea by describing the partnership between the two countries as "ironclad" (Al Jazeera, 2023).

PLA and other Chinese officials registered strong determination to protect Chinese territory and territorial claims, including areas having strategic resources such as oil and gas (Sutter, 2010). Once Beijing controls the South China Sea, China may achieve easier access to the critical sea lanes further south and possibly put Southeast Asia under its influence (Ming-Te and Tai-Ting Liu, 2011). Ott believes that China expects that Southeast Asia will be progressively subordinated to Beijing's strategic interests. Perhaps the closest analogy would be the assertion, in time, of a kind of Chinese Monroe Doctrine for Southeast Asia (Ott, 2006). Monroe's Doctrine was essentially designed to prevent the interference of European powers in nineteenth-century Americas, and Mearsheimer argues that we should expect China to come up with its own version of the Monroe Doctrine, as Imperial Japan did in the 1930s (Mearsheimer, 2010). By doing so, China could produce a buffer zone in its immediate neighborhood, undermine American and European influences, and take control of essential maritime routes. Currently, it is in the interest of Southeast Asian countries to play along since Chinese investments represent a lifeline for many—for instance, China is facilitating Joint Development Agreements (JDA) and research in the South China Sea (Heydarian, 2018). All this shows a complex relationship between the countries involved in the dispute, as well as the dual symbolism of the South China Sea. While some view it as the only place where China's military might can be projected and displayed, others solely see it as China's weak spot—primarily because it undermines its soft power projection within neighboring countries.

ASSERTIVE CHINA: THE ROLE IN THE GLOBAL GOVERNANCE

In the beginning of the new century, the Bush Administration invited China to be a responsible player on the international stage. Not long after, China became an important actor in resolving the US–North Korean conflict as a mediator between the two governments and aided in addressing the crisis in Sudan. In order to satisfy domestic constituents and elites and avoid the perception of accommodation to the United States, the Chinese leadership has systematically and carefully chosen foreign policy issues of interest over the past two decades. Christiansen reveals that, according to many Chinese observers, Beijing should refuse to assist the United States in pursuing what Beijing believes to be US core national interests (Christensen, 2011). In addition to ongoing activities through the work of the Security Council, China recently took a more active role in global governance by engaging in several important events—one of those being the case of mediation attempts in the 2021 Israeli–Palestinian conflict (Xinhua, 2021). Moreover, the recent agreement between Iran and Saudi Arabia to reestablish diplomatic and economic ties was also directly mediated by China, who, in the process, called for a stable and secure Persian Gulf region (Haghirian and Scita, 2023).

The outreach of China has improved, primarily because of its technology—best seen in the example of the push in Latin America, Africa, and Europe. Still, although many authors claim that Pax-Americana is no longer viable, and China exerts some level of global engagement, it is questionable whether China wants to engage in global affairs in the way the United States does. When looking at the relevant power indices like the Asia Power Index 2020, published by the Lowy Institute, we see that the United States is still ranked first in most parameters, even in China's immediate backyard. Nevertheless, China can be encouraged by the fact that it takes first place in significant parameters that could affect the title of superpower in the future and improve the mobility of its soft power—primarily with future resources and diplomatic influence (Lowy Institute, 2020). Still, the overwhelming narrative in Chinese media attempts to highlight the idea of the "shared future of all mankind," thus excluding unilateralism as an acceptable option (China Daily, 2022). China has so far demonstrated a willingness to learn and adequately apply or adjust traditional American concepts, giving it "Chinese characteristics." First, through BRI, China challenged the foundation of the American westward expansion, where the goal is to go west toward prosperity. Furthermore, China pursues its own Monroe Doctrine in the immediate neighborhood, in order to protect interests and create a buffer zone. Finally, the core concept within American social and political life is the notion of the American dream, which was challenged by President Xi Jinping, who introduced the so-called "Chinese dream."

CONCLUSION

In recent years, the American focus shifted from the Middle East to the Indo-Pacific, resulting in Barack Obama's "Pivot to Asia." The construction of the artificial islands and the growing dissatisfaction of Chinese neighbors have led to the emergence of the term "Thucydides trap," which explains the possibility of a war conflict between the United States and China. Currently, China wants to dominate only in its immediate neighborhood—a strategy that could be referred to as the Monroe Doctrine for Southeast Asia. Still, China has a difficult time exercising its soft power because of the South China Sea dispute but is also trying to reach a better position than the United States through soft-balancing strategies. Neighboring countries have a high strategic significance for China and represent a prolific ground for applying "Chinese characteristics" to traditional American concepts such as the Monroe Doctrine, American Dream, and Westward Expansion. China's current goal is to undermine the United States, establish dominance in the immediate neighborhood, and ensure the safe flow of goods, energy, and services. Therefore, this action produces a buffer zone that can protect mainland China from any intervention by the United States and its partners in the region. Some authors even suggest that we live in a post-American world, where the relative strength of the United States is in constant decline, and that assertive actors such as China could take advantage and undermine its position. The United States, which is still the dominant power in the world, doubtlessly views China's rise with skepticism. However, it seems unlikely that China will take the place of the United States in a global order, as well as the title of superpower since its soft and conventional power(s) are significantly lower—meaning that China's power is still lacking mobility. However, this could change in the future, in case China becomes the sole leader in technology development and improves its soft power capabilities.

NOTE

1. M. Hirkić. University of Sarajevo, Bosnia and Herzegovina. Email: muamerhirkic@gmail.com

To write this chapter, the author revised and used parts of his master's thesis project, defended at the Faculty of Political Science, University of Sarajevo, on December 24, 2019.

BIBLIOGRAPHY

Al Jazeera. 2021. "US, EU Concerned at China's 'Problematic' Actions in Disputed Sea." Accessed December 5, 2021. https://www.aljazeera.com/news/2021/12/3/us-eu-concerned-at-chinas-problematic-actions-in-disputed-sea.

Al Jazeera. 2023. "'Ironclad': Biden, Marcos JR Affirm US-Philippines Security Ties." *Al Jazeera*, May 2, 2023. https://www.aljazeera.com/news/2023/5/1/military-ties-top-agenda-as-biden-meets-philippines-marcos-jr.

Allison, Graham. 2015. "The Thucydides Trap: Are the US and China Headed for War?" *The Atlantic* 24. Accessed February 1, 2021. https://www.theatlantic.com/international/archive/2015/09/united-states-china-war-thucydides-trap/406756/.

Araya, Daniel. 2019. "The Future Is Asian: Parag Khanna on the Rise of Asia." *Forbes*. Accessed February 1, 2021. https://www.forbes.com/sites/danielaraya/2019/01/31/the-future-is-asian-an-interview-with-parag-khanna/.

Ariffin, Eijas. "Can China's Militarisation of the South China Sea Lead to Armed Conflict?" *The ASEAN Post*. Accessed February 1, 2021. https://theaseanpost.com/article/can-chinas-militarisation-south-china-sea-lead-armed-conflict-0.

ASEAN. 2012. "Declaration on the Conduct of Parties in the South China Sea." Accessed February 1, 2021. https://asean.org/?static_post=declaration-on-the-conduct-of-parties-in-the-south-china-sea-2.

Asia Maritime Transparency Initiative. 2019. "South China Sea Energy Exploration and Development." Accessed February 1, 2021. https://amti.csis.org/south-china-sea-energy-exploration-and-development/.

Beckley, Michael. 2018. *Unrivaled: Why America Will Remain the World's Sole Superpower*. Ithaca: Cornell University Press.

Blanton, Shannon, and Charles Kegley. 2016. *World Politics Trend and Transformation*. Boston: Cengage Learning.

Buszynski, Leszek. 2003. "ASEAN, the Declaration on Conduct, and the South China Sea." *Contemporary Southeast Asia* 25, no. 3: 457–475.

China Daily. 2022. "Xi's New Year Speech Shows China's Firm Resolution Towards Building Community with Shared Future." Accessed January 3, 2022. https://www.chinadaily.com.cn/a/202201/02/WS61d10c09a310cdd39bc7eb35.html.

Christensen, Thomas J. 2011. "The Advantages of an Assertive China." *Foreign Affairs* 90, no. 2: 22–33.

Council on Foreign Relations. 2020. "Territorial Disputes in the South China Sea." Accessed February 1, 2021. https://www.cfr.org/global-conflict-tracker/conflict/territorial-disputes-south-china-sea.

Dominguez, Gabriel. 2023. "Is Taiwan the Next Ukraine? It's More Complicated." *The Japan Times*. Accessed May 5, 2023. https://www.japantimes.co.jp/news/2023/02/19/asia-pacific/ukraine-war-anniversary-taiwan-comparison/.

Dreyer, June Teufel. 2007. "Chinese Foreign Policy." *Footnotes: The Newsletter of the Marvin Wachman Fund for International Education* 12, no. 5: 1–6.

Economy, Elizabeth C. "Obama's Big China Win at APEC: Not What You Think." Council on Foreign Relations. Accessed February 1, 2021. https://www.cfr.org/blog/obamas-big-china-win-apec-not-what-you-think.

Fox, William T.R. 1980. "The Super-Powers Then and Now." *International Journal* 35, no. 3: 411–430.

Gill, Stephan. 2010. "China's Soft Balancing Strategy and the Role of Resource Investment." *PEAR - The Yonsei Journal of International Studies 2,* no 2: 247–258.

Haghirian, Mehran, and Jacopo Scita. 2023. "The Broader Context behind China's Mediation between Iran and Saudi Arabia." *The Diplomat*. Accessed May 5, 2023. https://thediplomat.com/2023/03/the-broader-context-behind-chinas-mediation-between-iran-and-saudi-arabia/.

Heydarian, Richard. 2021. "Crossing the Rubicon: Duterte, China and Resource-Sharing in the South China Sea." Accessed February 1, 2021. http://www.maritimeissues.com/politics/crossing-the-rubicon-duterte-china-and-resourcesharing-in-the-south-china-sea.html.

Ikenberry, John. 2008. "The Rise of China and the Future of the West." *Foreign Affairs* 87, no. 1: 23–37.

Khanna, Parag. 2019. *The Future Is Asian: Commerce, Conflict, and Culture in the 21st Century*. New York: Simon & Schuster, Inc.

Kong, Lingjie. 2015. "The Belt and Road Initiative and China's Foreign Policy Toward Its Territorial and Boundary Disputes." *China Quarterly of International Strategic Studies* 1, no. 2: 215–233.

Lowy Institute. "Asia Power Index 2020." Accessed February 1, 2021. https://power.lowyinstitute.org/countries/?profile=CN.

Lynch, Allen C. "Deng's and Gorbachev's Reform Strategies Compared." Accessed February 1, 2021. https://eng.globalaffairs.ru/articles/dengs-and-gorbachevs-reform-strategies-compared/.

Mazza, Michael. 2019. "An American Strategy for Southeast Asia." American Enterprise Institute. Accessed February 1, 2021. https://www.rsis.edu.sg/wp-content/uploads/2019/03/An-American-Strategy-for-Southeast-Asia.pdf.

Mearsheimer, John. J. 2010. "The Gathering Storm: China's Challenge to US Power in Asia." *The Chinese Journal of International Politics* 3, no. 4: 381–396.

Ming-Te, H. and Tai-Ting Liu, T. 2011. "Sino-US Strategic Competition in Southeast Asia: China's Rise and US Foreign Policy Transformation since 9/11." *Political Perspectives* 5, no. 3: 43–60.

Missile Defense Advocacy Alliance. 2018. "China's Anti-Access Area Denial." Accessed February 1, 2021. https://missiledefenseadvocacy.org/missile-threat-and-proliferation/todays-missile-threat/china-anti-access-area-denial-coming-soon/.

Ott, Marvin. C. 2006. "Southeast Asian Security Challenges: Americas Response?" *Strategic Forum* 222: 1–8.

Palmer, James. 2023. "Why XI Is Rebranding Chinese Cultural History." *Foreign Policy*. Accessed May 5, 2023. https://foreignpolicy.com/2023/04/19/xi-china-global-civilization-cultural-history-rebrand/.

Poling, Gregory. 2018. "Kyaukpyu: Connecting China to the Indian Ocean." Accessed May February 1, 2021. https://amti.csis.org/kyaukpyu-china-indian-ocean/.

Rapp-Hooper, Mira. 2015. "Before and After: The South China Sea Transformed." Accessed February 1, 2021. https://amti.csis.org/before-and-after-the-south-china-sea-transformed/.

Reuters. 2021. "Xi Warns Against Foreign Bullying as China Marks Party Centenary." Accessed December 1, 2021. https://www.reuters.com/world/china/beijing-set-celebrate-centenary-chinas-communist-party-2021-06-30/.

Shear, Michael. 2015. "Obama Calls on Beijing to Stop Construction in South China Sea." *The New York Times*. Accessed December 1, 2021. https://www.nytimes.com/2015/11/19/world/asia/obama-apec-summit-south-china-sea-philippines.html.

South China Morning Post. 2016. "What's China's 'Nine-Dash Line' and Why Has It Created So Much Tension in the South China Sea?" Accessed February 1, 2021. https://www.scmp.com/news/china/diplomacy-defence/article/1988596/whats-chinas-nine-dash-line-and-why-has-it-created-so.

Stuart-Fox, Martin. 2003. *A Short History of China and Southeast Asia: Tribute, Trade and Influence*. Crow's Nest: Allen Unwin.

Sutter, Robert G. 2010. *US-Chinese Relations: Perilous Past, Pragmatic Present*. Lanham: Rowman & Littlefield Publishers.

The Diplomat. 2019. "Saving the China-ASEAN South China Sea Code of Conduct." Accessed February 1, 2021. https://thediplomat.com/2019/06/saving-the-china-asean-south-china-sea-code-of-conduct/.

Wang, Y-K. 2006. "China's Grand Strategy and US Primacy: Is China Balancing American Power?" The Brookings Institution - Center for Northeast Asian Policy Studies. Accessed February 1, 2021. https://www.brookings.edu/wp-content/uploads/2016/06/wang2006.pdf.

Xinhua. 2021. "China Puts Forward Four-Point Proposal Regarding Palestine-Israel Conflict." Accessed December 12, 2021. http://www.xinhuanet.com/english/2021-05/17/c_139950043.htm.

Zakaria, Fareed. 2017. "Say Hello to a Post-America World." *The Washington Post*. Accessed February 1, 2021. https://www.washingtonpost.com/opinions/say-hello-to-a-post-america-world/2017/07/27/aad19d68-7308-11e7-8f39-eeb7d3a2d304_story.html.

Part II

THE CHANGING NATURE OF WARFARE AND WEAPONRY

Chapter 5

A Profitable Enterprise

The Emergence of Private Military Companies as Stakeholders in International Security

Ushmayo Bhattacharya[1]

INTRODUCTION

Cultural analysis, as a method of inquiry into strategic behavior, had existed for centuries before scholars of international relations decided to begin incorporating it into modern analyses. However, strategic cultural analysis (in the contemporary sense of the term) was first begun by scholars such as Jack Snyder in an attempt to delve deeper into the reasonings behind the actions of the Soviet Union during the final years of the Cold War. Since that time, several waves of scholarship on strategic culture have appeared with different research agendas (Johnston, 1995). This chapter seeks to focus on the somewhat sidelined Second-generation scholarship on strategic culture and its usage in advocating for a shift in the direction of research on strategic behavior.

Edward Lock points to the importance of the question of agency in discussions on strategic behavior (Lock, 2010). He further highlights a key point that strategic culture is a concept that is subject to active manipulation by all actors within a security community (Lock, 2010, p. 701). This chapter attempts to draw attention to this question of agency, in particular to the Private Military Company (PMC) as an increasingly important actor influencing the strategic behavior of a security community. This chapter contends that the monopoly over the legitimate use of violence by states (another key assumption of strategic cultural analyses) is now being challenged by PMCs, which in turn translates to them having a greater voice in what passes as military practice within a security community.

The chapter begins with a detailed look at the Second Generation of Strategic Cultural scholarship, elaborating on the theoretical bridgeheads it provides to introduce the idea of Private Military Companies as possible actors of importance. It then focuses on the nuances of PMCs as actors within a security community, along with elaborating on the reasons why it has a crucial impact on strategic behavior. The final section talks about how the monopoly of violence that states enjoy is being challenged by PMCs and how considerations on International Security could benefit from incorporating the role of PMCs when analyzing strategic behavior.

THE CRACK IN THE WALL: A RECONCEPTUALIZATION OF STRATEGIC CULTURE

Bringing Back the Second Generation

As Alastair Johnston notes, the idea of Strategic Culture emerged as a challenge to the over-determinism of the Realist school of strategic studies during the Cold War (Johnston, 1995, pp. 34–35). It championed the factor of historicity being an important determinant of strategic behavior within a security community, as opposed to the primacy of the idea of future utility as championed by Realists. David Haglund further contends that the primary reason cultural analysis should be assigned an important role in strategic studies is because culture is the primary tool through which human collectivities pass down knowledge over time (Haglund, 2004, p. 485). On a more practical note, cultural factors may be useful in understanding and predicting the actions of a possible adversary while in a state of conflict and during negotiations after a conflict, as Darryl Howlett notes (Howlett, 2006, pp. 3–4). Further, Jeffrey Lantis has written on how cultural analysis might be useful in understanding issues that plague modern strategic considerations specifically, such as the WMD crisis (Lantis, 2006, p. 3).

Each sub-school within the umbrella of Strategic Culture scholarship, dubbed "generations" by Johnston (Johnston, 1995), has its advocates and critics; but this chapter aims to draw attention to the Second Generation of Strategic Cultural scholarship. Edward Lock, one of the more prominent scholars of the Second Generation, aims to fill a gap that proponents of other generations have overlooked, namely the questions of agency and identity within security communities (Lock, 2010, p. 687). The primacy of the state as the holder of the monopoly of violence within a security community is the notion that Lock wishes to challenge, saying that other actors within such communities have a substantial say in what is considered as security (Lock, 2010, p. 687). This chapter argues, following Lock's logic, that the PMC is one such actor that has emerged on the security landscape.

According to Lock, the focus of analysis in second-generation scholarship shifts away from the origins of a particular actor's strategic culture and toward the effects that strategic behavior has on the interactions and relationships between communities (Lock, 2010, p. 687). A very important aspect of second-generation scholarship that Lock highlights is that it argues against taking certain security communities (especially states) for granted and instead suggests exploring the implications that strategic behavior has on these communities and their roles in broader strategy (Lock, 2010, p. 687).

The lock goes on to redefine the way second-generation scholars have chosen to work on the topic, with particular reference to the arguments forwarded by Bradley Klein. Klein's work, Lock notes, has strong influences from the work of scholars like Michel Foucault, Richard Ashley, and Marxist scholars like Antonio Gramsci, one of the reasons the latter postulates that Klein's ideas might have been overlooked by strategic culture scholars (Lock, 2010, p. 696).

Strategic Culture as a Prism of Analysis

Bradley Klein argues that a limitation of theories on strategy is their assumption that the objects of analysis and their inherent cultural attributes have been constant since their origin. In his paper, Klein pits two versions of the origins of strategic culture which have been mutually antagonistic since their inception against each other; the view of the world as imagined by Machiavelli and Thomas Hobbes as opposed to the worldview imagined by Marxian scholars such as Gramsci (Klein, 1988, pp. 133–134).

Klein then draws attention to the possible merit in the latter view, where Gramsci calls the modern state system to be a carefully constructed mechanism by a sophisticated elite bourgeoisie to extol cooperation instead of coercion from the working class in order to maintain power (Klein, 1988, pp. 134–135). This argument is what Klein and then Lock emphasize. They argue that the *primary purpose of strategic culture is to problematize the taken-for-granted status that states enjoy in strategic studies* (Lock, 2010, p. 697).

Klein further shows several examples (such as John Mearsheimer's argument predicting post–Cold War Europe would be characterized by Germany acquiring nuclear weapons) of theorists who choose to ignore the agency of the various agents present in security communities and take the state and its goals for granted and as the sole unit of analysis (Klein, 1994, p. 19). Klein then mentions Barry Buzan and how the latter challenges the realist assumption of a neatly ordered world composed of the individual, state, and international levels in which the interactions of all three follow a hierarchy. Klein asserts that the interactions between these levels are far more fluid, possessing the ability for mutual influence in security decisions (Klein, 1994, p. 20).

Buzan, Klein claims, further says that all assertions and predictions regarding the understanding of security have remained almost completely state-centric, not acknowledging the crucial point that it is possible for states and non-state actors to have interdependency in matters of security (Klein, 1994, p. 21).

The key takeaway from Klein is his analysis of the nature of modern conflict and how it starts to deviate from the more traditional ways of warfare, which states are still geared toward. He mentions "low-intensity" conflicts as the current norm and how the main problem that states have today is how to dole out small portions of force to meet the challenges that conventional military threats can mount (Klein, 1994, p. 26). As Lock argues in his paper, strategic culture is produced by the actions of the various actors within a security community, and to get a complete understanding of modern conflict, the proper agency should be given to these actors (Lock, 2010, p. 700).

This article argues that one such actor is the PMC, the increasing importance of which in broader conceptions of strategy and security has been noted by several scholars (Leander, 2005; Singer, 2002). Taking the cue from Lock's argument about the question of agency, this article would like to suggest that one shortcoming of existing literature that PMCs might successfully challenge is that of the state monopoly on the use of force, the cornerstone of realist examinations of strategy.

Stefano Guzzini hints at why a strategic cultural prism might be a useful lens to look at this emerging phenomenon. In his discussions on structural power, Guzzini highlights the concept of *Doxa*, which he paraphrases from the work of Pierre Bourdieu (Guzzini, 1993, p. 466). Doxa, he writes, is a system of normalized recognition that is a result of *continuous practice*, which empowers at an intersubjective level where knowledge and acting spaces are defined. Normalized recognition through continuous practice is the cornerstone of the establishment of cultural practices. It can thus be argued that Anna Leander's argument of "epistemic power" (Leander, 2005, p. 5), which is the ability of an actor to determine what counts as a security issue, is a manipulation of what counts as normalized recognition in terms of security. Looking at it through the lens of strategic culture, the power that PMCs bring to bear on prevalent security discourse is extremely significant.

SUBTLE BUT SIGNIFICANT: THE POWER OF PRIVATE MILITARY COMPANIES

The Methods of PMC Influence Assertion

A key issue that has reemerged in International Security Studies since the late twentieth century is the privatization of armed forces (Singer, 2002, p. 193). An extensive debate has ensued over how this phenomenon affects the understanding of security; the traditional premise within which security has been considered for the better part of the twentieth century is the monopoly states have enjoyed over providing security and over the authorized use of violence in general. With the advent of PMCs, however, any organization or individual has the capability to utilize armed force, provided they have the financial means to procure it. Anna Leander argues that the importance of PMCs is overlooked because of the traditional and restrictive idea of power, which focuses solely on formal decision-making capacity, which is invariably held exclusively by states. The popular view is that PMCs are, at best, a strategic tool used to further the military influence of states, and they cannot be looked at as independent actors in global security considerations.

Leander points to the rising involvement of PMCs in international conflicts, mapping an exponential rise from the Gulf War to the Iraq conflict, which clearly showcases their rising influence in global security considerations. Leander argues that there are two different types of power that PMCs can wield in the evolving scenario. She talks of *structural* power, that is, their ability to refashion the evolving logic of legitimate expertise on security, and *epistemic* power, that is, their ability to influence understandings of security (Leander, 2005, p. 5).

The author goes on to show how PMCs in the United States integrate themselves into the functioning of the national military and the upper echelons of government, giving such organizations unprecedented access to sensitive and often classified information regarding American security concerns. Most major American PMCs, Leander says, offer technical or advisory services, often leading them to manage specific equipment or weapons systems (Leander, 2005, p. 6). With modern armies increasingly dependent on sophisticated technology in combat, the expertise that PMCs can guarantee is often the difference between deployed armies being effective or in disarray. Given their increasingly intimate involvement in conflict scenarios, and correspondingly rising government dependence on their expertise, PMCs are beginning to exercise *epistemic* power in influencing "what is told (and what is left out)" (Leander, 2005, p. 14), in security discourse.

To Leander, what this represents is a shift from the order established after the Vietnam War, when it was decided that "security was too important to be left to the generals" (Leander, 2005, p. 18). With the specialized expertise that PMCs now bring to security decisions, the stage is set for what Leander argues is the "remilitarization" (Leander, 2005, p. 18) of security discourse. The central issue that Leander discusses in her article is that the importance of PMCs in security discourse cannot be measured with the traditional understanding of power as formal decision-making capacity. As her article attempts to show, the ability to influence decision-making bodies must also be a factor in determining power.

Leander mentions that while most PMCs draw the lion's share of their profits from government contracts, it does not necessarily follow that they are answerable to the government for every action taken on the field. Given the fact that conflicts are often unclear, inconclusive affairs, the PMC retains control over most of the clauses of a particular contract, given the sizeable risk and investment it has to undertake. The most crucial of these include the right to back out of a contract if the corporation thinks that the risk is no longer worth the effort (e.g., the Ghurkha Security Guards in Sierra Leone abandoned their client after their commander was reportedly cannibalized by opposing forces; Leander, 2005, p. 8). Conversely, given that the expenditure states or international organizations have to incur in employing these PMCs is astronomical, as clients they too are anxious to see their investment bring tangible results.

The mutual profit motive is thus a very significant motivator for the open-ended nature of such contracts. As Hannah Tonkin argues, this effectively translates to clients not being involved in the day-to-day activities of the PMCs in the field of operations (Tonkin, 2012, p. 98). Further, even if contractors from PMCs work side by side with national armies deployed in the region, they are not under the command of the chief of the deployed armed forces.

The very expression "PMC" is another important particularity. The novelty in the private military market today is the fact it is organized into corporate organizations, instead of the traditional, individualistic pattern followed before; the mercenary. Singer highlights the differences between the traditional mercenary and private military organizations, given the different ramifications postulated in international humanitarian law for each (Singer, 2002, p. 6).

Article 44 of the Geneva Convention of 1977 states that a mercenary cannot be recruited from the territories of any of the parties in a particular conflict (Schuller, 2008, p. 4), and this is in direct conflict with the interest of several PMCs who often rely on local employees to provide general and on-ground intelligence. By corporatizing, PMCs thus get away with not being as accountable under international law and are most generally classified as being "civilians taking a direct part in hostilities" (Schuller, 2008, p. 4). The protection this offers PMC operatives is significant since they cannot be tried as war criminals.

The Hollow Premise of Accountability

Hannah Tonkin argues that PMCs enjoy such benefits due to the niche role they play in the current security discourse. By utilizing private contractors, a state can effectively double the number of men and equipment it has on the field in a conflict situation, without legislative approval or popular resentment, like the US military presence in both Iraq and Afghanistan. She further states that contractors issued the task of interrogation at Abu Ghraib were reported for abuse to the extent that the US Congress had to pass legislation to reserve that role for the army (Tonkin, 2012, p. 102). Based on her example, Tonkin is of the opinion that states and non-state actors have begun to push for more accountability regarding the actions of PMCs, culminating in the Montreux Document of 2007 (Tonkin, 2012, p. 103), which contained specific measures states could take to ensure increased accountability in the private military industry.

Amol Mehra critiques the idea of the Montreux Document given the fact that it is not legally binding and does not carry any "clear categorization of applicable laws, although he concedes that it is currently espoused by 17 states, most of which liberally contract PMCs" (Mehra, 2009, pp. 328–329). He further adds that no provision in the Montreux Document declares the use of mercenaries an offense in itself. Moreover, no law yet enacted targets the corporate aspect of private military force, simply individual contractors (Mehra, 2009, p. 327).

The Montreux Document, in essence, represents a pushback by states employing private military force to try and make PMCs accountable and thus dependent on states. Scholars like Marcus Mohlin even argue for this (Mohlin, 2014). However, the infiltration of PMCs into established political structures of the state has led to state representatives themselves lobbying for an increased agency for the former (Leander, 2005, p. 808). This is a clear example of the epistemic power of PMCs.

CHALLENGING THE MONOPOLY OF THE STATE: THE RISING STAR OF PRIVATE MILITARY COMPANIES AND ITS IMPLICATIONS FOR INTERNATIONAL SECURITY

The Legal Ambiguity of PMC Activity

It is this epistemic power of PMCs that is leading to their increasingly extensive role in every theatre of international security. As Elke Krahmann argues, this is what is allowing PMCs to slowly push back against the established international norm of states being the only actor within a security community to have the monopoly over the use of force (Krahmann, 2013). Krahmann begins her paper by mentioning the Montreux Document, which talks of regulations and courses of action allowed by Private Military and Security Companies, signed by eighteen states in 2008, and goes on to say,

> Disregarding the issue of whether the Montreux Document will be effective in curtailing the impunity of PMSCs, this article takes the document as a point of departure for raising another question: Are we witnessing a transformation of the international norm of the state monopoly on the legitimate use of violence? (Krahmann, 2013, p. 54)

Krahmann then elaborates on the possible answers to this question by looking at it from two angles; the examination of the origins and the current execution of the norm of the state monopoly on violence and the analysis of the legal and practical aspects of the activities that PMCs have been engaged in in recent years (Krahmann, 2013, p. 55).

As discussed in the previous section, PMCs have taken pains to distance themselves from the title of “Mercenary,” have actively sought to carve out a separate existence for themselves, and have managed to evade the very stringent clauses that international law puts on mercenaries while engaging in the same operations, albeit under different names (Krahmann, 2013, p. 65). Krahmann then highlights the shortcomings of international law regarding the exact role that PMCs might be able to play in a conflict situation, given that the only way the sanctions that apply to mercenaries might be used against them is if they are involved in direct and active combat, something most countries that employ PMCs take explicit measures to ensure does not happen (Krahmann, 2013, p. 65). Krahmann uses US Central Command and official NATO records to show how the United States and even the United Nations make laws, on the one hand, preventing private security contractors from engaging in offensive actions while on the field with or without national militaries, while allowing them the full usage of lethal force while protecting assets or personnel during those same missions (Krahmann, 2013, p. 65).

Thus, as Sarah Percy puts it; given that PMCs engage in “defensive operations,” while mercenaries engage in “combat,” the former enjoys the leeway that the legal gray area they operate in allows them, while the latter has heavy international sanctions against their usage (Percy, 2007). Mention must be made here of the Nisour Square massacre carried out in Iraq by the firm Blackwater in 2007 and the caricature of legal battles that followed as its aftermath. In their analysis of the event, Katia Snukal and Emily Gilbert discuss the term "lawfare," that is, the legal acceptance of the actions taken by a private entity, and elaborate on how Blackwater was able to evade legal prosecution for seven years before four of their employees were successfully charged, still retaining however, the right to appeal the decision (Snukal & Gilbert, 2015, p. 661). Interestingly, one of the last acts of President Trump at the end of his tenure at the White House was to pardon the four main implicated contractors accused of participating in the Nisour Square massacre, which, despite being strongly condemned by both the United Nations and elements within the United States military, is further proof that PMC contractors do enjoy tacit state favor, and are to an extent immune from the normal restrictions that bind conventional militaries (Reuters, 2020).

This point is important as it relates to one of the questions posited by Lock, which points to an analysis of how certain sections of a security communities' use of military force are justified and elaborated on while others are subdued (Lock, 2010, p. 701). Given the apparent immunity that PMCs are beginning to enjoy legally, their versions of justifying the use of force and thus securitizing an issue might be gaining more prominence.

PMCs in Action: In the West and the Rest

As Herbert Howe notes, since the 1990s, private military companies have run rampant in Africa, becoming almost the sole protectors of state sovereignty in failing regimes such as Angola and Sierra Leone (Howe, 1998, p. 308). He writes,

> since 1993, Executive Outcomes (EO), the world's largest and best known "mercenary" group, has marketed itself as a defender of African state security in this post-Cold War era. (Howe, 1998, p. 308)

In the case of stable and indeed central powers such as the United States as well, the trend toward using PMCs has been increasingly more mainstream, as documented by Deborah Avant. She writes,

> As the US government downsized the military after the Cold War, it found itself committing troops in a broader and less predictable array of conflicts. The government turned to contractors for a wider array of services-and contractors mobilized to provide these. (Avant, 2013, p. 115)

Between 2008 and 2010, the presence of fully armed combat-ready private contractors in Iraq and Afghanistan went up from 6,000 and 3,184 to 11,030 and 16,398, respectively. Canada, the Netherlands, Germany, and France arc among many other countries which have leased out their commitments at least partially to PMCs (Krahmann, 2013, p. 60). The crucial takeaway from these deployments is that PMCs are slowly being accorded the status of actual combatants; as opposed to the support roles they had hitherto played (Krahmann, 2013, p. 60). As Ben Murray further points out, they are being awarded national honors for their services as well (Murray, 2006).

Further, as Hilde van Meegdenburg notes, PMCs are also being deployed to provide “back-end” support to nations and even international organizations such as NATO (Meegdenburg, 2015, p. 336). She states that this role of PMCs has far-reaching implications with relation to the duration for which forces deployed to a conflict sector can comfortably remain in it (Meegdenburg, 2015). As an example, she cites the French firm Sodexo which provided logistical support (from waste management to provisions and canteens) to the Norwegian contingent being deployed to Afghanistan after the firm was contracted by NATO (Meegdenburg, 2015). It is thus not just direct combat or combat-support roles that are reserved for PMCs. Logistical roles are now being opened up to them as well, which is fertile ground for private firms to strengthen their ever-expanding foothold in matters of conflict.

It must be noted at this point that the accountability of PMCs is further blurred by the actions of several states that are not ”Western,” an example of which is the curious case of the Wagner Group in Russia. The Wagner Group has been mired in controversy since its inception, and this has been further exacerbated by the murky legal area in which the firm operates. Kimberly Marten highlights two very important points in her paper about the Wagner Group; the first being that the actions of the Wagner Group seem to be limited to missions *outside* Russia, and the second being that according to Russian law, private military firms are *illegal* (Marten, 2019, pp. 182–184). Wagner group forces have been deployed in Crimea, eastern Ukraine, Syria, Sudan, the Central African Republic, and possibly Libya (Marten, 2019, p. 182). Marten further points out the link between the extended involvement of the Wagner group in all these foreign theaters and the apparent illegality of its existence. While in 2018, the Russian Parliament and other auxiliary government bodies refused to consider the proposition of legalizing the Wagner Group; Putin publicly mentioned the firm and stated as long as it remained within the purview of Russian domestic law, it could continue to do business as it saw fit later in the same year (Marten, 2019, p. 184).

This tacit recognition of the existence and activities of the Wagner Group, coupled with the fact that its activities fall exclusively outside Russian territory, is a legal loophole that the firm is continuing to exploit with the support of nuclear power, highlighted by Putin’s declaration that their activities are state secrets (Marten, 2019, pp. 184–185). Three Russian journalists trying to report on the activities of the Wagner Group in the Central African Republic were shot dead, and Denis Korotkov, a journalist who has done intensive reporting on Russian PMCs, was severely threatened for his comments on the activities of the Wagner Group (Marten, 2019, pp. 187–189). Marten further highlights a very important point in the activities of private military firms with a specific focus on firms like the Wagner group; one of the key reasons the former prefers to operate under a quasi-legal framework is because of the well-documented legal troubles firms like Blackwater have run into for their involvement and conduct in conflict situations (Marten, 2019, p. 185). This is undeniable proof that PMCs are adapting to new circumstances that are emerging for their regulation, in several cases with the active support of important states.

As Carolin Liss writes, another emerging arena for PMSC activity has been South-East Asia. An example of this can be the troubled situation in the Malacca Strait, comprised primarily of Malaysian and Indonesian territorial waters (Liss, 2014, p. 197). Yet, neither of these two nations are participant in the largest concerted effort to oppose the chief threat of piracy and robbery on the Malacca Strait, the Regional Cooperation Agreement on Combating Piracy and Armed Robbery against Ships in Asia (ReCAAP); which has been signed by the ASEAN members, China, Japan, India, South Korea, Bangladesh, and Sri Lanka (Liss, 2014, p. 200). This is chiefly due to the inherent insecurities felt by all the nations operating within the region and the mutual suspicion of motives. In such circumstances, regional cooperation to combat piracy and robbery falls short of requisite levels, which is why Private Military and Security Companies s are being deployed in the region to level the scales. Even in this case, it is the ambiguity regarding their regulation that is proving pivotal for the rising influence of PMSCs. As Liss writes, there are over ten different managerial bodies responsible for maritime security enforcement in Indonesia (Liss, 2014, p. 203). In such circumstances, there emerges a considerable "gray area" within which PMSCs can operate, either by themselves or cooperating with local government enforcement agencies. While piracy in the region is at an all-time low, it has caused increased tensions amongst local powers. The fact that PMSCs operating in the Malacca Strait have, at the very least, a token presence in Singapore is a cause for concern for both Malaysia and Indonesia since it could be interpreted as Singaporean influence in their territorial waters (Liss, 2014, p. 205). Moreover, with other PMSCs (such as Erik Prince's venture in Myanmar) also active in the vicinity (Wion News, 2019), these nations are liable to interpret such activity as foreign encroachments into their zones of influence. Such perceptions further tear at the fabric of the delicate balance of nations and influence in South-East Asia, and PMSCs are proving to be at the center of this emerging security scenario.

Another country that has increasingly relied on PMSCs for the propagation of its interests abroad is China. The Belt and Road Initiative (BRI) has been an ambitious project undertaken by China in recent years, with scores of countries involved. Chinese citizens have been involved more and more closely with foreign projects all across the world and are often present in countries with hostile elements. This is especially true in Central Asia, where success in the BRI initiative is vital for the propagation of Chinese interests. There are several Chinese PMSCs operating in Kyrgyzstan; such as Cityguard, the Shandong Huawei Security Group, Zhongjun Junhong, all of which have been granted permission by the Chinese Government to operate abroad, avoiding the strict Chinese laws which regulate the operations of Chinese PMSCs within China (Muratalieva et al., 2022, p. 10). These companies offer a variety of services ranging from personnel training to guarding key facilities and are most recently involved in a project which China has decided to launch across Central Asia. In Kyrgyzstan, the "Safe City" project, which involves a massive buildup of surveillance cameras in major cities to increase citizen security, is being implemented by Chinese PMSC Shenzhen Sunwin Intelligent Co. Ltd (Muratalieva et al., 2022, p. 12).

Challenging the Monopoly of the State

The key question that must be asked in the face of such increased deployment of PMCs in combat situations involving states worldwide is how this challenges the monopoly of the legitimate use of force that states have hitherto come to enjoy. Krahmann points to the answer being in the chronology of how states came to enjoy this status.

With the establishment of strong monarchies across Europe, the private armies that had been the retainers of the nobility who held vast estates in what would subsequently become nations began to be appropriated by the King and then, in turn, by bureaucracies and elected democracies. The regulatory bindings which followed these shifts led to the ultimate unofficial abolishment of the private use of force altogether in the nineteenth century (Opello and Rosow, 1999). Krahmann argues that with the use of PMCs becoming widespread once more, alongside there being a legal gray area in which they mostly operate, the unchallenged status of the state in terms of the monopoly of the legitimate use of force is now questionable. The cycle has seemingly moved back to states trying to legally regulate the activity of PMCs, allowing them significant leeway once more (Krahmann, 2013, p. 66).

This shift is exceptionally noteworthy because of the argument Leander makes in her article, when she asserts that PMCs possess "epistemic" power, and she writes,

> if we apply a more comprehensive power analysis PMCs appear to have gained considerable power over security understandings and discourses. They increasingly shape which issues and problems are "securitised"—turned into existential threats—and which kind of (re-)action is to be considered most appropriate. (Leander, 2005, p. 803)

This must be understood as an argument that compliments the challenge to the monopoly of force that PMCs are beginning to mount against the state while still being nominally under the latter's aegis. Leander's chief contention is that the influence of PMCs is beginning to be exhibited not only in the operations that they are a part of on the field but also in determining what those operations will be (Leander, 2005, pp. 807–810). This ability, Leander claims, comes from the noncombat services that PMCs are beginning to provide to states. She quotes former Central Intelligence Agency director James Woolsey who noted that 95% of all intelligence the CIA worked with came from open sources, mostly from private security firms (Leander, 2005, p. 813). She further mentions the firm AirScan, which was the prime source of intelligence for the United States in Bosnia, and now handles surveillance in Iraq (Leander, 2005, p. 813). Another example she gives is that of Space Imaging and Digital Globe, firms that supplied most of the surveillance for the United States in Afghanistan (Leander, 2005, p. 813). By beginning to control the information based on which states make threat perceptions, PMCs are thus beginning to have a greater say in what security and strategic operations a state will participate in.

CONCLUSION

While materialist factors undoubtedly have their place and priority within the field, as Stuart Poore argues, without adequate understanding of the cultural connotations behind strategic behavior, the end result of analyses on the latter is, at best, extremely narrow (Poore, 2003, p. 284). As the Second-Generation Strategic Culture theorists point out, the direction of investigation of the scholarship must instead go beyond the traditional boundaries of the actions of states to encompass several more actors within a security community. These are the actors who have had significant influence over the strategic behavior of that particular community but have thus far been sidelined by the all-important stature of the state in analyses of strategic connotations. The crucial point where strategic culture might have more to offer to strategic analysis is the fact that it offers a deeper insight into the actual reasoning and justification that actors within a security community might provide both to themselves and to the external world behind their use of military force.

This chapter suggests that with this new direction pointed out by Second-Generation scholars, it is increasingly clear that PMCs have been emergent in the security arena for quite some time. Their increasingly prominent presence on the battlefield, coupled with the sophisticated services they are capable of providing to states or other clients, has begun, as this chapter has argued, to shift the monopoly of force that states have hitherto enjoyed in the legitimate usage of force.

While it is true that this shift is still in its nascent stages, this does by no means indicate its triviality, and ignoring the importance of PMCs in analyzing international strategic behavior has the potential to be extremely detrimental. The agency of the various actors within a security community must be recognized for an adequate analysis of strategic behavior, and in that context, the increasing gravity of PMCs cannot be overlooked.

NOTE

1. U. Bhattacharya. Central European University, Vienna, Austria. Email: ushmayo95@gmail.com

BIBLIOGRAPHY

Avant, Deborah D. *The market for force: The consequences of privatizing security.* Cambridge University Press, 2005.

Booth, Ken. "Strategic culture: Validity and validation." *Oxford Journal on Good Governance* 2, no. 1 (2005): 25–28.

Desch, Michael C. "Culture clash: Assessing the importance of ideas in security studies." *International Security* 23, no. 1 (1998): 141–170.

Glenn, John. "Realism versus strategic culture: Competition and collaboration?" *International Studies Review* 11, no. 3 (2009): 523–551.

Gray, C. S. "Out of the wilderness: Prime time for strategic culture, prepared for the defense threat reduction agency advanced systems and concepts office." *Contract Nos. DTRA01-03-D-0017, SP0600-04-C-5982* (2006).

Guzzini, Stefano. "Structural power: The limits of neorealist power analysis." *International Organization* 47, no. 3 (1993): 443–478.

Haglund, David G. "What good is strategic culture? A modest defence of an immodest concept." *International Journal* 59, no. 3 (2004): 479–502.

Howlett, Darryl. "The future of strategic culture." *Report for the Defense Threat Reduction Agency: 209–234*(2006).

Howe, Herbert M. "Private security forces and African stability: The case of executive outcomes." *The Journal of Modern African Studies* 36, no. 2 (1998): 307–331.

Johnston, Alastair Iain. "Thinking about strategic culture." *International Security* 19, no. 4 (1995): 32–64.

Snukal, Katia, and Emily Gilbert. "War, law, jurisdiction, and juridical othering: Private military security contractors and the Nisour Square massacre." *Environment and Planning D: Society and Space* 33, no. 4 (2015): 660–675.

Klein, Bradley S. *Strategic studies and world order: The global politics of deterrence.* No. 34. Cambridge University Press, 1994.

Klein, Bradley S. "Hegemony and strategic culture: American power projection and alliance defence politics." *Review of International Studies* 14, no. 2 (1988): 133–148.

Krahmann, Elke. "The United States, PMSCs and the state monopoly on violence: Leading the way towards norm change." *Security Dialogue* 44, no. 1 (2013): 53–71.

Lantis, Jeffrey S. "Strategic culture: From Clausewitz to constructivism." In *Strategic culture and weapons of mass destruction: Culturally based insights into comparative national security policymaking, New York: Palgrave Macmillan* (2009): 33–52.

Lantis, Jeffrey S. "Strategic culture and national security policy." *International Studies Review* 4, no. 3 (2002): 87–113.
Leander, Anna. "The power to construct international security: On the significance of private military companies." *Millennium* 33, no. 3 (2005): 803–825.
Lock, Edward. "Refining strategic culture: Return of the second generation." *Review of International Studies* 36, no. 3 (2010): 685–708.
Liss, Carolin. "The privatisation of maritime security in Southeast Asia: The impact on regional security cooperation." *Australian Journal of International Affairs* 68, no. 2 (2014): 194–209.
Marten, Kimberly. "Russia's use of semi-state security forces: The case of the Wagner Group." *Post-Soviet Affairs* 35, no. 3 (2019): 181–204.
Muratalieva, Zamira Tulkunovna, Asia Tashtanbekovna Esenbekova, and Nadezhda Sergeevna Tatkalo. "China in the shadow of Russia: Covert tools for expanding China's influence over Kyrgyzstan's security." *India Quarterly* 78, no. 1 (2022): 88–103.
Mehra, Amol. "Bridging accountability gaps-the proliferation of private military and security companies and ensuring accountability for human rights violations." *Pacific McGeorge Global Business & Development Law Journal* 22 (2009): 323.
Mohlin, Marcus. "Commercialisation of warfare and shadow wars: Private military companies as strategic tools." *St Antony's International Review* 9, no. 2 (2014): 24–38.
Murray, Ben. "American, British contractors honored for work in Iraq." *Stars and Stripes*, June 28, 2006. https://www.stripes.com/news/american-british-civilian-contractors-honored-for-work-in-iraq-1.51466
Opello, Walter C., and Stephen J. Rosow. *The nation-state and global order: A historical introduction to contemporary politics*. No. 320.1 O6. Boulder: Lynne Rienner, 1999.
Percy, Sarah V. "Mercenaries: Strong norm, weak law." *International Organization* 61, no. 2 (2007): 367–397.
Poore, Stuart. "What is the context? A reply to the Gray-Johnston debate on strategic culture." *Review of International Studies* 29, no. 2 (2003): 279–284.
Reuters (Nebehay Stephanie). "Trump Pardon of Blackwater Iraq contractors violates International Law-UN." December 30, 2020. https://www.reuters.com/article/us-iraq-blackwater-un-idUSKBN294108
Schüller, Andreas. "Rules and responsibilities of employees of private military companies under international humanitarian law." *Sicherheit und Frieden (S+ F)/ Security and Peace* (2008): January 1, 191–196.
Singer, Peter W. "Corporate warriors: The rise of the privatized military industry and its ramifications for international security." *International Security* 26, no. 3 (2001): 186–220.
Tonkin, Hannah. "The power and accountability of private military and security companies." *Making Global Institutions Work* (2014): 120-140.
Van Meegdenburg, Hilde. "What the research on PMSCs discovered and neglected: An appraisal of the literature." *Contemporary Security Policy* 36, no. 2 (2015): 321–345.
Wion News. "Former Blackwater contractor Erik Prince in Myanmar security venture." March 22, 2019. https://www.wionews.com/south-east-asia/former-blackwater-contractor-erik-prince-in-myanmar-security-venture-204928

Chapter 6

The New Nuclear Arms Race

Implications for Global Security

Ghazala Yasmin Jalil[1]

INTRODUCTION

Today's international security landscape is characterized by deteriorating relations between the United States and Russia. These tensions in relations between the two great powers have been accompanied with a breakdown in the bilateral arms control regime. This, in turn, is threatening to reignite an arms race between the two countries which reminds us of their Cold War competition. The year 2019 saw the demise of the 1987 Intermediate-Range Nuclear Forces (INF) Treaty that was the cornerstone of European security which required the United States and the Soviet Union to eliminate and permanently forswear all of their nuclear and conventional ground-launched ballistic and cruise missiles with ranges of 500 to 5,500 kilometers. The last remaining bilateral treaty, the New Strategic Arms Reduction Treaty (START) was rescued at the last moment when the Biden Administration took over in January 2021. The United States withdrew from the Joint Comprehensive Plan of Action (JCPOA) in 2018, which put checks on the development of the Iranian nuclear programme. The Nuclear Non-Proliferation Treaty (NPT) has not made any substantive progress. The Comprehensive Test-Ban Treaty (CTBT) has been in limbo for over two decades. UN forums like the Conference on Disarmament have been ineffective in negotiating arms control arrangements. There is no progress on the much-needed arms control legislation in outer space. The United States has not taken any interest in arms control arrangements in outer space. In fact, it is developing space force that is exclusively devoted to combat and space operations.

The breakdown in arms control has been accompanied by a renewed emphasis on nuclear weapons and other weapons systems. It has set in motion a new era of arms races. Both the United States and Russia are developing an array of nuclear weapons and indulging in massive military modernization programmes. India is also indulging in military acquisitions and modernizing its nuclear forces. It has also made tremendous progress in the military space programme and even conducted an anti-satellite test in March 2019.

Moreover, with the Nuclear Posture Review (NPR) in 2018, while focusing on modernizing its existing nuclear force, the United States has also made it clear that it is going to develop a whole new range of nuclear weapons. This includes new intercontinental ballistic missiles, new long-range bombers, and ballistic missile submarines, as well as new tactical nuclear weapons. During the Cold War, the latter was deemed dangerous by both the United States and the Soviet Union, and they eventually agreed to eliminate these. The US plans to rebuild its nuclear arsenal are estimated at $1.7 trillion over the next thirty years (U.S. Strategic Nuclear Forces: Background, Developments, and Issues, 2021). US plans could push other countries like China and Russia to modernize their nuclear arsenals. This is setting off a new arms race that would bring more global instability (Zala, 2019).

In turn, Russia has also laid out plans for an array of new nuclear weapons in March 2018. In his speech, Russian President Vladimir Putin elaborated on these plans that include a modern hypersonic missile that cannot be intercepted and has no parallel in the world, a nuclear-power cruise missile, and a nuclear-powered underwater drone.

The brewing new arms race bodes ill for the two great powers as well as for international security. It is, thus, important to study the dynamics of this emerging new arms race.

On the other hand, the United States–China relations have deteriorated considerably in the last few years. The trade war between the two countries has heightened tensions. For over a decade, the West and especially the United States have seen China's rise as a threat (Mearsheimer, 2001; Glaser, 2011; Ikenberry, 2008). South China Sea has increasingly become a flashpoint between the United States and China. China sees the area as its sphere of influence, while the United States has an increasing presence and activity in the area. Thus, there is competition brewing between United States and China as well. US officials have been stating China's rising power as one of the factors for withdrawing from the INF since China was not a big factor when the treaty was negotiated in 1987 (Finnegan, 2018).

The chapter draws upon the theory of realism. Within the realist school, it takes guidance from the theory of security dilemma and theories of arms racing. Arms racing theories have three basic variants. These consist of the action–reaction model, the domestic structure model, and the technological imperative. The domestic structure or the bureaucratic model sees the driving causes of arms races as internal. More specifically, the major players in this model are the corporate interests of research and development organizations, interservice rivalry, and domestic politics. The technological imperatives model sees technological innovations and the lobbying by military–industrial complexes as the driving force behind arms races. John Herz first gave the theory of security dilemma, which essentially argues that in an anarchic world where all states are responsible for their own security, any efforts of a state to acquire power or secure themselves renders other states insecure. They, in turn, respond by acquiring power or countermeasures to secure themselves. Robert Jervis argues that states caught in a security dilemma see security as a zero-sum game. Thereby, an increase in the security of one state automatically reduces the security of the other one (Jervis, 1978, pp. 169–170). Barry Buzan calls it a power–security dilemma because the states are constantly engaged in power and security struggle (Buzan, 1983, p. 157). Accumulation of military power, nuclear weapons competition, and arms races stand as a distinctive feature of security dilemmas.

The chapter's primary focus would be on the emerging US–Russia arms race. The chapter's conclusions are drawn from a qualitative analysis of the gathered data. Thus, it argues that the arms race is fuelled by an action–reaction dynamic and a sense of insecurity embodied by a security dilemma whereby the increase in power of one country makes others insecure, causing them to pursue more power and weapons systems. Thus, the cycle of security and insecurity among great powers continues. This would bring instability in the global arena as well.

The international norms have clearly been moving away from arms control and disarmament. The emerging new arms races would push the international security landscape toward an emphasis on arms and the realist concept of self-help. This is a very dangerous development, one that needs to be monitored and studied. With the two superpowers going for unchecked weapons developments, other countries are also going to follow suit; with everyone developing weapons and constantly trying to secure themselves, the world would be less secure.

A NEW ARMS RACE—US AND RUSSIA

The United States and Russia are entering into a new arms race that resembles their Cold War competition. The United States built as many as 30,000 nuclear warheads in the 1960s, and the Soviet Union had as many as 40,000. Over the decades, they reduced a considerable number of nuclear warheads and still hold close to 13,000 weapons between the two countries (SIPRI Yearbook, 2021). While the number of overall nuclear weapons in the world has decreased, the deployed number of weapons has actually increased to 3,825 in 2021 from 3,720 in 2020. Of these 2,000, mostly belonging to Russia or the United States are kept in a state of high operational alert (SIPRI Yearbook, 2021).

While the two superpowers managed to avoid a nuclear confrontation during Cold War and negotiated some arms control deals, today, those very deals are being abrogated. Both the United States and Russia are going for the upgrade of their nuclear triads. The United States alone has plans to develop new intercontinental ballistic missiles, long-range bombers, and submarines capable of launching nuclear ballistic missiles. They also have plans to develop low-yield nuclear weapons. The NPR asserts that the pursuit of low-yield capabilities is not an effort to "match or mimic" Russia's arsenal but to "counter any mistaken perception of an exploitable 'gap' in US regional deterrence capabilities" (US Nuclear Posture Review, 2018). Russia is also reacting by developing a whole new range of nuclear weapons. However, the new arms race is likely to be deadlier because both countries can produce more sophisticated and technologically advanced weapons. Today, in the global arena, there are three major competing powers—the United States, Russia, and to a lesser extent China. Also, their arms race is likely to set off arms races in other regions. Many more countries possess nuclear weapons than they did during the first nuclear arms race. Besides the five nuclear weapon states, Israel, India, Pakistan, and North Korea also possess nuclear weapons. This would make the new arms race deadlier and more complex.

The US Nuclear Weapons

The US's declining power, a resurgence of Russian prominence, and the rise of China are once again altering the global balance of power. The United States sees it as a threat and is modernizing and increasing its nuclear forces. Russia and China also feel threatened by US plans to modernize. Russia and China are also modernizing and upgrading their armaments in response to the United States. The United States feels threatened to by Russia and China, Russia feels threatened by the United States, and China, in turn, feels threatened by the United States. Each tries to pursue sophisticated weapons to try and secure themselves against the opponent. Thus, the dynamics of a security dilemma are at play where each side is threatened by modernization by others and, in turn, pursues weapons and nuclear force modernization to secure itself.

At present, the United States has around 1,650 strategic nuclear warheads deployed on land, air, and sea and around 180 tactical nuclear weapons on bases in European countries. The United States has plans for massive modernization over the next thirty years with a cost of $1.7 billion (U.S. Strategic Nuclear Forces, 2021). The US nuclear arsenal is being upgraded at land, air, and sea. The US investment in upgrading and updating its nuclear forces is the largest in the world. With the new Biden Administration in power, it remains to be seen if the US modernization and development plans will go as scheduled or be scaled back.

The February 2018 NPR outlined and confirmed US plans for modernization of it nuclear forces. However, it also revealed plans for a number of new nuclear weapons. This included the development of tactical nuclear weapons as a flexible nuclear option. The logic behind this assertion is that since United States might hesitate to employ a high-yield nuclear weapon in response to a "lower level" conflict in which an adversary used a low-yield nuclear device. The NPR thus argues that expanding low-yield options is "important for the preservation of credible deterrence" in regional conflicts (Nuclear Posture Review, 2018). The NPR envisages a modification of some existing submarine-launched ballistic missiles (SLBMs) to carry low-yield nuclear weapons. NPR argues that there is no "one size fits all" for deterrence. Therefore, "the US will apply a tailored and flexible approach to effectively deter across a spectrum of adversaries, threats, and contexts" (Nuclear Posture Review, 2018). The document argues that tactical weapons are vital for the preservation of credible deterrence. The development of tactical nuclear weapons would mean lowering the nuclear threshold, which is dangerous thinking on the part of the United States. As both the United States and Soviet Union learned at the height of the Cold War, low-yield nuclear weapons could not be used for warfighting. The notion that nuclear weapons can be used in warfighting is problematic. It increases the chances of misperception and miscalculation and has command and control issues. It, thus, also lowers the nuclear threshold promoting the notion that low-yield nuclear weapons are "more usable."

The 2018 NPR calls for a modification to "a small number of existing SLBM warheads" to provide a low-yield option. It also calls for the development of a sea-launched cruise missile. This reverses the Obama administration's policy, and it's NPR of 2010 that called for the retirement of existing nuclear-tipped cruise missiles at sea. The NPR document argues that these weapons give the United States flexibility and diversity in its nuclear options.

The NPR also revives the superpower rivalry and specifically talks about threats from Russia and China and its strategy to counter them. It states that "While the United States has continued to reduce the number and salience of nuclear weapons, others, including Russia and China, have moved in the opposite direction" (Nuclear Posture Review, 2018). This heralds a comeback to Cold War-style rivalries and threats.

The United States is also modernizing its triad of nuclear forces. The United States has plans to replace its 400 Minuteman III Inter Continental Ballistic Missiles (ICBM), which are deployed by the Air Force. It has plans to develop 600 missiles, out of which 400 will be deployed through 2070. In the air B-2 and

B-52 bombers are being upgraded (US Nuclear Modernization Programmes, 2018). These will eventually be replaced by the B-21 Raider. The Air Force plans to purchase 100 B-21s. The United States has plans to equip its bombers with air-launched long-range cruise missiles (ALCM; Zala, January 2019).

The US ballistic missile submarine fleet currently consists of fourteen Trident submarines which can carry twenty Trident II (D-5) missiles (reduced from twenty-four missiles per submarine) to bring it under New START limits. The Trump Administration also deployed a new low-yield warhead on Trident II (D-5) missiles (U.S. Strategic Nuclear Forces, 2021). The Biden Administration has not made public an NPR 2022, but its National Security Strategy 2022 promotes the concept of integrated deterrence that seeks to achieve a seamless combination of capabilities to deter adversaries, including joint capability development with allies and partners (National Security Strategy, 2022).

Russia and Its Nuclear Modernization

Like the United States, Russia is also undergoing a modernization of its nuclear forces on land, air, and sea. Some modernization is to replace and upgrade aging systems, while some are in response to US weapons plans.

Less than a month after the United States released its NPR, Russian President Vladimir Putin announced plans to develop and field a range of new nuclear weapons. Putin, in a State of the Nation speech, said that Russia is developing nuclear powered underwater drone, a nuclear-tipped cruise missile, and a hypersonic missile that is unrivalled in the world and has the capability to defeat any missile defense system (Presidential Address to the Federal Assembly, 2018). He claimed that its new hypersonic missile could reach any point in the world. He said that Russia would soon have missiles that would be capable of destroying intercontinental targets with high precision and hypersonic speed, which are maneuverable in terms of course and altitude. He described the proposed cruise missile as low flying and difficult to spot, with unlimited range and unpredictable flight (Presidential Address to the Federal Assembly, 2018). He emphasized that both these missiles are invincible and cannot be detected by any missile defense system.

Russia has subsequently revealed an array of weaponry. The most significant is its hypersonic missiles, the Avangard intercontinental ballistic missile system, which uses a hypersonic boost-glide vehicle with the ability to travel at a speed twenty-seven times that of sound. Russia also has "Kinzhal," which is a guided cruise missile with a range of 1,200 kilometers and a speed of Mach 10. Russia announced the deployment of "Avangard" on December 2019 (BBC News, 2019). Russia is also developing "Tsirkon," which is a ship-launched hypersonic cruise missile capable of targeting on the ground and at sea at speeds of Mach 6–8 (Hypersonic Weapons: Background and Issues for Congress, 2020). Russia accelerated work on its hypersonic missiles once the United States withdrew from the Anti-Ballistic Missiles Treaty in 2002 and brushed aside Russian concerns over the deployment of missile defense systems, arguing that it was meant to safeguard against missile attacks from "rogue" states like Iran and North Korea.

Clearly, the action–reaction dynamic is at work here. Russia has, over the years, protested over the fielding of US missile defense interceptors in Europe. However, the United States has not paid any heed to Russian concerns. Russia has, thus, developed weapons, especially the hypersonic missiles that can penetrate US missile defense systems. Russian weapons developments are driven by security dilemma vis-à-vis the United States.

The Russian President also talked about a number of new or upgraded systems. These include 300 new weapons models consisting of 18 new ICBMs, 2 SLBMs and a number of submarines, and an increased number of long-range missiles. He also spoke of an underwater drone, 100 times smaller than a submarine, which would be nuclear capable (Presidential Address to the Federal Assembly, 2018). He claimed that no defense system could detect or defeat it.

Russian president emphatically said that these weapons were a response to US missile defense systems. The United States withdrew from the 1972 Anti-Ballistic Missile Treaty in 2002, which essentially prohibited the deployment of missile defense systems against strategic missiles. The United States went on to develop extensive missile defense systems and fielded interceptors in Poland and Romania which is too close to Russian borders for comfort. This heightened Russia's threat perception and led it to counter the instability in US–Russia deterrence equation. The roots of the present arms race, thus, go deeper.

Overall Russia is modernizing across all nuclear legs of the triad—on land, air, and sea. At sea, Russia is modernizing its ballistic missile submarine fleet. It has six Delta Class submarines. It also deployed a few Borei Class submarines in the last few years and has plans to induct 6 more Borei Class submarines bringing the total number of the submarine fleet to at least 12 that will field 192 SLBMs with approximately 580 warheads (Podvig, 2018) since most missiles are equipped with multiple independently targetable reentry vehicles (MIRVs). The Yasen Class attack nuclear submarines would carry SLCMs. In the air, Russia is planning to replace its existing bomber fleet TU-160 with the stealth bomber PAK-DA. On land, the Topol-M is being modernized. It has deployed MIRVed version of the Topol-M, the RS 24 Yars. It currently deploys 180 ICBMs carrying 480 nuclear warheads. A new, more advanced Sarmat ICBM is being developed and deployed after 2020 (Trenin, 2019).

US development of missile defenses threatened Russia, and it has developed an array of weapons to counter and defeat United States. They are both massively modernizing their arsenals in order to deter threats from each other and other major powers in the world. The action–reaction dynamic and security dilemma characterizes the relations between United States and Russia. Their arms race is not just confined to this field but extends to nonnuclear field, offensive and defensive strategic systems, space, and cyberspace as well.

BILATERAL ARMS CONTROL REGIME AND ITS BREAKDOWN

The new arms race has been accompanied with worsening relations between the United States and Russia and a breakdown in bilateral relations. The breakdown of bilateral arms control started with US withdrawal from the ABM treaty in 2002.

The second causality of the breakdown in bilateral arms control is the 1987 INF Treaty. It was signed between the two Cold War superpowers to keep ground-based nuclear weapons out of Europe and prohibited manufacturing and deploying missiles with ranges of 500 to 5,500 kilometers. It led the United States and Russia to remove thousands of nuclear missiles aimed at each other. Under the INF, the Soviet Union eliminated 1,846 missiles while the US 846 (Woolf, 2019). The US accused Russia of developing a cruise missile that violated the terms of the treaty. The said missile was the ground-launched cruise missile Novator 9M729. Russia, in turn, accused the United States of violating the treaty as well. It alleged that the missile defense interceptors that the United States has deployed in Europe can be turned into offensive weapons with minor modifications (Gorbachev, 2018).

The United States has stated China as one of the reasons for withdrawing from the INF. US Secretary of State Mike Pompeo stated, "the US would no longer cede military advantage to a revisionist state like China that is threatening the US and its allies" (Finnegan, 2018). This suggests that the United States made Russian noncompliance an excuse for withdrawing from the INF. It is no longer perceived to be in United States interests to forgo an entire category of ballistic missiles.

The demise of the INF has serious repercussions as it leaves Europe vulnerable to the danger of medium-range ballistic missiles. It leaves the United States and Russia to develop and field intermediate-range nuclear missiles, which lessens the security of Europe. Also, if the United States deploys IRBMs in China's neighborhood it would threaten China. China would react by building and fielding weapons of its own.

Another arms control treaty that remained under threat during the Trump Administration is the New START. It was signed between United States and Russia in April 2010. It limits the deployed strategic nuclear warheads and bombs to 1,550 deployed missiles and bombers at 700 and the total number of launchers at 800. This is also a landmark treaty under which the United States and Russia eliminated thousands of nuclear warheads and launchers. New START was set to expire in February 2021 and needed to be extended for a further five years through mutual agreement (Klotz, January–February 2019). The United States dragged its feet on extending the treaty saying that new arms control treaties should be negotiated that also includes China. China refused to negotiate any such trilateral arms control arrangements saying that its nuclear arsenal is very small and does not threaten any great power. With the Biden Administration taking charge in January 2021, New START was renewed for a further five years with barely days to spare on the deadline to extend the treaty (Reif and Bugos, March 2021).

In one of the latest developments, Russia has suspended its participation in New START. Moscow has stopped all information exchanges with Washington envisioned under the New START and has not allowed inspections under the terms of the treaty. The suspension comes in the backdrop of the Ukraine war. The New START may become the next arms control causality that would bode ill for regional and global stability (Jalil, April 2023).

The degeneration of multilateral and bilateral arms control structure is destabilizing not just for United States and Russia but for the entire world and is likely to fuel an unchecked nuclear arms race and may even result in a domino effect around the world with other countries pursuing unchecked arms races.

CHINA'S NUCLEAR MODERNIZATION

The past decade or so has increasingly seen a growing competition between United States–China. Relations have deteriorated considerably during Trump Administration. The South China Sea and Taiwan have increasingly become a flashpoint. The United States increasingly sees China's rise as a threat. China also perceives a threat from the United States in its spheres of influence. Thus, there is growing competition between the two countries.

The US nuclear modernization, its abrogation of arms control treaties, and rising tensions in bilateral relations with China are creating incentives for the latter to modernize its nuclear forces. China has a modest nuclear programme compared to the United States and Russia. It only has a nuclear arsenal of roughly 280 nuclear warheads, compared to the approximately 4,000 nuclear arsenal of the United States (Neuneck, 2019). It has a triad of nuclear forces—based on land, air, and sea.

China is modernizing across all three legs of its nuclear triad. However, it is concentrated more on its ground-based forces and its sea-based capabilities. China is modernizing its ICBM force. It is adding road mobile DF-31A and DF-41. It has also developed a hypersonic glide vehicle DF-ZF which became operational in October 2019. It is designed to be mounted on DF-17. It also has two dual-use Cruise missiles—CJ-10 and CJ-20 (Kulacki, 2018). It has also introduced the intermediate range DF-26 being dubbed as the Guam killer intended against the threat of US forces in the Pacific (Zala, January 2019).

China is concerned about the US missile defense plans and its impact on Beijing's strategic nuclear deterrent. China is thus developing MIRV capable ICBMS in response to the US ballistic missiles defense plans. It has updated the DF-5 which was the main component of its strategic deterrence into MIRV-capable DF-5B. China is also developing technologies that can penetrate BMD systems, satellite capabilities that can potentially damage US space-based BMD systems, and also developing BMD system of its own (Arbatov, 2014).

China's pursuit of hypersonic missiles and nuclear force modernization is driven by the threat mainly from the United States. It is driven by concern that the US hypersonic could wipe out China's nuclear arsenal in a preemptive strike, and its BMD system would be able to intercept any remaining missiles (Zhao, 2018; Saalman, 2017). China is developing several hypersonic missiles, including the DF-17, a medium-range ballistic missile carrying the DF-ZF hypersonic glide vehicle with a Mach 10 speed. Beijing has tested the DF-41 ICBM, which can carry a nuclear hypersonic glide vehicle that would bring the United States within its range. Chinese hypersonic missiles also threaten the United States. China is also developing an air-launched CH-AS-X-13 missile with Mach 10 speed and a 1,500 kilometers range. China successfully tested Starry Sky-2, a nuclear-capable hypersonic vehicle prototype with Mach 6 speed, in 2018. Starry Sky-2 may be operational by 2025 (Sayler, 2021, pp. 15–16).

China is also planning to build a sophisticated missile defense system with the help of Russia (The Guardian, October 4, 2019). This could be a response to US plans to deploy intermediate-range missiles in Asia after the demise of the INF. This is likely to push China and Russia into deeper defense cooperation and may even lead to the creation of an integrated missile defense system.

At sea, China is developing the JL-2 submarine launched ballistic missiles (SLBM) with a range of over 7,000 kilometers. It has four submarines capable of carrying 12 SLBM each, and a fifth submarine is under construction (Kulacki, 2018).

China's ultimate goal is to make its nuclear forces more survivable and less vulnerable to a first strike. Thus, China's pursuit of modern weapons systems and nuclear force modernization is a manifestation of its security dilemma vis-à-vis the United States.

IMPLICATIONS OF EMERGING ARMS RACE FOR GLOBAL SECURITY

The brewing nuclear arms race, especially between the United States and Russia, and the accompanying demise of bilateral arms control has far-reaching effects for Russia and the United States but also for a rising China and the entire world.

The crumbling bilateral arms control between United States and Russia would negatively affect global arms control architecture, especially on the Non-Proliferation Treaty (NPT). It further weakens the NPT, which has not made much progress for years. The Nuclear weapons states have failed under article VI to pursue negotiation in good faith over for elimination of nuclear weapons. The emerging United States–Russia nuclear arms race goes counter to this article and the spirit of the NPT. In frustration, states in favor of nuclear abolition negotiated the Treaty on the Prohibition of Nuclear Weapons (TPNW) in July 2017. It has also revealed fissures in the nonproliferation regime and has hastened initiatives like Creating an Environment for Nuclear Disarmament (CEND) that the United States has been promoting (Paul Meyer, 2019).

The demise of the INF and the pursuit of the new nuclear arsenal and modernization means that the two great powers are stepping away from their promise to eliminate nuclear weapons. Instead, they are developing a range of new nuclear weapons. This would give impetus to nonnuclear weapon countries to pursue nuclear capability. It would give the wrong message to countries like North Korea, whose nuclear programme is a source of concern for the United States and the Western world. It would perhaps encourage others to go for nuclear capabilities.

The renewed emphasis on the role of nuclear weapons would also negatively affect global nonproliferation efforts. There would be no hope of CTBT entering into force. The technological race is also spilling into outer space. Both Russia and the United States have extensive military space assets and anti-satellite capabilities as well. The arms race and competition seem to be accelerating into space as well. Russia and China are also developing anti-satellite capabilities and other dual use technologies that can be used as space weapons. With the militarization and possible weaponization of space by the great powers, the prospects of any negotiation of treaties to keep space weapons-free would become a utopian idea.

In essence, the world is witnessing a fundamental change in the arms control norms. From traditional arms control to "normative" arms control discourse. The United States has emerged as the champion of the latter approach. It is a fluid approach that favors establishing norms of responsible behavior. Christopher Ashley Ford said, "We seek to develop and build upon like-mindedness with a wide range of partners willing to engage in good faith in trying to manage these challenges. We also seek to use this like mindedness as a foundation for collective action in response to reckless or destabilizing behaviours" (Christopher Ashley Ford, 2019). In essence, this means that there is a move away from arms control treaties that are legally binding and signatory states must adhere to. The arguments used are that given the tremendous advancements in technology, formal legal treaties and instruments cannot keep up with the pace of technology. In practice this means that the United States does not want its arms developments constrained by any bilateral or multilateral arms control agreements. This is perhaps why there has been an unravelling of the existing arms control arrangements and no political will to negotiate new ones or extend old arms control arrangements.

The new "normative" approach is manifested in United States initiatives like CEND. It was originally submitted as a working paper to the second preparatory committee for the 2020 NPT Review Conference 2018 (Meyer, 2019). It focuses on creating conditions where state relations are not driven by competition but are cooperative and free from conflict. This extends to biological weapons, outer space and cyberspace, and many other areas.

Thus, with the two global powers abandoning bilateral arms control, it essentially means that the international norms have clearly been moving away from arms control and disarmament. The emerging new arms races would push the international security landscape toward an emphasis on arms and the realist concept of self-help. This is a very dangerous development that the world needs to rigorously debate.

Today, competition dynamics are more complex than during the Cold War when there were only two great powers. The United States, Russia, and China are, in fact, embroiled in a trilateral security dilemma whereby each state is threatened by an increase in security of the other and reacts by building up its security and nuclear weapons capability. This would just lead to an unchecked arms race. The bipolar arms race has been replaced by a multipolar nuclear competition, which promises to be more volatile. The United States has to counter threats from Russia, China, North Korea, and others. Russia has to secure against threats from the United States, China, France, and the UK. China has to look out for threats from United States, Russia, and India. India has to secure itself against China and Pakistan, while North Korea is threatened by the United States (Schlosser, 2018). There are, thus, too many dyads of possible nuclear conflict and thus, the danger of a conflict turning nuclear to chances of misperception and miscalculation leading to a nuclear exchange. The world, thus, stands at a very dangerous crossroads whereby the risk of deliberate or accidental nuclear use is much higher than it was during the Cold War. This is why the Bulletin of Atomic Scientists has moved the hands of its Doomsday Clock to 100 seconds to midnight.

The nuclear arms race between Russia and the United States would have a cascading effect. It would fuel other arms races across the world. One can already see the worsening arms race between India and Pakistan. The two countries have been embroiled in conflict and an adversarial relationship for years. However, the deepening Strategic Partnership between the United States and India is fuelling India–Pakistan arms competition. It is providing technological advantages to India, and it is emboldening it in terms of its nuclear posture and encouraging preemptive tendencies. India has built its conventional forces massively and continues to build its nuclear forces. It has a triad of nuclear forces where it is working on ICBM capability and also operationalizing its submarine based naval nuclear capability. It has plans to build four to six nuclear attack submarines at sea in the next fifteen years. It has a range of nuclear capable missiles that are part of its naval nuclear strike capabilities. These include K-15 and K-4 missiles, Dhanush and Brahmos cruise missiles. It gives India a second-strike capability (Jalil, 2018). The United States has also approved the sale of twenty-four anti-submarine MH-60 helicopters worth $2.6 billion. This nuclearizes the Indian Ocean and makes Pakistan's limited naval nuclear deterrent more vulnerable.

India is also massively building its missile defense capabilities. Besides its indigenous systems it has negotiated a deal with Russia to acquire five S-400 missiles defense systems worth $5.5 billion. Two S-400 system have already been deployed which would give it capability to defend against incoming missiles and aircrafts. This negatively impacts on nuclear deterrence equation between India and Pakistan thus creating more instability in South Asia (Jalil, 2015).

India also conducted an anti-satellite test in March 2019. India has now carried the competition into space. Pakistan feels threatened and is working on upgrading all three legs of its nuclear forces. It is working on operationalizing its naval nuclear leg and has already tested Babar 3, which is a submarine launched ballistic missile (SLBM).

The global arms race thus has a cascading effect on regional arms races. The erosion of norms against the development and deployment of nuclear weapons, combined with the rapid demise of US–Russia bilateral arms control and the weakening of nonproliferation regime, directly and indirectly, fuels arms races across the world. It may also encourage a whole new round of nuclear proliferation (Arbatov, 2019). This will make the new arms race deadlier and more complex and the world a very dangerous place.

CONCLUSION

The new arms race promises to be deadlier and more complex than the first one during Cold War. Despite reductions in the overall number of nuclear weapons in the world, more states possess nuclear weapons today. The norms against the development and use of nuclear weapons are being eroded. With the development of tactical nuclear weapons and massive modernization programmes of great powers, the message that goes across is that increasing nuclear arms and even using them is ok. Arms control structure bilaterally between two great powers is crumbling, and international arms control regime is weakened. With the two superpowers going for unchecked weapons developments, other countries are also going to follow suit; with everyone developing weapons and constantly trying to secure themselves, there is a possibility that the world might descend into Armageddon. Humanity stands close to destruction and annihilation due to this new emphasis on nuclear arms. There has to be a global discussion to control and mitigate the dangers presented by nuclear weapons to avert a global disaster.

NOTE

1. G. Y. Jalil. Institute of Strategic Studies, Islamabad, Pakistan. Email: Ghazalay21@yahoo.com

BIBLIOGRAPHY

Arbatov, Alexei. (October, 2014). Engaging China in Nuclear Arms Control. *Carnegie Moscow Center*. https://carnegieendowment.org/files/Arbatov_China_nuclear_Eng2014.pdf

Arbatov, Alex. (June/July, 2019). Mad Momentum Redux? The Rise and Fall of Nuclear Arms Control. *Survival*, 61(3): 7–38.

Buzan, B. (1983). *People, States and Fear: The National Security Problem and International Relations.* Chapel Hill, NC: University of North Carolina Press.

Ford, Dr Christopher Ashley, Assistant Secretary of Bureau of International Security and Nonproliferation (December 13, 2019). Rules, Norms, and Community: Arms Control Discourses in a Changing World. Presentation at the European Union Conference on Nonproliferation, Brussels, Belgium. https://www.state.gov/rules-norms-and-community-arms-control-discourses-in-a-changing-world/

Finnegan, Connor. (December 4, 2018). Pompeo Says US Suspending Landmark Nuclear Deal Because of Russian Violations. *ABC News*. https://abcnews.go.com/Politics/pompeo-us-suspending-landmark-nuclear-deal-russian-violations/story?id=59602417

Glaser, Charles. (March/April, 2011). Will China's Rise Lead to War? Why Realism Does Not Mean Pessimism. *Foreign Affairs*. https://www.foreignaffairs.com/articles/asia/2011-03-01/will-chinas-rise-lead-war

Gorbachev, Mikhail. (October 25, 2018). Mikhail Gorbachev: A New Nuclear Arms Race Has Begun. https://www.sipri.org/commentary/essay/2018/crumbling-architecture-arms-control

Hypersonic Weapons: Background and Issues for Congress. (August 27, 2020). CRS Repot R45811. https://fas.org/sgp/crs/weapons/R45811.pdf

Ikenberry, John. (January/February, 2008). The Rise of China and the Future of the West: Can the Liberal System Survive? *Foreign Affairs*. https://www.foreignaffairs.com/articles/asia/2008-01-01/rise-china-and-future-west

Jalil, Ghazala Yasmin. (2015). Indian Missile Defence Development: Implications for Deterrence Stability in South Asia. *Strategic Studies*, 35(2): 29–46.

Jalil, Ghazala Yasmin. (Spring, 2018). India's Development of Sea-Based Nuclear Capabilities: Implications for Pakistan. *Strategic Studies*, 38(1): 34–47.

Jalil, Ghazala Yasmin. (April, 2023). New START: The Next Arms Control Casualty? Issue Brief. https://issi.org.pk/issue-brief-on-new-start-the-next-arms-control-casualty/

Jervis, Robert. (1978). Cooperation Under the Security Dilemma. *World Politics*, 30(2): 169–170.

Klotz, Frank. (January/February, 2019). Extending New Start is in America's National Security Interest. *Arms Control Today*. https://www.armscontrol.org/act/2019-01/features/extending-new-start-americas-national-security-interest

Kulacki, Gregory Kulacki. (January, 2018). China's Nuclear Force: Modernizing from Behind. *Union of Concerned Scientists*. https://www.ucsusa.org/resources/chinas-nuclear-force

Mearsheimer, John J. (2001). *The Tragedy of Great Power Politics*. New York: W W Norton & Company.

Meyer, Paul. (April, 2019). Creating an Environment for Nuclear Disarmament: Striding Forward or Stepping Back? *Arms Control Today*.https://www.armscontrol.org/act/2019-04/features/creating-environment-nuclear-disarmament-striding-forward-stepping-back

Neuneck, Götz. (2019). The Deep Crisis of Nuclear Arms Control and Disarmament: The State of Play and the Challenges. *Journal for Peace and Nuclear Disarmament*, 2(2): 431–452.

National Security Strategy. (October, 2022). https://www.whitehouse.gov/wp-content/uploads/2022/10/Biden-Harris-Administrations-National-Security-Strategy-10.2022.pdf

Nuclear Posture Review. (February, 2018). US Department of Defence, p. VIII. https://dod.defense.gov/News/SpecialReports/2018NuclearPostureReview.aspx

Podvig, Pavel. (2018). Russia's Current Nuclear Modernization and Arms Control. *Journal for Peace and Nuclear Disarmament*, 1(2): 256–267.

"Presidential Address to the Federal Assembly." March 1, 2018. http://en.kremlin.ru/events/president/news/56957

Reif, Kingston, and Bugos, Shannon. U.S. Russia Extend New START for Five Years. *Arms Control Today*, March 2021. https://www.armscontrol.org/act/2021-03/news/us-russia-extend-new-start-five-years

Russia Deploys Avangard Hypersonic Missile System. (December 27, 2019). BBC News. https://www.bbc.com/news/world-europe-50927648

Russia Is helping China Build a Missile Defence System, Putin Says. *The Guardian*, October 4, 2019.

Saalman, Lora. (August 15, 2017). China's Calculus on Hypersonic Glide. Stockholm International Peace Research Institute. https://www.sipri.org/commentary/topical-backgrounder/2017/chinas-calculus-hypersonic-glide

Sayler, Kelley M. (July 9, 2021). Hypersonic Weapons: Background and Issues for Congress. Congressional Research Service, R45811. p. 15–16. https://fas.org/sgp/crs/weapons/R45811.pd

Schlosser, Eric. (May 24, 2018). The Growing Dangers of the New Nuclear-Arms Race. *The New Yorker*. https://www.newyorker.com/news/news-desk/the-growing-dangers-of-the-new-nuclear-arms-race

Trenin, Dmitri. (2019). Russian Views of US Nuclear Modernization. *Bulletin of the Atomic Scientists*, 75(1): 14–18.

US Nuclear Modernization Programmes. (August 2018). Arms Control Association Factsheet. https://www.armscontrol.org/factsheets/usnuclearmodernization

U.S. Strategic Nuclear Forces: Background, Developments, and Issues. (December 14, 2021). CRS Report RL33640. Federation of American Scientists, https://fas.org/sgp/crs/nuke/RL33640.pdf

Woolf, Amy. (February 1, 2019). U.S. Withdrawal from the INF Treaty. *CRS Insight*. https://fas.org/sgp/crs/nuke/IN10985.pdf

Kristensen, Hans M. and Korda, Matt. World Nuclear Forces (2021) in *SIPRI Yearbook 2021: Armaments, Disarmaments and International Security*. Oxford University Press, pp. 333–412.

Zala, Benjamin. (January, 2019). How the Next Nuclear Arms Race Will Be Different from the Last One. *Bulletin of Atomic Scientists*, 75, pp. 36–43(1).

Zhao, Tong. (July 23, 2018). Conventional Challenges to Strategic Stability: Chinese Perceptions of Hypersonic Technology and the Security Dilemma. Carnegie-Tsinghua Center for Global Policy. https://carnegietsinghua.org/2018/07/23/conventional-challenges-to-strategic-stability-chinese perceptions-of-hypersonic-technology-and-security-dilemmapub-76894

Chapter 7

A Perilous Nexus

Military Drones, Power, and Risk-Taking

Hafssa Fakher Elabiari[1]

INTRODUCTION

On April 4, 2019, General Khalifa Haftar, commander of the Libyan Arab Armed Forces (LAAF), launched a military offensive to seize control over the capital Tripoli. As the Government of National Accord (GNA) launched the "Volcano of Rage" counteroffensive, Libya entered a new civil war that dashed the hopes of Libyans in creating a civilian state where sovereignty, dialogue, and cohesion prevail. In fact, the assault halted the negotiation process between Haftar and Fayez al-Sarraj and canceled the elections, as per the Paris Peace Forum and the Palermo Conference. In this fragile context, Haftar confirmed his de facto title as Libya's strongman, which changed the strategies of warring countries. On the one hand, Egypt, France, Russia, and the UAE sought to capitalize on the new phase of instability by providing military support in the form of weapons, financial flows, and diplomatic support. For instance, between September 2019 and July 2020, Russia deployed around 1,000 Wagner mercenaries to secure its interests in post-Qaddafi Libya (Ibrahim & Barabanov, 2021). Interestingly, the UAE deployed Chinese Wing Loong drones, known for their low cost and notorious for their lethality. In 2017, the UAE was already a client of China, purchasing 15 Wing Loong drones and 350 Blue Arrow-7 missiles (BBC, 2020). In August 2020, the UAE used a Wing Loong drone to strike the al-Watiya air base, killing twenty-six cadets. BBC-uncovered evidence captured the remnants of the Blue Arrow-7 missile (BBC, 2020). Evidence released by the United Nations showed that in Libya, Wing Loong drones are the only military aviation equipment capable of firing such missiles (Majumdar Roy Choudhury, 2019).

On the other hand, Haftar's territorial victories jeopardized the strategic interests of Turkey, Qatar, and Italy. Ankara, in particular, made a series of military and diplomatic moves, such as signing a maritime deal with the GNA and approving a bill to foster military and logistical cooperation with the GNA (Ramani, 2020). However, the signature of Turkey's involvement in Libya was the deployment of Bayraktar TB2 military drones. Arguably, these low-cost drones played a significant role in offsetting the balance of power between the GNA and Haftar. Indeed, Ankara managed to manufacture lethal technology at an affordable cost, test it on a battlefield, and establish an identity to itself as a drone power. Consequently, Turkish drone sales have skyrocketed over the past two years, with Turkey supplying drones to countries like Azerbaijan, Ethiopia, Morocco, and Ukraine (Spicer et al., 2021; Iddon, 2021).

On June 3, 2020, GNA-affiliated militias regained complete control over Tripoli International Airport, and they subsequently recovered Tarhunah and the Sharara oil fields. Consequently, Haftar's foreign backers started suffering a string of defeats because they realized that their protégé might lose the battle for leverage. For example, Egypt threatened to intervene in the event of a GNA control over Misrata and Sirte, two strategic cities that form a frontline between western and eastern Libya and a gateway to oil fields. Similarly, the UAE became reluctant to support Haftar as the latter was facing major setbacks. Indeed, supporting a losing side would shrink Emirati influence in Libya. If it were to continue, it would rely on a country that can provide advanced weaponry to outstrip Turkish maneuvers (Eljarh, 2020). Hence, it was clear that Turkey, a country whose military power is not equate with the UAE's, managed to offset the balance of power between Haftar and the GNA. But what exactly has made Turkey's operational efforts successful? Here, the tactical reasons are many, but the extensive use of military drones is of paramount importance. The UAE followed the same logic, except that it did not manufacture its military drones and instead relied on drone deployment and mercenary funding. With this, Libya possibly became, as former head of the United Nations Mission in Libya Ghassan Salamé said, "the largest drone war theater in the world" (Brookes & Schroeder, 2019).

This chapter examines the impact of military drone possession on power and risk-taking behavior in war-torn countries. Using the case study of Turkish and Emirati drones in Libya between 2019 and 2020 and drawing upon the concepts of real power and perceived power, it scrutinizes how the possession of military drones inflates a country's power and appetite for risk and erases the operational barriers linked to foreign intervention, thus creating an encouraging environment for reckless moves and clash durability. The choice of Libya as a case study stems from the uniqueness of the military drones involved (low-cost and lethal) and the drone expertise imbalance between Turkey (manufacturer) and the UAE (buyer). In the first part, the work explains how the possession of military drones inflates a country's real and perceived power and sets a limit beyond which the causation is no longer valid. The second part tackles how the possession of military drones enhances the propensity of decision-makers to take risky behavior confidently. The third section reviews how the possession and use of military drones extend the durability of wars. This work attempts to diminish the paucity of research on the security impact of military drones. It also generates a reflection on the concept of risk and power; two variables that influence security policies yet are not given sufficient attention. Finally, while this work is theoretical in nature, it can serve as a starting point for empirical research for the latter is much needed to advance the literature on emerging drone powers that are reshuffling conflict dynamics.

RELEVANT DEFINITIONS

The Fuzzy Concept of Power

The concept of power is central to the study of drone warfare from behavioral and military angles. In all sciences where the concept is relevant, there is profuse literature. However, a discipline's nature is what delineates the concept's boundaries. Natural sciences, like physics, have, in general, more precise conceptualizations and operationalizations of power compared to social sciences like political science or psychology. In fact, social sciences possess a subjective component that opens room for divergence and, sometimes, misconception. Whereas this difference posits the elusiveness of power as a challenge, it also presents a window of opportunity because scholars can always draw upon existing literature to conceptualize and operationalize power in a way that fits their research's scope and objectives. In this section, this is exactly how I proceed: I develop a solid overview of leading international relations (IR) and political theory literature on power to build a suitable definition that allows me to differentiate between real power and perceived power.

IR and political theory, as specializations of political science, share common notions when it comes to the concept of power. Generally, power involves control, action against someone's will, and the ability to modify the status quo (Read, 1991; Dahl, 1957). While the reference to Hobbes and Dahl does not depict all perspectives on power, it certainly samples a predominant perspective associated with positivist approaches to international relations. Dahl (1957) defines power as actor A's ability to push actor B to do something it would not otherwise do and develops three conditions under which power exists. In a situation where two actors, A and B, interact, there should exist intent from A to cause behavior change in B, conflicting aspirations between A and B, and A's possession of substantial resources that can push B to take a particular course of action. Dahl's conceptualization is paradoxical because it equates influence with power and places the latter within a context of consciousness and rationality. The unintended consequences of an action by A against B do not make A powerful.

For Barnett and Duvall (2005, p. 3), power is "the production, in and through social relations, of effects that shape the capacities of actors to determine their circumstances and fate." This definition is an attempt to overcome the bias surrounding the conceptualization of power. The concept is, de facto, the exclusive domain of realist scholars like Carr and Mearsheimer. Besides, some nonrealist scholars have tended to undermine the importance of power for the mere fact that their theories do not rely on power to account for world developments. By developing a fourfold taxonomy, Barnett and Duvall explain the forms of power and the factors that undermine or allow actors to determine their fate. Interestingly, their conceptualization delves into the social aspect of power and does not associate with any theoretical approach. According to Barnett and Duvall (2005), the purpose is to encourage international relations scholars to address the concept by connecting the dots between existing definitions to develop a solid conceptual framework. Hence, they do not set for themselves the theoretical barrier that guides the conceptualization process.

Morgenthau and Mearsheimer, theoretically different from Barnett and Duvall, associate with realism, and that constrains their ability to define power. Morgenthau, the so-called father of classical realism, places power at the heart of his political power theory. For him, "power is always the immediate aim" of states, hence the title of his book *Politics among Nations: The Struggle for Power and Peace* (Morgenthau, 1948, p. 13). No matter what goal(s) a state pursues, it can only achieve them by "striving for power" (Morgenthau, 1948, p. 13). The emphasis on power in international politics and the absence of a robust definition illustrates the weakness of realism. Morgenthau defines power as "man's control over the minds and actions of other men" and does not go beyond that (Morgenthau, 1948, p. 13). For Mearsheimer, a state's power depends on its military force, precisely its land force. In his works about offensive realism and balancing behavior, Mearsheimer overemphasizes the importance of power calculations. As we cannot dissociate economics from money, we cannot separate international relations from power (Mearsheimer, 2001, p. 65). This is understandable because the pillars of offensive realism all revolve around the balance of power, power acquisition, and power maximization. However, the theory should not subjugate the conceptualization process; the two should be complementary.

Gilpin (1981, p. 31) distinguishes between power and prestige, emphasizing military assets and to a lesser extent, economic capabilities. Whereas the former describes state A's capabilities, the latter refers to other states' perceptions of A's capabilities and readiness to exert power. Put simply, power is "the everyday currency of international relations"; prestige is the "reputation for strength in war," and it is a variable that allows a country to achieve its goals without necessarily using power (Gilpin, 1981, p. 31). For Baldwin, power is not a property to claim that actor A or B is powerful. Power is a relational concept that depicts a relation between two or more actors; thus, power relations are not static. For example, if country A possesses more military drones than country B, A is more powerful than B regarding drones or overall air power. However, if B manufactures its own drones, then it is more powerful than A regarding drone expertise. While Baldwin's work on power is relevant to the literature, it does not explain what makes some actors seek more power than others. Nagel shares Baldwin's relational approach by arguing that one cannot speak about power "without specifying power to do what" (Nye, 2021). Keohane and Nye's conceptualization also underpins the relational aspect of power. In their coauthored book, they define power as "the ability of an actor to get others to do something they otherwise would not do (Keohane & Nye, 1989, p. 10). They also tackle the independence-control nexus and argue that asymmetrical dependency sets the stage for vulnerability, thus, for influence (Baldwin, 2016, pp. 157–158). Nye's seminal works about power advanced the concept of soft power. While hard power orbits around force, coercion, and payments, soft power is an actor's ability to achieve its goals "through attraction rather than coercion or payments" (Nye, 2004, preface). To borrow Nye's (2021) metaphor, "hard power is like brandishing carrots or sticks; soft power is more like a magnet."

In the disciplines of psychology and organizational behavior, scholars have also attempted to conceptualize power amid elusiveness and fuzziness. Overbeck distinguishes between social power and personal power. The former is "the control or the domination of others" (power over), and it is by default, relational. At the same time, the latter refers to "the ability to carry out action" (power to; Overbeck, 2010). Overbeck, a psychologist in training and profession, follows the international relations theorists' train regarding the relationality of power. For their part, Torelli and Shavitt (2010) define power as "an individual's relative capacity to modify others' states by providing or withholding resources or administering punishments." Interestingly, Torelli and Shavitt's (2010) study is their distinction between personalized power and socialized power and the role of culture in predicting an individual's "power affiliation." Here, the two powers' conceptualization differs from Overbeck's. Personalized power refers to "status and personal achievement," and socialized power is about "benefiting and helping others" (Torelli & Shavitt, 2010). Other scholars have also tackled the social aspect of power. Ellyson and Dovidio (1985, pp. 1–28), power is the ability to exert social influence. To speak about power is to talk about resource asymmetry between actors. For Fiske and Russell (2010, pp. 231–250), power is "asymmetrical control over resources," the resources being physical, economic, or social. While this definition is relevant, one should be wary of its empirical applications because asymmetrical control does not always translate into a power relation.

Again, there is no right conceptualization and operationalization of power. Each definition fits a particular context. Hence, merging relevant works is useful for providing a robust conceptual framework. In this chapter, I conceptualize and operationalize power to fit the study of military drones.

Country A and Country B, enemies, possess robust military apparatuses. They regularly acquire sophisticated weaponry respectively from countries C and D. While one part of A's arms purchases is devoted to counter tangible threats such as terrorism and insurgency, another part is used to keep the power gap with B as large as possible. Power is a condition of relative immunity to material and/or ideational risks in a given time, space, and domain. The state of immunity can emerge overnight, and this is the result of misconceptions and misperceptions. Say, for example, that actor B misinterprets a signal emanating from A (e.g., military acquisition) and subsequently prompts bilateral behavior change toward A. In that case, A becomes immune concerning X in time T1, but it does not become powerful. Following this logic, immunity can entail power if and only if it stems from the actor's rational weighing of risks and payoffs per its interests. Also, a condition is, by default, relative; thus, it is susceptible to change. Relativity concerns time, space, and domain.

A power gap between actors A and B exists if and only if:

- It can bolster or drain B's resources and capabilities to prompt behavior change several times, at least in one domain, without external help (i.e., resorting to allies, asking for material support) and during a defined period.
- It possesses and controls more resources than B does.
- It benefits from prestige.

For this study's purpose, the concept of power has a military connotation, and it is divided into two types: real power (RP) and perceived power (PP). The first refers to a country's military apparatus, capabilities, and technology. The second refers to how decision-makers conceive their country's power. We differentiate between real and perceived power because there is often a mismatch between the two. The latter is a function of three factors:

1. Leaders' personality and ego (clearer in autocratic and semi-democratic countries).
2. Country's history, particularly the political one.

3. Country's regime (important because a democracy curbs the propensity of decision-makers to implement policies that reflect their egos and personal goals).

In this chapter, real power is measured using the expression below:

> RP = military expenditure (in US$) + local drone capability + imported drone capability

Since there is a mix of binary and numerical data, local drone capability and imported drone capability are quantified as 0 (absent) and 1 (present). Military expenditure is set on a scale of 1 to 7 (7 referring to a 7-digit annual military expenditure). In the 2015–2019 period, the UAE's annual military expenditure was six digits (SIPRI, 2020). Moreover, the country does not currently develop indigenous military drones and instead acquires them from China, so its real power is RP (UAE) = 7.

The Concept of Military Drone

Defining what a military drone is not easy. As Rothstein (2015, Preface, ix) articulates: "we know what a drone is. But at the same time, we don't." This difficulty lies in the fact that new technological inventions are improved versions of old inventions. A drone is a robot, a transportation means, an aircraft, and a computer (Rothstein, 2015, Introduction, x). But what about military drones? What makes them different from civilian ones? Why do military drones challenge conventional warfare?

A military drone is an aircraft that lacks an onboard pilot but is humanly controlled on the ground and can carry out target acquisition, intelligence, surveillance, and reconnaissance (ISR). Military drones are also labeled Remotely Piloted Aircraft (RPA), Unmanned Aircraft Systems (UASs), Unmanned Combat Aerial Vehicles (UCAVs), and Unmanned Aerial Vehicles (UAVs). Military drones or UAVs, two designations I interchangeably use, possess three features.

1. A military drone exclusively refers to a flying system.
2. A military drone is operated remotely.
3. A military drone does not carry an onboard pilot.

MILITARY DRONES AND POWER

For a long time, nuclear weapons were considered "great equalizers" for their ability to shrink power gaps between major and minor powers and deter hostile behavior (Paul, 2012). The proliferation of drone technology has made of military drones power equalizers. Just like the possession of a nuclear arsenal by country A refrains country B from attacking because it cannot absorb nuclear retaliation damage, UAVs' possession exerts the same effect under one specific condition. In a bilateral power relation, country A should possess UAV capability but not country B. In this section, I show how the possession of military drones inflates a country's real and perceived power while shedding light on the case when two countries, like Turkey and the UAE, possess military drones.

Low Cost-Lethality Combo

Compared to military aircraft, military drones are an attractive alternative as far as cost and lethality are concerned. In comparison, a MiG-29 fighter and an F-15 Eagle cost approximately US$23.8 million and US$43.1 million, and a Bayraktar TB2 or a Wing Loong II cost between US$1 million and US$2 million (Ritsick, 2020; Sabbagh, 2020). The price difference gives Turkish and Chinese UAVs a competitive advantage, especially because they also possess advanced lethal capability. Wing Loong II, an improved version of Wing Loong I, carries out ISR. Also, it has an endurance of 30 hours and a 480 kilograms payload capacity (Nacouzi et al., 2018). On the other hand, Bayraktar TB2 is a semiautonomous system manufactured by Baykar Makina, and it is capable of conducting ISR and target elimination (Baykar Makina, n.d.). Its payload capacity is 150 kilograms, and its endurance is 27 hours. It is important to note that the leading figure in Turkey's drone industry is Selçuk Bayraktar, a Massachusetts Institute of Technology graduate, who is President Erdoğan's son-in-law. This family relation is significant because it shows that the president and his circle keenly support the drone industry. In 2019, Erdoğan issued a presidential decree to support the production of military drones with some US$106 million (Bilgic, 2019). Note also that Bayraktar TB2 is not the sole drone Turkey manufactures. Other military drones include Bayraktar Akıncı System, Bayraktar VTOL UAV, and Bayraktar Mini UAV. These two details indicate the importance of Turkish leadership in developing the country's lethal drone power to counter the growing security challenges.

Turkish and Chinese UAVs are cheaper than American counterparts like MQ-9 Reaper or MQ-1 Predator. In Turkey, the possession of UAV capability is power-enhancing because Ankara has access to sophisticated drone technology without encountering the restrictions imposed on UAV acquisition. The same logic is valid for the UAE because Beijing neither imposes strict restrictions on purchasing clients nor determines the goals that cannot be achieved using UAVs (Boudot, 2018). Indeed, China is not a member of the Missile Technology Control Regime (MTCR), which grants it flexibility in choosing how to implement military export controls.

Drone Warfare, Virtual Warfare

Conventional war had long been known as a social institution that involves a cause, actors (e.g., states), and individuals (e.g., soldiers, combatants). Yet, the deployment of military drones has transformed the nature of war for three reasons. First, physical risk (injury or death) has become one-sided. The deployment of a Bayraktar TB2 or a Wing Loong II creates an asymmetrical exposure to physical risk. On one side, the drone pilot is perfectly safe in a control station that is hundreds if not thousands of kilometers far. On the other side, the target is fully exposed to death without even realizing it. Moreover, fear of violence and trauma, two basic emotions in war zones, are also one-sided. In a war zone where there is a civilian population and where UAVs are extensively deployed, people are likely to suffer from post-traumatic stress and malaise. As Chamayou (2015, p. 45) puts it, permanent drone surveillance culminates in "psychic imprisonment within a perimeter no longer defined by bars, barriers, and walls, but by the endless circling of flying watchtowers up above." While this logic does not always apply to drone pilots, some tend to suffer from traumatic disorders. This is what Gusterson (2016, p. 80) labels "remote stress," in reference to the drone pilots who fall victim to the moral dilemma of remote killing.

Second, the use of military drones reduces the battlefield's complexity. A battlefield is where an "unusual activity" like fighting occurs between forces that understand that they cannot fight beyond that battlefield (Mégret, 2011). The battlefield, in this sense, is a field and an idea that marks a war's beginning and ending in time and geography. It is also a force that legalizes exceptional acts like killing by setting unique norms. Yet, military drones transform the field into space by blurring its boundaries. In other words, the battlefield becomes impersonal because (Fakher Elabiari, 2020):

Drone operators conduct a fourfold loop—watch, target, decide, fire—in every drone strike, transforming the battlefield into an action game in which the player watches a virtual terrain for hours and then uses a joystick to shoot when the target appears.

Third, the possession of military drones enhances a country's real and perceived power. Suppose that countries A and B are fighting on a battlefield for political ends, and B possesses drone power, either local or imported. In that case, the fighting gets asymmetrical, and B becomes more powerful. Because B controls a resource that A does not, it can influence A's behavior in each period T and a specific domain D. Also, the possession of military drones adds to B's international prestige, for when the latter is present, B's real power is automatically recognized. So, the probability of retaliation from A decreases because it is aware of the power gap and the possibility that it will incur tremendous costs if B retaliates using drone power.

Furthermore, perceived power tends to outpace real power, especially in countries where the will is that of leaders and a small political elite. However, if A acquires military drones, that power gap shrinks significantly. This means that the probability of retaliation from A and B increases at an equal level because both possess military drones. So, the actions of both would not be subject to restrictions because attacking is simply using UAVs.

Consequently, when drone power is no longer extraordinary, the power gap shrinks. Therefore, military drones' possession enhances drone power to create a power gap if and only if one actor in a bilateral interaction has them. Still, the evolution of the perceived power of B does not change when A acquires military drones. This leads us to the third section, where a link is established between perceived power, overconfidence, and risk-taking.

MILITARY DRONES AND RISK-TAKING BEHAVIOR

When perceived power rises exponentially, overconfidence takes over. Overconfidence is "the tendency to overestimate the probability of achieving one's objectives" (Fabre & François-Heude, 2009). Overconfidence manifests itself in several ways. The first is miscalibration, that is, when an actor's probability assigning of an event exceeds its accuracy rate. One example of miscalibration is a country that launches a military intervention overseas while believing the outcomes would surely be positive. The second manifestation is called the better-than-average effect, and it is when an actor has an extraordinarily positive perception of itself. The third is the illusion of control an actor has when it believes it can control the course of a particular event. This is a miscalculation of real power. Note that randomly succeeding to control an event does not make the actor powerful. The successful use of military drones in instance T_1 increases an actor's overconfidence and propensity to take risky behavior in instance T_2. When overconfidence stems from past successes, it impacts the prospects of refraining from making specific decisions in the future. Demir (2017, p. 9) attributes the relation between past outcomes and future risk-taking to the excessive focus on opportunities. For him, an overconfident actor focuses more on the likelihood of gain rather than the likelihood of failure, and this inaccuracy culminates in biased risk assessment (Demir, 2017, p. 9).

There is a one-way relationship between overconfidence and risk-taking. In everyday life, actors that are supposedly rational have the propensity to move from situation 1 to situation 2. Before doing so, they weigh the risk associated with the move, that is, the likelihood that they would fail to achieve their intended outcomes. Yet, when the variable of overconfidence intervenes, the actors are more interested in weighing the payoffs associated with the move, that is, the likelihood that their action would succeed and the various benefits they would get. Here, we are talking about the same scenario, except that the judgment direction is different. But why is it different? The answer to this question lies at the heart of the Behavioral Approach System (BAS), a central mechanism in psychology responsible for controlling motivation. According to Stange et al. (2013), the BAS is a mechanism that activates approach behavior in response to positive signals such as rewards, success, and victory. It is, herein, contrary to the Behavioral Inhibition System (BIS), responsible for sensitivity to punishment signals.

The model below illustrates the cycle of positive and negative relationships between UAV possession and risk-taking behavior (figure).

Military drones' possession activates a country's decision makers' BAS and turns off their BIS, thus reviving past successes and minimizing the probability of failure. In fact, there is a negative relationship between power and risk perception. The more a country is powerful with respect to military drones, the higher the probability that it will misperceive risk and engage in risky behavior.

MILITARY DRONES ON THE BATTLEFIELD

One of the factors that speed up the process of conflict resolution is the urgency of ending the war. This urgency can be bound to several reasons, economic, political, and diplomatic. When a country uses military drones

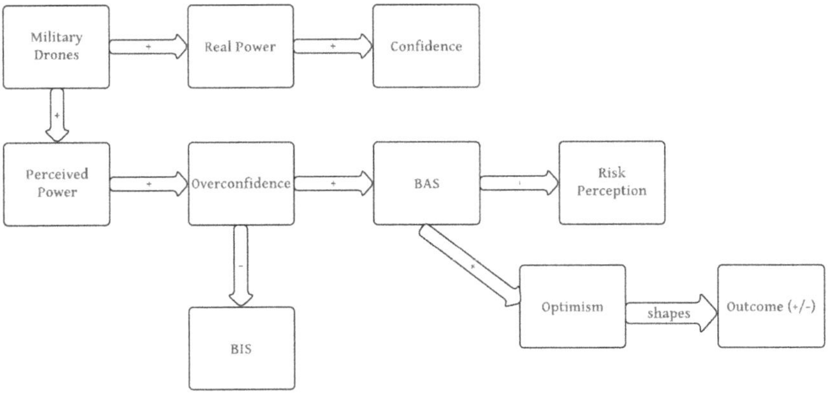

Figure 7.1 Diagram Showing the Relationship between Drone Possession and Various Variables. *Source*: This diagram was designed by the author.

in a remote war zone to uphold a mix of strategic interests, the urgency to resolve war decreases. In fact, the battlefield's elusiveness alters the mechanisms of transparency and accountability. In Libya, Turkey, and the UAE maintain a degree of separation from the consequences of their actions. Thus, it is difficult to determine who does what and who is responsible for that. In November 2019, a military drone attacked a biscuit factory in Wadi al-Rabie, south Tripoli, killing eight civilians and wounding twenty-seven others (Human Rights Watch, 2020). In January 2020, Tripoli's military academy was subject to a drone attack that killed twenty-six cadets in military training ("UAE implicated," 2020). The two attacks' perpetrators were not immediately identified because a drone attack remains secret by default as long as the responsible parties do not divulge information and other parties have not obtained intelligence information. However, the remnants' examination in both cases showed that they belonged to the Blue Arrow-7, a missile carried by the Chinese Wing Loong II that is operated exclusively by the UAE. Still, the Emirati officials continued to deny their relations with the attacks against non-legitimate targets (civilian people and unarmed cadets).

Chris Cole argues that Libya has become an epicenter for drone wars because many countries are involved, but "nobody is precisely sure who is doing what" (Sabbagh et al., 2019). The absence of a framework of accountability translates into the absence of a referent. When the UAE or Turkey launches a drone strike in Libya, they are responsible vis-à-vis what and who? Is it their respective citizens, the civilians who died from collateral damage, the Libyan authorities, or the three altogether? Here, the framework is political and moral because the debate on military drones has primarily been moral. Enemark (2020) develops a framework for conceptualizing responsibility in which drone-using countries should normally consider five objects for them to be responsible drone users. First, they should respect the sovereignty of states where they launch "defensive" drone strikes; second, they should obtain the citizens' consent on accepting the risk of retaliation; third, drone-using countries should commit violence only in the context of war and law enforcement; fourth, they should minimize the risk of collateral damage; and fifth, they should protect the military staff against physical risk. Enemark's framework shows us the paradox between what drone uses should be and what it is. Morally speaking, drone-using countries are the primary beneficiaries because UAVs' deployment does not create domestic discontent and political resistance. Indeed, discontent stems from economic pressure when the country is engaged in several war fronts whereas political resistance stems from the regular reporting of casualties among the military personnel. So, in the absence of moral, political, and economic barriers to retaliation, the risk of retaliation grows, creating a logic of carte blanche warfare, where the warring parties are not constrained.

CONCLUSION

This chapter explains how military drones, power, and risk-taking form a perilous nexus. The Libyan case provides enough evidence to assert that military drones' possession inflates power and appetite for risk through overconfidence and the BAS and BIS mechanisms. However, this reality opens room for reckless moves and is likely to stretch wars' durability because military drones alter the logic of deterrent behavior and diminish the risks associated with retaliation and escalation. This reality shifts the battlefield from a geographical arena where extraordinary actions and practices like killing and violence are allowed under restrictions to an impersonal space where actors are given carte blanche as long as they possess drone power.

The proliferation of military drones poses a significant challenge to security in the Middle East and North Africa, and worldwide. This chapter is only an attempt to initiate multidisciplinary research on military drones, which is very much needed. Future research can cover questions like: How is agency, an attribute of individuals, becoming an attribute of fully autonomous blind planes? How does the use of military drones impact conflict dynamics like intensity? How can international law uphold accountability to protect civilians in conflict zones?

NOTE

1. H. F. Elabiari. Istanbul, Türkiye. Email: fakher.hafssa@gmail.com

BIBLIOGRAPHY

Baldwin, David Allen. *Power in International Relations: A Conceptual Approach.* Princeton: Princeton University Press, 2016.

Barnett, Michael, and Raymond Duvall. "Power in International Politics." International Organization 59, no. 1 (2005): 39–75. https://doi.org/10.1017/S0020818305050010.

Baykar Makina. "Bayraktar TB2 UAS." (n.d.) https://baykardefence.com/upload/ingilizce/Bayraktar_tb2_UAS_brochure_eng.pdf.

BBC. "UAE Implicated in Lethal Drone Strike in Libya." BBC. August 28, 2020. https://www.bbc.com/news/world-africa-53917791.

Bilgic, Taylan. "Turkish Drone Maker Baykar Makina Gets Government Support." Bloomberg. September 5, 2019. https://www.bloomberg.com/news/articles/2019-09-05/turkish-drone-maker-gets-government-support-to-boost-output.

Boudot, Flore. "Le Succès des Drones de Combat Chinois." Institut de Recherche Stratégique de l'École Militaire. April 2018. https://www.irsem.fr/data/files/

irsem/documents/document/file/2809/N165%20-%20Note%20-%20Le%20succes%20des%20drones%20de%20combat%20chinois.pdf.

Brookes, Peter, and Terra Schroeder. "Game of Drones: Coming to a Military Theater Near You." The Heritage Foundation. October 8, 2019. https://www.heritage.org/defense/commentary/game-drones-coming-military-theater-near-you.

Chamayou, Grégoire. *A Theory of the Drone*. New York: The New Press, 2013.

Dahl, Robert. "The Concept of Power." *Behavioral Science* 2, no. 3 (1957): 201–215. https://doi.org/10.1002/bs.3830020303.

Demir, Imran. *Overconfidence and Risk Taking in Foreign Policy Decision Making: The Case of Turkey's Syria Policy*. Cham: Palgrave Macmillan, 2017

Eljarh, Mohamed. "Turkey's Intervention in Libya Disrupts the UAE but Opens the Door for Russia." Washington Institute. 2020. https://www.washingtoninstitute.org/policy-analysis/turkeys-intervention-libya-disrupts-uae-opens-door-russia.

Ellyson, S.L. and Dovidio, J. F. *Power, Dominance, and Nonverbal Behavior*. Edited by Steve L. Ellyson and John F. Dovidio, 1985 New York: Springer-Verlag

Enemark, Christian. "On the Responsible use of Armed Drones: The Prospective Moral Responsibilities of States." *The International Journal of Human Rights* 24, no. 6 (2020): 868–888. https://doi.org/10.1080/13642987.2019.1690464.

Fabre, Bruno, and Alain François-Heude. « Optimism and Overconfidence Investors' Biases: A Methodological Note." *Finance* 1, no. 1 (2009): 79–119. https://doi.org/10.3917/fina.301.0079.

Fakher Elabiari, Hafssa. "How Military Drones Are a Game-Changer in the Libyan Conflict." Morocco World News. April 12, 2020. https://www.moroccoworldnews.com/2020/04/299366/how-military-drones-are-a-game-changer-in-the-libyan-conflict/.

Gilpin, R. War and Change in World Politics. Cambridge: Cambridge University Press, 1981.

Gusterson, Hugh. *Drone: Remote Control Warfare*. Cambridge: The MIT Press, 2016.

Human Rights Watch. "Libya: UAE Strike Kills 8 Civilians." Human Rights Watch. April 29, 2020. https://www.hrw.org/node/340983/printable/print.

Ibrahim, Nader, and Ilya Barabanov. "The Lost Tablet and the Secret Documents: Clues Pointing to a Shadowy Russian Army." BBC. https://www.bbc.co.uk/news/extra/8iaz6xit26/the-lost-tablet-and-the-secret-documents.

Iddon, Paul. "Bayraktars and Harops: Is Morocco a Rising Drone Power?" Forbes. December 22, 2021. https://www.forbes.com/sites/pauliddon/2021/12/22/bayraktars-and-harops-is-morocco-a-rising-drone-power/.

Keohane, Robert O., and Joseph S. Nye. *Power and Interdependence*. Boston: Longman, 2012.

Majumdar Roy Choudhury, Lipika, Luis Antonio de Alburqueque Bacardit, Amanda Kadlec, Moncef Kartas, Yassine Marjane, and Adrian Wilkinson. Final Report of the Panel of Experts on Libya Established Pursuant to Security Council Resolution 1973. United Nations Security Council. 2011. https://www.securitycouncilreport.org/atf/cf/%7B65BFCF9B-6D27-4E9C-8CD3-CF6E4FF96FF9%7D/S_2019_914.pdf.

Mearsheimer, J.J. *The Tragedy of Great Power Politics*. New York: Norton, 2011.

Mégret, Frederic. "War and the Vanishing Battlefield." *Loyola University Chicago International Law Review* 9, no. 1 (2011): 131–151. https://lawecommons.luc.edu/cgi/viewcontent.cgi?referer=https://www.google.com/&httpsredir=1&article=1013&context=lucilr.

Morgenthau, H. J. (1948). Politics Among Nations. The Struggle for Power and Peace. New York, Knopf.

Nacouzi, G., J. D. Williams, S. Brian, L. Anne, L. David, X. Colin, S. Jia, G. Yuliya, M. Daniel, and M. H. Decker. *Assessment of the Proliferation of Certain Remotely Piloted Aircraft Systems: Response to Section 1276 of the National Defense Authorization Act for Fiscal Year 2017* (RR-2369-JS). (2018). https://www.rand.org/pubs/research_reports/RR2369.html

Nye, J. S. *Soft Power: The Means to Succeed in World Politics*. New York: Public Affairs, 2004.

Nye, J. S. "Soft Power: The Evolution of a Concept." *Journal of Political Power* 14, no. 1 (2021): 1979–2019. https://doi.org/10.1080/2158379X.2021.1879572.

Paul, Thazha V. "Disarmament Revisited: Is Nuclear Abolition Possible?" *Journal of Strategic Studies* 35, no. 1 (2012): 149–169. http://dx.doi.org/10.1080/01402390.2012.645369.

Ramani, Samuel. "Turkey's Military Intervention in Libya: A Surprise Triumph for Erdogan." *Royal United Services Institute* 40, no. 5 (June 26, 2020). https://rusi.org/explore-our-research/publications/rusi-newsbrief/turkeys-military-intervention-libya-surprise-triumph-erdogan.

Read, James H. "Thomas Hobbes: Power in the State of Nature, Power in Civil Society." *Polity* 23, no. 4 (1991): 505–525. https://doi.org/10.2307/3235060.

Ritsick, Colin. "25 Most Expensive Fighter Jets." Military Machine. January 1, 2020. https://militarymachine.com/most-expensive-military-jets/.

Rothstein, Adam. *Drone*. New York: Bloomsbury, 2015.

Russell, Ann Marie, and Susan T. Fiske. "Power and Social Perception." In *The Social Psychology of Power*, edited by Ana Guinote, and Theresa K. Vescio, 231–250. New York: The Guilford Press, 2010.

Sabbagh, Dan, Jason Burke, and Bethan McKernan. "'Libya Is Ground Zero': Drones on Frontline in Bloody Civil War." *The Guardian*. November 27, 2019. https://www.theguardian.com/news/2019/nov/27/libya-is-ground-zero-drones-on-frontline-in-bloody-civil-war.

Sabbagh, Dan. "UK Wants New Drones in Wake of Azerbaijan Military Success." *The Guardian*. December 29, 2020. https://www.theguardian.com/world/2020/dec/29/uk-defence-secretary-hails-azerbaijans-use-of-drones-in-conflict.

Spicer, Jonathan, Giulia Paravicini, and Orhan Coskun. "Exclusive U.S. Concerned Over Turkey's Drones Sales to Conflict-hit Ethiopia." Reuters. December 22, 2021. https://www.reuters.com/world/africa/exclusive-us-concerned-over-turkeys-drone-sales-conflict-hit-ethiopia-2021-12-22/.

Stange, Jonathan P., Benjamin G. Shapero, Shari Jager-Hyman, David A. Grant, Abramson, Lyn Y. Abramson, and Lauren B. Alloy. "Behavioral Approach System (BAS)-Relevant Cognitive Styles in Individuals with High vs. Moderate BAS

Sensitivity: A Behavioral High-Risk Design." *Cognitive Therapy and Research* 37, no. 1 (2013): 139–149. https://doi.org/10.1007/s10608-012-9443-x.

Stockholm International Peace Research Institute. *Military expenditure by country, in constant (2018) US$ m., 1988–2019* [Table]. 2020. https://www.sipri.org/sites/default/files/Data%20for%20all%20countries%20from%201988%E2%80%932019%20in%20constant%20%282018%29%20USD.pdf.

Torelli, Carlos J., and Sharon Shavitt. "Culture and Concepts of Power." *Journal of Personality and Social Psychology* 99, no. 4 (2010): 703–723. https://doi.org/10.1037/a0019973.

Chapter 8

US-Da Afghanistan Bank Sanctions

An Inelegant Solution to a Self-Imposed Problem

Michael Larrick[1]

INTRODUCTION

On February 11, 2022, the US government issued Executive Order 14064 (the "Order"), which blocked the foreign reserves of Da Afghanistan Bank ("DAB") within US jurisdiction.[2] This Order demonstrates how domestic issues can drive international and national security policy. It also provides a lens to understand sanctions regimes and the domestic and international legal mechanisms states use to leverage financial mechanisms to achieve national security goals. Seen in a larger context, the Order offers insight into the evolution of the US use of sanctions, and their detrimental effects on legal legitimacy, developing nations, and global finance.

As the government-owned central bank of Afghanistan, DAB's assets consist of the private property of Afghan citizens, civil society organizations, foreign investment, and financial institutions.[3] It administers these funds on behalf of depositors and holds some of these assets abroad as International Foreign Exchange Reserves of the country to implement monetary policy, facilitate international trace, and stabilize the financial sector.[4] Neither DAB, nor the past or present government of Afghanistan, nor the US government nor US taxpayers "own" these funds. Ultimate ownership and title of the approximate $6 billion rests with the depositors, the majority of which are the people of Afghanistan.

THE ORDER

The Substance of the Order

The Order is brief and lights on detail, blocking all DAB funds in the US and transferring them to the Federal Reserve Bank of New York. Simultaneously, the Office of Foreign Asset Control ("OFAC") issued a license splitting the funds into two separate accounts.[5] Finally, the Department of Justice filed a Statement of Interest in two Federal Court cases seeking to attach the DAB assets to enforce uncontested monetary judgments against the Taliban.[6]

The Order's preamble establishes the legal basis and states its intent. The president relies on the International Emergency Economic Powers Act[7] ("IEEPA") and the National Emergencies Act ("NEA").[8] He declares a national emergency to deal with an undefined humanitarian crisis in Afghanistan and orders the preservation of DAB property held in the United States to resolve the national security threat and preserve the welfare of the Afghan people.[9]

To achieve its mission, the Order "blocks" DAB's US property and interests from legal claims, transfer, payment, exportation, withdraw, or other dealings. It instructs US financial institutions holding DAB property to immediately transfer covered assets to a consolidated account at the Federal Reserve Bank of New York.

The same day, OFAC issued a license transferring half the property (and liquidating if necessary) into a $3.5 billion to a separate fund. These funds are set aside, allowing the Secretary of State to appoint individuals under the Federal Reserve Act ("FRA")[10] to control and dispose of the property "for the benefit of the people of Afghanistan."[11] The remaining funds are subject to the jurisdiction of several domestic court proceedings.

The SDNY Court Cases

The primary impetus for the Order involves two court cases in the Southern District of New York ("SDNY"), *John Does 1 Through 7 v. The Taliban et al.* ("Does")[12] and *Fiona Havlish et al. v. Sheikh Usamah Bin-Muhammed Bin-Laden et al.* ("Havlish").[13] In both cases, the plaintiffs sued and won default judgments for damages resulting from the September 11 attacks against several defendants, including the Taliban.[14] Since the Taliban and others did not have meaningful assets within US jurisdiction, these judgments were regarded as largely symbolic and went unsatisfied.

This changed when the Islamic Republic of Afghanistan dissolved, and the Taliban assumed control of Afghanistan in August 2021. The plaintiffs filed writs to attach DAB property, asserting that the Taliban, as the government, now controls DAB.[15] Therefore, the plaintiffs should be allowed to satisfy their judgment against the Taliban by tracing the DAB's foreign reserves in New York or with New York-based financial institutions and, therefore, subject to SDNY jurisdiction.

To succeed, the plaintiffs in both cases must show a sufficient connection to attach their judgment that the Taliban "owns" the DAB assets. The plaintiffs must convince a judge to (1) recognize the Taliban as the government of Afghanistan, (2) accept that the State of Afghanistan inherits the Taliban's preexisting legal debts, and (3) accept that the DAB assets are available to satisfy this judgment.

These cases have created a conflict between the Judicial and Executive branches of American Federalism. Normally, the Executive enjoys exclusive power to set foreign policy or national security goals.[16] The Executive Branch of the US Government is invested in *not* recognizing the Taliban as the legitimate government of Afghanistan or giving it control over DAB property.[17] The Judicial branch undermines these aims if an SDNY judge recognizes the Taliban as the government of Afghanistan and owner of DAB assets through an enforcement order. But due to the Separation of Powers, the Executive cannot directly interfere with the judicial process and explicitly shut down Havlish and Does' cases by using a blocking order to put the assets in question out of reach of the plaintiffs.

Reason for the Order

The Order, Statement of Interest, and OFAC license are the Biden Administration's attempt to cut through the Gordian Knot presented by the Havlish and Does writs. The Order uses legal mechanisms to centralize and remove DAB's assets from Taliban control while setting aside half (more than is at stake in either Havlish or Does) to satisfy potential court judgments, avoiding the appearance of improperly influencing the judiciary. Simultaneously, a Statement of Interest reminds the judges that the foreign policy and national security implications of granting the writs are outside the Judiciary's scope. The remainder held in trust for "the benefit of the people of Afghanistan" until the Executive decides what to do with it. And the Order avoids directly mentioning the Taliban or the government of Afghanistan, sidestepping explicitly recognizing any Taliban claim to the government of Afghanistan or DAB assets.

Despite this tidy picture, the Order neither strictly complies with legal procedure nor achieves its ambiguous goals. This chapter seeks to: (1) determine if the Order's inconsistencies are unusual or serious by examining these inconsistencies through domestic national security law and international law of sanctions, and (2) divine what this says about sanctions as a national security tool and how concerned parties might respond.

SANCTIONS UNDER US LAW AND HOW THE ORDER IS DERIVED FROM PAST PRACTICE

The Order uses the legal mechanism of sanctions, which leverages the United States' position as a financial center to control the assets of countries, groups, or individuals to achieve foreign policy and national security goals.[18] The Order roughly follows the form required but deviates in key respects, which undermine its claim to legality, although few grounds exist to challenge either the Order's measures or sanctions generally.

To act unilaterally without the consent of Congress, the president first needs to declare a national emergency pursuant to the NEA. This authority is *very* general, requiring only an executive order specifying the law permitting the president to take specific acts, notice to Congress and publication.[19]

To implement IEEPA sanctions, the president must invoke a national emergency to respond to an "unusual and extraordinary threat[s]" to national security, foreign policy, or the US economy originating outside the United States.[20] IEEPA grants the president three general powers:

(1) To investigate, regulate or prohibit foreign exchange transactions, transfers of credit, or import/export of currency or securities;
(2) Investigate and block during that investigation, any property of a foreign country or national; and
(3) Confiscate any property that belongs to a foreign country or national that the president deems is involved in hostilities or attacks against the United States to vest in an agency or person designated by the president, dealt with as he proscribes.[21]

The president's jurisdiction to apply these powers extends to the property physically in the United States or property that "come within the United States, or . . . within the possession or control of US persons."[22]

The president may renew an emergency declaration and indefinitely expand the scope or targets of IEEPA sanctions.[23] For example, every subsequent president has renewed annually the original September 11 attacks sanctions and expanded the list of targeted individuals/organizations.[24]

The first two powers make up the core of most US-issued sanctions.[25] "Block" is a legal term of art specific to IEEPA with an expansive definition that includes preventing the "use" of that property by its owner. While a contextual reading requires an investigation to block property, that pretext is rarely used today.[26] Despite sanctions depriving owners of the ability to exercise their rights to the property, US courts have held that the owner does not lose "title" or legal ownership, so blocking does not constitute a taking or expropriation.[27] This means the US government does not need to follow the normal Constitutional requirement of compensating owners for depriving them of their use over the property.[28]

The third power was added by the 2001 USA PATRIOT Act.[29] This expanded the president's powers from blocking and freezing property to seizing property without a Congressional declaration of war.[30] Perhaps because it is a significant expansion of power, it has only been exercised once, in 2003, against "the Government of Iraq and its agencies, instrumentalities, or controlled entities."[31] Due to its limited use, it is unclear whether this constitutes a taking, but it seems likely that it does since, unlike a block, the owner does not lose "use" temporarily but permanently.

A common administrative matter of sanctions is to centralize assets by liquidating property not easily transferable, such as real estate, and transferring all liquid assets to a central account held in the Federal Reserve. This crystalizes the assets under US jurisdiction and reduces the chances that the sanctioned party and conspirators will find a way to evade the measures, making off with all or part of the assets.

The transfer of foreign state or foreign central bank assets to the Federal Reserve engages additional FRA responsibilities. To receive, control, or dispense such property requires the approval of an authorized representative of the foreign state recognized by the Secretary of State.[32] Since assets "blocked" under IEEPA do not cease to belong to a foreign state or central reserve, an authorized representative must be found to approve any dispensation of that property.

EVALUATING THE ORDER UNDER US DOMESTIC LAW

If we compare this Order to the legal foundations of US sanctions, then we would find that while it mostly follows the *letter* of the law, it does not follow the *spirit*. The minimal requirements, justification, acts taken, and proposed resolution are all present on paper but do not match up with what we know of *why* the order exist in the first place.

The Order declares a national emergency, asserting the humanitarian and economic crisis in Afghanistan presents an "unusual and extraordinary threat to the national security and foreign policy of the United States."[33] The Order invokes the first two powers of IEEPA, preventing all transactions and "blocking" the assets subject to US jurisdiction by virtue of touching and concerning regulated US financial institutions. Acknowledging that a foreign state claims ownership of the assets, the OFAC License and Statement of Interest recognize the need for an authorized representative.

However, the justification for the freezing of the DAB assets is troubling. IEEPA powers may "only" be used in response to an unusual and extraordinary threat "and may not be exercised for any other purpose."[34] What exactly constitutes an unusual and extraordinary threat to the national security, foreign policy, or economy of the United States is not defined.[35] Humanitarian and economic reasons have been put forward before, although usually, the Executive is clearer what, exactly, the crisis is.[36] However, it is clear that the national security threat is not the *only* reason for the Order. A significant and admitted reason why the sanctions exist is to address the domestic difficulties raised by domestic court cases like Havlish and Does 1–7.[37] The Order's purpose, at least in part, is to find a way out of that conflict, which means that, however generously interpreted; the justification for the sanction of DAB assets is faulty at law.

In substance, the Order is creeping from "blocking" toward outright expropriation through confiscation and redistribution of a nonhostile party's assets. There is a barrier between the president's power to "block" and to "confiscate" under (2) and (3) above a block is a permissible taking because it is temporary and the title remains with the owner.[38] Confiscation requires the target to be engaged in armed hostilities against the United States and revokes full title to the property from the owner, and vests it in an agency. This power is Constitutionally dubious and invoked so rarely.[39] Further, while it might be possible to argue the Taliban have engaged in armed hostilities, they are absent from the Order itself. It seems incredible to argue the DAB or Afghan government is engaged in armed hostilities against the United States. The power of confiscation was not available to the Executive in this instance.

Yet the Executive is expanding the definition of the power to block to fully expropriate and use the funds as they want while retaining the legal safety of a "block" and without the need for hostilities against the United States as required for "confiscation." The Order stresses the definition of block in two ways: First, it orders the assets to be liquidated, which strains the definition of retaining title. Their use is not simply blocked pending investigation; some of the assets have changed form. Second, the remaining funds are held "for the benefit of the people of Afghanistan" via humanitarian and other means. This foreshadows confiscation and redistribution of the DAB assets, whether approved by a State Department approved official or not; any use *other* than for achieving and maintaining a sound economy is outside the scope of what the funds are for.[40]

If the United States redistributes the blocked funds, it faces a final legal challenge in finding a legitimate representative to approve. Now that the funds are sitting in the Federal Reserve, FRA Section 25B requires the State Department to identify an approved person to sign off on any dispersal of funds.[41] With the collapse of the former government and civil society in

Afghanistan and appointing a Taliban representative out of the question, such an individual is elusive. If a suitable candidate could be found, any use of the funds *other* than for the DAB's statutory mandate of stabilizing the Afghan economy would seemingly invalidate the legitimacy of that candidate. This rules out the stated intent in the Order of humanitarian relief.

The Order has the façade of legal legitimacy, but it lacks structural stability and reaches beyond the powers granted by Congress. While it may have seemed a tidy solution to Havlish and Does, the complications presented by those cases and avoiding recognizing the Taliban resulted in legally corrupted sanctions. Unfortunately, due to the unique situation and overall difficulty, it is likely the measures will continue unchallenged unless Congress decides to intervene, an unlikely proposition. This sets a dangerous precedent to support further expansion in future US sanctions.

SANCTIONS UNDER INTERNATIONAL LAW AND THE DAB MEASURES

International law plays an important role in state issued sanctions, setting limits on state national security policy. Through state practice and the opinion of international judicial bodies, the right to unilaterally sanction is recognized for national security purposes in response to an internationally illegal act. This power is wide but not unlimited—it must be validly exercised and minimize conflict with other international laws or obligations. These relationships shape the way we view the Order and its legality or validity.

Defining a Sanction in International Law

The definition of an economic sanction in international law is broad and eclectic. Generally, sanctions involve the "deliberate, government-inspired withdrawal or threat of withdrawal of customary trade or financial relations," which are seen as preferable to physical conflict.[42] They can be multilateral coordinated efforts or unilateral measures recognized as a customary right. States justify unilateral sanctions targeting other states or individuals and organizations as countermeasures, a "self-help" response to the target's internationally wrongful act or breach of an international obligation or law.[43] The imposing state may, but need not necessarily be, the state directly aggrieved by that harm.[44] But closer proximity to the effect of the harm certainly lends any response more legitimacy. The goal is to rectify the target's international standing, and coerce it back into compliance with its obligations.[45] Measures should be proportionate to the harm, not solely punitive, and terminated promptly once compliance is achieved.[46]

Validity of Unilateral Sanctions in International Law

While exact definitions vary, sanctions must wrestle with questions of validity and conflict with other principles of international law. Validity weighs whether a measure is appropriate or legitimate compared to the norms of sanctions under customary international law: Was there an internationally wrongful act attributable to the target of the sanctions? Is imposing sanctions justified? Is the response proportionate to encourage future compliance? These are questions of law and fact that often give rise to internal and external criticisms of states imposing sanctions.

To provide guidance on a proportionate or valid response, states can look to the ILC Articles on the Responsibility of States for Internationally Wrongful Acts ("ILC Articles").[47] Although nonbinding, they provide a roadmap for legitimate sanctions.[48] For instance, the ILC Articles describe when sanctions are justified, separating acts attributable to a state such that a state incurs international responsibility (such as acts by a government organ or by an insurrectional movement that later attains governmental control) from acts disconnected with the state (such as those carried out by non-state actors, or when the state is acting only in a commercial capacity).[49] The ILC Articles help shape state action and may guide tribunals tasked with deciphering the validity of sanctions.

Conflicts with Other International Law Principles—Noninterventionism

Entangles with validity, sanctions also conflict with other principles of international law, such as the principle of noninterventionism, human rights, and restrictions on trade or the ownership of property. Noninterventionism is grounded in mutual respect for sovereignty, whereby states try to avoid coercive action in the affairs of another state.[50] Foreign states often enjoy "sovereign immunity," a degree of exemption from domestic law when acting in the capacity of the state. This can include control over and dispensation of foreign state-owned property under central bank reserves performing state functions.[51]

These boundaries of sovereignty can conflict. A state's right to prevent foreign goods from entering its territory is in opposition to the right of states to trade with other countries.[52] This context is important when a powerful state imposes sanctions on a state with a developing economy, which may be especially vulnerable to coercive pressure or intervention by developed economies. The principles of noninterventionism and sovereign immunity seem diametrically opposed to, and must be balanced against, the goal of sanctions, to use economic forces to coerce a target state.

Conflicts with Other International Law Principles—Human Rights

Sanctions also have a broad negative impact on human rights. Directly, sanctions deprive targets of the right to property and the right to be heard.[53] As an example, a sanction deprives a person of the use of their property. States are generally permitted to expropriate property within their jurisdiction, if the taking is either justly compensated or justified to prevent a greater harm under a state's police powers. But if a sanction expropriates without compensation or sufficient nexus to a security exemption, it violates the individual(s) right to property. Most states will justify the expropriation as a national security prerogative, but the legitimacy of that justification should not go unchallenged.

Due to sanctions freezing the targets and those near them out of markets, there are severe indirect human rights impacts on individuals. Their lives are immiserated by lack of opportunity and lack of development brought by sanction's direct effects and ostracization.[54] Often those who feel these effects acutely are not the targets of sanctions. A country's poorest citizens are much more vulnerable than the rich to economic sanction's impacts, despite having little-to-no input or control over the events that lead to the imposition or lifting of sanctions.

The practice of secondary sanctions, or criminal penalties on people who transact with sanctioned parties, compounds these impacts. Trade partners operating outside the jurisdiction of sanctions may decline to trade for fear of reprisals on assets subject to the sanctioning state's jurisdiction. This has a freezing effect, ostracizing the target from trade. If the sanctioning state is large and influential enough, it may make the target a pariah since few third parties would consider themselves outside the state's jurisdiction and independent enough to avoid sanction themselves.

Sanctions conflict with, and should account for, human rights impacts. Most sanctions regimes exempt medical supplies, humanitarian aid, or food from sanctions to lessen the human rights impact. But these exceptions are largely superficial because these sectors are inextricable from the larger economy. How is a state supposed to effectively manage an economy with a partially frozen budget? How are individuals to afford necessities with a currency devalued or sell goods and services when partners fear reprisals from secondary sanctions? To mitigate sanction's impact on human rights, states should limit the scope and duration of sanctions as much as possible.

Due Process and Sanctions

Sanctions also conflict with due process, a principle that there should be minimum protections for persons' rights, such as fair treatment and protection from arbitrary or discriminatory state acts.[55] To increase sanctions effectiveness, as little notice as possible is desirable. Further, the shield of state police powers and expansive national security laws can make judicial recourse difficult, if not outright impossible. There are also "soft" aspects that make the challenge difficult: targets are likely not popular or sympathetic in the national image or lack the capacity to have their voice heard while under sanction. If a state cannot minimize these effects and guarantee a baseline of treatment for sanction targets, there is a concern the sanctioning state is not meeting its due process obligations.

States imposing sanctions know their measures are vulnerable to critiques of validity or conflict with other international legal principles. They often take pains to publicize both domestically and abroad that their measures are valid and that any imposition on other principles is either proportional and justified or minimized.[56] But the imposing state should not be allowed to unilaterally decide that sanctions conform to international law. Whether an imposition of sanctions or countermeasures is valid is almost never a binary choice but an approximate weighing of the evidence by the public, civil society, and other states.

Who will do this weighing is unclear. Targets would prefer to avoid the prejudice of sanctioner courts. But a general mechanism to compel dispute resolution does not exist, rather a checkerboard of coverage from treaty and ad hoc agreement. With a fair hearing in domestic courts unlikely and no standing body to adjudicate sanctions disputes, sanctions strain the principle of due process.

Analysis of the Order through the Lens of International Law Surrounding Sanctions

The Order has the hallmarks of a sanction valid at international law that acknowledges and seeks to balance conflicting legal obligations. But concerns lurk that the DAB sanctions constitute invalid countermeasures. Further, the measures are disproportionate in their improvement to United States and Afghanistan national security when balanced against the impact to Afghanistan's sovereignty and individual human rights.

Regarding validity, the Order justifies the freeze of DAB assets as a response to the national security and foreign policy threat posed to the American people by the humanitarian crisis in Afghanistan. Generously, that threat could be construed as a response to a security threat posed by a hostile government or "various groups," or to a government that cannot meet its human rights obligations to its people. There are exemptions for "agricultural commodities, medicine, medical devices, and personal, noncommercial remittances." This hits the notes for justified and proportionate response to a breach (or threatened breach) of international obligations.

These notes of justification are discordant, however. Afghanistan has not attacked the United States, nor is the United States is not at "war" with the Taliban.[57] Perhaps there is a legitimate concern the funds might end up in unfriendly hands, but the lack of connection between the DAB, the assets, and any breach of international obligation or threat to national security renders this speculative.

The other justification is on humanitarian grounds, that Afghanistan cannot meet its obligations to protect the human rights of its people and the United States must intervene on the people's behalf (which will be good for US security). Certainly after twenty years of occupation and the complete dissipation of the US backed government, the United States owes Afghanistan ongoing humanitarian support. But it beggars belief these sanctions will improve the economic or humanitarian situation in Afghanistan, which darkens by the day.[58] Similarly, the humanitarian carveouts are cruel jest as the currency value plummets and the fear of secondary sanctions chills trade and assistance.[59] The idea that the Order does not conflict, but augments human rights, rings hollow.

The unspoken but clear justification is the United States wants to keep the money out of the Taliban's administration to cripple any chance of effective governance. Certain quarters also suffer from "buyer's remorse," believing the funds belong to the United States since it provided aid to the previous government. These *real politik* maneuvers may enjoy public support, but they are not legitimate justifications under international law to violate another state's sovereignty.

The proportionality of the measures is also lopsided. Since the justification is muddled, it is difficult to accurately judge if the measure is reasonable to coerce Afghanistan into compliance. But certainly, an indefinite freeze of 90% of Afghanistan's foreign reserves is unwarranted at a critical juncture for the state.[60] The assets are critical to the functioning of the Afghani economy, and the sanctions have exacerbated a crisis of currency value and liquidity.[61,62] Meanwhile the United States seems unaffected by events in Afghanistan one way or the other. Despite the difficulties in measuring proportionality stemming from a weak justification, the power disparity is dizzying and the impact dwarfs the marginal gains.

Finally, there is a concern the United States is expropriating private property of persons without notice, hearing, or appropriate compensation. Despite strong concerns over the legality of the sanctions issued under the Order, it is unlikely they will face a meaningful challenge as a violation of international law. There is simply no treaty or other agreement granting a forum to hear such a dispute. The sanctions will likely never face scrutiny under international law.

The Sanctions issued under the order deserve harsh criticism when viewed under international law. While unilateral sanctions are generally allowable, these specific measures lack a coherent justification, seem disproportionate in scope and capacity, and directly conflict with other international legal principles in a way that raise serious concerns. While a formal legal dispute remains unlikely, states should continue to pressure the United States toward international compliance.

THE ORDER IN CONTEXT

The Order is not unique for its sparse compliance with United States and International law. Rather, it represents the Executive branch's latest use of sanctions to expand its own power and push the limits of acceptability in national security. The employ of sanctions to resolve short-term political goals undermines the effectiveness of sanctions, stability of centralized financial markets, and the legitimacy of law. The resolution of the DAB assets will prove how far the Executive is willing to push these limits.

The United States has increased its use of sanctions as a politically palatable alternative to military intervention.[63] During this time, the Executive has pushed its interpretation of national security law to shrink IEEPA's already minimal limits to rote formulization to expand its own power, in contradiction of Congressional intent.[64] The lack of legal connective tissue undermines the legitimacy of national and international security law.

Taken on its own, it is easy to see the Order as an aberration. Certainly, the political issues created by Havlish and Does 1–7 presented an unusual legal and political challenge to the US government. Yet the core legal concerns over justification of a National Emergency, appropriateness and scope of sanctions, and ultimate use of targeted funds, are not new or unique to the Order.

Compare the Order to E.O. 13224, the original sanctions on the suspected perpetrators of the September 11 attacks.[65] The present Order scantly covers all the elements, makes a minimal effort at explaining their legal nexus, and takes for granted the connection between them. Further, it openly advocates for blurring the legal lines between freezing and expropriation. E.O. 13224 references a specific action and how that impacts national security as grounds for declaring a national emergency. It contains all the required elements for IEEPA sanctions, elucidates them, and explains the connection between them.

Compared to the present Order, E.O. 13224 is a model draft for implementing sanctions. Yet E.O. 13224 faced contemporary criticism for pushing the limits of what "under investigation" meant for freezing orders, targeting charities with tenuous-to-no connection to the perpetrators of the 9/11 attacks.[66] The expansion of sanctions from countermeasures between states to non-state actors itself was controversial in the 1990s.[67] The Executive has been pushing the limits of sanctions for decades.

It may seem this expansion of sanctions power is a positive, especially when the alternative is overt violence. However, this expansion is not motivated by principle, which would advocate for a consistent use of sanctions in specific scenarios. Instead, this expansion comes from a desire to turn sanctions into an all-encompassing national security tool to solve any political inconvenience. This removes sanctions from their intended use—as a justified and proportionate response to encourage a rogue party's compliance—to a mere expression of power. The respect of sanctions as a national security tool is diminished by this lack of principle, which adversely affects their effectiveness.

The overall effect is a weakening of legitimacy of law, both domestic and international. Regulations that follow the rote formula of the law but undermine the spirit are arbitrary, unmoored from principled logical or moral foundations. Achieving a consistent idea of justice is not the goal; rather the Executive acts in its immediate advantage. Certainly, this strong-arm approach has many adherents in US foreign policy and national security circles. But with each step toward arbitrary expression of power, the perception of legitimacy of US authority is diminished. Other states may disregard US sanctions as illegitimate and decline enforcement or cooperation. More powerful states may see it as a blueprint for their own power-rather-than-principle based sanctions. Malevolent actors may curate opinion and law to provide a fig-leaf justification for sanctions to expropriate desired assets and subvert human rights, private property and due process concerns. This severely damages sanctions as a legitimate and coherent body of domestic and international national security law.

This delegitimization is not contained to the law of sanctions or national security. It also undermines faith in the interconnectedness of global finance. Developing countries and those potentially adjacent (charities, civil society organizations, and people in these states), often keep reserves in US jurisdiction either as a requirement of World Bank, IMF or other aid, or for general convenience as a stable and centralized financial hub. If the US government may freeze and confiscate those assets overnight because the political situation has changed, these traditionally "safe" places to park foreign reserves are not as stable as they seemed.

The US message is that assets are not safe from political intervention if the country or organization is on the fringe or particularly vulnerable to Washington's favor. Prudence calls for increased diversity of assets spread across jurisdictions and away from US adjacent financial centers. This diversification comes at a cost to some of the benefits of centralization—relatively stable currency, predictable legal frameworks, and ease of commerce with others—which potentially hampers free global trade. Secondary sanctions compound this effect, further chilling trade beyond the physical limits of a state's jurisdiction. Central reserves and others potentially subject to sanctions should add the threat of sanctions into their long-term monetary policy and consideration of loans/aid, and particularly how entangled they want to be with US dominated finance.

The Order is not an aberration but rather a continuation of a decades long push to expand the reach and power of sanctions. As the Order shows, sanctions may seem like an expedient solution to modern political problems. It is convenient and useful for a state to have expanded tools to address national security threats, doubly so where those tools do not require direct military intervention. But this is not without consequence: using sanctions for illegitimate ends with little regard to means or substance stretches sanctions to the detriment of legitimacy of law and trust in global finance. The longevity of sanctions as an effective national security tool requires elements of fairness and predictability than twisting them to fit immediate problems.

CONCLUSION

The Order was borne of the US Executive's immediate political need to keep funds from the Taliban and avoid recognizing them as the legitimate government of Afghanistan while also avoiding the appearance of interfering with the judiciary. The Executive saw sanctions as a neat legal solution to achieving these national security aims.

However, that solution is imperfect—the sanctions are lacking in form and substance when measured by the standards of domestic and international law. This deficiency is not an accident but part of a long push by the Executive to expand the utility of sanctions in its national security toolkit. This trend is leading to a shift in perceptions of sanctions from principled to arbitrary. The consequence of this push is an undermining of legitimacy of sanctions and national security law, as well as mistrust of centralized global finance.

Ultimately what happens in the Havlish and Does cases is irrelevant. The real wrongful act was freezing the funds on nonsensical grounds to begin with, depriving DAB and Afghanistan of funds at a critical moment for the country, an unconscionably cruel act. The damage from this act cannot be undone even by returning ownership of the funds now. That ownership is, coincidentally, still up in the air. The United States seems in no hurry to do anything with the DAB assets. A second wrongful act could still occur, which would be dispensing the funds for anything—including humanitarian aid—other than DAB's mission of stabilizing the Afghan economy.

An admission by the executive that the Order was a mistake and repealing the Order would help to reset the status quo for sanctions. But is unlikely. Nor can the damage be undone of crippling the Afghan economy because of domestic court cases and sour grapes after the United States retreated from Afghanistan, its proxy government immediately dissipated, and the Taliban regained control. What can be done is to unfreeze and return these funds to DAB so it can provide badly needed assistance to a country destabilized in no small part by these very sanctions. To achieve this, citizens, civil society, and other states must exert continual political pressure on the United States Unfreezing these funds would help to restore order to national security principles, law, and finance, but most importantly would actually benefit the people of Afghanistan.

NOTES

1. M. Larrick. Queen Mary University of London, UK. Email: mlarrick@gmail.com
2. Executive Order on Protecting Certain Property of Da Afghanistan Bank for the Benefit of the People of Afghanistan (Feb. 11, 2022).
3. Michelle Nichols, *U.N. has millions in Afghanistan bank, but cannot use it,* Reuters (Feb. 3, 2022).
4. Press Release Of Da Afghanistan Bank On The Decision Of United States Of America Regarding The Foreign Exchange Reserves Of Afghanistan (Feb. 12, 2022).
5. LICENSE No. DABRESERVES-EO-2022-886895-1 (Feb. 11, 2022) OFAC.
6. Statement of Interest of the United States of America (Feb. 11, 2022) Dept. of Justice, *filed in: John Does 1 through 7 v. Taliban et al; In Re: Terrorist Attacks on September 11, 2001; Havlish v. Bin-Laden et al.*
7. Codified at 50 U.S.C. 1701 *et seq.*
8. Codified at 50 U.S.C. 1601 *et seq.*
9. The Order, *preamble.*
10. Federal Reserve Act (1913), Sec. 25B.
11. OFAC License, *supra* note vi.
12. *Does 1 through 7 v. The Taliban et al.,* (SDNY) No. 20 Misc. 740 (KPF).
13. *Havlish v. Bin-Laden et. al.*, (SDNY) No. 03 Civ. 9848 (GBD) (SN).
14. Final Default Judgment, *Does 1 through 7 v. The Taliban et al.,* SDNY (Jan. 4, 2016); *and* Final Default Judgment, *Havlish v. Bin-Laden et. al.*, SDNY (Dec. 22, 2011).
15. Emergency Motion for Writ of Execution, *Does 1 through 7 v. The Taliban et al.,* SDNY (Aug. 26, 2021), Misc Action No. 1:20-mc-00740-KPF; Writ of Execution, *Havlish, el al. v. Iran, et al.,* Case No. 03-cv-9848, ECF No. 526-1.

16. Corn, G., *et al.* (eds), *National Security Law: Principles and Policy, Second Edition* (2019) pp. 138.

17. Scott R. Anderson, *What's Happening with Afghanistan's Assets?*, Lawfare (Feb. 18, 2022).

18. https://home.treasury.gov/policy-issues/financial-sanctions/faqs/topic/1501

19. National Emergencies Act (1967) 50 U.S.C. § 1621. NEA § 1631.

20. International Emergency Economic Powers Act (1977) 50 U.S.C. § 1701.

21. IEEPA § 1702.

22. Newcomb and Roberts pp 1369, quoting 31 C.F.R. § 536.201(a).

23. *The International Emergency Economic Powers Act: Origins, Evolution, and Use*, Congressional Research Service, Updated March 25, 2022 (the "CRS Report").

24. Newcomb and Roberts pp. 1345.

25. CRS Report pp. 24.

26. Ortblad, V. (2008) *Criminal Prosecution in Sheep's Clothing: The Punitive Effects of OFAC Freezing Sanctions* in Journal of Crim. Law and Criminology, Vol. 98 pp. 1440.

27. Newcomb and Roberts pp. 1362–1364.

28. Newcomb and Roberts pp. 1362.

29. Uniting and Strengthening America by Providing Appropriate Tools Required to Intercept and Obstruct Terrorism (USA PATRIOT) Act of 2001, P.L. 107-56, 115 Stat. 272.

30. CRS Report at pp. 13.

31. CRS Report at pp. 14.

32. FRA 25B.

33. The Order.

34. IEEPA, 35 U.S.C. § 1701 (b).

35. Newcomb and Roberts pp 1359 discuss the requirement to define the threat under IEEPA.

36. Newcomb and Roberts pp. 1356.

37. The Order and Statement of Interest at pp. 11.

38. Newcomb and Roberts pp. 1362.

39. CRS Report pp. 14 (In fact, the third power has only been used once, in 2003 against Iraqi assets under E.O. 13290).

40. See Da Afghanistan Bank Law, 2003 Article 2: Objectives.

41. 12 U.S.C. § 623.

42. Hufbauer, et al. (2007, cited in Cameron, I. and Moiseienko, A. 2021. *International Sanctions.* Available at: https://www.oxfordbibliographies.com/view/document/obo-9780199796953/obo-9780199796953-0220.xml?rskey=vU8zlt&result=2&q=international+sanctions#firstMatch (Accessed: 9/10/2022)).

43. Ruys, T. (2016). 'Sanctions, Retorsions and Countermeasures: Concepts and International Legal Framework' in van den Herik, L. (ed.) *Research Handbook on UN Sanctions and International Law.* Cheltenham: Edward Elgar Publishing Limited, pp. 17–18.

44. International Law Commission (2001, vol. II) *Responsibility of States for Internationally Wrongful Acts*, Article 38 (the "ILC Articles").

45. Ruys at pp. 1, citing J. Law and E.A. Martin (eds.), *A Dictionary of Law* (Oxford: OUP)(2014), "sanction."

46. Ruys at pp. 2.

47. ILC Articles.

48. See ILC Articles Part Two, Chapter I: *General Principles.*

49. ILC Articles, Part One, Chapter II: *Attribution of Conduct to a State.*

50. Jianming Shen, *The Non-Intervention Principle and Humanitarian Interventions Under International Law*, Int'l Legal Theory, Vol. 7(1) (2001).

51. Supra note xiv, pp. 148.

52. Ruys at pp. 10.

53. Ruys at pp. 17.

54. Mortimer Sellers, *The Legitimacy of Humanitarian Intervention Under International Law*, Legal Theory, Vol. 7(1) (2001).

55. Ortblad at pp. 1460.

56. Ruys at pp. 10.

57. U.S. Relations With Afghanistan, U.S. Dept. of State (published Aug. 15, 2022) *available at* https://www.state.gov/u-s-relations-with-afghanistan/.

58. *Economic Causes of Afghanistan's Humanitarian Crisis*, Human Rights Watch (Aug. 4, 2022).

59. Newcomb and Roberts pp. 1359.

60. *Afghanistan Central Bank Reserves*, Congressional Research Service (Feb. 23, 2022) pp. 1.

61. Supra note lvi.

62. IF12052 p1

63. Newcomb and Roberts pp. 1345 and 1354.

64. CRS Report pp. 8.

65. Executive Order 13224 (2001).

66. Otblad at pp. 1461.

67. Newcomb and Roberts pp. 1331–1332.

BIBLIOGRAPHY

Afghanistan Central Bank Reserves, Congressional Research Service (Feb. 23, 2022).

Corn, G. *et al.* (eds.), *National Security Law: Principles and Policy, Second Edition* (2019).

Da Afghanistan Bank Law, 2003 Article 2: Objectives.

Does 1 through 7 v. The Taliban et al. (SDNY) No. 20 Misc. 740 (KPF).

Economic Causes of Afghanistan's Humanitarian Crisis, Human Rights Watch (Aug. 4, 2022).

Emergency Motion for Writ of Execution, *Does 1 through 7 v. The Taliban et al.*, SDNY (Aug. 26, 2021), Misc Action No. 1:20-mc-00740-KPF; Writ of Execution, *Havlish, et al. v. Iran et al.*, Case No. 03-cv-9848, ECF No. 526-1.

Executive Order 13224 Blocking Property and Prohibiting Transactions with Persons Who Commit, Threaten to Commit, or Support Terrorism (Sept. 23, 2001).

Executive Order on Protecting Certain Property of Da Afghanistan Bank for the Benefit of the People of Afghanistan (Feb. 11, 2022).

Federal Reserve Act (1913).

Final Default Judgment, *Does 1 through 7 v. The Taliban et al.*, SDNY (Jan. 4, 2016); *and* Final Default Judgment, *Havlish v. Bin-Laden et. al.*, SDNY (Dec. 22, 2011).

Havlish v. Bin-Laden et al. (SDNY) No. 03 Civ. 9848 (GBD) (SN).

Havlish v. Taliban/In re 9/11 Attacks - Frozen Afghan Assets (Amicus), Center for Constitutional Rights (Apr. 25, 2022).

Hufbauer et al. (2007, cited in Cameron, I. and Moiseienko, A. 2021. *International Sanctions*. Available at: https://www.oxfordbibliographies.com/view/document/obo-9780199796953/obo-9780199796953-0220.xml?rskey=vU8zlt&result=2&q=international+sanctions#firstMatch (Accessed: 9/10/2022)).

International Emergency Economic Powers Act (1977) 50 U.S.C. § 1701.50 U.S.C. 1601.

International Law Commission (2001, Vol. II) *Responsibility of States for Internationally Wrongful Acts*, Article 38 (the "ILC Articles").

LICENSE No. DABRESERVES-EO-2022-886895-1 (Feb. 11, 2022) OFAC.

Michelle Nichols, *U.N. has Millions in Afghanistan Bank, but Cannot Use It*, Reuters (Feb. 3, 2022).

National Emergencies Act (1967) 50 U.S.C. § 1621. NEA § 1631.

Ortblad, V. (2008). Criminal Prosecution in Sheep's Clothing: The Punitive Effects of OFAC Freezing Sanctions. *Journal of Criminal Law and Criminology*, Vol. 98: 1439–1465..

Press Release of Da Afghanistan Bank on the Decision of United States of America Regarding the Foreign Exchange Reserves of Afghanistan (Feb. 12, 2022).

Ruys, T. (2016). Sanctions, Retorsions and Countermeasures: Concepts and International Legal Framework. In van den Herik, L. (ed.), *Research Handbook on UN Sanctions and International Law*. Cheltenham: Edward Elgar Publishing Limited.

Scott R. Anderson, *What's Happening with Afghanistan's Assets?*, Lawfare (Feb. 18, 2022).

Sellers, M. (2001). The Legitimacy of Humanitarian Intervention Under International Law. *Legal Theory*, Vol. 7, No. 1: 1440–1466.

Shen, J. (2001). The Non-Intervention Principle and Humanitarian Interventions Under International Law. *International Legal Theory*, Vol. 7, No. 1: 1–32.

Statement of Interest of the United States of America (Feb. 11, 2022). Dept. of Justice, *filed in: John Does 1 through 7 v. Taliban et al; In Re: Terrorist Attacks on September 11, 2001; Havlish v. Bin-Laden et al.*

The International Emergency Economic Powers Act: Origins, Evolution, and Use, Congressional Research Service, Updated March 25, 2022 (the "CRS Report").

U.S. Relations with Afghanistan, U.S. Dept. of State (published Aug. 15, 2022). https://www.state.gov/u-s-relations-with-afghanistan/.

Uniting and Strengthening America by Providing Appropriate Tools Required to Intercept and Obstruct Terrorism (USA PATRIOT) Act of 2001, P.L. 107-56, 115 Stat. 272.

Chapter 9

US Withdrawal from Afghanistan and Its Impact on War on Terror and Peace and Stability in South Asia

Aslam Khan[1]

INTRODUCTION

Afghanistan has always been the center of attraction due to its geostrategic location, foreign intervention, religious fundamentalism, drug trade, and Terrorism. Its strategic importance is evident as all the superpowers of their times have engaged or confronted with Afghanistan. Afghanistan has been the buffer state in the "Great Game" between British India and the Russian Empire. British concern of Russian influence in Afghanistan led to First Anglo-Afghan War (1838–1842), Second Anglo-Afghan War (1878–1880), and the Third Anglo-Afghan War (1919) (Khan, 2022: 1). To end the Second Anglo-Afghan War, the Treaty of Gandamak was signed between the British government and Afghan ruler Yaqub Khan to enable peace between both countries (Marsden, 2010: 9). This treaty gave right to Britishers to conduct the foreign relations of Afghanistan and Yaqub Khan was promised to safeguard Afghanistan from foreign aggression (Smith, 1986). After the Third Anglo-Afghan War, Great Britain lost control in Afghanistan due to a truce signed on August 08, 1919 (Marsden, 2010: 10). The most important development took place in 1893 when Afghan ruler Abdur Rahman Khan and British bureaucrat Sir Henry M. Durand agreed to mark the boundary between Afghanistan and British India known as Durand Line, where the interests of the local tribes and other indigenous people were ignored (Rasanayagam, 2011: 11). A closer look of nineteenth century reflects the great diplomatic endeavor between Soviet and British Empire. The demarcation of Afghanistan's border with the USSR and the signing of a Friendship Treaty in 1921 reflects a deep strategic outlook of Russia in Afghan affairs. World War II concluded with the fall of the mighty British Empire, and the Soviet Union, along with the United States emerged as the superpower changing the political course of South Asia. The newly independent state Pakistan, after the partition of India, became a strategic ally of America. The US-drafted it's South Asia policy by considering Pakistan to counter Soviet influence in Afghanistan. The Soviet invasion of Afghanistan in 1979 again provides Pakistan a chance to play in US Chessboard.

SOVIET INVASION OF AFGHANISTAN

On December 24, 1979, the Soviet Union invaded Afghanistan under the pretext of upholding the Soviet-Afghan Treaty signed in 1978 (Smith, 1986). This resulted in Soviet-Afghan War in the 1980s against Mujaheddeens having the support of Pakistan and the United States. The making of Mujahedeen and training and support to other warlords through Pakistan was a masterstroke of the United States that resulted in the defeat of the USSR and one of the major causes of Soviet disintegration. "Operation Cyclone" the largest covert operation by US President Nixon provided economic and military assistance through Pakistan (Greentree, 2019). The United States also provided Stinger Missiles to Mujaheddins to down the Russian jets and helicopters. US military aid to Mujahedeen channeled through Pakistan ranged from US$30 million to $280 million making it the biggest Central Intelligence Agency (CIA) covert operation anywhere in the world (Rasanayagam, 2011: 105). By early 1988, the Soviets started withdrawing from Afghanistan without victory. But the fall of the Berlin Wall on November 08, 1989, resulted in the end game for the USSR (Hellfeld, 1989).

This war has changed the political landscape of Afghanistan as the emergence of various extremist groups like Al Qaeda was the outcomes of this long war. But, at the same time, the new dimension of terrorism was also the outcome of US policies in Afghanistan. The geostrategic situation of South Asia changed dramatically as, on the one hand, acquiring nuclear power by both India and Pakistan and their rivalry brought Afghanistan into the limelight as the same mujahedeen were fighting from the side of Pakistan in Kashmir that had direct implications for India's security and, on the other hand, deteriorating relations between the United States and India resulted in the deep strategic partnership between India and Russia and the United States–Pakistan.

THE RISE OF TALIBAN

After the collapse of the Soviet Union and the United States low importance to the region gave Mujahedeen a chance to expand further. As Mujahedeen fought against the Soviet Union in the pursuit of Jihad, an element of religious fundamentalism could not consolidate the unity and power interests that gave rise to factionalism. The emergence of the Taliban (a group of religious students and scholars) on the pretext of security, and polity under the religious code of conduct got popular support and became a strong political force within a short period. Starting from Southern Afghanistan, by 1994, the Taliban took control of most of the provinces in the South from the other factions. By 1996 Taliban took control of the capital city of Kabul and almost 70% of the country. They got the recognition from Saudi Arabia, UAE, and Pakistan. Since the Taliban's initially had footprints of Wahhabist ideology that emerged from Saudi Arabia and also got huge funding for its spread Saudi Arabia is much closer. But soon after controlling the affairs of Afghanistan, the Taliban became the subject of criticism by their unwarranted actions such as the destruction of Bamiyan idols, several restrictions on women, and sharia punishments. The hosting of Osama Bin Laden, the Chief of the Al-Qaeda group in Afghanistan with the objective of liberation of the Islamic world from the non-Islamic influences and this exactly attracted the US attention as America was the sole superpower. Religious fundamentalism was all-time high as the presence of Jihadists from Kashmir to Central Asia to Uighur in China. But, the event of September 11, 2001, changed the course of Afghan affairs as planes slammed into the World Trade Center, the Pentagon and a Pennsylvania field and brought nearly 3,000 people to their deaths. The event shocked the United States and president called the attack the attacks "crusade" out of frustration. Reacting to the remark of Bush, the French Foreign Minister, commented that "We have to avoid a clash of civilizations at all costs." Reacting further, the Taliban's second in command Mohammad Hasan Akhund appealed to Afghani people to prepare for Jihad in the possibility of a US attack (Ford, 2001).

AMERICA'S GLOBAL WAR ON TERROR

For the 9/11 attacks, Al-Qaeda was held responsible by President Bush, and he immediately started his campaign to get international support to fight a war against terrorism. America got unprecedented support from all over the world as its adversaries such as China, Iran, and Russia, also offered support for the global war on terrorism (GWOT). The United States tried to get hold of Osama Bin Laden but the Taliban refused to hand over Al-Qaeda Chief. The United States launched a full-fledged attack on Afghanistan on October 7, 2001, with the allies, especially NATO and UK, and call the action "Operation Enduring Freedom." This operation changed the course of regional politics especially since Pakistan was caught between the Taliban and United

States. But, Pakistan took a U-turn from its Afghan policy and joined the US War on Terror. Uzbekistan was the first country where US special forces were present at the former Soviet Union airbase. Later the United States used Pakistani airbases for the attacks. Taliban could not resist long, and America took control of Afghanistan and formed an interim government led by Hamid Karzai after taking control of Kabul. After heavy United States and allies' presence in the region and the subsequent gorilla war technique used by the Taliban always kept the US forces engaged, and in the span of twenty years, the US-backed government never had full control of Afghanistan. On the other hand, the United States' long presence in Afghanistan was a cause of concern for both Russia and China. The United States, too, had the opportunity to look closely at four nuclear-armed states: Russia, China, India, Pakistan, and especially Iran. Another important point to be made here is that the whole US military strategy was completely dependent on Pakistan, and the latter took full advantage of the situation and got a huge amount of coalition support funds estimated at $33.4 billion till 2017 (Rana, 2017).

US PEACE TALKS WITH TALIBAN AND WITHDRAWAL FROM AFGHANISTAN

As time progressed, the cost of counter-terror operations and United States and coalition forces causality rose, and strong resistance and advancement of Taliban with the help of ISI of Pakistan and China made the United States rethink its strategies. If we go by a fundamental understanding of the State's behavior, we find State is a rational actor and goal-oriented, and its goals are consistent and cost-sensitive. States can change their strategies in the face of external constraints and opportunities changes.

The realist approach to the Afghanistan case indicates the cost of the War on Terror had a huge impact on the US economy and an uncertain outcome compelled the United States to assess the cost of war. As per the BBC report, more than 3,586 coalition soldiers have lost their lives since 2001 that includes two-thirds of American soldiers. The United States spending on Afghanistan, including military and reconstruction funds, also reached US$978 billion by 2020 (bbc.com, 2021). US peace talks with the Taliban can be better understood in the theory of defensive realism, where Kenneth Waltz and Stephen Walt focuses on a structural concept known as the offense–defense balance. They argued that the military might, at any point in time, be categorized as favoring either offense or defense. If defense has a clear advantage over offense great powers will have little incentive to use force to gain power and vice versa (Glaser and Kaufmann, 1998). After analyzing the on-ground situation in Afghanistan, President Obama announced the beginning of negotiations with the Taliban at Doha, Qatar, to achieve lasting peace in Afghanistan. Pakistan and Qatar were the architects of this peace negotiation initiative. Responding to the initiative, US Deputy National Security Advisor Ben Rhodes commented "The United States will be supporting a process that is fundamentally Afghan-led. We can play a role in talking to the Taliban as well in supporting that peace process—and because we have issues of our own to bring up with them" (Roberts, 2013). After Obama, President Trump negotiated a withdrawal agreement in February 2020 with the Taliban that completely excluded the Afghanistan government and agreed to release 5,000 Taliban, and May 1, 2021, was set as the date of final US withdrawal. Although, President Ashraf Ghani objected to the release of the Taliban. In the agreement, the Taliban agreed not to attack coalition forces, but time and again, they targeted Afghan Security forces. There was a lot of intelligence input from the CIA that the Taliban is working closely with Al-Qaeda, but the United States went as per the plans and started with the calling of US troops in phases.

The US Withdrawal became an issue in the US election, and Democratic Party candidate Joe Biden promised to bring back US forces from Afghanistan. After winning the election, Biden reviewed the deal during Trump Presidency, endorsed the terms, and announced the final withdrawal by September 2021 (The White House, 2021). Biden went with the withdrawal plan set by Donald Trump, and finally, on April 14, 2021, Biden announced that all troops will be called back from Afghanistan by September 11, 2021 (Roberts, 2013).

But, in May 2021 heavy fight started between the Taliban and US-trained Afghan forces. Thousands of causalities were reported from the heavy fights, and the Taliban succeeded in controlling most of the provinces. The United States tried to back Afghan forces with massive airstrikes but to no avail. Later, the Taliban started gaining control without resistance, and finally, on August 15, 2021, Kabul fell to the Taliban with the accusation of gross human rights violations, especially against women. America was forced to deal with the Taliban for safe withdrawal as the great power competition rose again (Morton, 2021). This time China-Pak nexus is becoming more complex for the United States. The approach of US withdrawal from Afghanistan resulted in a swift control of the Taliban on Afghan affairs. The exit of US and NATO forces from Afghanistan created new challenges for Afghanistan and the region. From the Taliban's perspective, it was a moral win and outlined the influence of the Taliban in Afghan politics (Danvers, 2021). But a serious question raised here is why the United States is forced to strike a peace deal. Is the goal of eradicating terrorism or the phrase Afghanistan is the graveyard of empires true? The War on Terror has cost millions of lives, destroyed communities and livelihoods, and created massive refugee and humanitarian crises but with what achievement?

IMPACT OF US WITHDRAWAL

The humiliating departure of the United States from Afghanistan has severe implications for War on Terror. It can be termed as the beginning of the end of US hegemony and degraded the status of the sole Super Power. The hasty and bloody withdrawal was criticized at home and made the political environment hot. Bruce Riedel, a former CIA operative, called the withdrawal "the most egregious is the complete failure of strategic planning and diplomacy" (Harris, 2021). Trump used the words like "greatest embarrassment," and "greatest technical mistakes." In a statement, Trump said, "Afghanistan under Biden was not a withdrawal; it was a surrender. Will he apologize for the greatest tactical mistake in history, pulling the military out before the citizens?" (Hindustan Times, 2021). The Defence Secretary of the UK, Ben Wallace, called it a "failure of the international community" (Dawn, 2021). Iranian President Ebrahim Raisi commented that "The military defeat and US withdrawal from Afghanistan should offer an opportunity to restore life, security and lasting peace in that country" (Dawn, 2021). Terrorist outfits worldwide can further boost up to take power through violence and the act of terrorism. US Withdrawal is being debated as a defeat for the United States and its allies. The United States, which has been fighting for Al-Qaeda and Islamic State for decades and cornered them in one way or the other, will again strengthen and emerge as a big threat to the region and international community through terror and violence. The active transnational network of terrorists will have the serious implication for peace and stability in Asia, Africa, and the Middle East as the presence of Al-Qaeda, Islamic State, Al-Qaeda in Islamic Maghreb, and Boko Haram have the wider objectives of establishing the states based on violence and terror. The sectarian divide and deadly suicide bombing in religious places such as mosques are evident in the present situation. On October 08, 2021, ISIS-K carried out a deadly attack through suicide bombing at a mosque in Kunduz. This attack killed more than fifty people, and hundreds were left severely injured, and ISIS-K openly took responsibility for the attack (abcnews.go.com). The close association of various terrorist outfits with Pakistan's ISI is a cause of concern not only for the region but for Pakistan too, as the organizations like Tahreek-e-Taliban Pakistan (TTP) are continuously fighting with Pakistan's army (Khan, 2022).

While it is, an era of strong alliances and support for the weak ally is vital. The United States has lost its credibility as a reliable partner, and it can impact its interests in Vietnam, South China Sea, and more. The embrace of China to the Taliban regime and its offer of unconditional support threaten Western interests in South Asia. The only thing mostly visible is to make an appeal to the Taliban for respect for human rights, peace, and so on. The vacuum created by the United States was immediately taken over by the Chinese ambition of great power. The swift withdrawal of the United States and small resistance by Afghan forces already evident how much China was involved in the affairs of Afghanistan. The present withdrawal justifies the Chinese narrative of the United States in decline and its irresistible rise, especially in the context of smaller states in need of support and protection. The China–Pakistan axis has dismantled US designs in Afghanistan and the region (Khan, 2022). India has a great role in the reconstruction of Afghanistan after 9/11 and maintaining a great relationship with Afghanistan forced it to change their foreign policy in the changed strategic scenario as Indian security concerns were seriously ignored by the United States and its allies (Khan, 2022).

IMPLICATIONS TO REGIONAL POLITICS

The Asian balance of power has been shifted toward China by the chaotic withdrawal of the United States. The strange relationship with Pakistan also adds more trouble, as Imran Khan has already made it clear in a statement, "Nobody emerges victorious from wars. Even the winner is a loser. Pakistan had paid a high price in the past by becoming a part of the war on terror. Now Pakistan will not fight wars but bring countries together" (Raza, 2020). With the help of Pakistan, China has tightened its grip and outrightly supported the Taliban after the US withdrawal and is deeply involved with the Afghan establishment. India is the worst affected by this crisis, as there is always a security threat from Pak-Taliban designs in Jammu and Kashmir (Khan, 2022).

India is deeply concerned by the developments in Afghanistan as, time and again, the terrorist outfits from Afghanistan have been used to destabilize the Indian state of Jammu and Kashmir. Indian Prime Minister Modi raised his concerns in the meeting of the heads of the state of the Shanghai Cooperation Organization (SCO) and the Collective Security Treaty Organization on Afghanistan by mentioning that "the Afghan soil should not be used to spread terrorism in any country and called for having a code of conduct to prevent cross-border terrorism and terror financing. He further said the recent developments in Afghanistan would have the 'greatest impact' on neighboring countries like India and that there is a need for regional focus and cooperation in dealing with the issue" (The Print, September 17, 2021). He also raised concerns about the uncontrolled flow of drugs, illegal weapons, and human trafficking. The prime objective of the new Taliban establishment is to get recognition from the international community, and they badly need India for that purpose. Taliban's acting Foreign Minister, Amir Muttaqi has already ensured that its soil was not used against any country (The Economic Times, November 12, 2021). India's prime security concern is a two-front battle with Pakistan over the Line of Control (LOC) and China's Line of Actual Control (LAC). India and Pakistan have fought several wars over Kashmir. Pakistan has always suffered setbacks as there is no parity in conventional war. Therefore, Pakistan adopted the policy of cross-border terrorism. There is a long history of infiltration into Indian territory by Pakistan, and previously mujahedeen from Afghanistan have taken part after the withdrawal of the Soviet Union. As mentioned in an opinion on news18 that by 1993 alone, nearly 400 Afghan mujahideen of Hezb-e-Islami of Afghan warlord Gulbuddin Hekmatyar were present in Kashmir Valley, which increased subsequently. In the first two decades of the Kashmir insurgency, about 3,000 terrorists were killed by Afghan Mujahideens and Pakistanis (Beigh, 2021). Various terrorist outfits from Pakistan, such as Lashkar-e-Taiba, Lashkar-e-Jhangvi, and Jaish-e-Mohammed, can advance with the help of the ISI-Taliban nexus. These groups have been instrumental in carrying terrorist strikes in India, that is, Pulwama Strike, Mumbai terrorist attack, and the attack on Indian Parliament. The two hostile nuclear neighbors are not a threat to regional security but to global security as a whole.

In the case of Pakistan, the Taliban takeover is not as attractive as it was analyzed. Although Pakistan has great role in the Taliban Moment earlier and later but for now, the business is not as usual. Initially, the response of Pakistan PM Imran Khan after the Taliban's takeover of Kabul was, "Taliban have broken the shackles of slavery" (Muzaffar, 2021). Although Pakistan played a key role in Peace Deal, its role has been subjected to duality and suspicion. Their unconditional support to the Taliban on the one hand and a key partner of the United States in the war against terror on the other is highly contradictory. Pakistan's interest was visible in ousting the Afghan regime due to its close ties with India. It's a fact that Pakistan certainly has an advantage by the fall of Kabul, but it also has several challenges. The issues such as Durand Line, ISIS-K, TTP, and refugee influx continue to haunt Pakistan (Khan, 2022). Durand Line is a bone of contention between the two countries, as we have witnessed several border skirmishes recently. Pakistan is also facing a grave threat from TTP as they frequently execute several deadliest terror attacks inside Pakistan. The TTP is known for targeting the Pakistani Military and Intelligence agencies. Consequently, the Pakistani Army initiated "Operation Zarb-e-Azb in 2014," which resulted in a big blow to TTP and a sharp decline in terrorist activities by the TTP. But after the Taliban takeover, there was a sharp rise in terrorist activities by TTP. As per the report of the Brookings Institution, The TTP claimed 282 attacks in 2021 alone and said that it had killed more than 500 law enforcement personnel, and it also claimed an additional 42 attacks in January 2022 (Afzal, 2022). The massive influx of refugees and strong resistance in Baluchistan make the situation more fragile.

CONCLUSION

It is evident from the above discussion that the Global War on Terror has a strong jolt for the United States by falling into the hands of the Taliban and resulting in the decline of US power. The GWOT has cost more than 2,500 US soldiers along with 3,846 US contractors, and other Western allies have lost 1,144 service personnel while Afghan Military has lost 66,000 personals along with millions of civilians, aid workers, and journalists just for the flashback of Taliban regime of 1996 (Knickmeyer, 2021). The kind of swift surrender by Afghan forces reflects the Taliban as an unchallenged force in the politics of Afghanistan. A new strategic dimension has emerged in South, Central, and West Asia. The states are reshaping their policies to secure their national interest. China has the upper hand in South Asia due to the failure in Afghanistan. Americans are forced to reset their ties with long-term strategic ally Pakistan as Islamabad had always played the central role in American strategic goals. Although Pakistan has successfully dismantled the Indian strategy, still struggling with the fundamentalist groups that have the backing of the Afghan Taliban. Terrorism needs to be redefined if a superpower, along with NATO and other allies, fails to tackle such forces and is forced to strike a deal with the same actors. Now UN designated terrorists are enjoying ministerial birth in the new Taliban regime. While India and Pakistan need to identify their core interests, the radical elements can have a broader objective. Afghanistan again has proved that it is a graveyard of superpowers as they defeated all the mighty empires such as Great Britain, USSR, and the United States. The great game is not over yet, only the players are being changed as China's deep involvement and decline of Western influence is yet to write a new chapter.

NOTE

1. A. Khan. Mahatma Gandhi Central University, Bihar, India. Email: aslamamu@gmail.com

BIBLIOGRAPHY

Abcnews. (2021). ISIS-K claims responsibility of suicide attack at mosque. Retrieved from https://abcnews.go.com/Politics/live-updates/afghanistan-withdrawal-live-updates/?id=79482353

Afzal, M. (2022). Pakistan's ambivalent approach toward a resurgent Tehrik-e-Taliban Pakistan. Retrieved from https://www.brookings.edu/blog/order-from-chaos

/2022/02/11/pakistans-ambivalent-approach-toward-a-resurgent-tehrik-e-taliban-pakistan/

BBC. (2021). Afghanistan: How many refugees are there and where will they go? Retrieved from https://www.bbc.com/news/world-asia-58283177

BBC. (2021a). Taliban are back - what next for Afghanistan? Retrieved from https://www.bbc.com/news/world-asia-49192495

CNN. (2011). Obama announces Afghanistan troop withdrawal plan. Retrieved from https://edition.cnn.com/2011/POLITICS/06/22/afghanistan.troops.drawdown/index.html

CNN. (2021). US War in Afghanistan. Retrieved from https://edition.cnn.com/2013/10/28/world/operation-enduring-freedom-fast-facts/index.html

Dawn. (2021). 'Unfinished problem': World leaders react to Taliban's reclaiming of Afghanistan. Retrieved from https://www.dawn.com/news/1641001

Danvers, W. (2021). US withdrawal from Afghanistan creates challenges for China, Russia and Iran. The Hill. Retrieved from https://thehill.com/opinion/national-security/569861-us-withdrawal-from-afghanistan-creates-challenges-for-china-russia/ (accessed 13/05/2023).

Ford, P. (2001). Europe criges at Bush 'crusade' against terrorists. The Christian Science Chronicle Monitor. Retrieved from https://www.csmonitor.com/2001/0919/p12s2-woeu.html

Glaser, L. and Kaufmann, C. (1998). What is the offense-defense balance and can we measure it? (Offense, Defense, and International Politics). *International Security*, vol. 28, no. 4, p. 44. Retrieved from https://web.stanford.edu/class/polisci211z/2.1/Glaser%20%26%20Kaufmann%20IS%201988.pdf

Greentree, T. (2019). Afghanistan: Remembering the long, long war we would rather forget. Retrieved from https://warontherocks.com/2019/02/afghanistan-remembering-the-long-long-war-we-would-rather-forget/

Harris, S. (2021). After Afghanistan falls, the blame game begins. The Washington Post. Retrieved from https://www.washingtonpost.com/national-security/taliban-us-intelligence-afghanistan/2021/08/16/c59f4416-febd-11eb-85f2-b871803f65e4_story.html

Hellfeld, M. (1989). The fall of the Berlin Wall - November 9, 1989. Retrieved from https://www.dw.com/en/the-fall-of-the-berlin-wall-november-9-1989/a-4812768

Hindustan Times. (2021). 'Greatest tactical mistake': Trump's fresh salvo on Biden's hasty withdrawal from Afghanistan. Retrieved from https://www.hindustantimes.com/world-news/greatest-tactical-mistake-trump-s-fresh-salvo-on-biden-s-hasty-withdrawal-from-afghanistan-101629538480423-amp.html

Khan, A. (2022). Afghanistan Crisis and Its Implications on South Asian Peace and Security. In Verma. K.S. (Ed.), *Changing Dimensions of India's Foreign Policy*. Delhi: Victorious Publishers, pp. 342–354.

Knickmeyer, E. (2021). Costs of the Afghanistan War, in lives and dollars. Retrieved from https://apnews.com/article/middle-east-business-afghanistan-43d8f53b35e80ec18c130cd683e1a38f

Marsden, P. (2010). *Afghanistan Aid, Armies and Empires*. London: I.B. Tauris.

Muzaffar, M. (2021). Taliban have broken 'the shackles of slavery,' says Pakistan PM Imran Khan. Retrieved from https://www.independent.co.uk/asia/south-asia/taliban-pakistan-imran-khan-afghanistan-b1903821.html

Morton, B. (2021). UK confident it can get Britons out of Afghanistan, Ben Wallace says. BBC. August 2021. Retrieved from https://www.bbc.co.uk/news/uk-58228190 (accessed 13/05/2023).

Rasanayagam, A. (2011). *Afghanistan: A Modern History*. London: I.B. Tauris.

Raza, I.S. (2020). Pakistan not to take part in anyone else's war: PM. Retrieved from https://www.dawn.com/news/1527386

Riedel, B. (2013). Pakistan's Osama bin Laden report: Was Pakistan clueless or complicit in Harboring Bin Laden? Retrieved from https://www.brookings.edu/opinions/pakistans-osama-bin-laden-report-was-pakistan-clueless-or-complicit-in-harboring-bin-laden/

Roberts, D. (2013). Taliban peace talks: 'Peace and reconciliation' negotiations to take place in Qatar. The Guardian. June, 2013. Retrieved from https://www.theguardian.com/world/2013/jun/18/us-peace-talks-taliban-afghanistan

Shimko, K. (2016). *International Relations: Perspectives, Controversies and Readings*. Boston: Cengage Learning.

Smith, C. (1986). The Great Game in Afghanistan. Library of Congress. Retrieved from https://www.loc.gov/ghe/cascade/index.html?appid=a0930b1f4e424987ba68c28880f088ea&bookmark=3rd%20Anglo-Afghan%20War

The Economic Times. (2021). Taliban govt making all-out efforts to ensure that Afghan soil is not used against any country: Muttaqi. Retrieved from https://economictimes.indiatimes.com/news/international/world-news/taliban-govt-making-all-out-efforts-to-ensure-that-afghan-soil-is-not-used-against-any-country-muttaqi/articleshow/87673135.cms?utm_source=contentofinterest&utm_medium=text&utm_campaign=cppst

The Print. (2021). Developments in Afghanistan will have greatest impact on countries like India, PM Modi says. Retrieved from https://theprint.in/diplomacy/developments-in-afghanistan-will-have-greatest-impact-on-countries-like-india-pm-modi-says/735308/

The White House. (2021). Remarks by President Biden on the end of the war in Afghanistan. Retrieved from https://www.whitehouse.gov/briefing-room/speeches-remarks/2021/08/31/remarks-by-president-biden-on-the-end-of-the-war-in-afghanistan/

UN. (2000). Security council imposes wide new measures against Taliban. Retrieved from https://www.un.org/press/en/2000/sc6979.doc.htm

Waltz, K. (1979). *Theory of International Politics*. Reading: Addison-Wesley.

Part III

SOCIOLOGICAL APPROACHES TO CONFLICTS AND SECURITY

Chapter 10

Exploring the Organic Regional Security Model (ORSM) to Construct a Transborder Security Integration in the South Asian Region

Iqbal Shailo[1]

INTRODUCTION

The well-being of the South Asian region depends mainly on understanding the complex history and legacy of conflicts and contradictions among South Asian nations. As the region is geographically connected to neighboring countries, South Asia's socioeconomic growth and political and democratic development are seriously hampered by political instability, ethnic conflicts, insurgencies, internal and external terrorist attacks, and intrastate conflicts. It is a region that is home to one-fifth of the world's population, where poverty and hunger prevail, where ethnic tensions and civil wars are a recurring phenomenon, where disasters and deaths are everyday reality and where hope and aspiration remain alive for democracy, rule of law, justice, and a better future for the millions of people in the region.

The South Asian Association for Regional Cooperation (SAARC), however, has not proven its effectiveness since its inception and has reportedly failed to achieve its well-defined objectives. It is far from being an instrument for promoting a regional unity (Jones, 2009). The association (which includes Afghanistan, Bangladesh, Bhutan, India, Maldives, Nepal, Pakistan, and Sri Lanka) has not taken any bold initiatives to resolve internal conflicts among member states, including the issues of border disputes and border security between Bangladesh, India, and Pakistan.

This chapter is organized as follows: First, it briefly describes the SAARC and its role in transborder relations and regional cooperation. Second, it explores an alternative security paradigm, the Organic Regional Security

Model (ORSM), a new approach to regional security integration in the South Asia region to construct a collective identity and mutual trust. Third, it focuses on the major approaches of the ORSM, highlighting the benefits and advantages of the model. Fourth, it highlights that the ORSM needs to go through various evolutionary phases to accomplish the task of security integration in the region. Fifth, it suggests that constructing a regional organic security community does not require prior political ties, nor preexisting physical or cultural legacies, among its member states. Finally, it postulates that further research is required to engage regional political institutions to formulate mechanisms to construct the ORSM in the better interest of regional peace and economic development in South Asia.

THE ROLE OF THE SAARC IN REGIONAL SECURITY INTEGRATION

The role of the SAARC is limited in bringing forward economic and security issues in the region but each country within the SAARC wants to cooperate with the others (Shailo, 2010). The SAARC is largely seen as a redundant association, and political mistrust and lack of honesty are the two most important elements that damage relations; thus, India and Pakistan are no exception. India is exploring possibilities of increasing its friendship with neighboring countries. India had maintained good bilateral relations with its neighbors during President Parvez Musharraf's regime in Pakistan, as well as the United Progressive Alliance (UPA) led by former Prime Minister Dr. Singh's government throughout the period of 2004–2007.

As for the SAARC, economic and national security issues figure prominently in its charters for member countries, but it does not advocate or take initiatives to form a security alliance at the subregional or regional level. In building a security community, Jones (2008) places greater emphasis on India's specific role in moving away from "command heights" to initiate building functioning, sustainable civil society and media regionally, stabilizing interstate conflicts and strengthening relations with other powerful states in order to sustain its economic strength.

The SAARC has somehow focused on the issue of regional and global terrorism but has not reached a consensus on how to address it. If internal and external security issues are resolved through SAARC initiatives, economic ties and partnerships could grow. India and Pakistan are devastated by internal and external terrorist attacks that frequently interrupt or delay progress on negotiations, dialogues and overtures among other member states. Accordingly, a strong political will on both sides is required to actively run the SAARC.

Even the association's role in the past decade has not reaped any cooperation in the region due to the lack of trust and faith in two regional powers, India and Pakistan. Even they do not like to sit together bilaterally to bridge the gaps created by their own egos and ethos. The role of both Indian and Pakistani prime ministers, Narendra Modi and Imran Khan, respectively, is very confusing as they have no intention of engaging in bilateral dialogues in recent days to find solutions to the ongoing crises and emerging problems that fundamentally depend on each other but have ignored the reality of the region by fueling incursions frequently on both sides of India's and Pakistan's borders.

THE ORGANIC REGIONAL SECURITY MODEL: A NEW APPROACH TO REGIONAL SECURITY INTEGRATION FOR THE SOUTH ASIA REGION

The ORSM of the South Asian region has focused its attention on the conceptual lenses for a negotiation of interests and identities. It asks the perennial question of how political actors imagine the region and how communities on different sides of borders visualize their own regions and foster solidarity and collective values to support an organic regional security integration concept.

I use the word "organic" as an alternative security framework for the South Asian region. According to the *Oxford English Dictionary* (2009), organic means "harmoniously related" or "characterized by natural development." At first glance, the word organic does not seem to fit the theoretical framework of any security concept. The word seems a bit confusing in the analysis of security, but I think the word itself is applicable to a South Asian context. Organic is generally thought to be more sustainable than conventional, and it brings practices from the essential elements, not by any imposed devices from external sources but by a power from within to keep it holy and pure from other interventions. Thus, the ORSM is an alternative security framework for the South Asian region.

South Asian regional security perspectives should involve economic, environmental, military, and societal sectors to reformulate the security paradigm at the bilateral, trilateral or regional level. Buzan (2000) suggests that individual security is rapidly taking on broader societal and political dimensions and, therefore, he advocates the inclusion of various *sectors* in the security complex, such as economic, environmental, societal, political, and military issues. For South Asia, the idea of *sectors* is essential, and, while these sectors have a distinct logic, they cannot be operationally separated from each other. The following can be considered to define an organic security paradigm for the South Asian region.

First, security can be redefined and reconstructed in terms of economic criteria. An economic-globalizing dynamic is the main factor that brings countries, mostly neighbors, closer to each other. Since the inception of the SAARC, South Asian countries have not shown any desire to sign a regional trade agreement. India has several bilateral trade agreements with Bhutan, Maldives, Nepal, and Sri Lanka. But, it has restricted some trade relations with Bangladesh and Pakistan by putting some barriers on the cross-border movement of goods. The member-countries have envisaged the initiation of a free-trade zone (South Asian Free Trade Area [SAFTA]) within the regional boundaries.

Second, the concept of security can be reformulated with respect to human security. While the concept of human security has earlier roots, its recent prominence comes from the 1994 *Human Development Report* of the United Nations Development Program (UNDP). The report has helped solidify the concept of human security, although recognition of people's security independent of state security is nothing new (Axworthy, 2001).

In respect to the subcontinent, millions of people are suffering from insecurity and anxiety. Ethnic conflicts in India (Muslims, *Dalits* and tribal), Pakistan (the *Shiites*, tribal and the *Ahmadiyyas*), and Bangladesh (conflicts occur sometimes between Muslims, Hindus, and other minorities including Indigenous groups for some religious/cultural and political issues fabricated by internal and external factors that occasionally turn into violent unrest) are dominating internal peace and harmony. The poverty-stricken people of the subcontinent are experiencing a lack of human rights, injustice and fair trial, which is an alarming situation for any nation, developing or advanced. Thus, security should be considered in human aspects, too.

Third, the environment is an important aspect of human security, and any threats to human security include environmental degradation. However, the environment as a security issue is not widely accepted and has not received enough attention either by the governments or the public in the South Asian region. Bangladesh, India, and Pakistan have also been facing environmental disasters, and the root of the disasters is regional, not local. Indian waters from Punjab and other tributaries often cause floods in Bangladesh and Pakistan, and Bangladesh is dependent on upstream states, including India, to meet its water needs (Chapman, 2003). The Farakka Barrage, built in India on the Ganges, has made the northern part of Bangladesh a desert, and people are gradually becoming climate refugees (Shailo, 2010). Thus, any security pact making environmental issues a priority would reduce the negative effects in national life.

Fourth, the concept of security in the subcontinent may include the issue of arms control and the theme of nonproliferation. The problem of nuclear nonproliferation has become an issue of anxiety in the region, and antagonism and hostility between India and Pakistan might accidentally escalate nuclear war, as some pundits have suggested, at any time for any causes. As a pre-emptive measure, both countries are holding various initiatives, meetings, and dialogues to reduce the risk of accidental use of nuclear weapons in the region.

Fifth, the subcontinent can expand security in terms of societal aspects, such as friendship and alliances with ethnic units/tribes/groups within the country. The subcontinent can drive for more engagement in cultural aspects, such as sports (cricket, soccer, and SAARC interstate games), cultural programs (musical programs, dances, poetry recitation programs, and competition in literary programs), and education and training (exchange of students, providing SAARC scholarships, and cross-country tours).

These five major approaches, as described above, are an attempt, primarily, to discuss a possibility of an ORSM (much more space is needed to analyze a detailed elaboration of the ORSM to test my model in South Asia.). The security of South Asia is connected to a social, cultural, political, economic, and environmental constellation. South Asian discourses are not different from those of other regions, and they are political resources to deal with the particular events of international order and to justify the actions of any state and its domestic and regional political behavior.

CONSTRUCTION OF THE ORGANIC REGIONAL SECURITY MODEL

India and Pakistan, two regional nuclear powers, do not have any security pact as of yet, and they do not belong to any bilateral security interdependence, although both countries are associated with a body of economic cooperation under the umbrella of the SAARC, which mostly deals with export, import, trade, and commerce. Any regional security integration in South Asia must be established not only through the maintenance of treaties and economic agreements, but also by taking into account ecological, cultural, and societal issues, as they are integral to pushing countries and communities to cooperate in regional security integration. Nowadays, the actors behind any regional cooperation are no longer states, but, instead, there are many stakeholders, such as political elites, civil societies, think tanks, NGOs, different types of institutions, advocacy organizations, people's movements, and mass populations.

The ORSM is an innovative regional security-integration building process drawing inspiration from the deep-rooted culture and customs of the surrounding areas of the South Asian region. It seems that any evolutionary phase of security communities requires a collective concept that can ensure the competencies of each member by defining their role and developing a decision-making mechanism.

If the political players and groups of civil societies are sincere, dedicated, and committed, then South Asia may be able to establish a viable security community in the days ahead. According to Adler and Barnett, South Asia is a pluralistic security community as a transnational region comprised of sovereign states whose people maintain dependable expectations of peaceful change (Deutsch et al., p. 29). They emphasize certain core values necessary to the formation of security communities, such as *depth of trust*, the nature and degree of *institutionalization of governance systems*, mutual aid to construct *collective system* arrangements and possessing a *system of rule* that forms a *collective security system* (Ibid., p. 29).

The ORSM cannot be implemented in a short span of time in South Asia, as the model needs to go through various phases of evolutionary mechanisms to accomplish the task of security integration. Adler and Barnett (1998a, pp. 48–57) have emphasized three different evolutionary phases to imagine a mature security community (see figure 10.1). Both scholars divided the evolutive process of security into three phases—nascent, ascendant, and mature—emphasizing a reasonable period of time to establish the process perfectly.

In the *nascent* phase, community member-states begin to recognize that a community is necessary and desirable, and member-states coordinate their relations in order to *increase mutual security*; *lower transaction costs*; and *encourage further exchange and interactions*. These *trigger mechanisms* have led to the creation of institutions or organizations to foster their relations and interaction to develop new institutions. Thus, the South Asian region, including Bangladesh, India and Pakistan, can initiate security networks that emphasize the role of the SAARC to proceed among the high officials of the member country to table frameworks at now-defunct annual prime ministerial meetings of the region.

In the *ascendant* phase, new regional interactions are established among the member-states, and "regional institutions are created, leading to increasingly dense networks and structures of interaction and deepening level of mutual trust" (Jones, 2008, p. 187). This phase for the South Asian region will contribute to increasing networks; the construction of new institutions and organizations; decreasing fear and threats; promoting the level of mutual trust; and encouraging collective identities. figure 10.1

In the *mature* phase, member-states are comfortable with each other, and war is extremely improbable and unpredictable at this stage. Institutions are functional in both domestic and regional settings, and they share a regional identity. This phase is more balanced, more worthy, and more transparent in that it pushes countries toward accountability of the political elites and

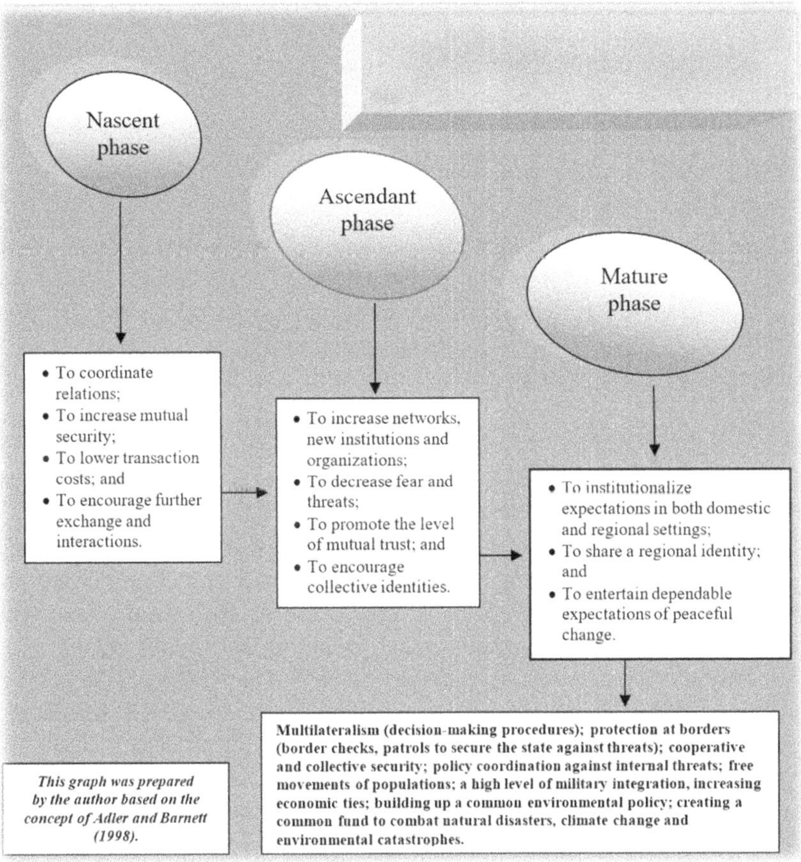

Figure 10.1 Evolution of Different Phases of Proposed Organic Regional Security Model (ORSM) in the South Asian Region. *Source*: This graph was prepared by the author based on the concept of Adler and Barnett (1998).

of member-states, and "there is an informal governance system based on shared meanings and a collective identity; and, while there remain conflicting interests, disagreements, and asymmetric bargaining, there is the expectation that states will practice self-restraint" (Ibid., p. 187). If member-states of the South Asian region reach this phase, there should not be any chaotic atmosphere between and among the members. They can easily change their fate through the following mechanisms: Multilateralism (decision-making procedures); protection at borders (border checks, patrols to secure the state against threats); cooperative and collective security; policy coordination against internal threats; free movements of populations; a high level of military integration, increasing economic ties; building up a common environmental policy; and creating a common fund to combat natural disasters, climate change, and environmental catastrophes.

CHALLENGES AND PROSPECTS IN CONSTRUCTING THE ORSM IN THE REGION

Establishing the ORSM under the SAARC mandate would definitely bring people together, although the people of each region would have to wait for a couple of years to implement this new organic security integration approach. Given this scenario, one could not start thinking of establishing any security integration in South Asia without India's help.

Now, certain questions may arise: Is South Asia ready to form an ORSM? Should South Asia try to establish a South Asian security alliance? The answer is no. But, if it is taken hypothetically that there might be some possibilities for establishing such a community in the region, then questions arise concerning what the basic elements for formulating a security community in the region would be. Peter Jones (2008) believes that any development toward formulating a security framework in South Asia would rely on the active participation of India. Quoting Adler and Barnett, Jones (2008, p. 188) states, "The existence of powerful states that are able to project a sense of purpose, offer an idea of progress, and/or provide leadership around core issues can facilitate and stabilise this phase."

Any sense of security community or regional security integration can take place through nonviolent means. The members of such an organic regional security community—political elites, civil societies, and the mass population—share similar values and a nonviolent attitude, which is characterized by a superior ethical perception that encourages the growth of mutual trust and confidence-building not only between the member-states but also among groups of member-states, as well as ordinary members of the community. Security integration needs a political transition between and among the communities of the region. So, the question may arise: Is it happening soon in South Asia? Is South Asia ready to embrace it? Does South Asia require any waiting period to establish it?

The idea of an organic security model is to study community-building processes to form a pluralistic and inclusive community. I have constructed some major approaches to explain the ORSM and how they facilitate a regional security model and peaceful environment in the South Asian region. These approaches—interpersonal trust, sense of community, integrative behavior, and free-trade enterprise—can formulate an organic security paradigm for South Asia. I think Adler and Barnett's (1998b) three phases of Security Communities (see figure 10.1) can work in this regard.

Both the *nascent* and the *ascendant* phases of evolutionary mechanisms can initiate to develop a ground of mutual trust. Foreign policy and regional affairs of the region can begin to reinterpret the conflicts of the past, and a process of reconciliation can begin. Thus, gradually, the member countries can enter into the final stage—the *mature* phase—and then, the region would:

a) Enjoy a high degree of trust;
b) Share a collective regional identity;
c) Initiate multilateralism (decision-making procedures) for the common interest of the members through "consensual mechanisms that automatically incorporate the interest of all members";
d) Uphold cooperative and collective security (cooperative in dealing with security problems that arise within the community and collective in dealing with problems that occur from outside the community);
e) Frame policies to look at internal threats that may arise at any time;
f) Ease free movements of populations; and
g) Undertake a high level of military integration, if needed, for any threats.

The foreign and security policies of the region are bound to accommodate people's views and popular cultures, and constructions of the geopolitical approaches depend on the popular views of the nation to which they belong. The thematic structure of security integration/ community has long been discussed in political science, international relations, and security studies. European integration theory has played a pioneering role, with its indigenous theoretical culture, in regional integration approaches. A key message of European debates is that one model/approach may be irrelevant to another.

The current governments of India, Pakistan, and Bangladesh are aware of the mutual benefits of remaining friendly and cooperative as they would remain in power for a few more years, which is, as political pundits suggest, an appropriate time to find solutions to their mutual problems while establishing a better atmosphere in the region. Mistrust, suspicion, and confusion are regular phenomena in any initiatives taken by India, Pakistan, and Bangladesh.

If the member-states of the region are cooperative and determined to establish an organic security integration model in South Asia, the region needs to develop a collective identity, mutual trust, and social interactions between governors and for the people to be governed within each state in the region. Being a strong country among its neighbors, India should build an image and attitude that will sow the structures of cooperation and strengthen Confidence Building Measures (CBMs) so that India can uphold its favorable geostrategic position. Unlike EU countries, South Asian nations face poorly developed political institutions, a lack of social and political cohesion, dependency, large economic disparities, and strong ethnic and religious groups.

CONCLUDING REMARKS

The approaches of the South Asian organic regional security integration explore options to broaden the social reach in generating public opinion and collective solidarity in constructing narratives on the ORSM. Thus, the construction of an organic regional security paradigm does not require prior political ties among the states nor preexisting physical or cultural legacies. Any region has to continue its institutional efforts to form its own collective identity beyond the national level, which is crucial for achieving peace, development, and prosperity.

The chapter contributes to the disciplines of international relations and security studies, and it encourages scholars and practitioners of global politics and international relations to consider exploring the prospects and challenges of the ORSM. It contains innovative ideas, approaches and methods, especially for South Asian scholars and regional security proponents.

Thus, the ORSM can serve as an alternative explanatory case study for other global security integration projects. A comprehensive research is needed to build a better understanding in which domestic and international factors would interact with the analysis of regional security integration from a South Asian perspective. The approach of the ORSM will be a unique case study for greater accumulation of knowledge where various theoretical and discursive methods complement each other rather than constantly arguing to make unsustainable grand theories. In addition, further initiatives are needed to engage political institutions to formulate mechanisms to construct the South Asian ORSM in the better interest of regional peace and development of the South Asian region.

NOTE

1. I. Shailo, Senior Program Advisor,the Federal Government of Canada. Email: iqbalshailo@gmail.com

BIBLIOGRAPHY

Adler, E., & Barnett, M. (1998a) "Security Communities in Theoretical Perspective." In E. Adler & M. Barnett (Eds.), *Security Communities*. Cambridge University Press:, pp. 29–66

Adler, E., & Barnett, M. (1998b) "A Framework for the Study of Security Communities." In E. Adler & M. Barnett (Eds.), *Security Communities*. Cambridge University Press, pp. 3–28

Axworthy, L. (2001) "Human Security and Global Governance: Putting People First." *Global Governance* 7 (1):19–23.

Buzan, B. (2000) "The Logic of Regional Security in the Post-Cold War World." In B. Hettne, A. Inotai, & O. Sunkel (Eds.), *The New Regionalism and the Future of Security and Development*. The Macmillan Press, pp. 1–25.

Chapman, G.P. (2003) *The Geopolitics of South Asia: From Early Empires to the Nuclear Age*. Routledge.

Deutsch, K.W., et al. (1957) *Political Community and the North Atlantic Area: International Organization in the Light of Historical Experience*. Princeton University press.

Jones, P. (2008) "South Asia: Is A Regional Security Community Possible?" *South Asian Survey* 15(2): 183–193.

Jones, R. (2009) "Geopolitical Boundary Narratives, the Global War on Terror and Border Fencing in India." *Transactions of the Institute of British Geographers* 34: 290–304.

Oxford English Dictionary. (2009) Oxford University, UK.

Shailo, I. (2010) "The Maritime Boundary Claims of Bangladesh, India and Myanmar: The Challenge of Security Integration in South Asia." *Pentagon's South Asia Defence and Strategic Year Book*. The Pentagon Press, pp. 131–141.

Chapter 11

Trauma, Ontological Insecurity, and States' Conflictual Behaviors

The Case of Iran, the UK, and the US

Siavash Chavoshi[1] and Mohammad Reza Saeidabadi[2]

INTRODUCTION

Over the past few decades, discussions on states' desire for recognition and ontological security have responded to a series of questions in conflict and security studies which encourages scholars to reflect more systematically on the social dimension of international society (Wendt, 1999, 2003). In this way, by the quick rise of social theories of international relations, IR scholars often have taken the concept of "conflict" and "war" out from the mainstream neorealist perspective. Scholars have often shifted IR theories toward social recognition theory and ontological security discussion to unravel states' conflict-seeking incentives (Ringmar, 1996; Mitzen, 2006a; Steel, 2008). Instead of confining states' noncooperative and conflictual behavior with the actor's innate tendency to achieve a relative gain in the anarchic system, often IR theorists expound on how states seek to gain a self-sufficient social identity through other established powers or the so-called significant "Others" to become a socially recognized identity with ontological security (Murray, 2018, p. 80).

On the other hand, ontological security denotes an individual's demand to achieve a "constant self" or a self-sufficient social identity by gaining recognition from the established forces in society (Innes & Steele, 2014). In particular, ontological security refers to a condition where individuals or states initiate to fully acknowledge each other's distinct identity markers. Otherwise, the feeling of ontological insecurity would put one of the parties into an identity crisis and fuel conflicts and irrational behaviors

(Fehl & Kolliarkis, 2015). This argument assumes that without achieving recognition and ontological security, no sense of self-identity and self-fulfillment will be truly constructed. Ontological security refers to the condition in which subjects or states freely become whomever they truly desire as an independent social identity in society (Fehl & Kolliarkis, 2015). Through the feeling of ontological security, actors can become recognized and acknowledged through their own unique and distinct identity markers (Steel, 2008, p. 3). Therefore, demanding social recognition and ontological security assist states in safely articulating their aspirant identity markers instead of being subordinated as an inferior actor in the international system. However, achieving a self-sufficient social identity is often costly, time-consuming, and conflictual (Esteves et al., 2020, pp. 10–30). States as social entities vastly desire to respond to their ontological needs in the international society. In other words, once states' inner desire for recognition and ontological security is ignored by the significant "other"(s), ontologically insecure states often delve into an identity crisis and adopt conflict-seeking behaviors to mitigate their social anxieties (Wolf, 2011, pp. 120–132).

As a result, this chapter will focus on two main purposes. Initially, this literature opens up a nonmaterialistic interpretation of states' Irrational and conflict-seeking behavior through recognition theory in a Hegelian fashion. It highlights some key arguments on master and slave dialectic to explain the roots of state conflictual behavior regarding individuals' and states' feelings of traumatic experiences, misrecognition, and ontological insecurity in society. Second, it will demonstrate that once a state's desire for recognition and ontological security is not well responded to by the established powers, both weak and rising states discursively use their collective historical trauma to justify their conflictual-seeking behaviors. In particular, by picking on the US and UK's decades of noncooperative and conflict-seeking relations with Iran, this chapter underscores the West and Iran's historical relations have been immersed in historical traumas and ontological insecurity.

THE STRUGGLE FOR RECOGNITION AND THE ROLE OF TRAUMA

In the Phenomenology of Spirit (1977), Hegel narrates the story of two beings or self-consciousnesses (Selbstbewüßtein) in a famously described parable referred to as the master and slave dialectic. In this dialectic, two protagonists symbolically strive to prevail or supersede1 (Aufheben) each other to achieve an identity. Throughout the competition, each of the subjects ceaselessly desires to subordinate the other subject as an inferior social being to gain "self-certainty" of their being via the struggle for recognition or the battle to death.

Broadly, Hegel extensively addresses the protagonists' (self-consciousnesses) "desire" for recognition and sets the stage for both beings to equally articulate their desired identity as independent subjects against each other. In *the Phenomenology of Spirit* (1977), Hegel explores the social dimension of human interactions through the master and slave dialectic. After examining the realm of "consciousness" and "self-consciousness" (Selbstbewüßtein), Hegel steps into a new section where he introduces two leading characters or "beings" in the dialectic. In this conceptually equivocal part, Hegel traces the nature of human conflict-seeking behaviors in virtue of individuals' so-called "desire" for recognition (Anerkanntes). By emphasizing some of the salient components of the human social dimension, the "self-consciousness" or "beings" are indicated as two subjects that constantly desire to be acknowledged or recognized intersubjectively via the other "self-consciousness" (Williams, 2000, pp. 33–40).

In this social battle, both characters ceaselessly desire to subordinate the other "self" to articulate their own so-called "pure I" (true identity). However, as soon as each "self-consciousness" begins to interact with the other "being," they realize that both "beings" are in fact in "itself" and at the same time outside of "itself" as Hegel reiterates. What seems to be significant is that the "self-consciousness" can only receive its states of total recognition only through an external "other." At its core, for Hegel, no social existence will get fully constructed on a unilateral basis. It is in this moment when Hegel reminds the reader that each of the self-consciousnesses to undergo through the self-formation process always requires an "other being" to become a self-sufficient social identity since individuals are only intersubjectively constructed and meaningful (Pinkard, 1994; Pippin, 2008; Epstein et al., 2018, 788–800).

In the course of this struggle, the inner desire for recognition maintains once one of the self-consciousnesses chooses to protect his own "physical" security by simply losing the competition to the other "self" in the recognition game. For one of two self-consciousnesses, achieving recognition appears less significant than protecting his physical security. As a consequence, as one of the self-consciousnesses fails to attain recognition, the balance between the self-consciousnesses suddenly becomes "unequal" and "opposed" (Hegel, 1977: 113–114). In this phase, the master only by resisting the fierce competition pushes his whole existence to the other "self" and defines himself as the leading figure or the Herr (master) and the other self-consciousnesses transforms into a *Knecht* (slave). As both characters move forward, the master gets to display himself as the only meaningful unity or the "essential" being or the "pure I" in the dialectic. As indicated in figure 11.1, one of the self-consciousnesses ultimately gets to live for "itself" as the master, and the other "self-consciousness" who did not risk his physical existence and resisted less, lives as a dependent self-consciousness or as *Knecht* (slave; Hegel, 1977, p. 115). Later, the winning side of the competition, by offering a fragile physical existence to the other "self," becomes the master or the ruling "self-consciousness" and puts the other "self" (slave) into total servitude and subordination.

Broadly stated, master and slave dialects initiate once two undeveloped characters begin to live as two independent characters under the pretext of master and slave in the Phenomenology. Interestingly, this process does not simply terminate here. Hegel also opens up a social space for more discussions by arguing that both characters, by defining new roles for each side, begin to define new social identities for the other "beings" as well. Therefore, his account precedes by emphasizing how both characters continue living unbalanced life according to their newly constructed social identities. From a closer look, as the concept of "slavery" constructs, the slave or the "impure" social identity seems to possess no capacity to develop beyond the master domination (essential reality) in the dialectic. On the surface, the slave only seems to live miserably on his own and is devoid of any subjective role to put "objects" in real shape after his disgraceful defeat to the master. Consequently, the traumatized self-consciousness (slave), who has lost their social identity in search of fragile physical security, only gets to offer one-sided services and receives nothing but humiliation and disrespect in return. However, Hegel further defined that the slave ultimately discovers that slavery would roughly reside in social recognition and will confine the slave in total servitude forever. Afterward, although this form of social interaction seems beyond the slave's capacity to resist for a long time, the slave ultimately strives to acquire the truth of "itself" as the independent identity to retain its lost social identity (essential nature). Soon after his servitude, the slave retains the truth of "itself" through its interaction with

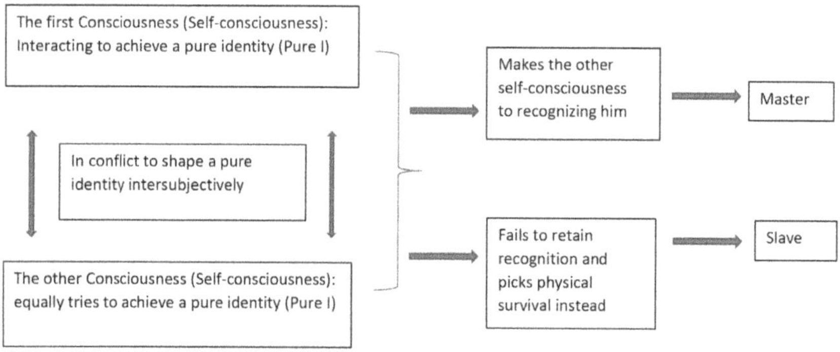

Figure 11.1 The Social Transition of Self-Consciousnesses. *Source*: Designed by the authors.

the master (Harr) and then improves its skills through the realm of thinghood or objects (diénen or bílden).

It is a strength of this exceptionally wide-ranging section that it raises far more discussions that "recognition" is never an easy task to achieve. However, understanding that the experience of "death" is an undeniable truth, the slave gradually decides to reach the condition of "self-realization" only by working and offering pure services to the master (Pippin, 2011, pp. 94–98). Interestingly, as the slave proceeds toward gaining self-certainty and truth (recognition), he becomes "seized with dread" as Hegel notes. This form of fear (*Furcht*) is emanated from the previously experienced moment of "death" by the absolute lord or the master. Looking at the slave, it is obvious how the earlier defeat and the experience of total servitude and slavery, as Hegel maintains, trembles the slave "in every fiber of its being" and shakes everything "solid" or "stable" to its roots (Hegel, 1977, p. 117). Here, the slave requires to deal with his so-called absolute fear and has to deal with a dominating figure called the "absolute master." Be that as it may, this form of fear is positive and as Hegel maintains, it is the beginning of "wisdom" in the dialectic. By moving into the dialectic, we later observe how the slave transforms and prevails over his inner fear in the long run. Therefore, through its formative activities, the slave, attains "objectivity," "permanence," and his lost "individuality" (Rauch & Sherman, 1999, p. 46).

As a result, four main arguments are highlighted in this section. First, the desire for social recognition will never evaporate completely, yet it may get postponed. Second, through his formative activities, the slave not only gets to realize his potent capabilities, but it comes to apprehend that the state of physical security does not fully satisfy and respond to his desire for recognition. Third, individuals are roughly isolated from their past and traumatic experiences. Individuals constantly learn from their past trauma and shape their current behavior. Fourth, by learning from past experiences, the traumatized slaves develop their skills and seek to regain their lost identity for mastery. By recalling the past trauma, the slave realizes that physical security is only a fleeting experience where the slave is constantly humiliated and disrespected. As a result, the total stigmatization of the slave as inferior self-consciousness (traumatic experiences) teaches the slave to struggle for more than mere physical existence to get subjectivity and agency within society.

STATE'S DESIRE FOR RECOGNITION AND ONTOLOGICAL SECURITY: THE RISE OF CONFLICT

More concretely, states likewise individuals seek to maximize their desire for attaining recognition via the established powers. To fulfill actors' nonmaterial needs, states, as independent social entities, constantly attempt to validate their independent self-identity through an intersubjective interaction with the established forces. In consequence, achieving the condition of social recognition would guarantee states' social survival as a self-sufficient identity in international society (Ward, 2017, pp. 15–16). However, Realists suggest that the states' quest for "relative gain" and "uncertainty" leave almost no room for sustainable cooperation among actors (Grieco, 1988). In this setting, war is inevitable since the anarchic system is "competitive at its core one" (Morgenthau, 1973). States' defensive goals lead to sheer determination for self-survival and security in the anarchic system (Waltz, 1979; Morgenthau, 1973).

In this way, grassroots conflicts and irrational behaviors often require to be examined on a social basis in international society (Chavoshi & Saeidabadi, 2021; Mitzen & Schweller, 2011). Giddens (1984, p. 367) posits that the need for sustaining the sense of biographical continuity and historical routines would result in the feeling of ontological security at the social level. In a Hegelian fashion, states as social entities, also constantly desire to articulate their desired identity to get fully recognized by the established forces or the significant "Others" as legitimized actors. States seek to sustain their collective routines and their sense of biographical continuity to instantiate their unique social identity to gain agency and ontological security in the international social hierarchy. The feeling of ontological security will allow countries to feel fully acknowledged by other established forces as distinct and unique social identities. However, if states fail to recognize and acknowledge other actors' need for ontological security, countries would often delve into conflicts and jeopardize their material gains to preserve their national identity and social status rather than their material interests (Ringmar, 1996; Charoenvattananukul, 2020, pp. 182–185).

A Hegelian Interpretation of states' behavior indicates that actors often seek social recognition and ontological security under three conditions. Initially, states with strong national sentiments and historical narratives desire to articulate their unique identity markers and sometimes struggle for their national and territory identity (Ringmar, 1996; Ejdus, 2020). The desire for sustaining national narrative and territorial integrity intensifies states' feelings of ontological security. However, once a state's feeling of ontological security is disturbed or threatened by an external other, states would often rise against the intruder to defend their social identity as an independent self-consciousness. At this moment, disruption of the state's routines will consequently provoke ontological distress and social anxiety among the states. For instance, Ejdus's (2020, p. 26) nuanced exploration in a Weberian tradition, explains the Serbia and Kosovo conflicts in light of Serbia's anxiety over the secession of Kosovo. The author attempts to shine a light on how states intensely desire to sustain their "territories" (space) as national monuments and how much the concept of "space" has resonated with social significance to the public and the decision-maker in Serbia.

In the second condition, rising powers would often seek conflict and act irrationally as soon as they experience "social immobility" and "misrecognition" in the international society. Conflicts are often exacerbated when states realize that when an emerging state is recognized by established forces, the recognized actors achieve a secure and legitimate social status. As Ward (2017) notes, desiring a higher status usually has two significant effects on international society. Initially, it grants specific material advantages to rising states compared to other countries. Further, it offers self-esteem and domestic political legitimacy for a rising power to precede globally as who they truly aspire to become as a self-assured social being (Ward, 2017, p. 37). By and large, status provides countries with role identity. Rising states as social entities often struggle for recognition in pursuit of ontological security since rising states constantly feel insecure about their social position in the anarchic system. As noted, as rising states confront misrecognition, actors often adopt "recognitive practice" against the established forces by achieving great power voice, exemplary military power, and increasing their sphere of influence in response to the great powers. In this model, Murray (2018) relies on the concept of misrecognition of states' social identity as the main driver of most conflictual and irrational behaviors among growing powers.

Ward (2017, p. 2) favors a more middle-ground approach, who, like Murray, reflects on the state's feeling of "social immobility" in international society. He notes that the feeling of "status immobility" among the rising states is tantamount to the rise of the immense feeling of social discontent and humiliation in the system. Based on this analysis of international social hierarchy, this signifies that the rising states, before taking any provocative steps toward the established powers as the "radical revisionist states," strive to sustain their power, wealth, and territorial status as rational actors. This process usually assists states to guarantee their future chances for social recognition as a growing power by not getting countervailed by superpower coalitions.

However, Ward accordingly notes that revisionism usually takes place in two stages. First, the rising states fail to attain their desired status after getting constantly confined to a subordinated social level by the Significant "Others" (Ward 2017, pp. 24–31). Second, the rising powers experience normative and structural dissatisfaction from the international society. As highlighted, the feeling of uneven distributions of normative values and structural advantages would ultimately lead to radical revisionism. For Ward (2017), misrecognition is a lingering process, marked by the incessant feeling of humiliation and disrespect. Therefore, achieving a viable "social status" is normally impeded by great powers not only for safeguarding the international social structure but for determining the international "glass ceiling" and "status immobility" against the other rising powers (Ward, 2017, p. 3).

Admittedly, both scholars reflect on rising powers' conflict-seeking behavior only in regards to states' feelings of "misrecognition" and "dissatisfaction" without referring to states' collective traumatic experience as one of the main sources of states' feeling of ontological insecurity in the international society. Nevertheless, Murrays and Ward's examination offers important empirical and theoretical advances but falls short in several respects. More concretely, both scholars roughly reflect on states' historical injuries and never provide any explanations on how states might often usurp their historical trauma to justify their conflictual behavior. Sometimes rising states in search of recognition and ontological security articulate their social dissatisfaction by referring to their historical trauma to justify their provocative behaviors. In this setting, memories, and historical traumas can also lead to feelings of ontological insecurity and conflict among states (Mitzen, 2006a, 2006b).

ONTOLOGICAL INSECURITY AND TRAUMATIC EXPERIENCES: THE CASE OF IRAN AND THE WEST

The experience of historical trauma can also push states to delve into conflict and war. The experience of trauma is an ontologically painful feeling among the actors in the national society. Caruth (1996) describes trauma as an unconscious experience of sudden or catastrophic events, an uncontrolled response to an unexpected or overwhelming violent event (Caruth, 1996, pp. 91–92). In this view, traumatic memories can change the so-called "linearity of historical" and pursue individuals to seek a new form of social interaction in society. Caruth (1995) introduces these moments as "the moment the world changed" (Caruth, 1995, p. 254). In examining the role of past traumatic events, Fierke (2004) also suggests that the experience of trauma locates in both physical disaster, and loss of control and powerlessness. In this condition, the feeling of "helplessness" and "loss of control" is marked as vivid representations of traumatic experiences (Fierke, 2004, p. 473). Perhaps above all else, then, the experience of trauma often remains in individuals' collective memory. The experience of trauma can gradually operate as an intense reaction to an event which is naturally a wrenching, dislocating experience, followed by a sense of loss and anger (Sasley, 2014). Hence, once an individual is traumatized, their pure trust is "betrayed" (Edkins, 2003, p. 4).

While tracing the concept of trauma at the individual level, it is also noteworthy to examine the role of trauma at the state level. On the state level, the feeling of trauma takes place as the actors feel threats toward how their social image is perceived by other states. Past traumatic events not only upset a nation's idea of itself but also upset the nation's collective understanding. In this way, trauma generates ontological insecurity among the actors (Innes and Steele, 2014, pp. 19–20). Here, there is a tight connection between traumatic experiences and feelings of ontological insecurity. Trauma can cause ontological insecurity and disrupt state self-narrative and the sense of biographical continuity as a unified social identity. Once states' social identity as a distinct image is disturbed or disrupted, states attempt to articulate their desired social identity through conflict-seeking and irrational behaviors. For instance, Becker (2014) looks beyond the dominant narrative, which speaks to and emphasizes states' material power and suggests that memories can shape a state's identity. For Becker, trauma can leave a profound effect on states' self-image and foreign policy orientations. Thereby, the tendency for aggression and conflict highly correlates with the degree of countries' traumatic history. Narratives of victimhood can result in more aggressive postures (Becker, 2014, pp. 62–68).

Accordingly, trauma pursues states to seek ontological security as a victimized state against the well-established forces in the international social hierarchy. The traumatized states could select "chosen trauma" to justify their conflict-seeking behavior. Large groups, through "chosen trauma" offer fresh interpretations of their past traumas. From a wider look, US–Iran historical traumas have been influencing both states' level of engagement since the Islamic revolution (1979) and have often put Iran and the United States even close to a full-fledged war, for example, after the assassination of General Qassem Soleimani in Baghdad in 2020. Generally, Iranian have experienced various agonizing historical traumas directly or indirectly. On the Iranian side, we can refer to Britain and Russia's colonialism of Iran (the Anglo-Russian Convention of 1907),the US/British coup of 1953, the United Kingdom and the United States support for Saddam in the Iran–Iraq War (1980–1988), the securitization of Iran's nuclear program (2002 to present), the systematic dehumanization of Iranians through the mainstream media,[3] the US withdrawal from the Iran nuclear deal (2018), the devastating labyrinth of sanctions and immigration bans since 1979. To this end, to understand the West and Iran's noncooperative and conflict-seeking behavior on some of the most critical issues, such as the Iran nuclear agreement (The Joint Comprehensive Plan of Action) today, it is also essential to reflect on Iran's feeling of ontological insecurity to better conceptualize the west and Iran long history. As a consequence, two sets of arguments are valid. First, post-revolutionary Iran, as a new power, deeply suffers from the absence of an independent social identity with a respected and unique social identity as a Shia state in the Middle East. Second, Iran's relation with Western countries such as the United Kingdom and the United States is required to be traced back to Iranians' collective memory as a humiliated or traumatized nation.

The traumatic experiences among the United States, the United Kingdom, and Iran have convinced Iran to discursively seize historical trauma and past wounds to justify some of its behaviors in defense of its national identity and Islamic dignity against the Western powers in the Middle East. However, actors' approaches to their collective traumatic experiences are not linear at all. States chose whether to narrate an intense feeling of humiliation, depending on their social standing in the international social hierarchy. That is to say that traumatic events might sustain for a while within countries' collective understanding of themselves. Nevertheless, these are the actors themselves who will ultimately choose whether to resurrect a series of historical wounds to redefine their understanding of "self" or not (Kinnvall, 2002, p. 102). As a result, trauma can lead to "radical" ontological insecurity and the past "Selves" can shape an actor's present and future actions (Steel, 2008). In other words, the "chosen trauma" can construct countries' future "self" and actions (Kinnvall, 2004, p. 755).

With a closer look at Iranian authorities' speech acts since the Islamic revolution, two keywords are widely articulated: "humiliation" (تحقیر) and "dignity" (کرامت). These two concepts have played a decisive role in shaping the United States and the United Kingdom's history of noncooperation and conflict and also Iran's feeling of ontological insecurity. In this endeavor, some discussions have been widely articulated among Iranian conservative voices since the Islamic Revolution. In these views, the United States is portrayed as the significant "other" who refuses to fully recognize the Islamic Republic of Iran as an independent and distinct social identity in the liberal-led order. The United States is illuminated as an untrustworthy master in this discourse. Therefore, based on the intense historical traumas, western powers as the absolute masters no longer deserve to engage in Iran's national security discussions such as Iran's nuclear enrichment capacity, ballistic missile program, and Tehran's regional military engagements. In this view, both Britain and the United States are often depicted as a dominating "pure I" (master) who hold profound historical animosity toward the Islamic Republic of Iran's core social identity as a progressive Shia state within a Hegelian fashion. In addition, the humiliation of Iranian collective identity, as decision-makers usually indicate, has been always followed by the total negation of Iran's independent social identity as a great nation. From the Iranian perspective, the notion of "enmity" (دشمنی) is entrenched in the United States –Iran contemporary history of ups and downs. Subsequently, shaping a non-biased interaction with the western states is always far-fetched, costly, and full of disrespect for the Iranian elites. For this reason, the Supreme Leader of the Islamic Revolution, Ayatollah Khamenei, on the eve of the Tabriz uprising against the Shah dynasty in 2017, delineated how United States –Iran relations had been historically established through "humiliation" and "disrespect" in his speeches during the meeting with the people of East Azerbaijan.

> *The Islamic Revolution ended the era of humiliation of the Iranian nation; Previously, the Iranian nation was humiliated by foreigners and powers; There was scientific humiliation, there was political humiliation, there was social humiliation . . . Before the United States, the British played this role in the country; The Islamic Revolution came to end with this unbearable humiliation.*

From a conservative perspective, it is put forward that the "West" (برغ) has brought "nothing" but "misery" and humiliation. In particular, historical traumas as the main source of Iran's historical backwardness are utilized to portray the United States as the principal cause behind Iran's feeling of ontological insecurity as a unique and distinct social identity. A key precedent could be found in the narratives of historical traumas between Iran and the United States over the US–UK lead coup d'état-overthrowing Iran's first democratically elected prime minister Mohammad Mosaddegh in 1953. Mosaddegh was known as a defender of Iran's oil nationalization, secular democracy, and resistance to foreign domination (Risen, 2000). However, after more than four decades of the Islamic Revolution, the ghosts of the 1953 overthrow of Mosaddegh by Washington and London are signified as an agonizing historical trauma embedded in the Iranian psyche. Significantly, Prime Minister Mosaddegh's so-called historic "humiliation" and 1953 historical trauma never freezes in 1953. Conversely, the aforementioned historical wounds have gradually transformed and later impacted the Iranian postrevolutionary foreign policy orientations toward the western decision-makers until today. In this vein, the tragic experience of the US/British coup of 1953 has transformed into a discursive practice to underscore how the United States consciously brought down the Iranian independent democratic voices in 1953. Interestingly, the depiction of Mosaddegh's national humiliations and the way the United States has treated the Iranian democrats has been an effective tool to convince postrevolutionary leaders to conclude how "untrustworthy" the US officials are on various issues such as Iran nuclear deal (JCPOA). Later, the painful withdrawal of Trump from the Iran nuclear deal was also interpreted as an act of "distrust" and "shame" and evoked the memory of the US/British coup of 1953.

Over the past decades, Ayatollah Khamenei (2017), as one of the chief foreign policymakers since the demise of Ayatollah Khomeini in 1989, has repeatedly demonstrated that Iranian diplomats should never forget United States –Iran shared historical experiences. Beyond his reckoning with the strategic and political considerations, the US interference in contemporary Iranian history has depicted the United States as the main source of Iran's ontological insecurity. To illustrate, soon after the collapse of the US–Iran nuclear deal under Trump, Ayatollah Khamenei reiterated that the Iranian diplomats should understand that the "enemy cannot be trusted" and a clear example is "the nuclear negotiations or JCPOA." In this statement, preserving the Islamic Republic of Iran's historic "dignity" is more invaluable than achieving the so-called "agreement" with the United States. Meanwhile, Ayatollah Khamenei during a lecture titled "confidence in America" and "the 1953 coup d'état," referred to the future of United States –Iran negotiation by pointing to some of the intense historic traumas between both states during the meeting with pupils and students in 2018:

> *Negotiations will not go anywhere. Mossadegh made a similar mistake and trusted them. That is, they are not satisfied even with people like Mossadegh; They want a servant, they want a servant, they want a servant.*

In this view, the contemporary political hostilities among both sides have consistently shown that the United States does not recognize Iran as a legitimized actor in its political rhetoric. Therefore, Iran does not require offering any responses to US aspirations to negotiate on Iranian nuclear activities as a great nation with its glorious Islamic and Iranian past. In the meeting between the commanders and a group of employees of the Air Force of the Army of the Islamic Republic of Iran in 2013, Iran's supreme leader underscores that "negotiating with the United States does not solve the problem." He asks "Where did they (Washington) keep their promises?"

He goes on by noting that "It has been sixty years since 1953 until today, in every case that the American officials trusted the American government" so, "nothing has been brought about to the Iranians." In doing so, Ayatollah Khamenei posits that "we do not negotiate on regional issues, on the various issues we have, on the problems we have with the United States." He then concludes by saying that "let the enemy run after you (diplomates)" (Khamenei, 2019). Similarly, three years later, just before reaching a comprehensive deal over the Iran nuclear deal, the keyword of "distrust" and the US–Iran historical trauma continued up until Trump's administration. In Tehran Friday Prayer Sermons, Ayatollah Khamenei also emphasized that:

> *I said from the beginning, after the withdrawal of the United States from JCPOA, that these three governments were constantly talking, constantly gossiping, I also said the same day, I do not trust them, they will not do anything.*

In accomplishing the herculean task of integrating thoughtful analysis of the history of historical trauma and the feeling of ontological insecurity, there are two critical points to address. First, Iran's misrecognition and feeling of ontological security have shifted United States–Iran relations toward belligerent policies, conflict, and an atmosphere of hostility. Second, Iran deeply feels humiliated and disrespected by the US–UK role in the US/British coup of 1953 which often evokes the memory of the past crisis. Throughout these accounts, the discursive use of historical trauma as a sign of national humiliation has gradually pushed the west and Iran relations toward hostility, distrust, and conflict. From one side, Iran proactively quests for social recognition and desires to reach ontological security. On the other hand, such anti-Iran sentiments and collective traumatic experiences, discursively adopted by both parties, roughly leave room for both states to ease historical wounds and act peacefully. With strong national sentiments in the Iranian postrevolutionary discourses, conflicts have shifted from sole non-cooperation toward an identity struggle to achieve recognition and ontological security.

CONCLUSION

Having discussed the master and slave dialectic, it was demonstrated how states as individuals desire recognition and search for ontological security. The slave's desire for recognition never terminates by simply losing the recognition competition to the master or the so-called "pure I." This argument seemed to have twofold significance so far. First, the slave (the traumatized self-consciousness) ultimately makes a historic return to the dialectic once he realizes that he deserves more than sole physical security in the dialectic. Second, through past traumatic experiences, the slave educates himself to act in no subordination as he gets involved in informative activities through the realm of objects and the master. Subsequently, the real conflict arises when the fear of death likewise the past experiences convinces the slave to revolt and subordinate other self-consciousnesses (or slave) to achieve recognition.

To conceptualize Hegel's master and slave dialectic from a social perspective, we require to explain why states often act provocatively in international society. Clearly, unlike neorealist discussions, it noted that states' quest for recognition can push states to seek conflictual and irrational behaviors to gain social recognition in the international society. However, those rising states that seek legitimized status and recognition do not always achieve morally accepted role identity in the international social hierarchy. Here, historical traumas would encourage states to feel more ontologically insecure. The feeling of ontological insecurity would also pursue states such as Iran to take on military recognitive practices by intruding into wars or conflicts to acquire a self-assured social identity as a great nation in the eyes of the well-established powers.

NOTES

1. S. Chavoshi. University of Tehran, Iran. Email: siavashchavoshi1992@gmail.com
2. M. R. Saeidabadi University of Tehran, Iran. Email: sabadi@ut.ac.ir
3. For example, Not Without My Daughter and Saturday Night Live skits and Robocop.

BIBLIOGRAPHY

Becker, Douglas J. Memory and trauma as elements of identity in foreign policymaking. In E. Resende & D. Budryte (Eds.), *Memory and Trauma in International Relations: Theories, Cases and Debates*. New York: Routledge, 57–73, 2014.

Caruth, Cathy. (Ed.). *Trauma: Explorations in Memory*. Baltimore, MD: University of Nebraska Press, 128–157, 1995.

Caruth, Cathy. *Unclaimed Experience: Trauma, Narrative, and History*. Baltimore, MD: Johns Hopkins University Press, December 15, 2016.

Charoenvattananukul, Peera. *Ontological Security and Status-Seeking, Thailand's Proactive Behaviors during the Second World War*. Routledge, 2020.

Chavoshi, Siavash, &Saeidabadi, Mohammad Reza. The struggle for recognition, ontological security and the case of China as a rising power. *International Political Review*, 9, 390–411, 2021.https://doi.org/10.1057/s41312-021-00122-0

Edkins, Jenny. *Trauma and the Memory of Politics*. Cambridge: Cambridge University Press, 2003.https://doi.org/10.1017/CBO9780511840470

Ejdus, Filip. *Crisis and Ontological Insecurity Serbia's Anxiety over Kosovo's Secession (Central and Eastern European Perspectives on International Relations)*. London: Palgrave Macmillan, 2020.

Epstein, Charlotte. The productive force of the negative and the desire for recognition: Lessons from Hegel and Lacan. *Review of International Studies*, 44(5), 805–828, 2018. https://doi.org/10.1017/S0260210518000347

Epstein, Charlotte, Lindemann, Thomas, & Sending, Ole J. Frustrated sovereigns: The agency that makes the world go around. *Review of International Studies*, 44(5), 787–804, 2018.

Esteves, Paulo, Jumbert, Maria, Gabrielsen, & de Carvalho, Benjamin. *Status and the Rise of Brazil: Global Ambitions, Humanitarian Engagement and International Challenges*. Palgrave Macmillan, 226pp, 2020.

Fattah, Khaled, & Fierke, Karin M. Overview. A clash of emotions: The politics of humiliation and political violence in the Middle East. *European Journal of International Relations*, 15(1), 67–93, 2009.

Fehl, Caroline, & Kolliarakis, Georgios. *Recognition in International Relations: Rethinking a Political Concept in a Global Context*. Springer, 2015.

Fierke, Karin M. Whereof we can speak, thereof we must not be silent: Trauma, political solipsism, and war. *Review of International Studies*, 30(4), 471–491, 2004.

Giddens, Anthony. *The Constitution of Society*. Berkeley, CA: University of California Press, 1984.

Grieco, Joseph M. Anarchy and the limits of cooperation: A realist critique of the newest liberal institutionalism. *International Organization*, 42(3), 498–500, 1988.

Hegel, Georg W. F. *Phenomenology of Spirit* (Miller, A. V., & Findlay J. N., Trans.). Oxford University Press, 1977.

Innes, Alexandria J., & Steele, Brent J. Memory, trauma, and ontological security. In E. Resende & D. Budryte (Eds.), *Memory and Trauma in International Relations: Theories, Cases, and Debates*. London: Routledge, 15–29, 2014 .

Khamenei Sayyed, Ali. Speech to Iranian people on the logic of the Islamic Republic's confrontation with the United States. Tehran, November 3, 2019.

Khamenei Sayyed, Ali. Speech members of Friday prayer headquarters on turmoil, People's trust in the Islamic system, History of Mohammad Reza Pahlavi coming to power and rule. Tehran, 27 July, 2002.

Khamenei Sayyed, Ali. Speech to people of East Azerbaijan. On US-Iran relations. Tabriz, February 15, 2017.

Khamenei Sayyed, Ali. Speech to pupils and students on experience of JCPOA. Tehran, January 28, 2018.

Kinnvall, Catarina. Nationalism, religion and the search for chosen traumas: Comparing Sikh and Hindu identity constructions. *Ethnicities*, 2(1), 79–106, 2002.

Kinnvall, Catarina. Globalization, and religious nationalism: Self, identity, and the search for ontological security. *Political Psychology*, 25(5), 741–767, 2004.

Kojeve, Alexandre. *Introduction to the Reading of Phenomenology of the Spirit (Raymond Queneau Assembled)*. New York: Cornell University Press, 1980.

Lebow, Richard Ned. *A Cultural Theory of International Relations*. Cambridge University Press, 2008.

Lindemann, Thomas. *Causes of War: The Struggle for Recognition*. ECPR Press, 2010.

Mitzen, Jennifer. Ontological security in world politics: State identity and the security dilemma. *European Journal of International Relations*, 12(3), 341–370, 2006a.

Mitzen, Jennifer. Anchoring Europe's civilizing identity: Habits, capabilities, and ontological security. *Journal of European Public Policy*, 13(2), 270–285, 2006b.

Mitzen, Jennifer, & Schweller, Randall L. Knowing the unknown unknowns: Misplaced certainty and the onset of war. *Security Studies*, 20(1), 2–35, 2011.

Möller, Ulrika. *The Prospects of Security Cooperation: A Matter of Relative Gains or Recognition*. Göteborg: Göteborg Studies in Politics, 2007.

Morgenthau, Hans J. *Politics Among Nations: The Struggle for Power and Peace*, 5th ed. New York: Knopf, 1973.

Murray, Michelle. *The Struggle for Recognition in International Relations Status, Revisionism, and Rising Powers*. Oxford University Press, 2019.

Pinkard, Terry. *Hegel's Phenomenology*. Cambridge University Press, 1994.

Pippin, Robert B. *Hegel's Practical Philosophy: Rational Agency as Ethical Life*. Cambridge University Press, 2008.

Pippin, Robert B. *Hegel on Self-Consciousness Desire and Death in the Phenomenology of Spirit*. Princeton: Princeton University Press, 2011.

Rauch, Leo, & Sherman, David. *Hegel's Phenomenology of Self-Consciousness: Text and Commentary*. State University of New York Press, 1999.

Ringmar, Eric. *Identity, Interest, and Action a Cultural Explanation of Sweden's Intervention in the Thirty Years War*. Cambridge: Cambridge University Press, 1996.

Risen, James. *Secrets of History: The C.I.A. in Iran*. The New York Times. Retrieved November 3, 2006, 2000.

Sasley, Brent, E. Remembering and forgetting in Turkish identity and policymaking. In E. Resende & D. Budryte (Eds.), *Memory and Trauma in International Relations: Theories, Cases, and Debates*. New York: Routledge, 2014, 138–152.

Singer, Peter. *Hegel A Very Short Introduction*. Oxford University Press, 2001.

Steele, Brent J. *Ontological Security in International Relations Self-Identity and the IR States*. Oxfordshire: Routledge Taylor & Francis Group, 2008.

Waltz, Kenneth. *Theory of International Politics*. New York: McGraw Hill, 1979.

Ward, Steven. *Status and the Challenge of Rising Powers*. Cambridge: Cambridge University Press, 2017.

Wendt, Alexander. *Social Theory of International Politics*. Cambridge: Cambridge University Press, 1999.

Wendt, Alexander. Why a world state is inevitable. *European Journal of International Relations*, 9(4), 511, 2003.

Wolf, Reinhard. Respect and disrespect in international politics: The significance of status recognition. *International Theory*, 3(1), 112, 2011.

Williams, Robert R. *Hegel's Ethics of Recognition*. Berkeley, CA: University of California Press, 2000.

Chapter 12

Socioeconomic Dynamics Fostering Antidemocratic Regimes in the Middle East and North Africa (MENA) Region

Ongoing Wars, Contemporary Issues, and Humanitarian Crises

Mehmet Babacan[1]

INTRODUCTION

As a part of the earth, a geographical region may mean more than a territory for humanity and history. The most suitable example of this situation is precisely the "Middle East" region. The international community almost daily talks about events or crises in the Middle East and North Africa (MENA) region. Today, all global powers have a particular agenda for this region. We must remember some historical conflicts between regional and global powers for the hegemony of the Middle East. Since the age of the Industrial Revolution, this region has occupied an indispensable geoeconomic and geopolitics role for Western countries. After the First World War, with the dissolution of the Ottoman Empire and Caliphate, Britain, and France were the region's dominant power (Cleveland and Bunton, 2016). Then with the end of the Second World War, countries in this region lived the effects of the "*Cold War*" (1945–1991) very strongly and heatedly. Nearly all worldwide crises during the Cold War occurred in the Middle East; *U-2 Crisis, Syrian Crisis, Suez Canall Crisis, 1973-OPEC Crisis, Invasion of Aphganistan and Kuwait War* . . . . At the same time, this region has *Mesopotamia*, where the first human communities were seen in history, and the first agricultural activities were carried out. The MENA region can be worked in various disciplines with other dimensions. Still, we can emphasize its political and social structure in recent years, especially during and after the *Arab Spring* revolutions, with the context of the main rules of international relations, foreign policy, and political science.

THEORETICAL AND CONCEPTUAL FRAMEWORK: "DEMOCRACY," "MIDDLE EAST," AND "SOCIAL STRUCTURE"

In recent years when we look at the books and articles that have been published about the Middle East region, generally, we see that they are focused on permanent instability, domestic wars, crises, and political, social, and economic disorder in countries with realist and/or neorealist perspectives (Danahar, 2015). Arguments about this situation generally unite on two points: (a) after the Arab-spring lots of crises and new failure states occurred, and security-based analyses have increased, (b) the region (the Middle East or MENA) is still a zone for world hegemony efforts between super/hyperpower as it happened in the past (e.g., Cold War).

Before moving on to the current unstable state of the Middle East region, we need to assess the reasons and processes that lead to this situation. The waves of the Arab Spring revolution still surround the Middle East. It is remembered with the internal conflicts, civil wars, and crises in this process as Libya, Syria, and Yemen. It has been stated that from the past to the present that democratization is a process that requires skill for the whole MENA region (Schmitter and Karl, 1991: 71–88). When we examine the views put forward about the reasons for this, the patriarchal, which is based on racial ethnicity, tribe, or sect, which we can call "*neo-patrimonial*," to consolidate the political authority of the Middle Eastern countries immediately after gaining their independence, they are determined to be a demand for the management with their social structure (Khoury and Kostiner, 1990).

The perspective that tries to explain the basis of the democracy debates in Middle Eastern countries by reducing the phenomenon of religion and cultural difference, and the *Orientalist* approach that includes theorists and authors such as Daniel Pipes, Samuel Huntington, and Eli Khedourie, is an opinion he adopts (Esposito and Piscatori, 1991: 427–440). As a reflection of this view, the rhetoric of Arab or Middle Eastern "*exceptionalism*" has been born in the literature on the Middle East. Therefore, it has been suggested that the social culture in the region is incompatible with liberal values, so an institutional democratic political system cannot be dominant in the region (Crystal, 1994).

However, since 2011, starting from Tunisia with a domino effect, the popular movements that have influenced the entire MENA geography have partially invalidated this rhetoric and demonstrated that democratic values could also spread in these countries with the dynamism of collective popular movements. As a general name given to the popular movements or uprisings that started to be seen in 2011, the "*Arab Spring*" was perceived by the rest of the world as the wave of democracy in which authoritarian regimes would collapse in this region and the Arab world of about 400 million would undergo a radical transformation. Indeed, while talking about *Arab exceptionalism* in the Middle East region, which is foreign to the liberal and democratic values system represented by the West and relatively late, the collective dynamism it demonstrated by the peoples of the region ruled by authoritarian regimes for years paved the way for the wave of democratization to spread in Arab societies.Huntington explains the process of democracy with the principle that an unelected government is replaced by a new, freely and honestly elected government and mentions the existence of waves of democratization in world history affecting political systems. According to Huntington, the first of the waves of democratization in the world that faced adverse waves was the United States (US) presidential elections in 1828, which were fed by the American and French revolutions, and the increasing spread of democratic-style elections and the governments in the world created. The second represents the process of *decolonization* with the end of the Second World War. The third wave of democratization follows the end of the Portuguese dictatorship (*Salazar regime*) in 1974 and the process of replacing authoritarian regimes in about thirty countries in Europe, Asia, and Latin America with democratic regimes (Huntington, 1991).

Referring to Huntington's *democratization waves theory*, it has been suggested that the popular uprisings seen in the MENA in 2011 were the fourth of these great waves. The presentation of the Arab Spring uprisings as the last wave of democratization demolished the dominance of the Arab or Middle Eastern exceptionalism discourse on the Middle East region for years. In addition, this situation has shaken the position and ideology of the Orientalist movement toward Middle Eastern countries. Also, Edward Said criticizes the idea of *Orientalism* that the region's political, cultural, and social structure and Islam, which is the dominant belief in the region, contradict democratic values (Said, 1988). The wave of the Arab Spring, in which the educated and urban youth with information and communication technologies are the locomotive, especially in countries such as Tunisia, Libya, Egypt, Yemen, and Bahrain, brought their demands to the regional and global agenda.

CONTEMPORARY ISSUES IN THE MIDDLE EAST AND NORTH AFRICA (*MENA*) REGION: *ARAB SPRING* AND REGIMES (CHANGING AND UNCHANGING REGIMES, OTORITERISM AND COUNTER-REVOLUTIONS)

As mentioned above, with the popular uprisings called the Arab Spring countries in the MENA, more demands on social justice, economic opportunities, and political freedoms have been brought to the agenda. Popular uprisings in Tunisia, where Mohammed Bouazizi, who constituted the beginning and the point of the inspiration of the Arab Spring wave, carried out the act of burning himself, actually coincides with the last months of 2010 (Yüksel and Bingöl, 2013: 315).The uprisings that turned into mass movements with the action of Bouazizi are not a phenomenon that occurs suddenly and reflects the expression that chronic problems that have developed over many years have become unbearable in society. Chronic problems, which are closely related to the social-economic and demographic structures of the Arab countries, especially in the last fifty years, are better understood when analyzed with some triggers. The rapid population growth in these countries in the MENA, the excess of young population, the deep feeling of unemployment and poverty among the public, dissatisfaction with justice services, the effects of fundamentalist movements, welfare, the high increase in food prices especially in 2010 and 2011, nepotism, lack of democracy, the persecution of autocratic oppressive regimes for years, complaints about low living standards they have been the primary triggers that ignited the popular movements (Idris, 2016). As a result of these uprisings, which were called the Arab Spring concerning the "*Prague Spring*" of 1968, the dictatorships that had ruled for many years, especially in Egypt and Libya, were destroyed. Still, the process was more difficult in Syria and Yemen.

As a result of the "*Jasmine Revolution*" that started in Tunisia on December 17, 2010, Zeinel-Abidin bin Ali, who ruled the country for twenty-three years, left the Presidency and his country on January 14, 2011. In the elections held afterward, the en-Nahda Party led by Rashid Gannushi, known to have ideological affiliation with the Muslim Brotherhood movement, won the majority in the parliament by taking 40% of the votes (AlJazeera, 2015). Millions of people who rebelled against the 30-year dictatorship of Hosni Mubarak in Egypt, where popular uprisings after Tunisia focused on the "*day of anger*" on January 25, 2011, filled Tahrir Square, and they demonstrated their reactions to unemployment, poverty, and political pressure. The ongoing internal turmoil in the country didn't stop despite the election of Mohammed Morsi as president on June 30, 2012, and the approval of the new constitution. Finally, with a military coup on July 3, 2013, the army took over the administration, and General Abdolfettah al-Sisi announced that Morsi was removed from his post. Following the constitutional amendment made in 2014 and the victory of General Sisi in the presidential election held in the same year, Morsi and many members of the Muslim Brotherhood were arrested and tried (Trager, 2015).

In Libya, where the public uprisings and events started on February 17, 2011, simultaneously with Egypt, the Western countries led by the United States of America (USA), Britain, and France followed a different policy. After the events in this country, NATO's air, land, and sea elements intervened on March 19. Moammar Gaddafi was caught and killed in Sirte on March 20, symbolizing a new era that began in Libya, where 30,000 people lost their lives. Today the country is divided into two due to the authority dispute between the Government of National Consensus, recognized by the United Nations (UN), and the warrior General Caliph Khafter and the social and economic life in the country has been paralyzed. Peaceful negotiations between both parties continue at international platforms led by the UN and European Union (EU). However, it should be said that after the overthrow of the dictator Gaddafi, Libya could not attain a real environment of peace and democracy as hoped (Winer, 2019).

And in Yemen, after the collapse of the national authority, the power vacuum is tried to be filled by local actors. Moreover, the use of these sectarian actors to eat by their neighboring two countries or regional powers, Iran and Saudi Arabia, constitutes the basis of the Yemeni Crisis. The main factor that makes Yemeni a regional security threat and crisis for the Middle East today is Houthi rebels against Mansour Al-Hadi, elected president in 2012 after Ali Abdullah Saleh, who founded a semi-authoritarian government in 1990, left his position. The Houthis, supported by Iran since the beginning, took over the administration in early 2015 and signed agreements with Iran in many areas, including oil, aviation, electricity, and maritime transport (Reuters, 2014). The expansionism of Iran, which is trying to expel the Shiite regime in the region, and its influence in Yemen prompted the Sunni bloc and Saudi Aarabian-led Arab League Members (Jordan, Kuwait, Egypt, and Morocco) have taken a military operation named "*Storm of Determination*" against the Houthi rebels in Yemen. Despite the United States' support for this military operation and providing logistical assistance, the Houthi rebels still dominate Yemen (Exum, 2017).

The demonstrations in Syria, which constitute one of the hardest and deepest links of the Arab Spring wave, started in March 2010 after four people were killed by the security forces in the city of Dera. The protests that started with democratic public demands gradually gained political content, and influenced by examples such as Egypt, Tunisia, and Libya, they turned to the Bashar al-Assad regime. The security forces' response to the demonstrators by firing heavy weapons caused the events to escalate, turn into a civil war, and turn the international community's attention there. The reaction against the Assad regime in Syria has become a regional and global crisis beyond an internal war. As a result of the civil war in Syria, 60% of the country's population has become refugees, and 11 million Syrians have needed humanitarian aid in the last ten years (Domazeti, 2020). In addition, the people of Syria and bordering countries such as Turkey, Jordan, and Lebanon have fallen to European refugee status. Besides , on August 21, 2013, approximately 1400 people lost their lives as a reult of the chmeical weapons attack in Eastern Ghouta. This was a truly brutal crime against humanity committed by the Assad regime. Today, it is cınsidered almost impossible organizing a military international operation against Syria. In addition to the existence of terrorist organizations such as ISIS (*Islamic State of Iraq and Syria*) and PKK/YPG (*Partiya Karkerên Kurdistanê/ Yekîneyên Parastina Gel)* in Syria ,the political authority is fragmented. With these terrorist organizations, Turkey, Iran and Russia also have military bases and forces in the country. Despite all this, the Bashar al-Assad regime resists leaving power and continues the civil massacres (Orhan, 2020).

In conclusion, we can say that; as a result of the widespread public uprisings seen in countries in the MENA geography since 2011 and the revolution called Arab Spring, the existing administrations were changed in countries such as Libya, Egypt, and Tunisia, in countries such as Syria, political systems and rulers continued their existence. During the Arab Spring, authoritarian regimes also showed the ability to adapt to new processes, learning from the Arab Spring protests (Heydemann and Leenders, 2011: 647–653).

UNDERSTANDING THE SOCIOECONOMIC DYNAMICS OF THE MENA REGION

The "Middle East" concept is artificial and a political geography term created for political purposes. Today's region, the Middle East, has a broad meaning of the lands extending from the Atlantic coast to India's Ganges river basin. The term Middle East was first used in history in 1902 by Alfred Thayer Mahan. After that, it is more broadly expressed by Valentino Chirol as the region covering all countries and territories on the road to the Indian colonies (Chirol, 1903). It is also argued that the concept of the Middle East originates from the name of the "*Middle Eastern Commmandership*" that Britain gave to its military units during the Second World War (Davison, 1960).

The Middle East region is more than just the name of a geographical region on earth, where the first agricultural activities were carried out on the fertile Mesopotamian lands where civilizations were born and where all three monolithic religions were born and developed is there. The city of *Jerusalem*, which is considered sacred for these three religions, is in this region. In addition to religious and historical elements, the region is rich in energy resources, containing 60% of the world's petroleum reserves and approximately 50% of natural gas reserves. It also has strategically important seaways, straits, and passages such as the Strait of Hormuz, the Strait of Aden, the Strait of Gibraltar, and the Suez Canal. The Middle East is a region where significant developments and changes have taken place that affect world history, except for the Industrial Revolution (Payind and McClimans, 2017: 8–9).

The region has been open to influence and intervention throughout history and has been the center of conflict and competition. One of the sources of conflict and competition in the region is the region's internal dynamics. Although the dominant belief of the region is Islam, Judaism, and Christianity are also mentioned as other active religions in the region. Ethically, it should be noted that besides Turkish, Arab, and Persian identities, Kurds and Jews also play an important role in the region. From the past to the present, there have been many conflicts stemming from the internal ethnic, religious, sectarian, and political dynamics of the region, such as the Israeli-Palestinian conflict, the Shiite-Sunni conflict, and the Ikhwan-Salafist struggle. Again, the economic structure in the region includes countries that differ greatly from each other depending on the form of political organization (Bates and Rassam, 1996). Firstly, there are "*rentier state*" countries whose economy is largely based on producing and selling natural resources (oil and gas); on the other hand, there are other countries with scarce resources. The economic and political organization in the region has a great impact on the social structure, such as religion, sect, and ethnicity. For example, in Egypt, where the per capita income is $3,000, some people rebelled within the scope of the Arab Spring due to unemployment, poverty, and other economic problems, while Saudi Arabia affiliated with the Palace bureaucracy, bribes and thanks to its neo-patrimonial rule, it freed itself from the effects of the Arab Spring (Kaldas, 2020).

Religion and Sectarian Issues

Religion has an important determinant role in the Middle East's current political issues and social and socioeconomic structure. In addition to the fact that the origins of *Christianity, Islam*, and *Judaism*, which are three important monolithic religions, are in this region, the fact that the prophets who preached these religions to the people were the first to declare their beliefs in the Middle East region also carries the subject to the historical dimension of theology and religions. With the three monolithic religions, the presence of other Middle East-centered minority religions, such as *Yazidism* and *Zoroastrianism*, shows the importance of the phenomenon of religion for the Middle East in every field. Although there are different races, languages, and religions in the Middle East, Middle Eastern states, countries, nations, and religions also differ. For example, there is not a single sect among the countries of the region regarding Islam, which is the dominant religion of the region, and there is a division into different sects (Halliday, 2005: 9).

The deepening of these sectarian differences in a way that reveals their own beliefs and identities by the states that exist in the region expands and strengthens the potential conflict areas in the Middle East. The rivalry between Saudi Arabia and Iran, which is the most important example that can be given in this regard, has turned the sectarian separation in the region into a regional leadership struggle in the situation. Today, Iran's support for Shiite militias in Syria, Lebanon, and Yemen is faced with strong opposition from the Sunni bloc in the region, especially from Saudi Arabia. While religions and sects shaped and gave identity to many Arab states in the Middle East, they gave the Jewish State identity by shaping it in the state of Israel, which was established in 1948. At the birth of Israel, as a spatial geopolitical discourse, has an important potential in the process of building the identity of both the state, the nation, and the society (Lee, 2014: 81). Since 1948, Palestine, which is in dispute with the Jewish State over the same religious places and sanctuaries, claims its religious perception especially on Jerusalem and to be effective in a way to highlight its religious belief works.

Despite having the same religious beliefs, Iran and Saudi Arabia, which are in regional competition over sectarian differences, are also based on a sectarian separation between Egypt and Saudi Arabia, and an understanding of Salafi and Muslim Brotherhood (*Ikhwan*) polarization can be mentioned. Therefore, while religion in the Middle East is often a source of legitimacy for political systems, it is often used extensively as a means of influencing other states and gaining influence over the region. This situation also leads to effects and conflicts that transcend the nation-state's borders (Razi, 1990).

Social Structure: Tribes and Ethnical Problems

It has a mosaic-like appearance regarding Middle Eastern national and ethnic identities and religions. Contrary to popular belief, the region is not a homogeneous structure; it is the living space of ethnic groups such as *Turkish, Arab, Persian, Kurdish, Armenian, Jewish*, and *Assyrian*, showing a heterogeneous character. *Turks, Arabs*, and *Persians*, the dominant ethnic elements in the region, emerged as the most important determinant of ethnicity in shaping the region in terms of civilization and history. However, it should be noted that *Kurds, Armenians*, and *Jews* are also ethnic groups that played an important role in shaping the region. Besides, there are many other ethnic minorities in every country. Kurds, for example, live significantly in Turkey, Iraq, Iran, and Syria, similar to Turkmen in Iraq. Besides, again in certain parts of Iran, it is known that Arab minorities exist. According to views based on historical reasons for the reasons of ethnic problems in the Middle East, the drawing of the borders of the countries by the imperialist powers in a way that does not conform to the nation-state logic after the First World War is the biggest factor that causes the conflicts. While the existing borders of the countries in the region were drawn arbitrarily by the Western states; as a result, divided societies that did not feel belonging to the state they lived in (Lu and Thies, 2013).

Ethnic diversity in the region and ethnic minorities within countries have created many conflicts, crises, and wars in the historical process. For example, Saddam Hussein used chemical poisonous gas against Kurdish minorities in the incident known as the *Halabja Massacre* in 1988, citing the uprisings of the Kurds in his country as an excuse. Before the war with Iraq (1980–1988), Iran claimed that the Arab minorities in his region, Khuzestan, were provoked by other Arab states, Iraq. And we know that since 1985 an armed rebellion (PKK) in Turkey has had a Kurdish minority. And a low-intensity war is taking place in the East and Southeast of the country (Gunes and Zeydanlıoglu, 2015).

Ethnic identities were as important as religious identities in the formation of the modern Middle East born. As an example, Saddam Hussein gave special importance to Arabs and Sunnis, who are minorities among Arabs, and even their countrymen (*Tıkritîs*), in his administration in Iraq. Similarly, while the Assad regime ensured the dominance of the minority ethnic identity of Syria against the Sunnis in the majority, the presence of local *Bedouin* elements supporting the Hashemite regime in Jordan is an example. In addition, the tribes that have held trade in Saudi Arabia for many years provide financial support to Ibn Saud to control the *Nejd* and *Hejaz* region during the establishment of the Saudi state, and these tribes are in a privileged position in the future it has enabled it to take place (Boulby, 2013).

The ethnic divisions that exist in countries in the Middle East have sometimes deepened as divisions that have the potential to return to conflict. Especially in the postcolonial period, powerful local families and tribes who held power saw the regime's interests that represented them as superior to the national interests. While this situation has created great dissatisfaction in the public base and affected social structure negatively over the years, the most appropriate examples of this can be seen in the thirty yearly Mubarak regime in Egypt and the Assad family, who are still active in Syria (Boulby, 2013).

Economic Structure

With the dissolution of the Ottoman Empire after the First World War, economically diverse countries and systems emerged in the Middle East. Effective colonial administrations in the region, especially France and Britain, gave more importance to politics in this region than the economy, and the countries in the region have ruled that their currencies are valid. This situation caused the extinguished countries to suffer great economic damage. In addition, another factor affecting the state structures and economic systems of the Middle Eastern countries is the Petroleum Concession agreements they signed with foreign powers, which represent indirect exploitation. For example, the concession first signed in Iran in 1901 is a prime example. Despite the reactions of the public, this situation in Iran continued until 1979, when the nationalization efforts of the Prime Minister Dr. Mohammed Musaddıq were interrupted by the *Ajax Operation* (Gelvin, 194).

Saudi Arabia and other Gulf countries (UAE, Kuwait, Bahrain, etc.), whose economy is mainly dependent on oil revenues and has the status of a *rentier state* in the region. These countries suffer more than other states in the event of an unexpected drop in oil prices and their economic incomes is fall sharply. This situation also accelerates social and political changes in the mentioned countries. The primary incomes of other states that do not have the status of a rentier state in the region and do not have petroleum incomes, except for natural resources, are foreign aids, agricultural incomes, small enterprises, and foreign exchange brought to take the country by the labor force working outside the country. For example, non-rentier states such as Jordan and Lebanon consistently receive foreign economic aid from actors inside and outside the region, as they do not have oil but are strategically and geopolitically important. However, this situation makes the domestic and foreign policies of these non-rentier states, which are defined as weak or small countries, open to the intervention of other actors and makes them their potential domain. This dependency relationship causes weak states to pursue an independent foreign policy rather than eliminate external factors (Sorli, Gleditcsh, and Strand, 2015: 147).

Military-Policy Relations

In the context of military-political relations, it can be said that the army has a determining role in the political systems of countries in the Middle East with authoritarian regimes. The fact that the army has an active role in the modernization process and that a large part of the income is devoted to defense expenditures reveals that domestic politics cannot be considered separately from a military organization. The new states established in the Middle East, especially after the collapse of the Ottoman Empire after the First World War, needed a strong army and charismatic leaders to build a strong central administration. Military coups in the Middle East came into force with the coup of Bekir Sıdkı in Iraq in 1936 for the first time in the Middle East in the postcolonial period. Saddam Hussein, who had an important place in the political life of Iraq, placed the army at the center of the state apparatus with his defense expenditures besides bringing the Baas party to the forefront. However, Egypt is the best example of the army's role in society and state life in the Middle East. The transformative and modernizing influence of the army on society in Egypt has a long history dating back to the Ottoman Empire. Nasser seized the Egyptian administration in 1952 and, after Britain withdrew from the Suez Canal in 1954, started to increase the number of police and security forces. The army's role in Egypt was understood more closely during the Arab Spring period, and the Supreme Military Council took over the administration after Hosni Mubarak left his position. It should be said that Abdulfettah al-Sisi, who currently rules Egypt, is a General, and the country is a military dictatorship based on military rule.

Shortly, we can say that military-political relations play an important role in the political life of the states in the Middle East, that the army intervened in the state life with coups and played an important role in suppressing the internal turmoil and opposition in the country (McNabb, 2017).

ONGOING WARS AND HUMANITARIAN CRISES

The MENA region have not survived the trauma of the Arab Spring, although ten years have passed. Today, the ongoing civil war and conflict environment in Libya, Syria, and Yemen has completely turned into a global crisis. Many global and regional actors actively participated in these crises and implemented a proxy war strategy. While the social, political, and economic life in these countries, where many terrorist organizations have emerged, has gradually deteriorated, people in these countries need humanitarian aid regarding food, economy, and health. Especially Syria and Yemen is a humanitarian crisis, and the people in these countries are hungry. In addition to all these, the COVID-19 global epidemic/pandemic, which started to emerge in 2019, seriously threatens the lives of the people of these countries under adverse health conditions. Furthermore, the regime change in these countries has not been fully realized, a well-functioning democracy has not yet been established, and economic and social life has not been settled (Middle East Institute, 2021).

It is a practice of proxy and attrition war in which all regional and global actors, large and small, take part in Syria today. To fulfill the functions of nation-states, especially after the Arab Spring, due to the extreme volatility of sectarian and regional alliances in line with strategic interests and the gradual weakening of existing nation-states, non-state actors emerged that got stronger. The leading terrorist organizations, ISIS, the PKK/YPG, and the Shiite-origin Hezbollah, have had an active presence in Syria. The emergence of these terrorist organizations and non-state actors, which are considered to be in addition to the opponents who are fighting the Bashar al-Assad regime in Syria, is far from the conditions of a Syrian society that will live in peace and stability. The most important reasons for the survival of the Assad regime, which symbolizes the Nusayri minority, which constitutes 16% of the population, to rule the rest of the society by autocratic methods, are supported by actors such as Iran and Russia, passive engagement of the United States and insufficient efforts of the international community. During the 10-year Syrian Civil War, approximately 14 million people were killed due to the torture of the Assad regime. At the same time, 5.6 million Syrians left their country and became refugees in Turkey, Jordan, Lebanon, and European countries. Approximately 60% of the country's population within the borders of Syria needs humanitarian aid, and hospitals, healthcare buildings, schools, and other important civil society buildings have been demolished during the ongoing civil war (BBC, 2016).

Yemen is the Middle Eastern country where a humanitarian crisis is experienced similar to Syria or even more severe. The political authority gap that emerged after the withdrawal of Ali Abdullah Saleh's administration in Yemen was wanted to be filled by local actors, especially the Houthi tribe belonging to the Zeydî sect. Even Zeydî seized the Capital City of Sana in 2014 and drafted a unilateral constitution. As we explained above, when the semi-authoritarian rule of Ali Abdullah Saleh, supported by Saudi Arabia, collapsed as a result of the Arab Spring uprisings and Shiite supporters started to take effect in the country, the Kingdom of Saudi Arabia is with its Sunni allies organized an air operation to this country together. In this situation in Yemen, while Iran openly supported the Zeydîs/Houthis, such as Nusayris in Syria, Russia demonstrated its support for Iran. On the other hand, the United States went to solidarity with Saudi Arabia and the Sunni bloc (Ghamarai, 2015: 47). But currently, the Joe Biden administration declared in its last statement that it would not support Saudi Arabia over the War in Yemen. While the armed conflicts continue in the country today, the people of Yemen are very dire; without the strength to stand in the face of hunger, poverty, disease, increased infant and child deaths, divided state structure, insufficient infrastructure, and instability draw the table. In Yemen, as in Syria, it is still unknown when the conflicts will end and when stability will be achieved (Pradhan, 2017: 96).

CONCLUSION

The Middle East is a region with an ancient civilization accumulation that has been the source of important developments in human history. This region has been the center of a global struggle throughout history due to its geopolitical location and energy resources. The competition to gain dominance in this region has affected the region's stability in all periods. At the same time, the regional leadership struggles of the states in the region have been mentioned. This geography, which has an important and special position in terms of religious, historical, economic, and geopolitical, remained under the rule of the Ottoman Empire for approximately 400 years; after the First World War, Britain and France established a mandate regime in the region. After the Second World War, the region, subject to the USSR and US's global competition, came to the agenda with the waves of social and political revolution called the *Arab Spring*, which started in 2011 after the Cold War. Authoritarian and antidemocratic regimes have generally dominated countries in the Middle East region for years. This is the main reason that started the popular uprisings. However, the ethnic diversity and religious minorities in every country in the MENA region, the frequent intervention of the army in politics, and the unstable economic structure are other important factors that reveal the popular movements. For example, the anger felt by the Sunnis, who make up about 70% of the population in Syria, against the oppressive regime of the minority Nusayri or the reaction of the people in Egypt to the economic inadequacies can be read from this perspective. In addition, the pressure of the Quaddafi tribe, to which leader Muammar Gaddafi belongs, on other tribes in Libya has been the reason for the popular uprisings in Libya. This collective public dynamism has also transformed the culturalist and orientalist literature, stating that democracy cannot rule over the region's people. However, the number of revolutions that have been successful in the current period is few, and the current situation resembles more of a winter than spring.

The ongoing civil war and conflict, especially in Syria and Yemen, has become a global humanitarian crisis. The war environment in Syria and Yemen continues due to the inability of local actors, supported by global and regional actors, to overpower each other. Besides proxy actors and proxy wars, the emergence of terrorist organizations such as ISIS, Hezbollah, PKK/YPG, and Al-Qaeda in Syria, Iraq, Libya, and Yemen further destabilized these countries. The countries in the region have used religious and ethnic minorities among each other for their strategic purposes and tried to create a sphere of influence. This situation continues during and after the Arab Spring.

NOTE

1. M. Babacan. Bursa Uludag University, Turkey/TR. E-mail: babacan_b27@hotmail.com

BIBLIOGRAPHY

Bates, Daniel and Amal Rassam (1996) *Peoples and Cultures of The Middle East*, New Jersey: Prentice Hall.

Boulby, Marion (2013) "Extra-Regional Interests, Authoritarian Elites and Dependent States Formation in the Arab World," in *State Formation and Identitiy in the Middle East and North Africa*, eds. Kenneth Christie and Mohammad Masad, New York: Palgrave Macmillan Press, 48–49.

Chirol, Valentino (1903) "The Middle East Question or Some Problems of Indian Defence," London: John Murray, Albemarle Street, 1–6.

Crystal J. (1994) "Authoritarianism and Its Adversaries in the Arab World," *World Politics*, 46 (2), 262–289.

Cleveland, William L. and Martin Bunton (2016) *A History of The Modern Middle East*, Boulder, CO: Westview Press.

"COVID-19 & Conflict in the Middle East," (2021) *Middle East Institute*, https://www.mei.edu/publications/covid-19-conflict-middle-east

Danahar, Paul (2015) *The New Middle East: The World After the Arab Spring*, New York: Bloomsbury Paperbacks.

Davison, Roderic H. (1960) "Where is the Middle East?" *Foreign Affairs*, 38 (4), 665–675.

Domazeti, Riad (2020) *Humanitarian Situation in Syria*, İNSAMER Research no. 130.

Esposito John L. and James P. Piscatori (1991) "Democratization and Islam," *Middle East Journal*, 45 (3), 427–440.

Exum, Andrew (2017) "What's Really at stake for America in Yemen's Conflict," *The Atlantic*, https://www.theatlantic.com/international/archive/2017/04/yemen-trump-aqap/522957/

Gelvin, James (2011) *The Modern Middle East: A History*, 3th edition, Oxford: Oxford University Press

Ghamarai, el Magdalena (2015) "Jemen: The Proxy War," *Securitologia*, (2), 43–56.

Gunes, Cengiz and Welat Zeydanlioglu (2014) *The Kurdish Question in Turkey: New Perspective on Violence, Representation and Reconciliation*, London: Routledge.

Halliday, Fred (2005) *100 Myths About The Middle East*, London: Saqi.

Heydemann S. and R. Leenders (2011) "Authoritarian Learning amd Authoritarian Resilence: Regime Responses to the 'Arab Awakening,'" *Globalizations*, 8 (5), 647–653.

"How Yemen's Houthis Control Sanaa and Alarm the West," (2014) *Reuters*, https://www.reuters.com/article/us-yemen-houthis-insight-idUSKBN0JN1OU20141209

Huntington Samuel P. (1991) *The Third Wave: Democratization in The Late Tweentieth Century*, Oklahoma: University of Oklahoma Press.

Idris, Iffat (2016) *Analysis of the Arab Spring*, (GSDRC Helpdesk Research Report 1350). Birmingham: GSDRC, University of Birmingham.

Kaldas, Timothy (2020) "Egyptians Are No Better Off Than Before the Arab Spring," *Bloomberg Opinion* https://www.bloombergquint.com/gadfly/egyptians-are-no-better-off-than-before-the-arab-spring

Khoury Philip S. and Joseph Kostiner (1990) *Tribes and Tate Formation in the Middle East*, Berkeley, CA: University of California Press.
Lee, Robert D. (2014) *Religion and Politics in the Middle East: Identity, Ideology, Institutions and Attitudes*, Boulder, CO: Westview Press.
Lu, Lingyu and Cameron G. Thies, (2013) "War, Rivalry and State Building in the Middle East," *Political Research Quarterly*, 66 (2), 239–253.
McNabb, James Brian (2017) *A Military History of The Modern Middle East*, Westport, CT: Praeger Publishing.
Orhan, Oytun (2020) "10th Years of Syria Crisis," *Ortadogu Analiz/Middle East Analysis*, 11 (93): 44–47.
Payind, Alaim & Melinda McClimans (2017), *Keys to Understanding the Middle East*, Columbus, OH: The Ohio State University Press.
Pradhan, Prasanta K. (2017) *Arab Spring and Secterian Faultlines In West Asia: Bahrain, Yemen and Syria*, New Delhi: Pentagon Press.
Razi, Hossein (1990) "Legitimacy, Religion and Nationalism in the Middle East," *The American Political Science Review*, 84 (1), 69–91.
Said, Edward (1988) *Orientalism*, New York: The Vintage Books.
Schmitter, P.C., and T.L. Karl (1991) "What Democracy Is … and Is not." *Journal of Democracy*, 2 (3), 75–88.
Sorli, Mirjam E., Nils Petter Gleditsch and Havard Strand (2005) "Why Is there so Much Conflict in the Middle East?" *The Journal of Conflict Resolution*, 49 (1), 141–165.
"Syria: The Story of the Conflict," (2016) *BBC*, https://www.bbc.com/news/world-middle-east-26116868
"Tunisia Parliament Approves Unity Government," (2015) *Al-Jazeera*, https://www.aljazeera.com/news/2015/2/6/tunisia-parliament-approves-unity-government
Trager, Eric (2015) "Egypt Two Years After Morsi," *The Washington Institute (TWI)*, https://www.washingtoninstitute.org/policy-analysis/egypt-two-years-after-morsi
Winer, Jonathan M. (2019) "Are The Foreign Patrons of the Libyan War Ready To End It?" *Middle East Institute*, https://www.mei.edu/publications/are-foreign-patrons-libyan-war-ready-end-it
Yüksel, Başak Akar ve Yılmaz Bingöl (2013) "The Arab Spring in Tunisia: A Liberal Democratic Transition?" *Electronic Journal of Social Sciences*, 12 (47), 310–327.

Part IV

COERCION, CULTURE, AND ENVIRONMENT IN INTERNATIONAL RELATIONS

Chapter 13

Coercion in International Affairs

Nature, Forms, and Mechanisms—A Theoretical and a Practical Perspective[1]

Jean Yves Ndzana Ndzana[2]

INTRODUCTION

The use of threat and, to some extent, of force as an instrument of foreign policy is not recent. From Antiquity with warrior pharaohs like Tuthmosis III or Ramses II to the Napoleonic conquests of the eighteenth century, military force has always been a strategic instrument for achieving political objectives. To avoid the disastrous consequences of the two World Wars of the twentieth century, the post-war international system was built on cooperation and international law as the main instruments for resolving international disputes. However, States increasingly resort to coercion as a foreign policy tool, making it an increasing hallmark of our post–Cold War era. In light of the Iranian nuclear crisis, this chapter aims to analyze the notion of coercion in international relations. Thanks to the process-tracing method, we will explore the various coercive strategies adopted by the US administration to compel the Iranian republic government under Ahmadinejad to reverse its nuclear program. In this regard, we will mainly rely on primary sources (remarks and comments of Iranian diplomats and Western leaders) and secondary sources (books and articles) to explain the outcomes of the coercive dynamics between the two States mentioned above. The scope of this chapter does not include the transformations of the international system which led to the current circumstances; instead, the first subpart (A) emphasizes the theoretical aspects of coercion, its nature (1), its forms (2), and its different mechanisms (3). The second subpart (B) will analyze the coercive dynamics between Iran and the United States during the Ahmadinejad presidency.[3]

COERCION IN INTERNATIONAL RELATIONS, A THEORETICAL PERSPECTIVE

The Nature of Coercion

The notion of coercion has two etymologies: on the one hand, an old French origin (*cohercen*) and, on the other hand, a Latin root (*coercere*). The former refers to restraining or constraining by force of law or authority, while the latter refers to *controlling, securing,* (*and*) *shutting up together* (Online Etymology Dictionary). From this perspective, coercing an actor (individual, group, State) designates the act of having recourse to a means or leverage to compel actors to do something they would not have done in other circumstances. Therefore, the core idea of coercion is rationality, the ability of an actor to decide and behave based first and foremost on his/her benefits over the costs. In addition, by emphasizing the necessity to use leverage (usually force) to modify the behavior of the target, coercion studies belong to the Realist school of thought in International Relations. From the previous etymologies, one would expect a consensual definition of coercion. Yet, there is no consensual definition of the notion of coercion. Robert Pape defines coercion as the "efforts to change the behavior of a State by manipulating costs and benefits" (Pape, 1996, p. 4). But Robert Art and Kelly Greenhill define it as *the ability to get an actor—a state, the leader of a state, a terrorist group, a transnational or international organisation, a private actor—to do something it does not want to do* (Greenhill and Krause, 2018, p. 5). Although these definitions encompass both the rationality dimension of coercion and broaden the spectre of the actors who might be subjected to a coercive policy, they do not explicitly highlight the instruments used by the coercer. Rob De Wijk fills this gap as he defines coercion as *the deliberate and targeted use—or threat to use—of power instruments to manipulate and influence the politico-strategic choices of an actor, or player, defined as an entity that plays an identifiable role in international relations* (De Wijk, 2014, p. 16).

Considering the previous definitions, coercion usually but not always requires using (military) force to compel an actor to behave accordingly. However, warfare does the same, for States also employ troops and weapons against others to implement their agenda. What's, then, the difference between coercion and war? Alexander George was the first to set a benchmark to distinguish the use of force in a coercive context from a warfare context; indeed, he described the coercive use of force as *an exemplary use of quite limited force to persuade the opponent to back down,* (meaning) *the use of just enough force of an appropriate kind to demonstrate resolution to protect one's interests and to establish the credibility of one's determination to use more force if necessary* (George and Simons, 1994, p. 73). Though

George already sets a difference between coercion and warfare, the adjective "exemplary" does not refer to a clear, tangible, measurable criterion.

Blechman and Kaplan go further on this issue as they argue that *armed forces may be used as political or martial instruments. When used as a martial instrument, a military unit acts to seize an objective (e.g., occupy territory) or to destroy an objective (e.g., defeat an invading army). (. . .) When used as a political instrument, the objective is to influence the behavior of another actor. That is, to cause an actor to do something that he would not otherwise do or not do something that he would do otherwise* (Congressional Research Service, 1980, p. 33). In other words, coercion should be assessed based on the effect of force on the target, especially on the modification of its perceptions. By highlighting the necessity of considering the rationality of the target, this approach captures a core element of the notion of coercion. It emphasizes the coercive mechanism which led to the target's reaction. However, one cannot predict in advance whether the reaction of the target will be proportional to the expected outcomes of the sender or the coercer or not. In fact, the target may or may not react according to the initial calculus of the sender or may even exceedingly behave accordingly. For example, a regime's collapse after a coercive policy cannot be considered a success if the initial goal of the sender was a change of policy from the target. Hence, a coercive policy can be identified based on the initial goal of the sender, the level of the military force deployed, and the actual effects on the target. A couple of variable plays a role in determining the form of coercion.

The Different Forms of Coercion

Depending on the reaction the coercer expects from the target when adopting a coercive policy, we have two forms of coercion: first, compellence and second, deterrence. The notion of deterrence comes from the Latin etymology *de-terrere*, which means "away" with "fear or frighten." Hence, deterrence refers to the action of preventing an actor from following a specific pattern of behavior based on the fear caused by one's retaliatory measures. In this case, the target will comply with the coercer's demands because the gains from maintaining the status quo, thus refraining from acting, surpass his loss. One of the boldest illustrations of a deterrent coercive policy in the recent history of international relations was the Mutual Assured Destruction (MAD) doctrine that characterized the Cold War era. The MAD doctrine refers to a *defence strategy based on the concept that neither the United States nor its enemies will ever start a nuclear war because the other side will retaliate massively and unacceptably* (Parrington, 1997, p. 6). In this case, conscious of the catastrophic consequences of the willing or unwilling use of their nuclear arsenal, neither the United States nor the USSR dared attack each other, and whenever they did, it was always indirectly or through proxy governments.

From its double Latin and old French etymologies, compellence respectfully refers to driving together, driving *to one place* and *to drive or urge irresistibly by physical or moral force*. The term compellence was coined by Thomas Schelling, who describes it as a scenario where the sender *initiates an action (or an irrevocable commitment to action) that can cease or become harmless only if the opponent responds (favorably)* (Schelling, 2008, p. 72). It is *a coercive strategy based on hurting the target (or threatening to do so), to force the target to change its behavior* (Greenhill and Krause, 2018, p. 5 - a). In other words, it implies that a coercer changes the course of actions already taken by an adversary or marked by the threat or actual use of force. Hence, compellence differs from deterrence in many regards: first, in the action's timing and initiative. Deterrence sets the stage; that is to say, it draws a red line not to cross. In this regard, deterrence is a reactive strategy. Second, compellence involves initiating the action—that is, taking the lead-which will not be stopped until the target has agreed on our demands. From this perspective, compellence is a proactive strategy.

However, Alexander George criticized the term compellence on two bases: first, it did not shed light on the offensive or defensive motivation of the coercer, and second, it emphasized too much on threats. As he noticed, "the term compellence, which Thomas Schelling introduced into the literature [. . .] is often employed to encompass both coercive diplomacy and blackmail and sometimes deterrence as well. [. . .] It is useful to distinguish between defensive and offensive use of threats; compellence does not. Second, compellence implies exclusive or heavy reliance on coercive threats, whereas I wish to emphasise the possibility of a more flexible diplomacy" (George and Simons, 1994, p. 73). To address those issues, he coined the notion of coercive diplomacy, which differs from blackmail. While the latter describes the offensive-based use of threats or actual use of force, the former describes the defensive-based use of coercive actions. Yet, coercive diplomacy refers to the defensive use of threats or symbolic use of force and helps make a difference with military coercion.

Several researchers argue that military coercion *seeks to achieve an outcome not by imposing it directly but by persuading another actor to behave in a particular way* (. . .). *It threatens the use of force, and sometimes includes its use—though when it does, it does not do so in ways that themselves determine the outcome of the confrontation* (Sisson, Siebens, and Blechman, 2020, p. 33). Phil M. Haun agrees as he believes that *military coercion threatens or employs limited violence to convince a target to comply with demands* (Greenhill and Krause, 2018, p. 79 - b). Yet, these definitions are not different from the classic definition of coercion, as we previously analyzed. Peter Viggo

Jakobsen provides a more accurate definition of military coercion as he considers it to be *the use of military threats and/or limited force to stop or undo undesirable actions already undertaken by other actors* (Jakobsen, 2011, p. 56). This definition highlights the exclusive reliance on military instruments in the coercive strategy. The exclusive reliance on military instruments can be explained by the nature of the demand formulated to the target, hence the strategic interests at stake in the conflict. Robert Pape describes this particular context in these terms: "in military coercion, the State issuing the threat (assailant) seeks to persuade the target state (victim) to concede territory or other political values that the assailant has not yet achieved on the battlefield. These goals may include compelling the target to reduce political or territorial aims, agree to a ceasefire, withdraw forces, or even surrender" (Pape, 1992, p. 425). Military coercion can be implemented using air strikes (Pape, 1992a), gunboats (Cable, 1994) or cyber-attacks. However, cyber-attacks can also be used in the context of diplomatic coercion or coercive diplomacy.

Alexander George defines coercive diplomacy as *a defensive strategy that is employed to deal with the efforts of an adversary to change a status quo situation in his own favor* (George and Simmons, 1994, p. 6). G. R. Berridge and Alan James Emeritus define coercive diplomacy as a *euphemism for the threat or use of force against an opponent in order to foster a more cooperative cast of mind* (Berridge and James, 2001, p. 36). While the former definition highlights the aim of coercive diplomacy, it fails to identify the instruments used for the purpose. Also, Berridge and James's definition does not clearly distinguish military coercion and coercive diplomacy. Therefore, it is essential to emphasize that coercive diplomacy implies the combination of threats or actual use of *exemplary force* with nonmilitary and classic diplomatic resources. Alexander George distinguishes two types of coercive defensive diplomacy depending on the coercer's objective. First, "type A," whose aim is to coerce a target before it achieves its objective. Second, "type B" consists of compelling an actor to undo an action. "Type C" is the most difficult one to implement as it consists of forcing an actor to make changes in the government or the nature of the political regime (Jentleson, 1991). According to John C. Harrison, there is a "type D" coercive diplomacy, which aims at creating a government in a country that does not have one. It's state-building-based coercive diplomacy (Harrison, 1995).

Coercive diplomacy can be implemented thanks to several political, economic and, to some extent, military instruments. Political-based coercion usually aims to sever diplomatic relations between the target State and the *international community*. This can be done differently, but a preferred strategy is a diplomatic isolation (Klotz, 1999). There are two main types of diplomatic isolation: bilateral and multilateral. Bilateral diplomatic isolation can take the form of diplomatic demarches, the withdrawal of ambassadors, (and) the denial of visas to officials (De Wijk, 2014, p. 110). Multilateral diplomatic isolation can take the form of UN resolutions, sports and cultural boycotts (De Wijk, 2014, p. 110). Another strategy of diplomatic coercion is naming and shaming campaigns, which refer to publicly saying that a person, company, and so on has behaved incorrectly or illegally. Finally, Timothy Crawford developed a theory of coercive isolation which refers to a specific diplomatic practice focusing on isolating an adversary in other to render him more vulnerable to military force and more exposed to the costs of fighting. He demonstrated how the Soviet compellence strategy against the Japanese during the Mongolia-Manchuria border war was only effective when the Soviet Union successfully deprived Japan of the military and political support it expected from Germany through the Nazi-Soviet pact (Crawford, 2013).

Concerning economic coercion, it's essential first to analyze the notion of economic statecraft. Economic statecraft refers to "all the economic means by which foreign policymakers might try to influence other international actors" (Baldwin, 1985, p. 40). Depending on the decision maker's goal, they can be grouped into two categories: positive and negative sanctions. Positive sanctions usually aim to incite or reward a State and can take the form of preferential tariffs, subsidies, foreign aid, investment guarantees, and preferential taxation of foreign investment. Conversely, negative sanctions aim at punishing a State for compelling him to change its behavior; they can take the form of embargoes, boycotts, punitive taxation, aid suspensions, and asset freezes. This negative aspect of economic assets is similar to the notion of economic warfare, which Thomas Schelling defines as the financial and trade means by which damage is imposed on other countries or the threat of harm used to bring pressure on them (Baldwin, 1985, p. 37).

There is no consensual definition of the notion of economic coercion. Murray Scot Tanner defines it as the efforts at coercive or threatening economic behavior by an initiating government directed against a target government; [it] includes the deliberate disruption, or threat of disruption, of "customary" trade, financial, or other economic relations (Tanner, 2007, pp. 4–5). *Daniel Drezner* defines economic coercion as *the threat or act by a sender government or governments to disrupt monetary exchange with the target State unless the target acquiesces to an articulated demand* (Drezner, 2003, p. 643). Those two definitions reinforce each other: the first one includes the deliberate use of economic means by the coercer to influence the behavior of the target; however, it does not insist on the dimension of rational choice imposed by the coercer as the second definition does. Jonathan Kirshner identified four main types of economic coercion: foreign aid, monetary power, financial power, and trade (Kirshner, 1997). In addition to the previous instruments analyzed, coercive mechanisms also play a strategic role in the dynamics of coercive diplomacy.

TYPES OF COERCIVE MECHANISM

From its Latin etymology *mechanismus*, a mechanism refers to *the structure of a machine, engine, or other contrivance for controlling or utilizing natural forces. From* the Greek etymology *mēkhanē*, a mechanism describes a "machine, instrument, or a device." The Merriam-Webster Dictionary defines a mechanism as *a process, technique, or system for achieving a result* (The Merriam-Webster Dictionary). Regarding coercive diplomacy, Daniel Byman considers a mechanism as a "process by which the threat or infliction of costs generates adversary concessions" (Byman and Waxman, 2002, p. 48). Thereof, the mechanism is the transmission belt between the coercive strategy and the coercive effect, which leads to a specific outcome. Byman identified four main coercive: power-base erosion, unrest, decapitation, weakening and denial. The power-base erosion refers to a process through which the target is expected to comply with the coercer's demand due to the risk of losing its core domestic support; this is a domestic application of the international coercive isolation analyzed previously. The coercer usually triggers this mechanism by putting "pressure on the adversary's constituency, which in turn causes an unhappy populace to pressure the government to alter its policy." (Romaniuk and Webb, 2015, p. 109) The pressure can be imposed via measures like economic sanctions, travel bans or other forms of actions which usually fall under the punishment strategy umbrella.

On the other hand, decapitation: In this case, the coercer aims to threaten the top leadership's security, which could be replaced by a less hawkish leader eager to comply. Byman argues that "actual assassination can bring to power a different individual or regime that may change the policy" (Byman and Waxman, 2002, p. 72). Concerning the denial mechanism, denial strategies aim to make the adversary realize its counter-coercive strategy's inefficiency. As a mechanism, it occurs when the leader is dissuaded from continuing on its controversial track or pattern. Byman emphasizes the necessity of distinguishing coercive denial and warfare denial. While the former *hinges on the perception* (*of the target*) *that benefits will not be achieved*, the latter *rests on making that perception a reality.* (. . .) *While coercive denial focuses on convincing an adversary that future benefits are unattainable, conventional warfighting focuses on physically stopping an adversary regardless of what its leadership believes* (Byman and Waxman, 2002, p. 78). The fourth mechanism analyzed by Byman is weakening. The weakening mechanism usually occurs when the coercive strategy aims to undermine the coercee's core infrastructures to incapacitate the entire country. According to Rob de Wijk, a synonym of the weakening mechanism is "incapacitation," and it aims to target critical infrastructure, communications and other institutions that make up a country's economic strength and political cohesion (De Wijk, 2014, p.

140). For the weakening mechanism to lead to the target's compliance, the coercer should focus on the target's "pressure points," which refer to the points that the adversary cannot "impenetrably guard," as Byman rightly put it. This was the case, for example, when the United States compelled the British to stop their invasion campaign against Nasser's Egypt in 1956 by threatening to deny them access to financial assets, which could lead to an economic crash in the UK (Byman and Waxman, 2002, p. 77). However, the weakening mechanism cannot be effective against autocratic regimes, which usually deviate from the coercive effects toward the political opposition. The next subpart will analyze the coercive dynamics between the United States (Bush and Obama) and Iran (Ahmadinejad).

The Iranian Nuclear Crisis: A Practical Case of Coercive Diplomacy

The Iranian nuclear program was officially revealed in 2002 by the National Council of Resistance of Iran, a dissent political organization calling for the toppling of the Islamic regime since 1981. From those ground-breaking revelations in 2002 till the signing of the landmark nuclear deal—between Iran and the Permanent members of the Security Council (SC) together with Germany (E3+3) in 2015—the Iranian nuclear crisis can be divided into four critical periods. The first period goes from 2002 to 2006 (negotiations between the EU and Iran), the second period goes from 2006 to 2009 (when the United States, China, and Russia joined the Iranian nuclear talks), and then from 2009 to 2013 (President Obama took office) and the last period from 2013 till 2015 (President Rouhani stepped in as the new Iranian president); we will focus on the third period. However, the inputs from the dynamics that occurred during the two previous periods will serve as a backdrop for our chapter. Furthermore, the chapter will focus only on the coercive measures adopted by the UN, the EU, or the United States, and we will analyze Iran's international response to these measures.

When President Obama was elected as the 44th President of the United States, one of his top foreign policy goals was to solve the Iranian nuclear crisis. Unlike his predecessor, President Obama opted for a more respectful and conciliatory approach toward the Iranians. As he declared during his speech in Prague, "my administration will seek engagement with Iran based on mutual interests and mutual respect. We believe in dialogue. (. . .) We want Iran to take its rightful place in the community of nations, politically and economically" (The White House, 2009a). Beyond his declarations, President Obama made several bold moves to materialize his intentions regarding the Iranian nuclear program. Among them was his best wishes message addressed to the Iranian people and leaders on the celebration of Nowruz (Persian New Year).

He specifically stressed the commitment of his administration to diplomatically tackle the bones of contention between the two countries. Mindful of the failure of the former administration's approach, he emphasized that the process could not be achieved by "threats, instead engagement that is honest and grounded in mutual respect" (The White House, 2009b). Obama's actions were unprecedented, especially regarding the tumultuous bilateral relations between Tehran and Washington. Concerning the formal aspects of the videotaped message, the fact that the US President had resorted to public diplomacy by sending a video message that could be accessed by millions of Iranians—without any official censorship—prevented the Iranian leaders from framing the debate regarding the intentions of the Americans. But how did the Iranian authorities interpret those gestures of goodwill?

Regarding the videotaped message, the Iranian leaders were surprised by Obama's message. Nonetheless, they provided a lukewarm answer to the US President's goodwill gestures. On the one hand, they welcomed the new administration's shifting approach, but they remained sceptical about the sincerity of the words of the new President. In a mirror policy move, Supreme Leader Khamenei decided to respond to Obama's videotaped message during a speech from the city of Mashhad on the Nowruz celebration. At a glance, the speech seemed to be a complete dismissal of Obama's "extended hand" as the Supreme Leader first recalled all the historical grievances between the United States and Iran, from the interference of Washington in Tehran's domestic affairs to his continuous support for Israel, through the United States support to Saddam's war against Iran in 1980. *Before the Revolution, Iran was in the hands of the United States, its vital resources were in the hands of the United States.* (. . .) *They showed Saddam* (*the late Iraqi president*) *a green light. This was another plan by the US Government to attack Iran*, Khamenei argued (Cole, 2009). Yet, due to domestic politics and the hope that the election of President Obama had sparked, the Supreme Leader cautiously conceded the possibility of Iran negotiating with the United States over its nuclear program. But President Obama discovered later that addressing the Iranian nuclear challenge was tougher than expected.

Negotiating with Iran was difficult, considering the acrimonious bilateral relations between the United States and Iran, and the controversy over the 2009 election demonstrated this. There were fierce domestic critics of the 2009 election, which officially acknowledged the reelection of President Ahmadinejad. Thanks to the support of the Revolutionary Guards and other paramilitary groups within Iran, the Iranian leaders did not struggle to send back the protesters to their houses. Despite the worldwide critics, President Obama first refrained from criticizing the brutal repressions of the protestors, probably because he wanted to avoid being accused of interference in Iran's domestic politics. Nevertheless, after the election chapter had been closed, the nuclear talks between Iran and the E3+3 group were under the US leadership. Those nuclear talks resumed a specific context, one characterized by deep tensions as three Western leaders (Obama, Sarkozy, and Brown) disclosed the existence of a hidden nuclear site in Qom. Reflecting on the gravity of the issue, President Sarkozy indicated that Iran would face sanctions if there were not an in-depth change by December 2009; in the same line, Prime Minister stressed that "the international community has no choice but to draw a line in the sand" and the UK "was prepared to implement further and more stringent sanctions" (The White House, 2009c). Tehran rejected the accusations of nuclear weapon activities at that site, claiming that it was a backup plant considering the possibility of a military attack against the other nuclear sites. To signal the resolve of the United States to solve the Iranian nuclear issue and compel Tehran to comply with the demands of the E3+3 group, the SC adopted several Resolutions.

As we previously mentioned, we will focus on one UN Resolution on the Iranian nuclear issue and analyze the counter-coercive response of Iran. One of the most rigid UN Resolutions in this regard was Resolution 1929 on June 9, 2010. In line with the previous Resolutions, the United Nations Security Council (UNSC) continued to rely on a coercive denial strategy as it decided that all "States shall prevent the direct or indirect supply, sale or transfer to Iran, (. . .) any battle tanks, armoured combat vehicles, large calibre artillery systems, combat aircraft, attack helicopters, warships, missiles or five missile systems as defined for the purpose of the United Nations Register of Conventional Arms" (Art. 8). Furthermore, Res. 1929 also called upon States *to inspect all cargo to and from Iran, in their territory, including seaports and airports, if the State concerned has information that provides reasonable grounds to believe the cargo contains items the supply, sale, transfer, or export of which is prohibited by paragraphs 3, 4 or 7* (Art. 14). In requesting the International Atomic Energy Agency (IAEA)to submit a report within ninety days on the compliance by Iran with the provisions of Res. 1929, the Security Council aimed at creating a "sense of urgency."

To strengthen Res. 1929, the EU also adopted a set of new sanctions against Iran under Council Decision 2010/413/CFSP. Relying on the coercive denial strategy, the EU also imposed nuclear-related trade sanctions on Iran. For example, they prohibited the supply, sale or transfer of "items, materials, equipment, goods, and technology contained in the Nuclear Suppliers Group and Missile Technology Control Regime lists" (Art. 1a). In addition, "any additional items, materials, equipment, goods and technology, determined by the Security Council or the Committee, which could contribute to enrichment-related, reprocessing or heavy water-related activities, or to the development of nuclear weapon delivery systems" (Art 1b). However, President Obama was perfectly aware that targeting only the nuclear establishment and the political elites did not represent a credible leverage to compel Iran to adopt a more conciliatory approach. Thus, he adopted several unilateral sanctions.

The first set of nuclear-related unilateral sanctions that the United States imposed upon Iran was the Comprehensive Iran Sanctions, Accountability, and Divestment Act (CISADA), voted by Congress and signed on July 1, 2010, by President Obama. The CISADA mainly targeted the oil and bank sectors, especially companies involved in Iran's ballistic and nuclear programs. This legislation prohibited foreign financial institutions from pursuing several activities related to the Iranian nuclear program. Among them was, for example, money laundering. By targeting the financial sector and limiting international trade with Iran, the adoption of the CISADA inaugurated the era of the coercive punishment strategy. The effects of its provisions were visible. For instance, they substantially reduced the gasoline deliveries to Iran, which heavily depended upon that to produce its oil. As foreign partners were now reluctant to trade with Iran due to the sword of Damocles of sanctions, "gasoline deliveries to Iran dwindled from about 120,000 barrels per day before CISADA to about 30,000 barrels per day in the following months" (Macaluso, 2014, p. 10). What was Iran's reaction to these coercive measures?

Despite the coercive measures adopted by the Great Powers against Iran, Tehran maintained its defiant nuclear policy. Indeed, the Iranian authorities rejected the new UN sanctions. As then Iran's envoy to the IAEA, Ali Asghar Soltanieh, hammered, "nothing will change. The Islamic Republic of Iran will continue uranium enrichment activities" (Black and Macaskill, 2010). Consequently, the Iranian government expanded the scope of its nuclear enrichment capabilities by installing new centrifuges. This was a clear counter-denial strategy crafted by Tehran, as the goal was to demonstrate to Washington the ineffectiveness of their sanction policy. A Senior Iranian official described it in these terms: "we escalated our nuclear activities to show what pressure would produce. Perhaps we really didn't need some of the nuclear facilities and activities we engaged in, but we deemed it necessary for breaking the mentality of the other side" (Parsi, 2017, p. 118). The intransigence of the belligerents greatly fuelled tensions between both parties, especially as the spectre of a military intervention loomed over the Iranian nuclear program.

As all the initiatives to solve the Iranian nuclear issue so far had not been successful, the Obama administration found itself in a very uncomfortable situation. Indeed, the nuclear deadlock was progressively leading the administration toward a dilemma between inaction and the recourse to military force, something President Obama wanted to avoid. Indeed, not only would this have meant a failure of one of his top foreign policy goals, but it would have emboldened proponents of force against Iran, like PM Netanyahu. Fortunately, a middle ground was found with the recourse to covert actions, including cyber-attacks. Launching cyber-attacks was an attractive foreign policy in many regards. From a political perspective, it was less costly than launching military strikes with unpredictable consequences. From a technical perspective, it would seriously damage the nuclear infrastructure of Iran, which would satisfy Israel regarding Iran's growing nuclear capabilities. Consequently, with the help of Israel, the United States developed what Zetter (2014) called *the world's first digital weapon* under the code name Olympic Games: the Stuxnet malware. The malware was introduced in the nuclear infrastructures of Iran through a Universal Serial Bus (USB) stick that infected computers connected to the centrifuges. Many experts agree that they destroyed around 1,000 centrifuges which could be considered a success, provided the original goal of the Stuxnet was to destroy a more limited number of centrifuges and set back Iran's progress in operating FEP (Albright, Brannan, and Walrond, 2010).

The Iranian authorities acknowledged the cyber-attacks, though they downplayed their impact on the nuclear program. For instance, President Ahmadinejad declared that "they (the United States and Israel) succeeded in creating problems for a limited number of our centrifuges with the software they had installed in electronic parts. But the problem has been resolved" (Hafezi, 2010). Regarding the killing of key nuclear scientists, President Ahmadinejad immediately accused Israel and the US government, who had "undoubtedly" played a strategic role in the killing of those scientists but insisted that it would not deter Iran from improving its nuclear program. Despite the consensus over the condemnation of the killing of members of the Iranian scientific community, there were still political rifts among key elites, especially between Ahmadinejad and Khamenei. Indeed, despite his endorsement by the Supreme Guide, Ahmadinejad still lacked political confidence from many elites. Hence, the deal signed with Turkey and Brazil would have been a suitable way to regain political legitimacy, as it could have reduced the economic pressure of the sanctions. However, the Supreme Guide's technical requirements prevented the success story Ahmadinejad had envisioned.

As time was going and no concrete solution loomed on the horizon, Congress increased its pressure on the Obama administration, calling for additional sanctions against Iran. In a letter sent to the President, nienty Senators expressed their anxiousness regarding the evolution of the Iranian nuclear program. "We remain seriously concerned that Iran continues to accelerate its uranium enrichment and ballistic missile programs. (. . .) We must do more to increase the economic pressure on the regime. In our view, the United States should embark on a comprehensive strategy to pressure Iran's financial system by imposing sanctions on the Central Bank of Iran (CBI) or Bank Markazi" (USIP, 2011). Considering Iran's gesture of goodwill regarding the Russian proposal, this clearly showed that the United States had skipped the diplomatic pattern and preferred the pressure track. Nonetheless, the increased pressure did not come only from the United States but also from Israel. Indeed, Israel had been contemplating the possibility of a nuclear strike against the Iranian nuclear infrastructure. "No option should be removed from the table,'' Ehud Barak, Israel former Defence Minister, declared in an interview with BBC (Marx and Goebel, 2011). Nonetheless, the Great Powers privileged more economic sanctions over the military option.

To compel Iran to meet the IAEA's demands, the EU adopted Council Decision 2012/35/CFSP on the January 23, 2012. This Decision was a clear coercive punishment strategy. Indeed, it mainly imposed trade sanctions on Iran as it prohibited, among others, "the import, purchase or transport of Iranian crude oil and petroleum products" (Art. 3a). In addition, "the sale, supply or transfer of key equipment and technology for the petrochemical industry in Iran, or to Iranian or Iranian-owned enterprises engaged in that industry outside Iran" were prohibited under Art. 4a. The EU also focused on nonpetroleum sectors like gold and precious metals, which the sale of was forbidden. The EU also imposed financial sanctions upon Iran: "the granting of any financial loan or credit to enterprises in Iran that are engaged in the Iranian petrochemical industry" (Art. 6a). But one of the strongest and most popular financial sanctions the EU had taken against Iran was probably the decision to ban Iran from the SWIFT system. The EU adopted Council Decision 2012/152/CFSP on the March 15, 2012, which prohibited to supply of specialised financial messaging services, which are used to exchange financial data, to the persons and entities referred to in paragraph 1 (Decision 2010/413/CFSP—Council Decision 2012/152/CFSP, 2012). Combined with the Executive Orders (Executive Order 13599, 2012) signed by President Obama simultaneously, those sanctions had a devastating effect on Iranian domestic politics.

Despite the poor economic situation that the country was facing, President Ahmadinejad surprisingly maintained a firm and assertive nuclear policy. A couple of factors can explain this outcome. Among them was yet again the support of the Supreme Leader. Indeed, notwithstanding the chorus of criticism against his nuclear and hence economic policies, President Ahmadinejad was still enjoying the political support of key political figures and the IRGC. This situation created a deep political hostility among key elites and could have ended up in a power-base erosion. To avoid such an outcome that threatened the regime's survival, Ayatollah called for political unity and support for the Presidents irrespective of one personal and political opinion. He relied on the framing strategy and described the sanction policy as a strategy of the West to topple the regime, a threat all the Iranians should fight against. Oliver Borszik confirms it in these terms: "by declaring the sanctions an external attack against the revolution and the entire system, the supreme leader evoked a "rally around the flag" effect. In this way, Khamenei used the sanctions as an external stimulus to prompt the political elite to do away with the latent intra factional disputes" (Borszik, 2014, p. 18). This argument was politically valid since several international Media echoed Israel's plans to strike Iran's nuclear facilities. Although it was never considered a credible threat by the Iranian authorities, the Israel military threat was a perfect political springboard to keep the country united. What lessons can be learned from these coercive dynamics between Iran and the United States?

The previous dynamics between the United States and Iran indicate that the United States failed in its goal to compel Iran to stop its nuclear enrichment activities. Several factors can explain the causes of this surprising failure, considering the abysmal gap in power capabilities between the United States and Iran. The first factor is the nature of demand formulated by the United States. The nuclear program, in general, and mastering the fuel cycle symbolized national pride for the entire country. Consequently, requesting a Messianic country like Iran (former Persia) to relinquish a technological achievement that strengthened its position in a region surrounded by its foes was simply unacceptable. In addition, the US leaders miscalculated the domestic effects of the economic sanctions and covert actions in Iran. While the former substantially crippled the Iranian economy, it was capitalized by the Iranian leadership, which presented them to public opinion as an attempt by the United States to topple the regime. Considering the deeply rooted historical relations between Iran and the United States, such action was a golden opportunity unwillingly granted to the Iranians by the Americans. The subsequent rally effect in the Iranian landscape seriously undermined the expected unrest the US administration and the US leadership had envisioned. Consequently, the Iranian leadership maintained a firm stance regarding its nuclear policy. This indicates the absence of strategic empathy within the US decision-making system when confronting their enemies. A core element for the success of any coercive strategy and which explains why the United States, despite their overwhelming power capabilities, has failed to challenge foes with lesser capabilities.

CONCLUSION

The goal of this chapter was to provide a substantial analysis of the notion of coercion in international politics. The first part of the chapter dwelled on the philosophical understanding of the notion of coercion, from its etymological definition to the theoretical legacy of the scholars who worked on this relevant issue. The second part emphasized the practical aspect of coercion by analyzing the coercive dynamics between the United States and

Iran regarding its controversial nuclear programme during President Ahmadinejad's mandate. Though the scope of the chapter did not allow a lengthy analysis of those coercive interactions, it nevertheless highlighted the nature and weaknesses of the coercive strategy of the United States. As the chapter has demonstrated, one critical condition of a coercive policy's success is the coercer's ability to understand and exploit the vulnerabilities of its target, something which, unfortunately, the United States has been unable to do whenever challenging most of its adversaries. This conclusion espouses an intellectual tradition (Tsu, 2007; Slantchev, 2011) which emphasizes the need for the coercer to adjust his coercive strategy proportionately to the features of the enemy that one faces.

NOTES

1. We sincerely thank Leeandra Boodlal for the time and energy she spent to review this article and provide insightful feedback.
2. J. Y. N. Ndzana, Leiden University, Leiden, Netherlands. Email: j.y.ndzana.ndzana@fgga.leidenuniv.nl
3. The data are partly drawn on our PhD research project on the successful conditions of coercive diplomacy in the context of nuclear proliferation. More information on the author's PhD project are available on https://www.universiteitleiden.nl/en/research/research-projects/governance-and-global-affairs/understanding-coercive-dynamics-in-non-proliferation-issues.-a-structured-focused-comparative-analysis-of-iran-libya-and-south-africa

BIBLIOGRAPHY

Books

Baldwin, D. (1985) *Economic statecraft*, Princeton, Princeton University Press.
Berridge, G. and James, A. (2001) *A dictionary of diplomacy*, London, Palgrave Macmillan.
Bracken, P. J. (1983) *The command and control of nuclear forces*, New Haven: Yale University Press.
Byman, D. and Waxman, M. (2002) *The dynamics of coercion: American foreign policy and the limits of military might*, Cambridge, Cambridge University Press.
Cable, J. (1994) *Gunboat diplomacy*, 2nd ed., London, Palgrave Macmillan.
Congressional Research Service (1980) *Should the United States significantly increase its foreign military commitment?* Washington, DC, Library of Congress.
De Wijk, R. (2014) *The art of military coercion: Why the West's military superiority scarcely matters*, Amsterdam, Amsterdam University Press.

George, A. and Simons, W. (1994) *The limits of coercive diplomacy*, 2nd ed., Colorado, Westview Press.
Greenhill, K. M. and Krause, P. (eds) (2018) *Coercion: The power to hurt in international politics*, New York, Oxford University Press.
Harrison, J. (1995) *The limits of type D coercive diplomacy in Somalia*, Washington, DC, PN, Reprint Edition.
Kirshner, J. (1997) *Currency and coercion: The political economy of international monetary power*, Princeton, Princeton Press University.
Pape, R. (1996) *Bombing to win: Airpower and coercion in war*, New York, Cornell University Press.
Parsi, T. (2017) *Losing an enemy*, London, Yale University Press.
Romaniuk, S. and Webb, S. (2015) *Insurgency and counterinsurgency in modern war*, Boca Raton, Routledge.
Schelling, T. (2008) *Arms and influence*, London, Yale University Press.
Slantchev, L. B. (2011) *Military threats: The costs of coercion and the price of peace,* London, Cambridge University Press.
Sisson, Siebens and Blechman (2020) *Military coercion and US foreign policy: The use of force short of war*, 1st ed., London, Routledge.
Tanner, S. M. (2007) *Chinese economic coercion against Taiwan: A tricky weapon to use*, California, RAND.
Tzu, S. (2007) *The art of war*, Minnesota, Filiquarian.
Zetter, K. (2014) *Countdown to zero day: Stuxnet and the launch of the world's first digital weapon*, New York City, Crown.

Chapters of Books

Haun, P. (2018) 'Airpower, sanctions, coercion and containment: When foreign policy objectives collide', in K. M. Greenhill and P. Krause (eds) *Coercion: The power to hurt in international politics*, New York: Oxford University Press, pp. 77–93.
Klotz, A. (1999) 'Diplomatic isolation', in N. C. Crawford and A. Klotz (eds) *How sanctions work: Lessons from South Africa*, London, Palgrave Macmillan, pp. 195–213.

Journal Articles

Borszik, O. (2014) 'International sanctions against Iran under President Ahmadinejad: Explaining regime persistence', GIGA Research Paper, (260):18.
Crawford, W. T. (2013) 'The strategy of coercive isolation in US security policy', RSIS working paper, (260): 1
Drezner, D. (2003) 'The hidden hand of economic coercion', *International Organization*, Vol. 57 (3): 643.
Jakobsen, V. P. (2011) 'Pushing the limits of military coercion theory', *International Studies Perspectives*, Vol. 12 (2): 156.

Macaluso, A. (2014) 'The apparent success of Iran Sanctions. Iran, Rouhani, and the nuclear deal', The Hague Institute for Global Justice, Working Paper (2): 10.

Parrington, A. J. (1997) 'Mutually assured destruction revisited: Strategic doctrine in question', *Airpower Journal*, Vol. 11 (4): 6.

Pape, A. R. (1992) 'Coercion and military strategy: Why denial works and punishment doesn't', *Journal of Strategic Studies*, Vol. 15 (4): 425.

Online Articles

Albright, D., Brannan, P. and Walrond, C. (2010) 'Did Stuxnet take out 1,000 centrifuges at the Natanz enrichment plant?' Institute for Science and International Security, December 22:1.

Online Resources

Black, I. and Macaskill, E. (2010) 'UN imposes new sanctions on Iran', *The Guardian*, June 9. UN imposes new sanctions on Iran | Iran | The Guardian, accessed on the March 12th, 2021.

Cole, J. (2009), 'OSC: Khamenei's speech replying to Obama', *Informed Comment*, March 23. Accessed on the March 24th, 2021 from https://www.juancole.com/2009/03/osc-khameneis-speech-replying-to-obama.html

Hafezi, P. (2010), 'Iran admits cyber-attack on nuclear plants', *Reuters*, November 29. Accessed on the March 8th, 2021 from https://www.reuters.com/article/us-iran-idUSTRE6AS4MU20101129

Marx, B. and Goebel, N. (2011) 'Iran warns West against military strike', Deutsche Welle (DW), November 7. https://www.dw.com/en/iran-warns-west-against-military-strike/a-15515091, accessed on the April 11th, 2021.

Online Etymology Dictionary, coerce, coerce | Origin and meaning of coerce by Online Etymology Dictionary (etymonline.com), accessed on the March 30th, 2021.

The Merriam-Webster Dictionary, mechanism, Mechanism | Definition of Mechanism by Merriam-Webster, accessed on the March 28th, 2021.

The White House (2009a), 'Remarks by President Barack Obama in Prague as delivered', April 5, Remarks by President Barack Obama in Prague as Delivered | whitehouse.gov (archives.gov) accessed on the March 27th, 2021.

The White House (2009b), 'Videotaped Remarks by the President in Celebration of Nowruz', March 20, Videotaped Remarks by The President in Celebration of Nowruz | whitehouse.gov (archives.gov), accessed on the March 27th, 2021.

The White House (2009c) 'Statements by President Obama French President Sarkozy and British Prime Minister Brown on Iranian nuclear facility', September 25, 2009. Statements by President Obama French President Sarkozy and British Prime Minister Brown on Iranian Nuclear Facility | whitehouse.gov (archives.gov).

The White House (2012) Executive Order 13599—Blocking Property of the Government of Iran and Iranian Financial Institutions, February 5, CFR-2013-title3-vol1-eo13599.pdf (govinfo.gov), accessed on the April 13th, 2021.
USIP (2011) '90 Senators: Sanction Iran's Central Bank', *The Iran Primer*, August 11. Accessed on the March 15th, 2021 from https://iranprimer.usip.org/blog/2011/aug/11/90-senators-sanction-irans-central-bank

International Legal Documents

The Council of the European Union (2010) 'Council Decision 2010/413/CFSP', Official Journal of the European Union, Brussels, July 26, L_2010195EN.01003901.xml (europa.EU), accessed on the April 14th, 2021.
The Council of the European Union (2012), 'Council Decision 2012/35/CFSP amending Decision 2010/413/CFSP concerning restrictive measures against Iran', Official Journal of the European Union, Brussels, January 23, https://eur-lex.europa.eu/LexUriServ/LexUriServ.do?uri=OJ:L:2012:019:0022:0030:EN:PDF, accessed on the April 13th, 2021.
The Council of the European Union (2012) 'Council Decision 2012/152/CFSP amending Decision 2010/413/CFSP concerning restrictive measures against Iran', Official Journal of the European Union, Brussels, March 15, Council Decision 2012/152/CFSP of 15 March 2012 amending Decision 2010/413/CFSP concerning restrictive measures against Iran (europa.eu) accessed on the April 13th, 2021.
The Security Council (2010) 'Resolution 1929', The United Nations, New York, June 9, S/RES/1929%20(2010) - E - S/RES/1929%20(2010) -Desktop (undocs.org), accessed on the April 13th, 2021.

Chapter 14

Does International Relations Theory Fully Understand Culture?

Tamta Tskhovrebadze[1]

INTRODUCTION

Even though culture is everywhere in the modern world, international relations research and contemporary theories still need further exploration. Culture is everywhere; its subsequent impact is evidenced by cultural policies influencing nation-building, state formation, and capacity, including thorough constitutional policies and governance. Despite the recently mentioned acknowledged importance of culture on political behavior and political decision-making processes, we should analyze the consecutive causal inference of the culture on politically active individuals and their actions.

The research dimension of international relations involves three levels of analysis—state level, regional, and global. By focusing on the state level, analysis of a nation-state can imply that the belongings, history, experience, and practice of people form a nation. The belongings like common ethnicity, history, language, religion, and culture are the most important sources of the shared identity and ideology not only in intrastate but also in interstate dimensions. The global level analysis centralizes civilization as the legacy of nationalism, the inheritance that influences trends in global relations even nowadays.

Studying culture as a separate concept in international relations requires surfing attitudes and applications of various theories. Understanding interconnections, identifying their effects, and defining contexts are not quite easy to define.

UNDERSTANDINGS OF CULTURE IN INTERNATIONAL RELATIONS THEORY

To simplify arguments for readers unfamiliar with the topic, it would be suggested first to focus on conceptualization. The United Nations Educational Scientific and Cultural Organization (Bourdieu, Distinction: A Social Critique of the Judgement of Taste, 2015) defines culture as a "set of distinctive spiritual, material, intellectual, and emotional features of society or a social group, and that it encompasses, in addition to art and literature, lifestyles, ways of living together, value systems, traditions, and beliefs." Thus, culture is a set of knowledge, values, and beliefs building a homogenous society that binds its attributes or so-called cultural affinities.

Comprehensive analysis of a culture in international relations theory faces domestic and international dimensions. One of the most important turning points in analyzing culture and political intersections can be found in the early work of Almond and Verba's The Civic Culture: Political Attitudes and Democracy in Five Nations (1963). They identified three types of political culture: parochial, subject, and participant.

In the parochial political culture, people are only vaguely aware of the existence of a central government.

In the subject of political culture, citizens see themselves as subjects of a government rather than as participants in the political process.

In the participant political culture, citizens believe both that they can contribute to the system and that they are affected by it (as cited in Hague, Harrop & Breslin, 1992).

The most positive role of political culture is seen in a democratic society as mutual fruitful cooperation between the state and its citizens.

French sociologist Pierre Bourdieu introduced the idea of cultural capital in the twentieth century. He defined cultural capital as "familiarity with the legitimate culture within a society" (Bourdieu, 1986). He observed the logic that belongings with the legitimate culture were transferred to descendants, and families tried to make their children acquainted with the cultural capital they considered familiar. Families prioritizing education are more likely to raise educated children, encouraging them to centralize education as a core value for their future children too. There is a strong connection between economic, social, and cultural capital. Unequal possibilities logically lead to disproportional opportunities. A person who grows up in a wealthy family could be more readily offered an opportunity to study abroad and gain some valuable qualifications and experience. This advantage can be seen as a form of cultural capital. That could lead to the person being offered a position in a company. With this position, a person can expand social networks and build up more friendships, which is understood as social capital (Huang, 2019, p.

1). These situational examples visualize how disproportionally cultural capital can be attainable by individuals and effectively transferred to economic capital and social capital.

Despite the widely accepted idea that realism is all about exercising power and competing interests, proponents of the realist school make arguments relying on cultural assumptions. Culture is an indivisible part of nation-state creation, all those values and characteristics that identify a nation and often address its interests, especially characterizing imperialist instincts. Nationalist political realism later extended into geopolitical theories, which perceive the world to be divided into supranational cultures, such as East and West, North and South, Old World and New World, or focusing on the pan-national continental aspirations of Africa, Asia, and so on (Moseley, n.d.).

Let us focus on the dominant International Relations theory in the twenty-first century—Constructivism. Constructivism gained popularity after the end of the Cold War when the traditional theories of realism and liberalism failed to answer the politics of insecurity fully. From the constructivist's perspective, the world is socially constructed. It comprises central factors such as norms, ideas, knowledge, and culture, stressing the role played by "collectively held or intersubjective ideas and understanding on social life" (Jung, 2019). Alexander Wendt (1995) argues that "the concept of how the world is socially constructed involves two basic claims: that the fundamental structures of international politics are social rather than strictly material (a claim that opposed materialism), and that these structures shape actor's identities and interests, rather than just their behavior (a claim that opposes rationalism (Wendt, pp. 71–72). He proposed an example to better explain reality's social construction: "500 British nuclear weapons are less threatening to the United States than five North Korean nuclear weapons" (as cited in Hurd, 2008, p. 298). The logic of this puzzle seems quite simple, and as Wendt himself suggests, "the British are friends, and the North Koreans are not."

Countering to neorealist and neoliberal proponents, constructivist perspectives suggest building a bridge between those two and better explaining the change in world politics through its norm-based character. Now we are developing the controversial concepts of "friends" and "enemies." Assuming no "friends" and "enemies" exist in the international system, state interests still shape their relationships into partnerships or rivalries. Of course, this social and relational phenomenon is difficult to explain; a friend–enemy distinction is an important notion of contemporary international relations. Oelsner and Koschut facilitated the concept of normative friendship: "normative friends genuinely trust each other because their relationship is not based on instrumental rational thought process and utility-based cost-benefit calculations but is manifested as an emotional and moral disposition" (2014, p. 14). In other words, states having much in similar are more prone to cooperate than states with major disagreements. The partnership is more strengthened when states adhere to similar ideologies, interests, and values.

Following the interpretation of Kant's Democratic Peace Theory (1795), US President Woodrow Wilson, in his 1917 war message to Congress that the United States aimed to make the world "safe for democracy" (Oren, n.d.). The complexity of the democratic peace concept makes us analyze its different angles and perspectives. Some of the proponents of the Kantian vision claim that democracies are more peaceful in nature and are not confronting each other because of shared culture, while others argue that structural aspects of political culture urge democracies to work on peaceful conflict resolution mechanisms.

Zeev Maoz and Bruce Russett, in their article Normative and Structural Causes of Democratic Peace 1946–1986, confirm that democracies rarely fight each other, but not because they are less conflict-prone, rather there are common possessions between democratic states that prevent them from fighting and requires deeper causal analysis (1993, p. 624). It is also argued that at least one potential cause for democratic peace is the intention of wealthy states not to fight one another because they have far more to lose than to gain by doing so. Rich states are often engaged in heavy trading with one another. The costs of a war would be enormous, and the benefits would be little (as cited in Simpson, 2019, p. 111).

Bourdieu in Distinction (1987) argues "taste classifies, and it classifies the classifier. Social subjects, classified by their classifications, distinguish themselves by the distinctions they make, between the beautiful and the ugly, the distinguished and the vulgar, in which their position in the objective classifications is expressed or betrayed (Distinction, Intro). Combining this logic with the rational choice theory—which depicts that individuals are choosing the course of action more relevant to their preferences—taste and classifications are core signs of congruity between states while determining cooperation perspectives.

CONTEMPORARY INTERNATIONAL RELATIONS AND CULTURE

Through the lens of the "clash of civilizations" concept, international relations can be explained by the approach of a civilization-based world, where societies sharing cultural affinities cooperate. If we follow the logic mentioned above of cooperation, then why often do political scientists ignore the prominence of cultural industries and technologies?

Culture is mostly analyzed as a central characteristic of international order and a central trigger in remaking the new world order. Perhaps, the discipline of international relations deals with the culture by defining world politics as a state of nature, rather, it does not consider the concept of a state as formidably a cultural product. We can still identify certain directions where cultural explanations may not be neglected. These include the construction of world views, the issue of cultural diversity, culture as a source of conflict and cooperation, and the idea of cultural internationalism (Chatterjee, 2006). Yosef Lapid's concept of "Culture's Ship" suggests a metaphor for the ship of culture that comes, stays, and leaves the shores of IR only to return (as cited in Chatterjee, 2006).

Despite the differences, culture, and civilization are often interchangeably used concepts. The formation processes of civilizations underwent a revolutionary transformation with the onset of industrialization of the West (Harshe, 2006). Western civilization has soon become progressive, especially in the context of colonialism and imperialism, and molded as a political-economic phenomenon.

This distinction is even more popular nowadays because the upheavals of non-Western ideology proponents are quite substantial. If originally the "West" as a terminology was used to refer to the countries representing Western Christendom and similar cultural backgrounds evolved from the European Civilization, today the terminology is associated with liberal ideas and features.

Except for the Western civilization, the Chinese, Aztec, Ottoman, and other civilizations have been promoting development, living standards, infrastructure, and weaponry to facilitate their dominance and influence. Therefore, the reason for the prevailing "Western way" of thinking, living, and ruling for centuries remains quite debatable.

Ferguson's book "Civilization: The West and the Rest" proposes his contribution toward answering the issue. Europe's success came not as the result of any natural advantages but because it was able to develop just the right mix of political, legal, and social institutions that made it resilient enough to withstand the inevitable plagues, natural disasters, failed leaders or just plain bad luck (Pearlstein, 2012). If cultural traditions and values influence the attitude and behavior of the actors in international relations, Gadamer suggests that an individual's cultural tradition is developed because of their historical finitude. This is because cultural tradition is the source of human beings' "prejudices." Prejudice refers to "a judgment that is rendered before all the elements that determine a situation have been finally examined" (Lee, 2001). Historical identity is then built with relevant prejudices and cultural resources that conceptualizes people's way of looking and experiencing the world. Therefore, the division of the "West and the Rest" is quite logically explained, focusing on the cultural traditions and prejudices that are quite distinct between them. Despite the capacity and legacy of other civilizations,

Westernization processes and shared liberal ideology have overshadowed other developments. Hence, the non-Western part of the world has increasingly important strategic implications for the West. They are relatively higher in number than countries sharing Western affinities, rather fragmented in terms of their aspirations and interests, and have the potential to heavily influence the global peace and security architecture.

Although now discredited, Gobineau's Racial Theory enjoyed popularity in the twentieth century, centralizing racial inequality as a major determinant of the historical processes and the struggle for racial dominance as one of the most triggering factors of the historical identifications. Gobineau's theories were the product of years of historical, anthropological, and ethnological studies. They were part of a general European interest in biological and sociological determinism (The Editors of Encyclopaedia Britannica, n.d.). The theory asserts every historically developed culture is determined by the people, ethnicity, and race involved in a process; therefore, the question of the differences in terms of potential and possibilities arises. According to this philosophy, the West and especially Great Britain, which enjoyed the position on the higher hierarchical ladder, was entitled to the obligation and responsibility to spread civilization through virtuous and conscientious politics for facilitating the development of the less developed people of the East. This concept is already very controversial in its origin centralizing the division between the West and the East and highlighting the superiority of the Western culture as the most advantageous among the Aryans.

History remembers many violent examples of claiming superiority of one's culture over others. For instance, the superiority of Germanic culture served as a weapon in the hands of respective state officials, which determined Germany's hard power politics and hegemonic aspirations until World War II. Cultural imagination and nationalism have been becoming increasingly popular in the post-war period. Nationalizing culture has been a major source of discussions facing Americanization, Westernization, and China's nationalistic sentiments as illustration.

Western nations earlier rationalized their "civilizing mission" and became pioneers, whereas, in the second half of the twentieth century, new players came on the scene. Besides the fragmented Western countries in Europe in the post-war period, new players became actively engaged in remaking the new world's order. The Soviet Union soon took the lead as an increasingly influential and expansible actor full of inherited imperialistic instincts. Individual imperialist aspirations started prevailing in twentieth- and twenty-first century politics, unlike the preexisting imperialism practices to be understood as a unifying force, which was not again realized after the fall of the Roman Empire. USSR, the Third Rome Doctrine of Russia, the Islamic Civilization

Movement, Chinese ambitions, and other European and Asian powers diverse individual commitments and interests transformed imperialism into a divisive force.

Interpretations of imperialism can be categorized into four main categories. The first group focuses on economic explanation justifying the empires' claim to acquire more and more resources as a direct correlation with power. Suppose the state is self-sufficient economically and politically. In that case, security is strengthened by decreasing the dependency on other nations, further maintaining the logic of questioning whether trustworthy nations exist in the international system. Traditional analysis suggests self-sufficiency is a basis for forming national interests and aspiring nations to preserve high power. Great Britain's and other Western nations' initiatives to establish ties with neighboring regions can be considered an example, representing the aspiration of regaining international leadership and strengthening spheres of influence. Later this form gained even more intensity, as it went much further than economic prosperity and changed its concept into the "Crusaders Imperialism" image, influence, and coercion for maintaining ideological proliferation of values and culture. "Crusaders Imperialism" continues the logic of historical colonialism, focusing on Realpolitik and power politics, and well explains the complex and interconnected nature of imperialism types—Economic, Political, Military, Communication, and Cultural. Imperialism itself suggests motives for maintenance; the security argument claims that strong states are inherently imperialistic as they are consequentially searching for power, recognition, and prestige.

Whereas opponents suggest a different vision by proposing imperialism as a struggle for survival. The transformation of the new imperialism facilitated the appearance of the struggle between nations and races, and at the turn of the century, the coincidence of the popularity of evolutionary theories with the scramble for Africa gave rise to so-called scientific racism (Gomes, 2017). Imperialism enabled some to be predominantly prioritized, who's endowed with superior qualities and comparatively advantaged resources are destined to rule others. This imperial sentiment is rooted in different national and social concepts of the Social Darwinist theory of imperialism. Pro-colonial movements used a variety of arguments to promote national expansion (Barth, 2015).

In line with the relatively arguable debate of whether imperialism still a relevant concept is today, there is an assumption that it has never gone anywhere. Imperialism has always been with us as a form of world power exercised by the dominant states. Names of those dominant states, changes or not, do not alter the hegemonic competitiveness; rather, key components of imperialism can be altered over time.

ELEMENTS OF CULTURAL IMPERIALISM

We live in a dynamic and complex world, especially international processes. Complex interdependence and globalization prompt states to seek a comparative advantage of the explored specificities or, generally, culture. A strong concatenate among all three makes a country powerful, confident, and influential. Dominant states identify the core necessity of being acknowledged and followed; that is why they must propose policies relevant to the majority and use the globalization capacity to effectively address issues desired by many. While small states are vulnerable, dominant powers are trying to make them dependent economically, politically, militarily, and culturally by proposing harmony and well-being.

The uprising concern toward globalization is largely proposed by uncertainty in the international environment and the fragility of the states facing these global processes. Misinterpretation and similarity of Globalization with Americanization posed misunderstandings between those synonymizing "global culture" with the US soft power aspirations and dominance.

Contemporary international relations and politics are no longer synonymized with only military power rather, it represents the whole complex of political, economic, cultural, and social influence associated with the exertion of soft power tool by the most powerful countries over the less powerful ones. This logic is correlated by the rethinking of cultural imperialism and resistance, as this is an increasingly acute trend nowadays for countries with strong anti-hegemonic or self-hegemonic aspirations. These imperialistic relations and interests often explain the basis of originating concerns and threats to world peace and security.

UNDERSTANDING OF US CULTURAL IMPERIALISM—A CASE STUDY

Stuart Hall has argued that culture is a process, a set of practices. Primarily, culture is concerned with the production and exchange of meanings—the giving and taking of meaning—between the members of a society or group (cited in Grayson, 2015). Let us analyze the US global image as a dominant power. Apart from the straightforward vision of states' military and economic capabilities as central measurements of their strength and power, appropriate attention should be paid to cultural power characteristics.

Generally, states have institutionalized agencies for preserving and supporting national cultures. Usually in the form of ministries or departments. However, the United States does not have a department for culture by the claim they are not in need to. Some might think this happens because state support is not so substantial in the country, whereas this cannot be the case as can we speak of the non-substantial nature of US culture when the globe is considering it as cultural hegemon?

The real intentions of America are quite easily identifiable as Washington has been diligently trying to promote its imperialist aspirations starting from the political and encouraging to more on the cultural scale. American cultural imperialism relies on soft power practices to increase global reputation and popularize the American way of life by shielding the nondominant cultures globally. American sophisticated strategy of "cultural hegemony" requires defining a certain set of attributes and characteristics explaining its cultural dominance.

Legacy of British Imperialism. If we look through the prism of the United States, considered a result of British expansionist policy, we can consider it a successor of the European power. The country has adroitly developed its utility, inherited experiences and accomplishments, and integrated with the rest of the culture. Acquired physical and intellectual property, promoted liberal and democratic values, and nonaggressive encroachment to conformity governed the US capability to develop an imperialistic attitude and keep hegemony on the world. After the decline of the British Empire, the United States has shown up as a single ideological descendant capable of overweighting the influence and power aspirations of the Soviet Union. Therefore, ideological proximity, the English Language, and lessons learned from the British Empire, accompanied by smart policies under modern American cultural imperialism, resulted in reordering the world around American orbit.

"American Dream" Strategy. The twentieth century was a century of US upheaval. Through its very smart and intriguing policy of the greatest cultural export, the United States gave a born "American Dream" desirable for everyone in the world. Especially for those who were representing developing or newly independent nations and dreaming of the "American Dream" as something extraordinary precedential for better lives and ideal imaginations of prosperity. The rise of the consumer economy and the "American lifestyle" in the 1950s had a terrific impact on the world when American popular culture went global ("America's Cultural Role in the World Today," n.d.).

American "pop culture" expressed in films and music determined the country's popularization globally. People, mostly representing other than the Western (developed) part of the world, eventually become dreamers of something unattainable but extremely desired. Everybody in Georgia remembers the dark decade of the 1990s, a newly independent country with full of imposed threats and challenges to statehood and sovereignty, where each of the single children dreamt of a colorful and sparkling future shown on their screens and America as the symbol of development, freedom, and opulence. Then, the country has profitably exported the culture of democracy.

It constructed a role model transparent, free, and respectful society, thus, conferred buoyant expectations on democratic values, freedom, and respect of choice, expression, and the way of life for those who remained deprived in their home societies. In accordance with the Pew Research Center statistics of US image (2019), a median of 66% across thirty-two nations surveyed worldwide rated the United States favorably. However, a certain decline has been noticeable in developed nations in recent years. The share of adults voting for the United States favorably regarding human rights, freedom, and respect has declined in Germany, Canada, and Australia. The survey results among ten EU member states offer only a median of 43% favorable impressions of the country. The decline was remarkable during the Obama presidency, whereas considerably flawed during the Trump era (America's International Image).

Linguistic Imperialism. Language is one of the most basic determinants of cultural superiority. Linguistic superiority can be expressed by very close concepts of language nationalism and imperialism. This is still a penetration tactic from a dominant state; however, political power centralizes communication as its core value and tool. It is quite debatable whether certain signs of linguistic imperialism exist in spreading the English Language thought the world. In contrast, it is no doubt that the United States greatly benefited from the extending influences of the British Empire.

As the most spoken language in the world, 20% of the world and 1.35 billion speak English today (Lyons, 2021), with the majority speaking American English. American TV programs, films, video games, and music have a large domestic market of more than 300 million customers, in addition to their influence on the rest of the world. The United States also has a social and cultural impact on immediate neighbors such as Mexico, Canada, and North/Central America ("The USA's international influence," n.d.). The reach in the media is another advantage of the country, that is strongly encouraged by English speaking target audience in the world and innovational applications which are apparent in all spheres of the country. Literature, music, filmography, art, sport are yet another part of US cultural influence. Thanks to information technologies and the widespread English Language, people in most countries worldwide might have heard "Hollywood" names of well-known singers, actors, actresses, and sports players that automatically conjure up their visions and form identifications. Thus, linguistic influence can be considered one of the important sources of the US's deliberate imperialist intentions. The most applicable measurement for the success of US-promoted policies regarding linguistic dominance would be a worldwide belief that studying English is the key to success in life. In November 2011, The Bureau of Educational and Cultural Affairs in the US Department of State and the TESOL (Teachers of English to Speakers of Other Languages) International Association announced an initiation of launching a joint effort to connect teachers and resources for English language teaching (ELT) in the United States with parties or entities with ELT needs outside the United States. According to the US Department of State website, "The goal of the partnership is to utilize the networks, expertise, and resources of both the State Department and TESOL to respond to the global demand for English language teaching and learning." This deliberate policy for enhancing international outreach and enriching the target audience is supposed to further increase the tangible and intangible results of the country's linguistic imperialism aspirations.

International Political Marketing. Long-term and consistent policies of political marketing ensure its progress. Thus, how United States realizes imperialist aspirations through different policies and applications? There are several dimensions of this progress worth mentioning here. Technological achievements enabled politicians to access many tools, directly link to the electorate, and grasp virtual constituencies worldwide. Internet and social media enable people to be involved in political processes by keeping their finger on the political pulsation of society. Persuasion and leadership are very important, and it is the task of leadership to guide tradeoffs and articulate the parameters of what is possible. Slater and Narver have convincingly argued that marketing theory's consumer and market orientation conceptually involves "leading" and "following." The parallel motives of spreading influence can be found in political marketing theory as a tool to persuade other countries to adopt the same vision and similar sociocultural contexts (Henneberg & O'shaughnessy, 2008). The appearance of political marketing and campaigning on social media is a relatively new phenomenon, which was first introduced in the US Political marketing in the States has gained many different forms. Active online political marketing is easily visible in any recent campaigns in the United States.

In addition to international political communications, the US international political marketing strategy focuses on nation branding through public diplomacy. Promoting a facilitative public policy for prompting goals of microeconomic behavior of companies, firms, and consumers is a part of the national planning strategy of the country for accumulating national wealth and benefits. US political leaders are building the global image and reputation of the country by intensifying the transmission of information and getting a larger number of people involved in information-sharing processes. Plenty of cases and success stories prove political marketing's importance in attaining political success. Many alternative strategies and models exist; however, specific success stories assert that correct and purposive individualism is a useful tool for pursuing maximum benefits. Latest updates of the "America First" policies, imperialistic and nationalistic "America is back" vision serve the purpose of promoting the national product and remaining an influencer and architect of the global order. Indeed, a successful political marketing campaign pursuing imperialist ambitions is not always easy to plan. But the correct concentration, sustainable strategic decisions, market preferences and demands analysis, public diplomacy, loyalty, and advocation are keys to further success stories.

COUNTERCULTURE AND POLITICS

Counterculture has become a relatively controversial concept. Contemporary international relations revealed that there is room for theoretical and empirical innovations in analyzing relationships and the dependent nature of politics and culture. An important argument is the fact that culture is not rigid. It is a process that gradually builds up through interaction (Hassi & Storti, 2012).

By considering counterculture, we may think of inclinations of the countering positions as a result of the conflicting nature of the globalization of culture. Barber (1996) argues that governments are struggling to respond to the homogenization of cultures around the world brought on by globalization (cited in Sommerich, 2001). Barber proposes "Jihad vs. McWorld" as an example of this conflicting nature of globalization of culture, where locals struggle to preserve their culture and traditions by resisting the commercial interests of others.

Since culture classifies societies, it is considered the most valuable tool for distinguishing itself from others. In many parts of the world and over time, diverse groups have been trying to preserve their culture, gain independence, or attain dominance. This leads to many conflicts and clashes on different sides of the world among those striving for either power and influence or trying to remain independent from outer influences. For instance, the Basque nationalist and separatist group ETA has been trying to pursue their goals violently aimed to Basque independence, the Women's Movement for Civil Rights, Hippie Movement, and so on had also posed political implications as counterculture examples.

CONCLUSION

Depicted the importance and interconnectivity of culture and international relations extends perspectives and assumptions for researched findings highlighting the complex interdependence and focusing on relevancies matching internal and international political processes. Understanding culture and its role in international relations has its capacity and depends on the understanding and considerations of culture as goods, as policies, or as a power. Categorization of the state involvement and contributions often takes us to see the real aspirations of the states and is useful to establish some categorization of the state and culture polyhedral relationship phenomena.

Following the assumptions proposed by Samuel Huntington, "The problem is culture includes everything, it explains nothing" (Huntington, 2000). As much as the vitality of culture is easy to identify in all societies, it can have many different meanings and contexts, making it notably difficult to define. Despite the widely acknowledged idea that classical international relations theories are more concentrated on a state, power, security, relationships, and cooperation, culture plays an important role in defining itself as an intersubjective indivisible part of the discussion. The mutually dependent nature, influence, and trends of culture and international relations contradict the ignorant nature of some mainstream theories. As being defined as purely subjective in concept by beliefs, values, attitudes, and constraints, analysis of culture's role and influence in international relations can be controversial, centralizing the common views and values as core elements for adhesiveness.

NOTE

1. T. Tskhovrebadze. International Black Sea University, Tbilisi, Georgia. Email: ttskhovrebadze@ibsu.edu.ge

BIBLIOGRAPHY

America's International Image. (2016–2020). Retrieved from Pew Research Center, Global Attitudes and Trends: https://www.pewresearch.org/

America's Cultural Role in the World Today. (n.d.). Retrieved from Access to International English: https://access-internationalvg2.cappelendamm.no/c951212/artikkel/vis.html?tid=385685

Barth, B. (2015, March 4). *Imperialism.* Retrieved from International Encyclopedia of the First World War: https://encyclopedia.1914-1918-online.net/article/imperialism

Bourdieu, P. (1986). *The Forms of Capital.* New York: Greenwood.

Bourdieu, P. (2015). *Distinction: A Social Critique of the Judgement of Taste.* Routledge.

Chatterjee, S. (2006). Culture and IR Theory: Departure or Appropriation? Jadavpur Journal of International Relations, 10(1), 53–84.

Gabriel, A. A., & Sidney, V. (1963). *The Civic Culture: Political Attitudes and Democracy in Five Nations.* Princeton: Princeton University Press.

Gomes, C. L. (2017). A Man of His Time: The Scientific and Political Grounds for Kipling's Imperialism. *Anglo Saxonica*, ER. III N. 13 75–85.

Grayson, K. (2015, January 30). *The Rise of Popular Culture in IR: Three Issues.* Retrieved from E-International Relations: https://www.e-ir.info/2015/01/30/the-rise-of-popular-culture-in-ir-three-issues/
Hague, R., Harrop, M., & Breslin, S. (1992). *Comparative Government and Politics.* Retrieved from https://link.springer.com/content/pdf/10.1007%2F978-1-349-22276-6_6.pdf
Harshe, R. (2006). Culture, Identity and International Relations. *Economic and Political Weekly.* Vol. 41, Issue No. 37, 3945–51.
Hassi, A., & Storti, G. (2012, August 22). *Globalization and Culture: The Three H Scenarios.* Retrieved from IntechOpen: https://www.intechopen.com/books/globalization-approaches-to-diversity/globalization-and-culture-the-three-h-scenarios
Henneberg, Stephan C., & O'shaughnessy, Nicholas J. (2008). Theory and Concept Development in Political Marketing, Issues and an Agenda. *Journal of Political Marketing*, 6(2-3): 5–31
Huang, X. (2019, August 7). *Understanding Bourdieu - Cultural Capital and Habitus.* Retrieved from Review of European Studies: https://doi.org/10.5539/res.v11n3p45
Hurd, I. (2008, January 18). *Constructivism.* SPI Publications - Delhi. 298–316.
Jahn, B. (2000). *The Cultural Construction of International Relations: The Invention of the State of Nature.* PalgraveMacmillan.
Jung, H. (2019, February 27). *The Evolution of Social Constructivism in Political Science: Past to Present.* Retrieved from Sage Journals: https://doi.org/10.1177/2158244019832703
Koschut, S. A. O. (2014). *Friendship and International Relations.* London: Palgrave Macmillan.
Lee, H.-I. (2001). Cultural Confrontation and Compromise: The Response of Non-Western Societies to Western Political Ideas. *The International Journal For Peace Studies.* Vol. 6, No. 2 (Autumn/Winter 2001), 53–74.
Lyons, D. (2021, March 10). *How Many People Speak English, and Where Is It Spoken?* Retrieved from Babbel Magazine: https://www.babbel.com/en/magazine/how-many-people-speak-english-and-where-is-it-spoken
Maoz, Z., & Russett, B (1993). Normative and Structural Causes of Democratic Peace, 1946–1986. *The American Political Science Review*, Vol. 87, No. 3, 624–638.
Moseley, A. (n.d.). *Political Realism.* Retrieved from Internet Encyclopedia of Philosophy: https://iep.utm.edu/polreal/
Oren, I. (n.d.). *Democratic Peace.* Retrieved from Britannica: https://www.britannica.com/topic/democratic-peace
Pearlstein, S. (2012, January 13). Civilization: The West and the Rest, by Niall Ferguson. Retrieved from The Washington Post: https://www.washingtonpost.com/entertainment/books/civilization-the-west-and-the-rest-by-niall-ferguson/2011/12/28/gIQAVzQxwP_story.html
Reus-Smit, C. (2019, March 21). *International Relations Theory Doesn't Understand Culture.* Retrieved from Foreign Policy: https://foreignpolicy.com/2019/03/21/international-relations-theory-doesnt-understand-culture/
Simpson, S. (2019). Making Liberal Use of Kant? Democratic Peace Theory and Perpetual Peace. *Sage Journals*, Volume 33, Issue 1. 109–128.

Sommerich, C. D. (2001, May). *The Cultural Role of the State in Domestic and International Relations.* Retrieved from https://digitalcommons.unl.edu/cgi/viewcontent.cgi?article=1037&context=opentheses

The Editors of Encyclopaedia Britannica. (n.d.). Retrieved from Encyclopaedia Britannica: https://www.britannica.com/biography/Arthur-de-Gobineau

The USA's International Influence. (n.d.). Retrieved from BBC: https://www.bbc.co.uk/bitesize/guides/z6frqp3/revision/5

Wendt, A. (1995, July). *Constructing International Politics.* Retrieved from ResearchGate: https://www.researchgate.net/publication/265960638_Constructing_International_Politics

Chapter 15

Key Issues of Water Security in International Relations

Adriano Mortada[1]

INTRODUCTION

Water has always been essential to the survival of humankind and civilizations. Throughout history, there were traces of complex water irrigation systems that date back to 6,000 years ago, ranging from the earliest Mesopotamian civilizations to the Indus Valley civilization (Sijkar et al., 2002). Freshwater is an indispensable resource for prosperity, human health, and security. It is fundamental for equality, poverty eradication, preservation of ecosystems, and food security. There have been several successes regarding water security, such as water management, drought and flood protection, sanitation, and drinking water supply schemes. These water management schemes are far from optimal and can significantly function well, but there are some places where they could be more present. Due to the absence, billions globally face serious water security challenges, from water scarcity, lack of sanitation, poor quality, and water-related disasters. Water resources are under pressure from global drivers such as agriculture, climate change, and urbanization.

DEFINING WATER SECURITY

Water security is defined as sustaining the accessibility of acceptable quality and adequate quantity of water to sustain the populations' human well-being, livelihoods, and socioeconomic development (Gerlak et al., 2018, p. 84). This sustainability ensures the protection against anything related to water, such as pollution and disasters, and the preservation of the ecosystem in political stability and a climate of peace. This definition emphasizes that it can be sustainably managed throughout the water cycle and is implemented via interdisciplinary focus to reinforce societal resilience from any water-related impacts without compromising the ecosystem and population. To realize water security, transparency, and efficiency are required to satisfy basic human needs. This, if achieved within a reasonable time, can provide humankind the accessibility and affordability to usable water. The concept can be applied on all levels from individual to community to local, national, regional, and international (Bogardi et al., 2012).

The term water security also captures certain dynamic dimensions of water-related issues and offers perspective outlooks into addressing the challenges that we are presently facing. Even though some definitions of water security have a specific focus to represent narrow interests (Bhaduri et al., 2013). However, under the umbrella of water security, many interests are captured and also offered to consider the issues that are interrelated and have multiple causes toward upcoming consequences.

AGRICULTURE

Globally, various irrigation systems use over 70% of water for agriculture. According to this percentage, this makes water one of the most used commodities for human growth and the stability of civilizations. Water and food security are linked because, without water security, food security would diminish. Usually, for food to be produced per person, it generally requires about 3,000 liters of water which is clear that the reliability of water in food production is critical as wealth and population growth. Due to the price rise and global financial crash of 2008, the enhancement of food security was slowly undermined (Beddington, 2009, p. 1). The risk of food shortage concerning population growth is possible because undermining food security in countries that rely heavily on agriculture has led to social unrest in a number of countries, such as Syria or Haiti, which represents an early sign of upcoming food shortages globally.

Food production is heavily relied on natural resources, essentially water. According to the UN-Water, 70% of global water withdrawals are for agriculture, and four-tenth of the world population still works in agriculture. Even though global food production can feed the entire population, fundamental changes have yet to be made to enhance food security (UN Water, 2011, p. 1). Due to the lack of planning, there would need to be more availability of resources for feeding a burgeoning population with an increase in water demand for nutrition needs. In order to feed the increased global population, food production will need to double in the next forty years. If there is no change in the food chain or in dietary habits and the lack of improvement in water and land productivity, the consumption of global water in agriculture will be forcibly increased by approximately 70% to 90%. The challenge is based on more than just the increase of agricultural production to meet the demands of the global economy and growing population (UN Water, 2011, p. 2). However, in multiple developing countries, progress is always dependent on the availability of water and irrigation systems. The demand for irrigation systems in developing countries will increase concerning population growth. The largest increase in irrigation water requirements is projected mostly in Latin America and Africa (Fischer et al., 2007, p. 1093). Furthermore, the critical value of renewable freshwater exists in Africa and the Middle East due to population growth (Wallace, 2000, p. 108). Some countries are already experiencing economic water scarcity, and some are projected to experience scarcity. Scarcity occurs when investment in infrastructure development is needed to grow water demand but is constrained by human, institutional, and financial capacities (Mancosu, Snyder, and Gavriil, 2015, p. 981). Throughout the entire Arab countries, only around 14% of the area is considered arable land, and only 4% of the area is under cultivation. Agriculture in the Arab world plays an essential role in their economies as a generator of domestic food, foreign exchange, and feed demand satisfaction. The population growth in the Arab region shows increased water demand, but the demands exceed the region's supply. Freshwater is being used unsustainably in the Arab region due to the absence of regulatory mechanisms (Kharraz et al., 2012). Despite the existence of institutions, there is an extreme risk of vulnerability to water fluctuations which can result in water scarcity for domestic and agricultural purposes. If infrastructure is inadequate, then the existence of malnutrition is possible despite the presence of abundant water resources relative to the water needs.

Water scarcity will expand to two-thirds of the world population if there is further population growth. Currently, the global population is already exposed to the threat of water scarcity and water usage of food. The increase in food demand is mostly under pressure from freshwater resources and global land. The revaluation of land ownership was driven by the convergence of the global crisis in finance, food, and energy (Borras et al., 2011, p. 209). Due to the increased global demand for biofuel concerning the inclining oil price, the need for land has increased. To satisfy their energy and food needs, governments intend to acquire lands in foreign countries, the so-called "land grabbing" phenomenon. The phenomenon refers to large-scale land acquisitions mainly by private investors but also by public investors and agribusiness that buy farmland or lease it on a long-term basis to produce agricultural commodities (Margulis,

McKeon, and Borras Jr., 2013). Countries that attract foreign investors have weak and abundant land governance. Most of the land acquisitions by foreign investors occur in sub-Saharan Africa and South Asian regions, where they are more affected by hunger than any region in the world. For example, Kenya has been facing droughts for years that hurt its agriculture sector. Instead of Kenya addressing the issue, they decided to give the farmland to foreign investors for biofuel production, which requires much water (Sindayigaya, 2011). When the grabbed land is irrigated, it includes acquiring available freshwater resources, which reduces the downstream areas that can result in water stress, that is, insufficient moisture in the soil (Mancosu, Snyder, and Gavriil, 2015, p. 981). The water used for agriculture in multiple "grabbed" countries has shown that they are located in economic or physical water stress areas. The distrust in markets and the claim on natural resources and self-sufficiency had led many countries to rebuild their national stocks and agricultural investments in other countries to maintain the food supply. However, due to the lack of a code of conduct, the local population would start losing access to water, land, and resources that heavily depend on water and food resources (Beddington, 2009, p. 3).

The crops have multiple uses for industrial materials: fuel and food. Their production aims to exploit grabbed land from a certain economic point of view (Mancosu, Snyder, and Gavriil, 2015, p. 983). The biofuel commodities and crops can be flexibly interchanged. The growth of biofuels depends on the need for water and fertile lands with competition between food-crop resources and fuel production (Mancosu, Snyder, and Gavriil, 2015, p. 983). Biofuel production targets water resources, reducing smallholder farmers' access to land (Mancosu, Snyder, and Gavriil, 2015, p. 983). Therefore, the inclination of crop production for biofuels would increase the demand to use fresh water and it would worsen the water stress in some countries.

The increase in water scarcity would be a major challenge to food security, especially in the agricultural sector, since it remains the largest user of freshwater resources globally despite the domestic and industrial demands. Due to the increase of water demand in the nonagricultural sector, the quantity will be transferred from irrigation, resulting in the decline of water reliability in agriculture's water supply without improvement regarding water management investments and policies. This would intensify the issues related to water scarcity and competition that would, put pressure on food supplies and continuously generate concerns for global food security. To achieve water and food security, there should be an increase in water production in the agricultural sector. Every drop of water used in agriculture is essential for crop productivity. Even though production is one part, food security depends on the food trade. This is a complex and political international issue that needs urgent attention to include linkage with water security. The trade-water-food nexus is a significant issue regarding water for food production. Water security should be addressed globally to determine the balance needed concerning economic and population growth to increase the chance of success in food security.

CLIMATE CHANGE

Climate change is considered one of the most critical challenges the population faces today from an economic, environmental, and social aspects. The international organizations have repeatedly alerted the global community on the awareness of the vulnerability of freshwater resources. Water and food security are the key challenges under climate change as both are highly vulnerable to continuously changing climatic patterns. Studies have predicted that the average global temperature may increase by 1.4–5.8 °C, and there would be a substantial reduction in freshwater resources and agricultural yield by the end of the twenty-first century (Misra, 2014, p. 153).

Climate change presents a challenge to water security, and it has the potential to increase insecurity between nations; because it can drastically cause impact on the global water supplies in several ways. One of them is rising sea levels which can threaten coastal aquifers and infrastructure. A saltwater intrusion would compromise freshwater coastal aquifers used for groundwater extraction (Kemp et al., 2018, p. 13). A seaside country like Bangladesh is consistently impacted by salt intrusion, affecting the coastal areas' water and land. Due to Climate change, the impact expands toward the inland soil and water annually (Mahmuduzzaman et al., 2014). Glaciers will eventually become less reliable due to reduced precipitation and rising temperatures resulting in glaciers melting in multiple regions. River basins are mostly dependent on monsoon rain and glacier melts, which will continuously sustain the water demands in several regions. However, due to population growth, water demands will increase (Luttrell, 2014, p. 46). The Himalayan glaciers provide water for Afghanistan, India, Nepal, China, Bangladesh, Bhutan, Pakistan, and Myanmar. Around 2 billion people rely upon Himalayan glaciers for drinking, agriculture, energy, and so on. Due to Climate change, at least one-third of the Himalayas will disappear by 2050 (McCarthy and Sánchez, 2015). The increase in ice melt would generally result in an inclination of water flow into the oceans and rivers that would change the hydraulics of waterways. But the increased flow of rivers would disrupt river floods, flooding, and erosion. Some countries rely on rivers for food production, and the changes in these flows would impact the crop cycles and result in a decline in food production. The increase of sediments in river systems would also affect food security by disrupting the ecological balance and reducing the water quality and fish population (Luttrell, 2014, p. 47). Argentina is one of the countries that heavily rely on agriculture and cattle farming for the national economy. But it is also a country that is strongly affected by floods, such as in the area of sub-Meridional lowlands of Santa Fe where thousands of inhabitants are affected, and millions of hectares of productive land are depleted, causing economic damage (Latrubesse and Brea, 2009). In addition, the shifting precipitation pattern won't just intensify flooding but also droughts. The increased temperature would decrease soil moisture and increase surface drying. Different categories of droughts can cause disturbances in water security. The first type is the interannual drought which remained a mix-up with desertification. This climatic phenomenon is mostly man-made due to the negative correlation between erratic rainfall and GDP growth (Falkenmark, 2013, p. 3). The GDP growth is negatively affected because the erratic rainfall would cause harm to the agriculture that many countries relly on heavily for their econmy. A harm on the agriculture sector would lead to an incraese of the food price due to less food availability. As a result, governments would be forced to allocate resrouces which would contrain the countries financially. Also, the multiyear drought period forced the reduction of water allocation for irrigation. The farmers have greatly opposed the idea in the past, and there is no indication of them supporting it in the future. The reason for their opposition is that it would affect their agriculture production area (Falkenmark, 2013, p. 4). Secondly is the interseasonal dry spells, a global phenomenon concerning dry climate regions, where regions suffer from a lack of rainfall or short periods that directly affect food production and cause plant water stress (Falkenmark, 2013, p. 3). Each of these consequences mentioned above can potentially compound the complications created by each other. However, not all areas in the globe will be equally affected, but climate change will have a huge impact on the regions that already suffer from water insecurity. Iraq has been exposed to severe environmental issues that include drought and desertification. Iraq's agriculture accounts for a vast amount of water consumption, around 92% of fresh water for food production and irrigation. Due to drought conditions between 2005 and 2009, Iraq's agriculture was devastated, along with water shortages. If the environmental situation in Iraq continues, the Euphrates and Tigris, Iraq's two major water sources, may dry up by 2040 (Al-Obaidy and Al-Khateeb, 2013).

The rising of sea levels has been the most visible effect of climate change, and the rate will continuously rise in the coming decades. The oceans are currently rising at an average rate of 3.2 millimeters per year which is due to the polar ice melting concerning the geophysical phenomenon that is known as thermal expansion, that is, liquid water stores more heat while its volume increases (Kemp, Hagberg et al., 2018, p. 12). In addition, the rising sea levels can salinize coastal aquifers, and storm surges cause flooding in below-sea-level nations and threaten the island states (Kemp et al., 2018, p. 13). The rise of sea levels would also cause salt intrusion, threatening the groundwater aquifer, a source of sanitation and drinking water.

Greenhouse effect temperatures also threaten the key sources of freshwater, that is, mountain glaciers and snowpack. The melting of high-altitude ice and snow every season gradually provides water to the population for drinking, agriculture, and sanitation (Bhanoo, 2015). As the world gets warmer, the snowpack accumulation during the winter will decline, which will also decrease the freshwater runoff and reduce the availability of the water, which may be utilized in the summer for sanitation and drinking. The demand for freshwater will globally increase concerning population growth and agricultural goods. Other weather variables that are impacted by climate change include precipitation and drying. Warm air usually causes precipitation to fall in rain rather than snow and increases evaporation (Kemp et al., 2018, p. 14). As the temperature of the Earth increases annually, the level of water the atmosphere holds will also increase.

There is a general call for understanding the dynamics of climate, how it sustains the current economy, and how it will inevitably cause an economic crash, especially in most developing countries like Asia and Africa. This understanding of the now-changing dynamics is needed because their economies depend heavily on climate-sensitive sectors such as agriculture, fisheries, water, tourism, and energy (UN Water, 2011, p. 2).

Due to the uncertainties, climate change will continue to have an increased negative effect on the availability, quality, and distribution of water resources. This shift can impact livelihoods and lives, resulting in more suffering and upcoming conflicts with water management. Urban dwellers will be most affected and lack necessities such as adequate sanitation, safe drinking water, durable housing, secure tenure, and fair sanitation services (UN Water, 2011, p. 5). The challenge toward climate change is not just to ensure enough water but to effectively manage when and where there is too much water, that is, flooding, in the wrong place and time, or when its quality is dangerous for human consumption. This challenge will ensure that the quality and quantity of water are sufficient to meet environmental demands and human needs. Climate change aggravated the water security challenge and will need essential adaptation. Achieving sustainable water security against climate change is a challenge for adaptation. The requirement for adaptation to this challenge is needed and well explored. Furthermore, the challenge is reducing the negative impact of floods and droughts on human lives and livelihoods by reducing the risk of such disasters and building the resilience of people and communities. Prediction and monitoring are keys to developing early warning systems and disaster preparedness. Approaches should be holistic, considering the needs of communities, the built environment, and aquatic ecosystems within the river basin where they occur. Hence water-related disaster management needs to be integrated with other planning spheres at the catchment level and address the fact that many poor people live in high-risk locations. This is essential because, at the moment, only the poor people are and will be exposed to climate-related issues; however, if these issues are not addressed promptly, the entire world population will be affected. As mentioned in other parts of this chapter, accessibility to water and lack thereof will inevitably lead to war conflict.

World governance has struggled to allocate Earth's water for centuries, and this struggle for the resource has led to conflict. The degradation of water resources has been due to population growth concerning the rising demand for clean and usable water (Beddington, 2009, p. 4). The continued degradation of water resources will increase the probability of upcoming conflicts over water and negatively impact the vulnerable and poor regionally and globally. Freshwater scarcity is essential to the continued conflict within and between developing states. Within developing states, the scarcity of water can have a continuous violent role when water-dependent sectors like irrigated agriculture cannot sustain farming, which can destabilize migration flow.

CONFLICT

Conflict related to water often occurs locally rather than internationally but is inversely related to geographical scale (Wolf, 1999). Even though international water disputes do not cause violence, they can hamper development and interstate tension. Also, the local conflicts may impact the station at a national and regional level.

There are links between water and conflict derived from narratives within academic studies and media concerning experts in the field. One of them is access to adequate water supplies, the conflict occurs mostly when the dispute is involved in the access to adequate quality and quantity. Even though water supplies are not limited, the redistribution of water among different uses and users can be contested. When the water suppliers decline the terms of quality or quantity for irrigated regions, it can trigger migration flows that can politically destabilize locally or regionally. For example, the deterioration of water quality and reduced water availability in Iraq sparked across the region in 2018. Concerning the reduced flow of the Euphrates and Tigris rivers due to the development upstream in Syria, Turkey, and Iran, it is difficult for Iraq to maintain water supply to agriculture and cities (Schmeier et al., 2019). This has generated dissatisfaction with the government and forced people to migrate to other parts of the country with challenging security. In addition, the degradation quality of the water can pose a threat to health and increase scarcity which is a source of potential conflict (Wolf, Carius, and Dabejko, 2004, p. 60).

Secondly, water is essential in sustaining human livelihoods and can indirectly cause conflict. Water is a fundamental resource for agriculture, the largest livelihood source. The local population must search for career opportunities in other locations if sustainable livelihood is threatened. Migration occurs due to lack of water, sudden floods, droughts, natural disasters, or pollution can upscale tension between incoming and local communities, especially when there is pressure on resources that are already scarce. Livelihood loss used to be due to poverty, a common indicator of the cause of conflict in most civil wars that emerged in developing countries in recent and previous history (Ohlsson, 2000). For example, the significant droughts in Somalia constantly pressuring pastoral livelihoods. Droughts have caused herders to sell their livestock, leading to a deterioration in rural incomes. Due to the widespread poverty and lack of economic alternatives, part of the community has decided to join armed groups such as Al Shabaab, which offers revenues to their fighters (Detges, Pohl, and Schaller, 2017).

Thirdly, there are scenarios where it is not just the lack of water that would result in conflict but also the need for more management of resources. The failure in management includes a lack of adequate water institutions, overlapping functions, and a lack of transparency. This mismanagement tends to be extremely political by balancing interests over water allocation and water scarcity management. Disagreements and lack of shared responsibility in decision-making can lead to a divergent management approach that serves contradictions and provokes competing claims. The claims can contribute to disputes within countries without enforcement and monitoring. Furthermore, the controversy of mismanaged decision-making can be due to insufficient participation by water users and local communities, which fails to consider local practices and rights (Wolf, Carius, and Dabejko, 2004, p. 61). For example, due to the mismanagement of Yemen's water supply, water availability is declining dramatically, which impacts the population through unequal distribution and an imbalance in society due to nepotism and corruption. This issue has increased the frustration of the disadvantaged and fueled Yemen's security and political crisis (Detges, Pohl, and Schaller, 2017).

Water stress plays a role as a driver toward conflict under conditions in the community, such as the endurance of poverty, economic inequality, resistance to tensions, and human mismanagement. Water stress can result from a combination of factors such as policy failures, population pressure, water supply degradation, and unequal distribution between groups (De Bruin et al., 2018, p. 27). Through inaccessibility, economic scarcity, and drought, local water stress may intensify conflict over water claims. Lake Chad, bordered by Niger, Chad, Cameroon, and Nigeria, was classified as once the sixth-largest lake in the world. Since the drought began, the lake has shrunk by over 90% in the area. In the 1990s, the lake was used for irrigation and began compounding the problem of drought, which led to further shrinking of the lake. This natural catastrophe had an effective consequence for the region's 30 million people who depend on the lake for their survival. Frequent disputes between herdsmen and farmers and over-access to land and water often escalate into violent clashes (Iceland, 2017).

Conflict outbreaks can also depend on rainfalls because it is an essential key climate variable that significantly impacts society, such as social disruption. The lack of rainfall in regions can lead to drought, resulting in tension over water scarcity due to competition, depending on the political, social, and economic constellations (De Bruin et al., 2018, p. 28). This would increase livelihood insecurity, especially in the areas where pastoralists and farmers are heavily dependent on rainfall during their daily lives. Concerning the increase of livelihood insecurity, the migration pattern may increase. There has been communal conflict in Ethiopia and Kenya due to the decline in precipitation. countries rely heavily on agriculture because it dominates their economic sector. As such, they are vulnerable to adverse changes in the local climate. The changes in the local climate reduced the capabilities of people living in vulnerable environments where livelihoods depend on factors such as precipitation (Weezel, 2019).

Land degradation and water stress may induce local conflict over fertile land. The variables can be linked to a shortage of livestock crops due to land shortage which may result in conflict for fertile land availability. The insufficient water storage infrastructure and unsustainable land may intensify water stress which can intensify conflict on fertile land (Selby, 2014, p. 829). The availability of fertile land and land use is directly affected by water shortages, not just water stress but also inequality of access to land. Northern Lebanon has been going through land degradation due to illegal activities such as deforestation and quarrying. These activities damage the landscape that affects the agriculture sector and water resources (Kallio, 2015). This has led to armed conflict over land control. Water and land use conflicts can be connected to over land and water rights between landlords and the rural population (Goldstone, 2002, p. 3). Mostly it happens in developing countries where foreign investors cultivate for export and land grabbing (Hall et al., 2015, p. 467). The access to water and fertile land is unequally divided due to the increase of water stress that causes water conflict over what is left of the fertile land and increased biomass cultivation concerning biofuels linked to food prices and conflict over land use.

The construction of dams can lead to conflict between riparian countries due to the need for more governance mechanisms and distrust. Sharing river water resources between riparian countries often leads to collaboration rather than conflict (Wolf, 2007, p. 241). Still, the dam's construction can cause tensions by disrupting the water supply and increasing the water stress. Even though dams are constructed for sustainable energy, it is considered less important for ecology and human rights (Zarfl et al., 2015, p. 161). The dam's construction is mostly related to power issues and social distrust between countries that share rivers. The more the dams are constructed, the more they can alter tensions and create new ones from local to transboundary scales. For example, the Nile basin between Ethiopia, Egypt, and Sudan is historically strained due to political relations and conflict over agreements. Some agreements have given Egypt the right to use a huge a major percentage of the Nile. At the same time, Ethiopia can only use the least percentage of the Nile run-off. However, Ethiopia has been planning to construct dams that risk causing political conflict between countries and endanger the indigenous tribes' livelihoods (Arsano and Tamra, 2005). Water and food security are undermined; the local communities that live along the river banks are threatened to lose their livelihoods which can trigger migration (Abbink, 2012, p. 125). These possibilities can create an impact on an existing tension.

Through pathways that were discussed to link water security with conflict possibly. International and regional organizations can assess the basins at risk and give and build up an early warning process for regions with conflict potentials. This collaboration would enhance the institutional capacity between nations and encourage transboundary collaboration. The UN can improve facilitation and water management skills and also use water to build confidence and prevent conflict rather than triggering it.

URBANIZATION

The world is primarily shifting to urban landscapes, partly due to the domination of economic activities and human settlements, which are more suited to urban life. Over half of the global population lives in urban areas, which will grow exponentially by 2050 (DESA, 2019). Urban water security implication is necessary for national and municipal development agenda because urban areas are experiencing critical transitions and facing the pressure of demands due to the economic and population growth concerning climate change of droughts and floods. These transitions threaten socioeconomic development and water security, that is, inadequate sanitation services, water management, ecosystem degradation, and water quality (WWAP, 2019). Therefore, ensuring urban water security can be seen as a global challenge threatening humanity's economic, food, ecological, and national security.

The concentration of employment and homes in cities has a downside since cities are considered centers of production, waste, and consumption. This creates pressure on wastewater management, water supply, and built environments that include water and air pollution (Hoekstra and Wiedman, 2014, p. 1114). Mexico City suffers from water shortages since 40% of the water is imported from a distant port and has no large-scale operation regarding recycling wastewater (BBC News, 2018). Water pollution reduces the availability of healthy water, thus leading cities to rely on rural areas for water, food, and waste removal. In addition, drinking water consumption in cities is critical because cities with more than 100,000 are mostly located in water-scarce basins. This scarcity is because agricultural water consumption would deplete almost 90% of the basin (Hunger and Doll, 2008, p. 335). Due to the depletion of the basin, all water used for industrial and domestic purposes is eventually returned to the water body. For example, water cooling in power plants, flushing toilets, or wastewater management is returned to water bodies (Richter et al., 2013, p. 335). Since the produced water is not consumed again, reducing urban water use or recycling will not make a difference in alleviating water scarcity. Beijing also suffers from water scarcity because almost 40% of Beijing's water surface is polluted and unusable for industrial use or agriculture (BBC News, 2018). Furthermore, cities also generate a considerable amount of solid waste. But poor waste management ranges from ineffective disposal to a nonexisting collection system that causes water, air, and soil contamination. Unsanitary and open landfills also contribute to the contamination of drinking water, concerning the increase of transmitting and infectious diseases (Koop and Cornelis, 2016, p. 392). Cairo's main water source is the Nile River, but the water also leads to untreated agricultural residential waste (BBC News, 2018). Solid waste management can be considered a challenge for urban areas of all sizes.

Many countries are unaware of urban challenges toward water security, but some developments must be addressed. An estimation is that around 2 billion people will have a water shortage, and two-thirds of the world's population will suffer from scarcity (Koop and Cornelis, 2016, p. 393). In addition, immigration and world population growth will mostly occur in cities. Many cities are located in high-risk areas, and it is estimated that two-thirds of the world's largest cities might become vulnerable to sea-level rise, and some cities suffer from severe land subsidies. Due to these vulnerabilities, the threat to marine existence is plausible concerning increased fluvial flooding (Molenaar et al., 2015). Wastewater treatment in developing countries is inefficient, and the water supply demand would increase due to rapid urbanization. This would enhance biodiversity loss, and eutrophication threatens drinking water, aquaculture, and fisheries (Ligtvoet et al., 2014).

Urban areas have increasingly shaped water security as they grapple with water availability. Urbanization has created several obstacles to water availability by exacerbating competition for water concerning the depletion of water bodies and aquifers. Urbanization and environmental change are linked because they project an impact on water availability and an increase in the stress on water supplies due to the increase of surface water evaporation and altering the dynamics and timing of monsoons, rainfall, snowmelt, and other hydrological processes (Nielsen, 2013, p. 16). These changes can directly affect the replenishment of reservoirs and negatively impact urban areas, that is, droughts and floods. Urban areas and urbanization have indirectly and directly shaped water security due to significant changes in the population structure, economic growth, land use, and social practice. These imply that the urban process is an essential source of demands on water resources because it affects the hydrological cycle and habitant and land fragmentation dynamics (Grimm, 2008, p. 756). The difference in land use, function, and quality determine hazard risk and water availability. One is the change in vegetation cover that affects evapotranspiration and infiltration dynamics, influencing the risk of floods and rainfall-triggered landslides.

Wastewater management and urban water should be considered a threat to developing countries. Most cities cannot manage water consumption among users nor expand essential water services. The increase in low-income areas of cities also poses challenges in sustaining service delivery. The rapid growth of urbanization increases the need for improving water supply, waste management, and wastewater treatment services. But, this must consider impacts over a wide area, both upstream and downstream, as well as across basin and aquifer boundaries. Much more must be done to ensure that urban water and waste management is a vital key component of urban planning.

SOLUTIONS

Governments, academics, engineers, and scientists have critical roles in addressing water security challenges in achieving global water security. One of them is strengthening the institutions to promote water security through the emergence of new politics of water governance that reflect global economic and political power. This emergence requires new approaches and alliances within their developmental trajectories (Hope, 2012, p. 7). In addition, enhancing policy and enterprise partnerships must be mobilized significantly concerning the global demographic growth and economic opportunities within developing countries. Multinational companies with material dependency capabilities to develop reliable water availability should explore and recognize these opportunities and issues (Hope, 2012, p. 9). Furthermore, transforming hygiene behavior and sanitation services is essential to water security. To achieve this, One Water recognizes that wastewater and water supply interact and treat them collectively (Hope, 2012, p. 10). This approach can promote the design of adopting waterless toilets as a universal and low-cost approach that can be adopted by the poor as the rich.

To reduce water scarcity, water productivity is recommended by improving the supply chain, business practices, policies, and efficient technologies to put water on more environmentally and economically beneficial use (Richter, Bartak, and Caldwell, 2020, p. 319). In addition, the agricultural sector should reconsider improving their irrigation system by adopting mulching and no-till strategies that can increase soil moisture and reduce water consumption globally (Richter, 2017, p. 886).

There is a need in developing countries to manage and develop sustainable and appropriate water infrastructure. The link between finance experts and water needs to be built to tackle scarce funds and underinvestment. Improving water resources management is required to protect water quality and build the foundation for meeting future demands. Investing in policy and legal forms can help support and create underlying conditions to sustain improvements in water resource management (Beddington, 2009, p. 5). Government investments should address water quality and quantity issues through programs that help crosscutting programs that focus on development. Financing water resources management is directly related to good governance.

Increasing water security requires tailored policy responses adaptable to location, national, and international contexts. Policy responses would build a foundation for enhancing and strengthening the water systems to withstand upcoming uncertainties and changes. Countries with legal frameworks and policy foundations would enable them to adapt to the challenges (Zeitoun, 2016). Water allocation, planning, and pricing policies are needed because they aim to increase water security through efficient agricultural, domestic, and industrial water use. This strategy will ensure affordability, flexibility, and availability. Establishing policies on water pricing would reflect on the actual cost, including the cost of delivery service and treatment, infrastructure, and economic value of water. Virtual water trade flows can lift the burden on limited water resources in water-scarce countries, but it requires equitable international trade (D'Odorico et al., 2014). The policy of using unconventional water sources, such as wastewater management for reuse and recovery of water for use, is recommended. Wastewater can contribute toward achieving water security by transforming it from health constraints and environmental burdens into an economic asset willing to achieve water security (UN Water, 2013, p. 22).

Balancing social, environmental, and economic priorities as well as balancing "soft" (institutional) and "hard" (infrastructure) solutions such as investments, small and large scale, in storing and transporting water, and in protecting the resource itself (Beddington, 2009, p. 5).

CONCLUSION

The essence of water security is that concern for the resource base itself is coupled with concern that services exploit it for human survival and well-being (Beddington, 2009, p. 1). The challenges discussed in the chapter have increasingly become important as global changes threaten water availability. There is a need to develop equitable and sustainable ways of managing water cooperatively. Cooperation can be promoted by facilitating interdisciplinary and multilevel dialogues to foster development and peace. Enhancing water security is possible by strengthening the stockholders' capacity through anticipation, prevention, and managing water conflicts. The response to water scarcity can be classified under different categories, such as reallocation, supply augmentation, and water conservation. Some strategies for dealing with water scarcity are implemented locally and primarily by donor-assisted projects and government agencies. Water education needs to be improved even if the challenges are identified in the previous paragraphs. Water education must not just be hydrological sciences but also interdisciplinary and multidisciplinary. This approach would include advancing knowledge through training and increasing awareness regarding water issues aimed at water professionals and decision-makers. The awareness should reach out to media professionals so that they can globally communicate regarding water issues effectively and accurately.

NOTE

1. A. Mortada. University of Pavia, Italy. Email: adriano.mortada94@gmail.com

BIBLIOGRAPHY

Abbink, Jon. "Dam controversies: Contested governance and developmental discourse on the Ethiopian Omo River dam." *Social Anthropology/Anthropologie Sociale* 20, no. 2 (2012): 125–144.

Al-Obaidy, A. H. M. J., and Mukdad Al-Khateeb. "The challenges of water sustainability in Iraq." *Engineering and Technology Journal* 31, no. 5 (2013): 828–840.

Arnbjerg-Nielsen, Karsten, P. Willems, Jonas Olsson, S. Beecham, A. Pathirana, I. Bülow Gregersen, H. Madsen, and V-T-V. Nguyen. "Impacts of climate change on rainfall extremes and urban drainage systems: A review." *Water Science and Technology* 68, no. 1 (2013): 16–28.

Arsano, Yacob, and Imeru Tamrat. "Ethiopia and the Eastern Nile Basin." *Aquatic Sciences* 67, no. 1 (2005): 15–27.

AQUAOSO. "The Growing Prevalence of Flood Damage in Agriculture." Accessed: December 1, 2022. https://aquaoso.com/blog/flood-damage-in-agriculture/.

BBC News. "The 11 Cities Most Likely to Run out of Drinking Water—Like Cape Town." Accessed: December 1, 2022. https://www.bbc.com/news/world-42982959.

Beddington, John. "Global Water Security." *Global Water Partnership, no. 33* (2009): 1–5.

Bhaduri, Anik, Janos Bogardi, Afreen Siddiqi, Holm Voigt, Charles Vörösmarty, Claudia Pahl-Wostl, Stuart E. Bunn et al. "Achieving Sustainable Development Goals from a Water Perspective." *Frontiers in Environmental Science* 64, (2016): 1–13.

Bhanoo, Sindya N. "Billions of People Depend on Water From Shrinking Snowpacks," Nytimes.Com. Accessed: December 1, 2022. https://www.nytimes.com/2015/11/18/science/billions-of-people-depend-on-water-from-shrinking-snowpacks.html.

Bogardi, Janos J., David Dudgeon, Richard Lawford, Eva Flinkerbusch, Andrea Meyn, Claudia Pahl-Wostl, Konrad Vielhauer, and Charles Vörösmarty. "Water security for a planet under pressure: Interconnected challenges of a changing world call for sustainable solutions." *Current Opinion in Environmental Sustainability* 4, no. 1 (2012): 35–43.

Borras Jr., Saturnino M., Ruth Hall, Ian Scoones, Ben White, and Wendy Wolford. "Towards a better understanding of global land grabbing: An editorial introduction." *The Journal of Peasant Studies* 38, no. 2 (2011): 209–216.

Carius, Alexander, Geoffrey D. Dabelko, and Aaron T. Wolf. "Water, conflict, and cooperation." *Environmental Change and Security Project Report* 10 (2004): 60–66.

De Bruin, Sophie, Joost Knoop, Hans Visser, and Willem Ligtvoet. "Linking water security threats to conflict." (2018).

Detges, Adrien, Benjamin Pohl, Stella Schaller. "Editor's Pick: 10 Violent Water Conflicts." Climate-Diplomacy. Accessed December 1, 2022. https://climate-diplomacy.org/magazine/conflict/editors-pick-10-violent-water-conflicts.

D'Odorico, Paolo, Joel Carr, Carole Dalin, Jampel Dell'Angelo, Megan Konar, Francesco Laio, Luca Ridolfi et al. "Global virtual water trade and the hydrological cycle: Patterns, drivers, and socio-environmental impacts." *Environmental Research Letters* 14, no. 5 (2019): 1–33.

El Kharraz, Jauad, Alaa El-Sadek, Noreddine Ghaffour, and Eric Mino. "Water scarcity and drought in WANA countries." *Procedia Engineering* 33 (2012): 14–29.

Falkenmark, Malin. "Growing water scarcity in agriculture: Future challenge to global water security." *Philosophical Transactions of the Royal Society A: Mathematical, Physical and Engineering Sciences* 371, no. 2002 (2013): 1–14.

Fischer, Günther, Francesco N. Tubiello, Harrij Van Velthuizen, and David A. Wiberg. "Climate change impacts on irrigation water requirements: Effects of mitigation, 1990–2080." *Technological Forecasting and Social Change* 74, no. 7 (2007): 1083–1107.

Gerlak, Andrea K., Lily House-Peters, Robert G. Varady, Tamee Albrecht, Adriana Zúñiga-Terán, Rafael Routson de Grenade, Christina Cook, and Christopher A. Scott. "Water security: A review of place-based research." *Environmental Science & Policy* 82 (2018): 79–89.

Goldstone, Jack A. "Population and security: How demographic change can lead to violent conflict." *Journal of International Affairs* (2002): 3–21.

Grimm, Nancy B., Stanley H. Faeth, Nancy E. Golubiewski, Charles L. Redman, Jianguo Wu, Xuemei Bai, and John M. Briggs. "Global change and the ecology of cities." *Science* 319, no. 5864 (2008): 756–760.

Hall, Jim, and Edoardo Borgomeo. "Risk-based principles for defining and managing water security." *Philosophical Transactions of the Royal Society A: Mathematical, Physical and Engineering Sciences* 371, no. 2002 (2013): 1–22.

Hall, Ruth, Marc Edelman, Saturnino M. Borras Jr., Ian Scoones, Ben White, and Wendy Wolford. "Resistance, acquiescence or incorporation? An introduction to land grabbing and political reactions 'from below.'" *Journal of Peasant Studies* 42, no. 3–4 (2015): 467–488.

Hoekstra, Arjen Y., and Thomas O. Wiedmann. "Humanity's unsustainable environmental footprint." *Science* 344, no. 6188 (2014): 1114–1117.

Hope, Rob, Katy Hansen, Mutsa Mutembwa, and Sarah Schlessinger. "Water security, risk and society–key issues and research priorities for international development." Synthesis report submitted to UK collaborative on development sciences by Oxford University Water Security Network. Accessed: December 1, 2022.

https://www.ukcdr.org.uk/wp-content/uploads/2017/12/Water-Security-Risk-and-Society.pdf

Hunger, Martin, and Petra Döll. "Value of river discharge data for global-scale hydrological modeling." *Hydrology and Earth System Sciences* 12, no. 3 (2008): 841–861.

Iceland, Charles. "Water stress is helping drive conflict and migration." World Resource Institute. Accessed: December 1, 2022. wri.org/insights/water-stress-helping-drive-conflict-and-migration

Kallio, Enni. "Land degradation in war and conflict regions." Yale Environment Review. Accessed: December 1, 2022. https://environment-review.yale.edu/land-degradation-war-and-conflict-regions-0

Latrubesse, Edgardo M., and Daniel Brea. "Floods in Argentina." *Developments in Earth Surface Processes* 13 (2009): 333–349.

Mahmuduzzaman, Mohammed, Zahir Uddin Ahmed, A. K. M. Nuruzzaman, and Fazle Rabbi Sadeque Ahmed. "Causes of salinity intrusion in coastal belt of Bangladesh." *International Journal of Plant Research* 4, no. 4A (2014): 8–13.

Molden, David, ed. *Water for Food Water for Life: A Comprehensive Assessment of Water Management in Agriculture*. Routledge, 2013.

Kemp, Geoffrey, Luke Hagberg, Adam Lammon, Bianca Majumder, and Bradley L. Nelson. "Water crises, security and climate change." Accessed: December 1, 2022. https://cftni.org/publications/water-crises-security-and-climate-change/

Koop, Steven H. A., and Cornelis Johannes van Leeuwen. "The challenges of water, waste and climate change in cities." *Environment, Development and Sustainability* 19, no. 2 (2017): 385–418.

Mancosu, Noemi, Richard L. Snyder, Gavriil Kyriakakis, and Donatella Spano. "Water scarcity and future challenges for food production." *Water* 7, no. 3 (2015): 975–992.

Margulis, M. E., N. McKeon, and S. M. Borras Jr. "Land grabbing and global governance: Critical perspectives." *Globalizations* 10, no. 1 (2013): 1–23.

Misra, Anil Kumar. "Climate change and challenges of water and food security." *International Journal of Sustainable Built Environment* 3, no. 1 (2014): 153–165.

McCarthy, Joe, Erica Sánchez. "Billions Rely on Himalayan Glaciers for Water. But They're Disappearing." Accessed: December 1, 2022.

Global Citizen. https://www.globalcitizen.org/en/content/himalayas-melting-climate-change/

Molenaar, A., J. C. J. H. Aerts, P. Dircke, and M. Ikert. *Connecting Delta Cities: Resilient Cities and Climate Adaptation Strategies*. Rotterdam: Connecting Delta Cities, 2015.

Ligtvoet, W., H. Hilderink, A. Bouwman, P. Puijenbroek, P. Lucas, and M. Witmer. "Towards a world of cities in 2050." An outlook on water-related challenges. Background report to the UN-Habitat Global Report. PBL Netherlands Environmental Assessment Agency (2014).

Ohlsson, Leif. *Livelihood Conflicts: Linking Poverty and Environment as Causes of Conflict*. Swedish International Development Cooperation Agency (SIDA), 2000.

Richter, Brian D., Dominique Bartak, Peter Caldwell, Kyle Frankel Davis, Peter Debaere, Arjen Y. Hoekstra, Tianshu Li et al. "Water scarcity and fish imperilment driven by beef production." *Nature Sustainability* 3, no. 4 (2020): 319–328.

Richter, Brian D., James D. Brown, Rachel DiBenedetto, Adrianna Gorsky, Emily Keenan, Chantal Madray, Martha Morris, Devin Rowell, and Susan Ryu. "Opportunities for saving and reallocating agricultural water to alleviate water scarcity." *Water Policy* 19, no. 5 (2017): 886–907.

Richter, Brian D., David Abell, Emily Bacha, Kate Brauman, Stavros Calos, Alex Cohn, Carlos Disla et al. "Tapped out: How can cities secure their water future?" *Water Policy* 15, no. 3 (2013): 335–363.

Selby, Jan. "Positivist climate conflict research: A critique." *Geopolitics* 19, no. 4 (2014): 829–856.

Schmeier, S., J. Hartog, J. Kortlandt, K. Meijer, E. Meurs, R. Sasse, and R. ter Horst. "Water scarcity and conflict: Not such a straightforward link." ECDPM Great Insights Magazine, 8(4). Accessed: December 1, 2022. https://ecdpm.org/great-insights/complex-link-climate-change-conflict/water-scarcity-conflict/

Sindayigaya, Willy. *Foreign Investments in Agriculture–Land Grabbing*. GLS Treuhand, Zukunftsstiftung, 2011.

Sojka, Robert E., David L. Bjorneberg, and J. A. Entry. "Irrigation: An historical perspective." *Encyclopedia of soil science* 1, no. 1070 (2002): 745–749.

United Nations, Department of Economic and Social Affairs, Population Division. World Urbanization Prospects: The 2018 Revision (ST/ESA/SER.A/420). New York: United Nations, 2019.

UN-Water. "Water Security and the Global Water Agenda | UN-Water." Accessed March 3, 2022. https://www.unwater.org/publications/water-security-global-water-agenda/

UN Water. "Chapter 2 Challenges and opportunities for water in the transition to a green economy." Accessed December 1, 2022.

https://www.un.org/waterforlifedecade/green_economy_2011/pdf/watergreenconf_chap2_challenges_opportunities.pdf

USAID; U.S. Agency for International Development. "Addressing water challenges in the developing world: A framework for action." Accessed December 1, 2022. https://reliefweb.int/sites/reliefweb.int/files/resources/F619FB3C75EA4FEF492576F8000425CD-Framework_for_Action.pdf

Van Weezel, Stijn. "On climate and conflict: Precipitation decline and communal conflict in Ethiopia and Kenya." *Journal of Peace Research* 56, no. 4 (2019): 514–528.

Wallace, J. S. "Increasing agricultural water use efficiency to meet future food production." *Agriculture, Ecosystems & Environment* 82, no. 1–3 (2000): 105–119.

Wolf, Aaron T. "Shared waters: Conflict and cooperation." *Annual Review of Environment and Resources* 32 (2007): 241–269.

Wolf, Aaron T. *Water and Human Security (AVISO 3).* Victoria, Canada: The Global Environmental Change and Human Security Project, 1999.

Wolf, Aaron T., Shira B. Yoffe, and Mark Giordano. "International waters: Identifying basins at risk." *Water Policy* 5, no. 1 (2003): 29–60.

WWAP (UNESCO World Water Assessment Programme). "The United Nations world water development report 2019: Leaving no one behind." Accessed: December 1, 2022. https://en.unesco.org/themes/water-security/wwap/wwdr/2019

Zarfl, Christiane, Alexander E. Lumsdon, Jürgen Berlekamp, Laura Tydecks, and Klement Tockner. "A global boom in hydropower dam construction." *Aquatic Sciences* 77 (2015): 161–170.

Zeitoun, M., B. Lankford, T. Krueger, T. Forsyth, R. Carter, A. Y. Hoekstra, R. Taylor, O. Varis, F. Cleaver, R. Boelens, and L. Swatuk. "Reductionist and integrative research approaches to complex water security policy challenges." *Global Environmental Change* 39 (2016): 143–154.

Part V

EFFECTS OF RESPONSES TO THE COVID-19 PANDEMIC ON INTERNATIONAL ORDER

Chapter 16

Mask Diplomacy on the New Silk Road

The Implications of COVID-19 Pandemic for China's Quest for Global Leadership

Paulina Kanarek[1]

INTRODUCTION

Over the last few years, we have witnessed an increasingly assertive attitude of Chinese foreign policymakers and have heard multiple times that China, although is not willing to interfere in other countries' domestic issues, is aiming to become the world's most powerful country. In 2017, as Xi Jinping became the first Chinese leader to address the World Economic Forum in Davos, he set out to establish himself as the standard-bearer for globalization, and China as a beneficiary of globalization in the past and a leader in the future (Economy 2017).

The outburst of the COVID-19 pandemic brought criticism of the way in which China handled the crisis and deteriorated its image abroad. Therefore, this chapter argues that since 2020 China has been using its mask diplomacy to shift the narrative about the pandemic, improve the perception of China internationally, and project Beijing's influence in the areas that the People's Republic of China (PRC) considers of strategic importance. Using comparative case study approach, this chapter will show that the mask diplomacy reflects China's foreign policy goals.

Each country has unique relations with China; however, some common patterns can be observed. Using the case study of Hungary and Serbia, it will be demonstrated that China is more likely to make its mask diplomacy work in countries that are ruled by populist leaders, and the PRC's offensive is unlikely to fundamentally transform its image in countries like Italy or Spain. It will also be demonstrated that the recent surge in assertiveness in Chinese foreign policy is in fact a long-term trend, which has only become more visible during the pandemic. It will also be shown that there is a strong correlation between economic goals and mask diplomacy. Countries involved in the Belt and Road Initiative (BRI) and those who are issuing favorable narratives about China are more likely to get support.

This work is divided into six parts. Following this introduction, a short literature review and an analysis of China's foreign policy strategy will be provided. The next part will provide insights into Chinese policy in Europe since the pandemic's beginning, touching upon the issue of wolf warrior diplomacy and China's charm offensive. The case study analysis of selected European countries will show the differences in approaches toward China. Then, the next part will focus on analyzing China's foreign policy toward Latin America. The last part will summarize all findings.

LITERATURE REVIEW

The usefulness and effectiveness of soft power in diplomacy is a well-researched topic in literature. The political scientist Joseph Nye first articulated soft power as the ability to affect others to obtain the outcomes one wants through attraction rather than coercion or payment (Nye 1990, 2008). It is an important tool for policymakers, especially in the field of public diplomacy.

Nevertheless, some scholars argue that it is hard to define Chinese soft power (Breslin 2011) as it differs from the soft power of other countries (Bates and Huang 2006; Glaser and Murphy 2009). Although Chinese power of attractiveness and influence was initially considered weak (Holyk 2011; Nye 2012), its importance and significance have steadily grown over the last two decades. Joshua Kurlantzick argues that with growing support from nations in Africa, Latin America, and Southeast Asia, China could challenge US domination in international relations (Kurlantzick 2007).

Chinese soft power has brought different outcomes in various regions of the world. In the analysis of Chinese soft power goals in Europe, Ingrid d'Hooghe finds that Beijing wants to build the image of China as a stable, responsible, and reliable economic partner, a trustworthy member of the international community, and a rising power that is not to be feared (d'Hooghe 2011). There is no consensus among scholars regarding the outcomes of Beijing's soft power policies in Latin America. While some researchers argue that it is uncertain to what extent the Chinese soft power is attractive to Latin America's citizens (Leiteritz 2012; Steinmüller 2014), other scholars believe it is not very successful (Carreras 2017).

Mask diplomacy is an element of the current public diplomacy of China and an important tool in Beijing's soft power projection. Stojanovic (2020) emphasizes that mask diplomacy is a mix of soft power policy, political messaging, and aid shipments. This chapter aims to fill in the gap in the literature on China's most recent soft power strategies. It will build on the previous research about the effectiveness of Chinese soft power by analyzing the factors that impact the efficiency of mask diplomacy.

RECENT DEVELOPMENTS IN THE CHINESE FOREIGN POLICY

As Xi Jinping assumed power in 2012, Chinese foreign policy has profoundly changed. In the autumn of 2013, Xi Jinping publicly presented the idea of reviving the Silk Road by creating the BRI. The project consists of the Silk Road Economic Belt and the twenty-first century Maritime Silk Road, which aim to promote economic development and improve connectivity and cooperation on a transcontinental scale. According to the official sources published by the Chinese government, by the beginning of 2022, 146 countries have joined the Initiative. Nevertheless, as Nedopil (2021) notices, it is difficult to state how many countries are actually members of the BRI, as some of them have not published a confirmation of signing a full Memorandum of Understanding for the BRI.

The Initiative is one of the most complex and unclear foreign policy efforts of the twenty-first century. This multitrillion project has gained a high level of awareness, yet despite its recognition, there is little reliable information about how it unfolds in aggregate (Hillman 2018). Although China assures that the project's main aim is enhancing interregional connectivity, critics have noticed that the BRI builds Chinese soft power and serves as a geopolitical strategy to project Beijing's influence and development model worldwide (Interviewee 2 2021).

Over the past decade, it has become clear that China is striving for Xi Jinping's Chinese Dream, based on the great rejuvenation of the Chinese nation, a plan for China to emerge as a global superpower. This work believes that Chinese foreign policy has become more assertive over the last few years. Nevertheless, it was only when the COVID-19 pandemic started in late 2019 that China significantly changed its rhetoric and started projecting its influence in some parts of the world more boldly and openly. China is willing to continue promoting its development model, investing in infrastructural projects, and building its positive image abroad. With the newly developed strategy called mask diplomacy, China is gradually strengthening its position in countries severely impacted by the coronavirus pandemic. The next part of this chapter will show the outcome of this strategy in selected countries of two geographical areas—Europe and Latin America.

MASK DIPLOMACY IN EUROPE

In analyzing the Chinese foreign policy in Europe throughout 2020, this work observes two major trends: a more assertive narrative in the rhetoric used by the Chinese officials and a contrasting charm offensive visible in the new strategy of so-called mask diplomacy.

The second quarter of 2020 has witnessed the culmination of the growing number of strong statements made by officials from China, often described as wolf warrior diplomacy. The term originates from a Chinese patriotic action blockbuster titled "Wolf Warrior" and has now become a buzzword to criticize the confrontational style of diplomats in China (Chen and Hu 2020). Nevertheless, this work argues that the causality of this new rhetoric is difficult to determine. Several factors have influenced the shift toward bolder and firmer statements of Chinese officials.

Firstly, the long-term course toward more self-confident and less tolerant of criticism of China becomes more visible. In this case, it can be pointed out that China is gradually becoming more assertive, and the circumstances of the pandemic only shed light on this phenomenon.

Secondly, the wave of criticism toward China can be considered a major reason for some representatives of the Chinese government to become more defensive. The global anti-China sentiment has been rising since the beginning of the coronavirus crisis, with Europe and the United States being the major critics of China, blaming Beijing for the outbreak of the pandemic and accusing it of a lack of transparency. In this case, as Chen and Hu (2020) notice, China's pugnacious diplomatic action might be a counter-attack in a specific situation, not a new normal.

When asked about China's foreign policy, Chinese Foreign Ministry Spokesperson Hua Chunying said that aggressiveness is not China's tradition and cited Mao Zedong's words: "*We will not attack unless we are attacked. If we are attacked, we will certainly counterattack*" (Hua 2020).

This sharp rhetoric contrasts with China's EU charm offensive which we can observe through the analysis of mask diplomacy in various European countries. Raj Verma (2020) believes that China decided to provide medical assistance and vital health equipment, as well as offered to share its expertise in tackling the pandemic, to place Beijing in a positive light. Indeed, the mask diplomacy, which by the end of 2020 has changed into vaccine diplomacy, served the purpose of rebuilding China's image after the initial criticism and strengthening its position as a responsible global leader.

This work argues that the ultimate target of China's mask diplomacy in Europe was to strengthen its weakening position, rebuild trust, and encourage further cooperation with Beijing. Through the investigation of case studies, it will be shown that this strategy brought rather mixed results. It amplified preexisting political and economic challenges in the EU–China relations, which raised concerns in Europe regarding its overreliance on the supply of strategic goods. It showed a clear division and lack of coherence in Europe—while some Western European countries were accusing China of sending defective testing kits and medical masks, others were welcoming Chinese involvement in crisis management and publicly showing their appreciation for Chinese help (Chapple 2020). Analysis of Serbia and Hungary, along with an overview of the situation in Spain and Italy, will shed light on how Chinese assistance is perceived in Europe.

THE FRUITS OF MASK DIPLOMACY IN CENTRAL EUROPE

Serbia

Serbia was in the scope of China's interest before the pandemic outbreak. China signed a strategic partnership with Serbia in 2009, and both countries have strong and increasingly friendly relations. They also share political views with Beijing supporting Belgrade on the Kosovo issue, reflecting its situation vis-à-vis Taiwan and even Hong Kong (Le Corre and Vuksanovic 2019). Additionally, Serbia is the prime case of interparty cooperation with China (Szunomár et al. 2020).

Moreover, Serbia plays an important role in the BRI for China's flagship project in this part of Europe: Belgrade–Budapest high-speed railway. It can serve as an entry point into South-Eastern Europe, and since this Balkan state is not an EU member state, it has more flexibility than EU countries in the region in how it wants to shape its relations with China. Belgrade's motives behind tightening its economic connection with China can also be partially explained by the country's search for additional funds in the crisis caused by the pandemic.

The correlation between previous strong and friendly Sino-Serbian relations and the Chinese mask diplomacy in 2020 should be observed. The case study of Serbia supports the hypothesis that Beijing's mask diplomacy reflects its foreign policy goals in the region. It also shows some degree of conditionality of Chinese aid—the countries that speak favorably of Beijing are more likely to receive Chinese support.

This work argues that the media coverage of Chinese donations of masks and other medical equipment in Serbia was significantly more intense than in other countries. The Serbian government has made considerable effort to acknowledge Chinese assistance publicly and made sure that both Serbian citizens and Beijing observers saw Belgrade's gratitude. In the first half of 2020, in the streets of Belgrade, residents could see numerous billboards displaying the Chinese flag, the picture of Xi Jinping, and banners saying "Serbs And Chinese, Brothers Forever." The Palace Albania building in central Belgrade lit up in the colours of the Chinese flag in March 2020, and screens saying "thank you" to Chinese President Xi Jinping were displayed next to Serbia's National Assembly building (Chapple 2020). City authorities have paid for the displays of appreciation for China.

The highlight of this pro-China performance by the Serbian government occurred on March 21, 2020, when President Aleksandar Vucic greeted Chinese doctors who arrived in Serbia by kissing the Chinese flag in gratitude (CGTN 2020). This was well received by Beijing and widely covered in the Chinese media. Although the European observers were rather critical regarding the excessive enthusiasm of Serbian officials, the case study of Serbia shows that Beijing's mask diplomacy brought the expected outcome and gave Beijing exactly what it wished for.

Mask diplomacy strengthened the image of China as a responsible global leader and a generous partner among Serbian citizens. In Serbian public opinion, China is a reliable friend who did not disappoint them amid the coronavirus crisis. According to the report published by the Centre for Strategic and International Studies, a poll conducted in March 2020 showed that 40% of Serbians believed China was the biggest donor to their country, while only 17.6% believed the European Union was the largest donor (Conley et al. 2020). In reality, the European Union is responsible for most donations to Serbia, followed by Germany, the United States, and the United Nations (Conley et al. 2020). China falls in fifth place.

China's mask diplomacy in Serbia was very successful. Chinese medical assistance and economic activities have solidified Serbia's support for Beijing's foreign policy objectives. Using Serbia, Beijing showed that it rushed to help its European friends and thus created the narrative that it is a pioneer in crisis solution and a loyal partner. This is precisely what China wanted to achieve with its mask diplomacy in the region.

Hungary

Hungary is competing with its neighbors for Chinese investment. In 2011, the country adopted the "Opening to the East" policy, although China-friendly policies have preceded Orban's government (Szunomár et al. 2020). It goes in line with Beijing's interest, as China hopes to build highways, construct or reconstruct railways as well as expand power plants in Central and Eastern Europe (Szunomár et al. 2020).

Hungary has never criticized China when it comes to COVID-19. In fact, Sino-Hungarian relations accelerated during the pandemic. The air bridge between China and Hungary was opened to facilitate the delivery of coronavirus protection supplies from China. President Orban personally welcomed the arrival of a plane from China at Budapest airport, noting that eighty-six planes had arrived until mid-March with masks, tests, and ventilators (Szicherle and Kreko 2020). Government officials in Hungary repeatedly praised China and publicly demonstrated their gratitude to the Asian partner. The economic ties also boosted as Budapest and the Chinese Export–Import Bank signed a loan agreement to construct the Hungarian phase of the Budapest–Belgrade railway line (Szicherle and Kreko 2020).

After the initial success of the mask diplomacy in Hungary in the first half of 2020, Hungary became the European Union's first member state to approve China's Sinopharm COVID-19 vaccine domestically (Reuters 2021). By the end of January 2021, when Hungary purchased 5 million doses of the Sinopharm vaccine, it was still not approved by the European Medicines Agency (EMA). Assessing the attitude of the Hungarian government, it should also be noticed that a few weeks earlier, decision-makers in Budapest bought Russia's Sputnik V vaccine, which also has not been approved by EMA and was not yet purchased by any other EU member.

Hungary's decision to import a Chinese-made vaccine, which was not yet verified and tested by the EMA, was heavily criticized by several EU member states. Nevertheless, Budapest continued strengthening ties with China, hoping that Beijing would provide a replacement for shrinking EU subsidies. As Szicherle and Kreko (2020) notice, the Hungarian government and state media have provided highly favorable coverage of China for years. China sees the effort and rewards the partners who were supportive in the past; therefore, it is not a coincidence that amidst a shortage of medical equipment, Hungary received 6,500 ventilators by June 2020 from China.

Last but not least, political preferences were an important factor as well. The Hungarian government's relations with the EU were deteriorating; Hungarian leaders are known for keeping close ties with Moscow and Beijing. Cooperation with Budapest seemed to be very smooth for Beijing over the past few years. Hungary is another example that shows how China uses mask diplomacy to achieve its foreign policy goals and build a strong position in the region. Hungary has been an important gateway to Europe for China through its infrastructure and investment projects. Beijing used the opportunity provided by the coronavirus crisis to build its positive image as a global leader in the country. Moreover, it is also becoming apparent that China has used Central and Eastern Europe as a testing ground for more activist party diplomacy (Interviewee 2 2021).

Hungary and Serbia support China on political issues, and it should be noted that mask diplomacy proved to be a great success for the Chinese government in these countries. Beijing's help was acknowledged and received huge media coverage, which pleased Chinese donors. Nevertheless, Serbia and Hungary represent an exception rather than the rule. The brief overview of the situation in other EU countries will show that mask diplomacy was not as successful elsewhere.

SCEPTICISM AMONG OTHER EU COUNTRIES

Since early March 2020, the epicenter of the outbreak of the coronavirus pandemic shifted from China to Europe; therefore, Beijing decided to provide help to the countries which found themselves in a critical situation. Many European states, including Spain, Italy, France, Greece, the Czech Republic, Poland, and the Netherlands, received some medical aid and assistance. This was done via multiple bodies, such as the Chinese Red Cross, Huawei, Alibaba, and the government in Beijing (Billaudot 2020). Mask diplomacy in Europe served the purpose of improving China's image after the outbreak of the pandemic in Wuhan. Chinese help brought relief to those struggling, however, the experts argue that China has only scored points in the short term, but in the long run, European mistrust toward Beijing is not likely to change any time soon.

In March 2020, Italy's extremely high daily death tolls brought a serious threat to the European community. China did not take long to respond to the Italian crisis—before the end of the month, the Chinese team of medical experts and tonnes of medical supplies were sent to help. It is also worth noticing that Italy became more important to Chinese policymakers as it signed a memorandum of understanding in support of the BRI in 2019. Therefore, the Chinese generosity was partially explained.

Nevertheless, the Italian perception of China as a partner who provided much assistance during the most challenging time of the pandemic in Italy lasted only a short time. According to the poll conducted by the Italian Institute for International Political Studies (ISPI), the perception of China as a main global threat has drastically increased over the last year (ISPI 2021). Additionally, with time Italy also focused on more cooperation with the EU member countries to combat the pandemic and avoided depending entirely on China. It also became more obvious to public opinion that much of the mask diplomacy was not donations but a result of commercial transactions.

Spain was also among the EU member states most severely hit by the pandemic. Nevertheless, Esteban and Armanini (2020) believe COVID-19 did not convince Madrid to build stronger ties with China. Moreover, in Spain, studies have shown that even after several months of intensive efforts by Beijing to promote a better image of China as a reliable partner for Spain in the crisis, Spanish public opinion identified China as Spain's second-preferred ally outside the EU, after the United States (Esteban and Armanini 2020). Furthermore, the Spanish government is very careful when trading with China as it does not want to depend on Chinese suppliers of medical products and 5G communication networks.

Josep Borrell, High Representative of the European Union for Foreign Affairs and Security Policy, publicly stated that the EU must be aware of a geopolitical component, including a struggle for influence through spinning and the politics of generosity (Borrell 2020).

Analyzing the situation in selected European countries has shown that Beijing is using its mask diplomacy to project power and improve its image in Europe. It had various outcomes—from great success in Hungary and Serbia to doubts and scepticism in other EU member states. This dichotomy in the attitudes toward China is problematic for the EU, and it can be argued that China benefits from European disunity as it can establish stronger ties with selected countries.

CHINA'S RISING INFLUENCE IN LATIN AMERICA

By the end of January 2021, Latin America was the world's worst-hit region by the coronavirus pandemic. As Europe and the United States had to focus on managing their domestic crises, China found the perfect timing to project its influence in Latin America by offering medical equipment, vaccines, and support in rebuilding the economy.

Considered the United States' backyard, Latin America had somewhat limited relations with Beijing and joined China's BRI much later than most Asian and European countries. Nevertheless, China's growing appetite for raw commodities such as copper, iron, petroleum, and soybeans sparked its interest in South American natural resources long ago. China is Argentina's, Brazil's, and Peru's main trading partner and the main destination for exports from Brazil, Chile, Cuba, Peru, and Uruguay (Perez 2020).

At the same time, Latin American countries face a threat of another "lost decade" —over 60,000 demonstrations have been reported in Latin America and the Caribbean from 2018 to the present (ACLED 2020), inequality deepened, and infrastructure lacks investment. According to a study by the United Nations Economic Commission for Latin America and the Caribbean (ECLAC), nearly 45 million more Latin Americans will be impoverished due to the pandemic. According to the International Monetary Fund (2021), Latin America and the Caribbean experienced a 7.4% contraction in 2020.

China provided help to the majority of crisis-thorn Latin American states and has been delivering medical equipment to the region continuously since

March 2020. As Telias and Urdinez (2020) argue, donations made by the Chinese government and China's private companies were affected by two political determinants—strategic partnership status with China and the One China Policy. The best example which proves this theory is Paraguay. The government in Asuncion still officially recognizes Taiwan; therefore, the support it received was incomparably smaller than that of its neighboring countries, which recognize Beijing.

China has been projecting its influence in Latin America for many years, however, it only became more visible recently when the first COVID-19 vaccines were produced. By early March 2021, the following Latin American countries have approved at least one of the vaccines produced by China: Argentina, Brazil, Bolivia, Chile, Colombia, Dominican Republic, Ecuador, Mexico, Peru, Uruguay, and Venezuela. Therefore, this work believes that researching the current influence of China in Latin America is also adequate to talk about vaccine diplomacy, which can be considered a continuation of the mask diplomacy efforts. Both terms will be used interchangeably.

Chile

Chile joined the BRI in November 2018, hoping to increase trade exchange with China and encourage Chinese investment. Currently, China is Chile's top trading partner; over 32% of Chile's total exports were received by China in 2020 (Statista 2021).

In 2019 and 2020, trade between China and Chile surpassed $40 billion yearly, and China's presence in the Chilean market became more visible. In November 2020, Chinese state-owned company State Grid announced it would buy Chilean electricity distributor Compañia General de Electricidad (CGE). The Chilean government seems not to oppose the deal despite concerns over foreign control of an industry of strategic importance for national development (Guzman 2021). This tightening commercial cooperation has also been evident as one observes the Chilean vaccination campaign.

Chile became an undisputable leader in terms of vaccination programs, not only in Latin America but also globally. At the beginning of March 2021, the country's vaccination campaign was the fourth most successful globally, just behind Israel, UAE, and the UK (measured by COVID-19 vaccination doses per 100 people). The origin of the vaccines that Chile purchased is important. Unlike the European economies, Chile put its hopes on the CoronaVac vaccine, developed by the Chinese company Sinovac, and has ordered 60 million doses by early February 2021 (Diaz-Cerda 2021). Chilean President Sebastian Pinera personally welcomed the first shipment of vaccines developed by Chinese scientists.

Argentina

Over the past decade, Argentina has secured Chinese funds for projects, including railways, solar energy, nuclear energy, and dams, mainly through the Export–Import Bank of China (China Exim) and China Development Bank (Koop 2019). China has also received Argentine exports, mainly the primary goods. Argentina and China have to some extent, comparable diplomatic traditions, especially in the issue of nonalignment. In the political rhetoric between the two countries, they also often stress the similarities between Argentina's stance on Malvinas (Falkland Islands) and China's position on the issue of Taiwan (Interviewee 3 2021).

The Peronist government, which has been in power since the end of 2019, moved the nation in an increasingly left-populist direction, as well as contributed to the deepening of the country's relationship with the PRC. The outcome of the tightening relations became even more visible in April 2020, when China became Argentina's largest trading partner, displacing neighboring Brazil for the first time (Interviewee 3 2021). As the pandemic started, China rushed to support Argentina—in March 2020, the government in Buenos Aires received test kits, protective suits, masks, gloves, and digital thermometers. The donations, welcomed by Fernandez's government, were a projection of Chinese soft power, which arrived just on time, as Argentina was battling not only the coronavirus but also a severe economic crisis while renegotiating $110 billion in foreign debt with creditors (Garrison 2020).

It is believed that Argentine foreign policy is still, to some extent, dependent on the United States. Therefore, the fact that Argentina joined the BRI at the beginning of 2022 can be considered a major diplomatic victory for China in the region and an opportunity for Beijing to strengthen its influence in the continent further. Moreover, according to some experts in Sino-Argentine relations (Interviewee 3 2021), through its BRI, China is offering a new model of globalization and a long-term project—something that the crisis-thorn Argentine economy desperately needs in the near future.

CHINA'S TIES WITH OTHER LATIN AMERICAN COUNTRIES

Brazil is China's most important economic and political partner in South America. By 2019, bilateral trade reached over $100 billion, making China the main destination for Brazilian exports (Simoes 2020). Nevertheless, Bolsonaro's administration has adopted a highly pro-US approach and showed some anti-China sentiments, especially at the beginning of the pandemic.

As Ellis (2020) notices, despite some tensions between China and Brazil, Bolsonaro's economic interest in the PRC was stronger than his public scepticism toward the country. It also seems that China's agricultural, mining, and petroleum demand is strong enough to ignore some of the anti-Chinese rhetoric in Brazil (Ellis 2020). This also did not impede the cooperation after the outburst of the pandemic. As the crisis hit Brazil, which became the epicenter of COVID-19 in Latin America, the Brazilian government started seeking help in Beijing. In January 2021, Bolsonaro also publicly thanked China for the vaccines that Brazil has received.

Chinese vaccines reached Latin American states very quickly and made a significant contribution to the strengthening of South America's ties with Beijing. In February 2021, Peru announced the purchase of 38 million vaccine doses from state-run Chinese firm Sinopharm. Mexico has signed an advance-purchase agreement with another Chinese developer, CanSino Biologics, for 35 million doses. Ecuador ordered 2 million doses of the CoronaVac vaccine from the Chinese pharmaceutical company Sinovac. Latin American presidents contributed to improving China's image while publicly thanking Beijing for medical support. Chinese banks will also most likely extend concessional loans to the region (Interviewee 1 2021). Additionally, China's multibillion-dollar network of investment and infrastructure deals can be treated as a promise to tighten economic ties with the region further.

Latin America is very vulnerable to shocks from the global economy. Although China cannot solve all the continent's problems, it can offer a lot to Latin American partners. Furthermore, as the Chinese government is slowly abandoning its low-profile foreign policy, it will not be afraid of confrontation in the areas considered as the US sphere of influence. And with its abundant access to natural resources, political support, and enhanced economic cooperation, Latin America will be a valuable ally for China in the future.

Gerard Araud, formerly France's ambassador to the United States, has written that China wants a geopolitical status that reflects its recovered power and that would challenge the US hegemony. This phrase seems to be especially adequate to the current situation in Latin America. The pandemic proved to be a good time for Beijing to further strengthen its position in the region and build a positive narrative through vaccine diplomacy.

CONCLUSIONS

This chapter has demonstrated that the Chinese mask diplomacy reflects the goals of China's foreign policy. China is not afraid to challenge the world order that we know and aspires to become a global leader.

It was proved that mask diplomacy was supposed to strengthen China's position in the countries of strategic importance for China, as well as improve how China was perceived internationally. The charm offensive demonstrated through the mask diplomacy could be contrasted with the more assertive rhetoric of the Chinese diplomats. Nevertheless, this chapter has shown that it is not a new phenomenon—Chinese foreign policy has been growing increasingly assertive for a decade, and the COVID-19 pandemic only made this trend more visible.

Case study analysis of selected countries has shown that mask diplomacy tended to be more effective in the countries ruled by populist governments and those who have not received much aid from elsewhere—which is especially the case of Latin America. This chapter believes that with the successful results of mask diplomacy in some regions, China will continue to project its influence and gradually become more powerful.

The main limitation of this work is the number of countries researched. Mask diplomacy could bring different outcomes in other regions; therefore, more academic analysis in this field shall be conducted in the future.

In the early 1990s, Deng Xiaoping advised China's foreign policy to be good at maintaining a low profile, hide its capacities, and bide its time. The outburst of the pandemic in 2020 showed that China is no longer interested in maintaining a low profile and will keep challenging the United States, striving to become the world's largest economic power. Does it mean that the PRC no longer needs to bide its time, as its time has just come?

NOTE

1. P. Kanarek. MFA, Poland. Email: paulina.kanarekk@gmail.com

BIBLIOGRAPHY

Primary Sources

Borrell, J. 2020. "The Coronavirus Pandemic and the New World It Is Creating. Statement by the HR/VP." https://eeas.europa.eu/delegations/china/76401/eu-hrvp-josep-borrell-coronavirus-pandemic-and-new-world-it-creating_en

Hua, C. 2020. "Foreign Ministry Spokesperson Hua Chunying's Regular Press Conference on December 10, 2020." http://pl.china-embassy.org/pol/zglc/t1839270.htm

Interviewee 1 – Latin American Sinologist Affiliated with Peking University, Interviewed on February 12, 2021, via Skype.

Interviewee 2 – Sinologist, Lecturer at the University of Warsaw. Interviewed on March 2, 2021, in Warsaw, Poland.

Interviewee 3 – Historian Specializing in Sino-Argentine Relations, Lecturer at National University of Quilmes, Buenos Aires. Interviewed on February 20, 2021 via Skype.

Secondary Sources

ACLED. 2020. "Anti-Government Demonstrations in Latin America & the Caribbean: 2018–2020." Armed Conflict Location & Event Data Project Report. https://acleddata.com/2020/12/09/anti-government-demonstrations-in-latin-america-the-caribbean-2018-2020/

Bates, G. and Huang, Y. 2006. "Sources and limits of Chinese 'soft power.'" *Survival*, 48(2): 17–36. https://doi.org/10.1080/00396330600765377

Billaudot, S. 2020. "Chinese Aid to European Union Countries: A New Balance of Power Between East and West?" https://www.thenewfederalist.eu/chinese-aid-to-european-union-countries-a-new-balance-of-power-between?lang=fr

Breslin, S. 2011. "The Soft Notion of China's Soft Power." Chatham House Asia Programme Paper, February 1.

Chapple, A. 2020. "Public Displays of Affection? Chinese Signage in Serbia Sparks EU Ire." RFE/RL's Balkan Service May 27. https://www.rferl.org/a/chinese-signage-in-serbia-sparks-eu-ire/30637889.html

Carreras, M. 2017. "Public Attitudes toward an Emerging China in Latin America." *Issues & Studies*, 53(1). https://www.worldscientific.com/doi/abs/10.1142/S1013251117400045

CGTN. 2020. "Serbian President Kisses Chinese Flag as Support Team Arrives." CGTN Europe March 22. https://news.cgtn.com/news/2020-03-22/Serbian-president-kisses-Chinese-flag-as-support-team-arrives--P3FlpiEMBa/index.html

Chen, D. and Hu, J. 2020. "Is China Really Embracing 'Wolf Warrior' Diplomacy?" *The Diplomat* online publication September 9. https://thediplomat.com/2020/09/is-china-really-embracing-wolf-warrior-diplomacy/

Conley, H., Hillman, J., McCalpin, M., and Ruy, D. 2020. "Becoming a Chinese Client State: The Case of Serbia." Center for Strategic and International Studies (CSIS). http://www.jstor.org/stable/resrep26534

D'Hooghe, I. 2011. "The Limits of China's Soft Power in Europe: Beijing's Public Diplomacy Puzzle." In: Lee, S. J. and Melissen, J. (eds) *Public Diplomacy and Soft Power in East Asia*. Palgrave Macmillan Series in Global Public Diplomacy. New York: Palgrave Macmillan.

Diaz-Cerda, V. 2021. "How Chile Became an Unlikely Winner in the COVID-19 Vaccine Race."

https://theconversation.com/how-chile-became-an-unlikely-winner-in-the-covid-19-vaccine-race-154614

ECLAC. 2021. *Social Panorama of Latin America 2020*. Santiago: ECLAC Annual Report LC/PUB.2021/2-P/Rev.

Economy, E. 2017. "Beijing Is No Champion of Globalization." *Foreign Affairs* online publication January 22. https://www.foreignaffairs.com/articles/china/2017-01-22/beijing-no-champion-globalization

Economy, E. 2018. *The Third Revolution: Xi Jinping and the New Chinese State.* Oxford and New York: Oxford University Press.

Ellis, E. 2020. "The Future of Brazil–China Relations on the Context of COVID-19." *Global Americans* online publication September 18. https://theglobalamericans.org/2020/09/the-future-of-brazil-china-relations-in-the-context-of-covid-19/

Esteban, M., and Armanini, U. 2020. *China–Spain Relations Amid COVID-19 in a Comparative Perspective: An Enduring Partnership Facing Potential Uncertainties.* Budapest: China-CEE Institute Working Paper.

Garrison, C. 2020. "With U.S. Hit by Virus, China Courts Latin America with Medical Diplomacy." *Reuters.* March 26. https://www.reuters.com/article/us-health-coronavirus-latam-china-featur-idUSKBN21D346

Glaser, B. S., and Murphy, M. E. 2009. "Soft Power with Chinese Characteristics." In: Carola McGiffert (ed) *Chinese Soft Power and Its Implications for the U.S.*, 10–26. Washington, DC: Center for Strategic and International Studies.

Guzman, L. 2021. "State Grid Grows Presence in Chile with CGE Purchase." Dialogo Chino online publication February 1. https://dialogochino.net/en/climate-energy/39680-state-grid-grows-presence-in-chile-with-cge-purchase/

Hillman, E. 2018. "China's Belt and Road Initiative: Five Years Later." Center for Strategic and International Studies (CSIS) online publication January 25. https://www.csis.org/analysis/chinas-belt-and-road-initiative-five-years-later-0

Holyk, G. 2011. "Paper Tiger? Chinese Soft Power in East Asia." *Political Science Quarterly*, 126(2): 223–254. http://www.jstor.org/stable/23056992

International Monetary Fund 2021. "Latin America and Caribbean's Winding Road to Recovery" IMF online publication February 8. https://blogs.imf.org/2021/02/08/latin-america-and-caribbeans-winding-road-to-recovery/

Italian Institute for International Political Studies 2021. "Italy–China Relations in 2021: A Time to Regroup." ISPI online publication February 5. https://www.ispionline.it/en/pubblicazione/italy-china-relations-2021-time-regroup-29162

Koop, F. 2019. "Argentina Crisis Prompts Shift in Chinese Investment." Dialogo Chino online publication October 25. https://chinadialogue.net/en/energy/11606-argentina-crisis-prompts-shift-in-chinese-investment-2/

Kurlantzick, J. 2007. *Charm Offensive: How China's Soft Power Is Transforming the World.* New Haven: Yale University Press.

Le Corre, P., and Vuksanovic, V. 2019. "Serbia: China's Open Door to the Balkans." *The Diplomat* online publication January 1. https://thediplomat.com/2019/01/serbia-chinas-open-door-to-the-balkans/

Leiteritz, R. 2012. "China and Latin America: A Marriage Made in Heaven?" *Colombia International,* 75: 49–81.

Nedopil, C. 2021. "Countries of the Belt and Road Initiative." Green BRI Center online publication. www.green-bri.org

Nye, J. 1990. *Bound to Lead, the Changing Nature of American Power*. New York: Basic Books.

Nye, J. 2008. "Public Diplomacy and Soft Power." *The Annals of the American Academy of Political and Social Science,* 616: 94–109. http://www.jstor.org/stable/25097996

Nye, J. 2012. "Why China Is Weak on Soft Power." *New York Times*, January 17.

OBOReurope. 2020. "The China–Serbia Connection." OBOReurope online publication April 26. https://www.oboreurope.com/en/china-serbia-connection/

Oppenheimer, A. 2019. "China Is Becoming More Popular Than the U.S. in Many Latin American Countries." *Miami Herald*, April 26. https://www.miamiherald.com/news/local/news-columns-blogs/andres-oppenheimer/article229621934.html#storylink=cpy

Perez, C. 2020. "China and 'Mask Diplomacy' with Latin America." Atalayar online publication May 3. https://atalayar.com/en/content/china-and-mask-diplomacy-latin-america

Reuters. 2021. "Hungary Signs Deal for Chinese Sinopharm's COVID-19 Vaccine, First in EU." *Reuters*. January 21. https://www.reuters.com/article/us-health-coronavirus-hungary-vaccine-idUSKBN29Y0OD

Simoes, E. 2020. "Brazil–China Diplomatic Spat Escalates Over Coronavirus Supplies." *Reuters*. April 6. https://www.reuters.com/article/health-coronavirus-brazil-idINKBN21O23Y

Statista. 2021. "China as Share of Total Exports from Selected Countries in Latin America in 2019." Online Data Report. https://www.statista.com/statistics/1105815/latin-america-share-exports-china-country/

Steinmüller, H. 2014. "China's Growing Influence in Latin America." In: *South America, Central America and the Caribbean 2015*. The Europa Regional Surveys of the World (23rd). Routledge.

Stojanovic, D. 2020. "China's 'Mask Diplomacy' Wins Support in Eastern Europe." *AP News*. April 14. https://apnews.com/article/eastern-europe-czech-republic-china-russia-virus-outbreak-76dff4b113e82d85716262895909f151

Szicherle, P., and Kreko, P. 2020. "Hungary: The Success Story of Chinese Mask Diplomacy." Centre for Democratic Integrity online publication August 3. https://democratic-integrity.eu/patrik-szicherle-peter-kreko-hungary-the-success-story-of-chinese-mask-diplomacy/

Szunomár, A., Karindi, L., and Leonte, A. 2020. *Empty Shell No More: China's Growing Footprint in Central and Eastern Europe*. Prague, Czech Republic: Association for International Affairs (AMO).

Telias, D., and Urdinez, F. 2020. "China's Foreign Aid Political Drivers: Lessons from a Novel Dataset of Mask Diplomacy in Latin America During the COVID-19 Pandemic." *Journal of Current Chinese Affairs* online publication. https://www.researchgate.net/publication/344035590_China%27s_Foreign_Aid_Determinants_Lessons_from_a_Novel_Dataset_of_the_Mask_Diplomacy_During_the_COVID-19_Pandemic

Verma, R. 2020. "China's Diplomacy and Changing the COVID-19 Narrative." *International Journal*, 75(2): 248–258. https://doi.org/10.1177/0020702020930054

Chapter 17

The Rise and Fall of Militant Wings in the Wake of COVID-19

Maheen Farhat Raza[1] and Muhammad Ali Raza[2]

INTRODUCTION

The global pandemic has not only altered the geopolitical and geostrategic contours of world politics but also appears when the United States' dominance is waning. COVID-19 also has an impact on the militant landscape. New trends in global terrorism studies have been observed all over the world. The Global Terrorism Database did not include the COVID-19 era in the most recent 2020 Global Terrorism Index report (GTI-2020). The available literature, however, indicates that the global pandemic hampered the execution of the violent maneuvers. According to scholars, the significant decrease in violence results from the global lockdown. However, this is only one side of the coin. The status quo has not been disrupted for some militant organizations. The situation has served as a catalyst for the groups to become more lethal and difficult to comprehend. The chapter is intended to investigate the rise and fall of militant wings during the global pandemic. Over the last five years, the 2020 Global Terrorism Index (GTI) reported a 709% increase in fatalities from far-right motivated extremism (GTI-2020). On the other hand, all other forms of terrorism have decreased by 15%. This includes religious organizations as well. Similarly, according to 2019 figures, religious group attacks such as Islamic State have declined by up to 40% regarding lethality (GTD-2020). This drop compared to the far-right is steadfast, as it reflects the loss of the organization's professed caliphate, which covered large areas of Bagdad and Damascus. Therefore, on one side, the GTI has reported a rise in far-right terrorism; on the other, it has stated a decline in religious extremism. Thus, the chapter aims to explore the trajectory of the militant organizations. For this purpose, the researcher intends to apply the "Terrorist

Lifecycle" framework and seeks to answer the following questions in the following chapter:

> Why is far-right terrorism increasing over religious extremism?
>
> Which conditions compelled the militant outfits to either hibernate or recuperate during the outbreak of COVID-19?
>
> What are the factors that provide an impetus to terrorist groups to perpetuate violence in the wake of the global pandemic?

LITERATURE REVIEW

COVID-19 has hampered overall terrorist operationalization. In addition, such crises lead to the evolution of conspiracy theories. These theories are then used to garner popular support and to call for violence to target minority communities or to contest government legitimacy. Such crisis scenarios postulate that the current order has failed to address the core and central issues of the community (Comerford 2020).

For instance, the monitoring of several religious groups' online discourse revealed that the cadres of these militant outfits used this natural disaster to sensitize people about the need to establish a revolutionary Sharia-based Islamic State. Various organizations, including Syrian Jihadist groups, have labeled the pandemic as a "harbinger of the apocalypse" (Stalinsky 2020; Comerford and Davey 2020). *Hayat-Tahrir-al-Shaam* also posits the possibility of political and economic collapse and a geopolitical opportunity for their cause. Similarly, the virus has been dubbed as a "Soldier of God" by the ISIS magazine *Al-Naba* (Norlen 2020; Wall Street Journal 2020). Whereas the narrative of South Asian Afghan militant groups is such that the Taliban looks at the spread of contagion as a punishment for mankind's disobedience and sins (Botobekov 2021). In addition, the Islamic Revolutionary Guard Corps of Iran, a US-designated Foreign Terrorist organization, claimed that the outbreak resulted from a "Zionist biological terror attack" (Arabi 2020). On the other hand, *Al-Shabaab* blamed the spread of the coronavirus in Somalia on "crusader forces" (Shire 2020).

Also, Jihadi propaganda has attempted to highlight the shortcomings of democratic states in responding to COVID-19. Instead, these groups emphasized the efficacy of the Islamic response to the virus (Norlen 2020). By focusing on the same line, many religious groups have utilized their official social media channels to portray their state-building credentials and governing skills as superior to the contemporary governing regimes (Comerford and Davey 2020). The UN Counter-Terrorism Executive Department (UN CTED) has used this to endorse itself as an alternative service provider in areas with poor governance (United Nations 2020). The UN CTED has already cautioned the member states that the global pandemic supported the militants in accessing an increasingly online captive audience. The more tactical innovations spurred by the virus, the more opportunities it would present for radicalization and mobilization (UN CTED 2020).

In the same context, far-right groups (FRGs) have declared democracy a failure, citing the global health crisis. As a result, such factions appealed to wider extremist constituencies for insurrectional violence by disseminating conspiratorial hate speech. Various unregulated imageboard websites, discussion platforms, and encrypted messaging Android apps are used to spread extremist content. These include 8chan or 4chan, Voat, and Telegram, in that order (Institute for Strategic Dialogue 2020). These platforms explain how Liberals, Muslims, and Black Americans who were deemed enemies were attacked (Kyler and Azman 2020; New York Times 2020; Atlantic 2020). Over a million posts on the sites and platforms call for violent attacks (Pantucci and Ong 2021). The rapidly expanding Telegram Channels were also used to rally "broad-based anti-government supporters," colloquially known as *Boogaloo*, to join forces in armed conflict (New York Times 2020). This threat diversification poses a sophisticated security challenge.

The scholars of terrorism studies, such as Bruce Hoffman and Colin Clarke, described the global pandemic as a shift from a "monochromatic threat from Salafi-Jihadist groups like Al-Qaeda and IS to a kaleidoscope of new threats from the Boogaloo's and white supremacists" (Washington Post 2020; Comerford 2020). Similarly, the domestic terrorism threat posed by QAnon has increased during the lockdown (Ong 2020). Furthermore, during the COVID-19 crisis, several far-right pages and channels have seen a dramatic increase in interest in the elites. It has been claimed that prominent figures such as George Soros and Bill Gates are involved in a Jewish plot to gain social control (Broderick 2020). Economic downturns, geopolitical uncertainty, and societal polarization might lead to violent extremism and terrorism, with some wings rising and others falling. However, its applicability in the aftermath of COVID-19 is yet to be investigated.

METHODOLOGY

The chapter will present a qualitative and analytical study that uses secondary sources such as journal articles and archives kept by research institutions. The empirical data used in this study is based on news reports published in major newspapers. In addition, the statements of cadres from various factions of FRGs are given due consideration. These obtained statements are subjected to activist interpretation. Methodologically, the author concentrated on Telegram's secure Android platform for statement collection. This app was chosen because it is impossible to track users and thus contains authentic information about intended or perpetrated violent maneuvers. Furthermore, Facebook, Instagram, and Twitter were avoided primarily because information about violence is quickly removed from these social media sites. Aside from that, the chapter will use the Terrorist Life Cycle and Social Movement Theory to answer the research questions.

Terrorist Life Cycle Framework

Generally, militant organizations are ephemeral. According to critical terrorism scholars, 90% of militant outfits have existed for less than a year. This indicates that terrorist organizations' life cycles are short, and only a small number can continue with violent operations for an extended period. The transformation of militant organizations occurs due to the interaction of numerous factors that affect the overall trajectory of the violent movement.

The terrorist lifecycle is a framework for understanding and analyzing the trajectory of a militant organization. These organizations are too complex to comprehend (Phillips 2011). Therefore, all militant groups don't need to fit into all four stages of (a) Emergence, (b) Rise, (c) Downfall, and (d) Demise. The first stage elaborates on the birth of a social movement and the struggle the group has to bear for the initiation of violent acts (Phillips 2011). This stage is prolonged. A newly born organization has to undergo a constructive phase in which a commonly shared ideology is identified and accepted. This stage is the most crucial step as it derives popular support and helps recruitment. It inculcates zeal and zest among the cadres, which is fruitful for their training. A militant group cannot be created without the leaders' commitment, ability to organize the group, communication among the cadres, and a shared ideology (Iqbal and Silva 2013).

In the second stage of the terrorist lifecycle, the operational and strategic aspects of the violent movement are investigated (Iqbal and Silva 2013). The groups improve their operational capabilities (Phillips 2011). This is accomplished by increasing the lethality of violent assaults. Furthermore, grassroots support distinguishes this phase, resulting in additional funding, logistical assistance, and aiding the group in gaining political legitimacy. With all this, a company encourages its recruits to engage in violent behavior (Gupta 2008). The government retaliates as long as violence is used. This causes the terrorist organization to retaliate with violence, making it more lethal (Robert 1969). Violence is sometimes used to counter other competing movements (Iqbal and Silva 2013). Terrorist organizations may have a cooperative relationship with one another, but mostly it appears to be antagonistic (Sirseloudi 2005). This indicates that the group tries to exert its influence to coerce other militant outfits in the same political environment (Iqbal 2017).

The third phase is of downfall. Here, the organization loses its operational capacity to launch attacks. Therefore, a decline is observed in the frequency of violent acts from the perpetrators. This is due to the weakened political objectives, which ultimately cause a decline in popular support (Iqbal and Silva 2013). When a group loses popular support, it is extremely difficult for leaders to maintain cohesion among group members, and thus internal splits emerge. This causes instability and lowers the morale of the movement. It also reduces the militant group's funding and logistical support. As a result, the lethality of militant outfit attacks falls (Iqbal 2017).

The final stage is demise, which represents the terrorist organizations' renunciation of violence. Typically, a political goal's demise occurs because it is no longer relevant in a changing political environment (Phillips 2011). A leader's or other group members' death or incarceration could cause the group's demise (Cronin 2009). This lowers the morale of the group's remaining top-tier leadership, who maintain internal cohesion. Internal schisms can occasionally form new splinter groups, which are typically more lethal than their parent organizations (Iqbal 2017). Overall, this phase is distinguished by an end to all violent activities (Phillips 2011).

The theory is used to identify significant rise and fall causal factors. Among the "rise" contributing factors, the author paid special attention to popular support, which aids in the amplification of the recruitment process. Furthermore, commitment, operational capabilities in times of crisis, political legitimacy gained through pandemic framing to further political objectives, and the use of violence to counter rival movements are all critical. However, the fall has been attributed to a loss of operational capacity, weakened political objectives, a drop in popular support, sometimes due to internal splits, and a leader's assassination or imprisonment. During times of crisis, political goals can become irrelevant in a changing political environment (Cronin 2009).

This chapter is divided into three sections. The first section distinguishes between Far-Right and Religious Extremism. The second section focuses on the rise of far-right extremism in the aftermath of the global pandemic. The final section explains how the extreme right gained traction and which events bolstered their operational capabilities. The Analytical Discussion concludes the chapter.

DISTINGUISHING FAR-RIGHT EXTREMISM FROM RELIGIOUS EXTREMISM

Far-right extremism, addressing hatred, racism against minorities, ultra-nationalism, white supremacy, Islamophobia, anti-Semitism, and xenophobia (White 2020), is not a new phenomenon. Over the last year, the intensity of this type of extremism has increased (GTI-2020). Far-right extremism is a fluid and complex milieu of rebel movements that operate online and offline. There has recently been an increase in lethal attacks targeting transnational political objectives.

Many violent groups have religious traditions that are a part of their indigenous, cultural, or racial identity. Scholars of critical terrorism studies argued that religious outfits have peculiar objectives that refer to apocalyptic ideals, creating a theocracy, or capturing the land occupied by other religions (Gregg 2014). As a result, religious extremists are willing to kill because they believe in theologies that justify violence in the service of God. They have no sympathy for their victims because they regard them as God's enemies. And they are willing to give up their own lives because they expect massive and immediate afterlife rewards in exchange for "martyrdom" (Wintrobe 2003; Sprinzak 2000).

FINDINGS

2020 is the year where violence spread through contagion. White supremacists reaped the benefits of the global pandemic, especially when global security forces were more inclined to break down global jihadism. The most visible leaders are not organizational or spiritual figures but rather discrete attackers who have labeled themselves as Saint Crusius, Saint Breivik, and Hail Saint Tarrant, among others (Weiner 2020).

In recent years, social media sites have used significant resources to combat the spread of jihadi content (Pantucci and Ong 2021). Companies began to do the same for far-right extremists spreading COVID-19-related content and instructing their cadres to intentionally infect healthcare workers, security forces personnel, or minorities by coughing or sneezing (Vieten 2020). To combat such acts, Facebook deactivated many accounts associated with far-right extremists who planned to bring weapons to protests over George Floyd's assassination (Daily Mail 2020; Washington Post 2020).

Law enforcement and other agencies monitor various internet applications for this purpose. Europol, for example, is collaborating with the encrypted messaging app Telegram to contain jihadists by seizing thousands of their Android app accounts. Such initiatives proved to be a significant setback for religiously motivated groups, now attempting to rebuild through alternative means (Flashpoint 2020). However, the rate of content creation outpaced the rate of removal. This is significant because no comparable action has been taken against far-right extremists on social media platforms (Daymon and Criezis 2020).

RELATIVE SURGE IN FAR-RIGHT

The global pandemic has affected the militant trajectory in multiple ways. According to the Terrorist Life Cycle, terrorist organizations are typically exploitative, robust, and rigid in their ideologies and operational capabilities. Adversity enables militant groups to quickly adjust and adapt to any unexpected situation (Iqbal 2017). As a result, some violent far-right organizations are exploiting the current situation to recruit, radicalize, and launch violent maneuvers. The ulterior factors that describe the rise of far-right extremism over other traditional forms of terrorism are given below.

Online Recruitment

Firstly, in the last year, there has been an increase in online recruitment. This aided in the recruitment of more cadres/recruits. Consequently, because of the global lockdown, the groups increased their efforts to recruit new members via social media (Babb and Wilner 2021). So, the target of mainstream terrorist organizations has remained vulnerable to young people who spend more time on the Internet due to the closure of educational institutions, open-door activities, and the loss of employment opportunities (United Nations Institute for Training and Research 2020). As a result, global pandemic-related lockdowns with restrictions on freedoms and local authorities imposing preventive measures through force led to further tensions and disentanglement of various segments of the population (Wood et al. 2021).

Similarly, FRGs operate and organize online. This challenges law and enforcement agencies to identify potential violence perpetrators (Vynck and Nakashima 2021). The right wing uses a variety of online platforms, the most prominent of which are Facebook, Twitter, YouTube, Telegram, wire, line, and so on. These social media platforms host right-wing extremist ideologies because they are better framed (Vynck and Nakashima 2021). David Lane's Fourteen Words is one such example. He is a founding member of the white supremacist group "Order." The fourteen words are "We must ensure the survival of our people and a future for white children" (Ward 2021). Furthermore, to attract young people, these organizations use computer games and various mobile applications.

The far-right's operationalization is not limited to the Internet. Global anti-lockdown demonstrations featured racial, anti-government, and extremist narratives (Guardian 2020). It is most prevalent in the United States, where states with Democratic or liberal governors have enacted strict pandemic policies (Censky 2020). It is also marked by an increase in gun sales as well as armed militias raiding government buildings. This was done to coerce higher-level government officials into changing policies. The plots to kidnap Michigan Governor Gretchen Whitmer (Censky 2020) and Virginia Governor Ralph Northam are an extension of their predetermined strategy (White 2020).

In contrast, religious groups are well-organized networks with leaders and ideologies. As a result, their recruiting strategy is also sophisticated. The recruitment is done primarily through personal acquaintances (Martin 2021). However, religious groups are not only radicalizing on offline platforms; they are also radicalizing on online platforms. Many of the violent groups in this wing use public places to recruit new members (Comerford 2020). These cadres could have come from seminaries or madrassas, or they could have come from a vulnerable demographic, such as the youth (Comerford and Davey 2020). The faulty narratives of extremist organizations easily brainwashed the youth. Travel restrictions and a ban on public gatherings enforced by a global lockdown impede religious wing recruitment to a greater extent (United Nations Institute for Training and Research 2020).

Popular Support

Furthermore, popular support for COVID-19 is gained through misinformation, propaganda, and conspiracy theories. Using interpretive activist discourse, questions about the emergence and success of FRGs can be answered by dissecting the language and symbolism used by FRGs. For example, Hundred Handers, a loose network of inexperienced activists based in the United Kingdom, aims to encourage the mainstreaming of core identitarian principles through guerrilla sticker campaigns (BBC 2021). Most of the slogans, such as "no borders, no defense" and "pubs closed, borders open" (Cogley 2020), linked COVID-19 spread to globalization. Similarly, the *Nordiska Motstandsrorelsens*, or Nordic Resistance Movement (NRM), has been seen on the streets through leafleting, banners, flash mobs, and demonstrations. COVID-19, according to the leader of the NRM's Swedish branch, can bring national uprisings to international forums, ensuring the fortification of revolutionary political forces (Grewal 2020). The far-right specialized in such contemplative strategies, as well as how to frame crisis issues successfully. These propaganda techniques and conspiracy theories aid in recruitment as well. According to these schools of thought, the Coronavirus threat is a deliberate ploy to divert public attention away from more pressing issues.

One of the most significant conspiracy theories was that far-right extremist groups believed that the radiation emitted by 5G towers was spreading the virus. The New York Times reported an increase in the number of arson attacks on 5G technology towers in the United Kingdom. The assaults, according to government officials, were the result of an internet conspiracy theory that declares the spread of COVID-19 to ultra-fast wireless 5G technologies (Satariano and Alba 2020; Fildes, Stefano, and Murphy 2020). Other conspiracy theories have labeled the virus as a bio-engineered weapon designed to reduce the world's population and undermine Trump (Aljazeera 2020). Others created a number of graphics and memes depicting the virus's eagerness to be used as a biological weapon to coerce the masses (SITE Intelligence Special Report 2020). However, mainstream religious groups such as the Islamic State and others have not issued any official call (Kyler and Azman 2020). In conjunction with other environmental factors, the conspiracy theories advanced by FRGs aided violence and narrative development (Amarasingam and Argentino 2020).

Socioeconomic and Environmental Factors

Other reasons that suggest an increase in far-right extremism include socioeconomic and environmental factors. The global economic downturn, coupled with the loss of employment opportunities, provided fertile grounds for radicalizing and recruitment of far-right cadres, thereby increasing their operational capacity (Vieten 2020).

The economic stagnation caused by the global pandemic resulted in prolonged unemployment and subsequent mass impoverishment, forcing the government to close nonessential businesses (Vieten 2021). This has increased the likelihood of violent maneuvers. Some far-right extremists inflicted violence by criticizing local efforts to combat the global pandemic. The masses claimed that the state had taken away their liberties by requiring face masks in public indoor and large outdoor gatherings to prevent the spread of the contagion (Comerford 2020).

The economic downturn cast a negative impact on religious groups. While financing strategies such as using humanitarian relief operations as cover-ups for terrorist financing activities remain viable during the pandemic, the amount of money made or collected may decrease due to the global economic downturn. For example, Indonesian IS supporters have struggled with the economic consequences of COVID-19, as some have been laid off or have seen a decrease in their earnings (Arianti and Taufiqurrohman 2020). Coupled with IS's purported lack of financial support, the loss or significant decrease in income for IS cadres and adherents has resulted in declining revenues for pro-IS groups and cells in Indonesia, such as Jamaah Ansharud Daulah, Jamaah Ansharul Khilafah, and Jamaah Ansharul Khilafah (Arianti and Taufiq-ur-rohman 2020). This has limited these groups' ability to use their funds for violent maneuvers.

HIBERNATION OR RECUPERATION

No doubt, COVID-19 has reduced overall terrorist activity in many states. There has been a remarkable reduction in violence in contexts where extremism is primarily an urban phenomenon, coinciding with the global lockdown. However, COVID-19 appears to have had a significant impact on the trajectory of violence in settings where terrorism occurs as part of a larger conflict, including disputed regions. When operationalization becomes difficult, the militant organization hibernates (Iqbal 2017).

Mass casualty attacks on mosques in Christ Church, New Zealand mark the recuperation of the extreme right violence. The deadly assault claimed the lives of fifty-one people and inspired other shooters to use similar tactics (Pantucci and Ong 2021). Attacks by John Timothy Ernest, Patrick Crusius, Filip Golon, William John, and Stephen Balliet are just a few examples. All these people were said to have applauded Brenton Tarrant's heinous act of violence. The year 2020 represents a continuation and escalation of this threat posed by a large group of far-right militants. To ensure their survival, the ideologues of extreme right organizations have exploited the global pandemic (Pantucci and Ong 2021). The framing of their ideologies revolves around racism, anti-government policies, and anti-globalization ideals.

The convergence of issues in the form of a global pandemic, Black Lives Matter protests, rising political tensions in the run-up to the 2020 Presidential Election, and increased security risks has shed light on how far-right extremists exploit the issues. For example, anti-government fringe groups such as the Boogaloo Movement, QAnon, and the Proud Boys unite over "shared attitudes on the legitimacy of the global pandemic, lockdown orders, and the role of law enforcement and other government officials" (Atlantic 2020; New York Times 2020).

According to Social Movement Theory, the outbreak of COVID-19 provided militant organizations with a political opportunity to gain popular support. The strategies for forming coalitions differ depending on the group. Starting with migration, far-right organizations such as Hundred Handers, a decentralized organization primarily focused on Britain, claim that open borders spread the disease (Cogley 2020). As a result, the emphasis was shifted to border hardening. Other Identitarian groups, such as CasaPound (Bartlett et al. 2012), identified migrants as COVID-19 virus vectors. Along with this, some blame was placed on the Chinese government. Their activism was founded on the idea of "defending European borders." The far-right extremists claim that the spread of the virus could have been stopped by closed borders (Bieber 2020).

Globalization is another factor cited by FRGs. Virus spread is viewed as a by-product of globalization by organizations such as the German IBD (Caniglia 2020). They also agreed that the crisis would not be the last of its kind in this era. The underlying causes are multiculturalism and liberal values. The NRM, for example, has criticized free markets. Every state that relies on the free market, according to them, has failed and has not proven to work in times of crisis (Vieten 2020).

Another factor in the same context is the role of bad governance, which aided the extreme right's ability to extend violence. As interpreted by these groups, the contemporary era's capitalist themes also advocated for bad governance. The government, according to the hundred-handers, prioritizes the economy over the lives of its citizens. Similarly, NRM considered how poor governance influenced the demand and supply process. This refers to a lack of hospital or healthcare facilities, as well as police or military resources (Vieten 2020).

ANALYTICAL DISCUSSION

COVID-19 proved to be a catalyst, hypercharging the contemporary trends of global terrorism. According to the GT index, it may also catalyze the trend of political ferocity and depict a significant increase in far-right terrorism in Europe, North America, and Oceania. Previously, Asia was a fragile continent in this regard. Terrorists seeking to transform the system of governance, world order, and societies through violence, according to historical precedents, generally seek to exploit such crises to fulfill their objectives (Jones et al. 2020).

With the start of the COVID-19 crisis, some FRGs declared that democracy was a disaster and called for insurrectional violence. The goal was to opportunistically broaden extremist constituencies using the ongoing pandemic to spread conspiratorial hate speech.

One of the most important distinguishing factors between religious groups such as the Islamic State and the far-right in general is organizational setting. Religious organizations are centralized and managed by a hierarchical organizational structure. Although only for a short time, the Islamic State had established a quasi-government that had taken control of large swaths of territory in Iraq and Syria. Abu Musab Al Suri, a prominent figure behind Al

Qaeda's post-9/11 strategy, also argued that in order to ensure survival, the movement should be transformed from its traditional hierarchical structure to a decentralized setting. He described an organization's centralization as fragile and vulnerable (Amarasingam and Argentino 2020).

In contrast, the far-right is largely decentralized. The increased frequency of lone wolf attacks in recent years is due to the presence of multiple centers of influence. These online self-radicalized cadres of far-right ideologies attempt to seize control of the situation. Some even turned themselves into weapons to hasten the bioterrorism (Kyler and Azman 2020).

Militant organizations become more adaptable, flexible, resilient, innovative, and inclusive as they decentralize, and they may become more lethal as a result (Gunaranta 2002). Their less structured affiliations amplify the threat posed by more traditional militant organizations. The threat's disaggregated nature makes it difficult to predict, detect, anticipate, track, isolate, prosecute, and ultimately defeat (White 2020).

Framing is important in addition to the organizational setting. The formation of far-right organizations began on online platforms. These platforms function as an infinite number of virtual rallies where synchronization can take place in real-time despite vast distances. This facilitates "hive terrorism," as Koehler defines it, in which a spontaneously formed crowd quickly disperses after violence perpetration (Koehler 2019). Terrorist disbandment makes it difficult to counter, curtail, and, most importantly, identify them.

This operationalization of far-right terrorists contributes to the perception of global far-right extremism with a unified purpose. As a result, the far-right version of extremism, which was previously thought to be primarily local, is now considered a transnational movement.

When considering the likely increase in violence perpetrated by FRGs in the coming years, framing skills are critical. FRGs' actions are highly responsive to their political surroundings. To frame the crisis issues, these organizations used diagnosis, prognosis, and motivational elements. The diagnostic element, as the name implies, elaborates on the root causes of the global pandemic's spread. The COVID-19 crisis is deeply rooted in globalization, migration, and other issues, such as mal-governance for Identitarian and National Socialist FRGs.

Diagnosis is incomplete without prognosis, which helps to rule out a viable solution to the problem or key issue identified. For instance, for the identified migration problem, the suggested solution by the FRGs is the hardening of borders. Europe should eliminate the porous borders to curtail this disease (Jones et al. 2020). Similarly, the issues created by globalization can be countered by the adherence to Nationalism. And, for mal-governance, which is advocated by the capitalist themes, the possible way out deliberated by the FRGs is the need to counter capitalist themes.

FRGs mass mobilization is based on motivation (Auger 2020), encouraging individuals to participate in collective actions. Typically, catchphrases are used to entice the grassroots. For example, statements such as "open borders spread the disease" (Owen 2020), "Closed Borders: The Best Vaccine," and "No Border, No Defense" (Willson 2020; Emanuel et al. 2020) are used to oppose migration. While those FRGs that supported globalization coined phrases such as "Nationalism would have prevented this," "pubs closed, borders open" (Cogley 2020), and "our government valued the economy more than our lives" (Vieten 2020). Similarly, one of the statements presented with the mal governance diagnosis is, "inadequate hospital, police, and military resources, if to govern is to anticipate, we can consider that we are no longer governed."

Terrorists, according to Vincent Auger, regularly exploit the issues in novel ways. These crisis issues appear out of nowhere. They are terrifying because they cannot be predicted, nor can their tragic outcome be predicted (Auger 2020). One such crisis issue is the spread of the Coronavirus. Historical precedents can also demonstrate the ability of FRGs to exploit such grave concerns. Previously, the US Department of Homeland Security reported that the election of Barack Obama in 2009, as well as the economic recession, was being used by far-right organizations to increase recruitment and propaganda activity (Berger 2020). This also suggests that FRGs' framing strategies are commendable.

RESULTS

Online recruitment strategies, popular support, and socioeconomic and environmental factors fuel several far-right militant, violent assaults. Firstly, the increased screen time of the youth following the global lockdown increased recruitment opportunities. Second, it is known from the interpretive activist discourse that the FRGs gain popular support through propaganda and misinformation deeply rooted in appealing conspiracy theories (Al-Jazeera 2021). Other socioeconomic and environmental factors, such as poverty and job loss, are also at work, skillfully framed to coerce and radicalize a relatively larger segment of the population (Vieten 2020).

CONCLUSION

It has been empirically proven that the far-right has outperformed all other forms of terrorism in the West. However, a global surge is also expected. But this does not mean that religious extremism will vanish from the world. The extreme right organizations are on edge when it comes to framing crisis issues, such as the one presented to the world in the form of a global pandemic. Their framing abilities appear more logical than an abstraction accused of being deeply rooted in religion. Furthermore, as previously stated, the organizational structure in the form of decentralization strengthens the operational capacity of FRGs and presents some of the most significant challenges to law enforcement and security forces in countering violent maneuvers.

NOTES

1. M. F. Raza. National Defence University, Islamabad, Pakistan and Military College of Signals, (Affiliated with National University of Sciences and Technology), Rawalpindi Cantt. Email: maheenfarhatraza@hotmail.com

2. M. A. Raza. Air University, Islamabad, Pakistan. Email: prof.maliraza@gmail.com

BIBLIOGRAPHY

Amarasingam, Amarnath, and Marc-André Argentino. "The QAnon Conspiracy Theory: A Security Threat in the Making." *CTC Sentinel* 13, no. 7 (2020): 37–44.

Arianti, V., and Muh Taufiqurrahman. "The Impact of COVID-19 on Terrorist Financing in Indonesia." *Diplomat*, 11 November 2020. https://thediplomat.com/2020/11/the-impact-of-covid-19-on-terrorist-financing-in-indonesia/ accessed 2 April 2021.

Auger, Vincent A. "Right-Wing Terror." *Perspectives on Terrorism* 14, no. 3 (2020): 87–97.

Babb, Casey E., and Alex S. Wilner. "Exploiting Chaos: How Malicious Non-State Actors Leverage COVID-19 to Their Advantage in Cyberspace." In *Stress Tested: The COVID-19 Pandemic and Canadian National Security*, edited by Leah West, Thomas Juneau, and Amarnath Amarasingam, 33–50. University of Calgary Press, 2021. https://doi.org/10.2307/j.ctv25m8djx.6.

Bartlett, Jamie, Jonathan Birdwell, and Mark Littler. "The Rise of Populism in Europe Can Be Traced Through Online Behaviour." In *The New Face of Digital Populism*, 2011. London: Demos. https://demos.co.uk/wp-content/uploads/files/Demos_OSIPOP_Book-web_03.pdf.

Berger, J. M. "How White Nationalists Learned to Love Donald Trump." *Politico Magazine* 25 (2016). https://www.politico.com/magazine/story/2016/10/donald-trump-2016-white-nationalists-alt-right-214388/

Bieber, Florian. "Global Nationalism in Times of the COVID-19 Pandemic." *Nationalities Papers* 50, no. 1 (2022): 13–25.

Botobekov, Uran. "How Central Asian Salafi-Jihadi Groups are Exploiting the Covid-19

Pandemic: New Opportunities and Challenges." *Religious Studies* 21 (2021): 107.

Broderick, Ryan. "Qanon Supporters and Anti-Vaxxers are Spreading a Hoax That Bill Gates Created the Coronavirus." *BuzzFeed News* 23 (2020). https://www.buzzfeednews.com/article/ryanhatesthis/qanon-supporters-and-anti-vaxxers-are-spreading-a-hoax-that

Bryman, Alan. *Social Research Methods*. Oxford University Press, 2016.

Caniglia, Mattia, Linda Winkler, and Solène Métais. "The Rise of the Right-Wing Violent Extremism Threat in Germany and its Transnational Character." *European Strategic Intelligence and Security Center* 2 (2020). http://www.esisc.org/upload/publications/analyses/the-rise-of-the-right-wing-violent-extremism-threat-in-germany-and-its-transnational-character/ESISC_The%20Rise%20of%20the%20Right-Wing%20Violent%20Extremism%20Threat%20in%20Germany%20.pdf.

Cogley, M. "How the Alt-Right Is Using COVID-19 as Cover to Spread Propaganda." *Telegraph*, 16 June 2020.

"Coronavirus: Arrests Over 'Disgusting' Racist COVID-19 Stickers." *BBC News*, 16 April 2021.

Comerford, M. *How Have Terrorist Organizations Responded to COVID-19?* Sydney: Institute for Economics and Peace, 2020.

Comerford, Milo, and Jacob Davey. "Comparing Jihadist and Far-Right Extremist Narratives on Covid-19." *Global Network on Extremism & Technology*, last modified April 27, 2020.

Cronin, Audrey Kurth. *How Terrorism Ends: Understanding the Decline and Demise of Terrorist Campaigns*. STU-Student edition, Princeton University Press, 2009. JSTOR, http://www.jstor.org/stable/j.ctt7rjbs. Accessed 25 Sept. 2023. accessed 26 September 2023.

Davey, Jacob. "COVID-19 Disinformation Briefing No. 2." (2020).

Division for Peace, Impact of COVID-19 on Violent Extremism and Terrorism. Geneva, Switzerland: United Nations Institute of Training and Research, 2020. https://unitar.org/sites/default/files/media/file/Factsheet%20CT%20Printed.pdf .

Efrat, Asif, S. Hirsch-Hoefler, and M. Friedman. "Report on the Relationship Between Terrorist Threats and Governance Conditions in the European Union." (2021).

Emanuel, Ezekiel J., Govind Persad, Adam Kern, Allen Buchanan, Cécile Fabre, Daniel

Halliday, Joseph Heath et al. "An Ethical Framework for Global Vaccine Allocation." *Science* 369, no. 6509 (2020): 1309–1312.

Global Terrorism Index 2020: Measuring the Impact of Terrorism. Sydney, Australia: Institute for Economics & Peace, 2020. http://visionofhumanity.org/reports accessed 28 December 2020.

Gregg, Heather S. "Defining and Distinguishing Secular and Religious Terrorism." *Perspectives on Terrorism* 8, no. 2 (2014): 36–51.

Grewal, K. "Excuse to Destroy Our People': Far-Right Groups Weaponise Coronavirus to Further Their Agenda." *Print*, March 28, 2020.

Gunaratna, Rohan. "Inside Al Qaeda: Global Network of Terror." (2002).

Gupta, Dipak K. *Understanding Terrorism and Political Violence: The Life Cycle of Birth, Growth, Transformation, and Demise*. Routledge, 2020.

Iqbal, Khuram, and Sara De Silva. "Terrorist Lifecycles: A Case Study of Tehrik-e-Taliban Pakistan." *Journal of Policing, Intelligence and Counter Terrorism* 8, no. 1 (2013): 72–86.

Iqbal, Khuram. "The Downfall of Daesh in the Middle East and Implications for Global Security." *Corvinus Journal of International Affairs* 2, no. 2–3 (2017): 76–84.

Jones, Seth G., Catrina Doxsee, and Nicholas Harrington. *The Right-Wing Terrorism Threat in Europe*. Center for Strategic and International Studies (CSIS), 2020.

Koehler, Daniel. *Violence and Terrorism from the Far-Right: Policy Options to Counter an Elusive Threat*. ICCT Policy Brief, 2019. The Hague: International Centre for Counter-Terrorism, 2019.

Kosnar, M., and Phil Helsel. "FBI Says Man Killed in Missouri Wanted to Bomb Hospital Amid Coronavirus Epidemic." *NBC News*, March 25, 2020.

Lenthang, Es. "Facebook Removes Another 900 Accounts Linked." *Daily Mail*, June 17, 2020.

Martin, R. "Future Trends: Far-Right Terrorism in the UK—A Major Threat?" April 14, 2021.

McNeil-Willson, Richard. *Framing in Times of Crisis: Responses to COVID-19 Amongst Far-Right Movements and Organisations*. International Centre for Counter-Terrorism, 2020.

"Member States Concerned by the Growing and Increasingly Transnational Threat of Extreme Right Wing Terrorism." CTED Trends Alert, April 2020.

Norlen, Tova C. "The impact of COVID-19 on Salafi-Jihadi Terrorism." *Connections* 19, no. 2 (2020): 11–24.

Ong, Kyler. "Ideological Convergence in the Extreme Right." *Counter Terrorist Trends and Analyses* 12, no. 5 (2020): 1–7.

Ong, Kyler, and Nur Aziemah Azman. "Distinguishing Between the Extreme Far-right and Islamic State's (IS) Calls to Exploit COVID-19." *Counter Terrorist Trends and Analyses* 12, no. 3 (2020): 18–21.

Our Nine Political Points. Nordic Resistance Movement, 17 November. https://nordicresistancemovement.org/our-nine-political-points/ accessed April 28, 2021.

Owen, David. "Open Borders and the COVID-19 Pandemic." *Democratic Theory* 7, no. 2 (2020): 152–159.

Pantucci, Raffaello, and Kyler Ong. "Persistence of Right-Wing Extremism and Terrorism in the West." *Counter Terrorist Trends and Analyses* 13, no. 1 (2021): 118–126.

Peterson, Hannah. "Give Me Liberty or Give Me Death? A Comparative Analysis of Public Health Responses to the COVID-19 Pandemic, Their Efficacy, and Their Legal Implications." *Arizona Journal of International and Comparative Law* 38 (2021): 319.

Robert, T. G. *Why Men Rebel*. New Jersey: Princeton University Press, 1969.

Satariano, Adam, and Davey Alba. "Burning Cell Towers, Out of Baseless Fear They Spread the Virus." *The New York Times* 11 (2020).

Shire, Mohammed Ibrahim. "More Attacks or More Services?: Insurgent Groups' Behaviour During the COVID-19 Pandemic in Afghanistan, Syria, and Somalia." *Behavioral Sciences of Terrorism and Political Aggression* 14, no. 4 (2022): 288–311.

Sirseloudi, Matenia P. "How to Predict the Unpredictable: On the Early Detection of Terrorist Campaigns." *Defense & Security Analysis* 21, no. 4 (2005): 369–386.

Stalinsky, Steven. "What Jihadists Are Saying About the Coronavirus." *MEMRI Daily Brief* 216 (2020): 6.

Stephenson, M., and Stewart Bell, "Violent Extremists May Exploit Coronavirus Pandemic, Target Hospitals, Threat Report Warns." *Global News*, April 8, 2020.

"The Far-Right's Online Discourse on COVID-19 Pandemic." SITE Intelligence Special Report, March 26, 2020.

"The 'Superspreaders' Behind COVID-19 Conspiracy Theories." *Aljazeera*, February 15, 2021.

Timberg, Craig. "As Trump Warns of Leftist Violence, a Dangerous Threat Emerges from the Right-Wing Boogaloo Movement." *The Washington Post*, June 18, 2020.

Vieten, Ulrike M. "The 'New Normal' and 'Pandemic Populism': The COVID-19 Crisis and Anti-Hygienic Mobilisation of the Far-Right." *Social Sciences* 9, no. 9 (2020): 165.

Vynck, G. D., and Ellen Nakashima. "Far-Right Groups Move Online Conversations from Social Media to Chat Apps- and Out of View of Law Enforcement." *Washington Post*, January 18, 2021.

Ward, Janet. "Confronting Hatred: Neo-Nazism, Antisemitism, and Holocaust Studies Today." *The Journal of Holocaust Research* 35, no. 2 (2021): 67–74.

Weiner, R.U. "The Growing White Supremacist Menace: COVID-19 Has Been a Boon for Far-Right Extremists." *Foreign Affairs*, June 23, 2020.

Wilson, Jason. "The Rightwing Groups Behind Wave of Protests Against Covid-19 Restrictions." *The Guardian* 17 (2020).

Wood, Reed, Gina Yannitell Reinhardt, Babak RezaeeDaryakenari, and Leah C. Windsor. "Resisting Lockdown: The Influence of COVID-19 Restrictions on Social Unrest." *International Studies Quarterly* 66, no. 2 (2022): sqac015.

Conclusion

Emerging Trends of Multipolarity and Geoeconomics in Global Governance

Lorenzo Fiorito[1], Senthan Selvarajah[2], and Nesrin Kenar[3]

It is clear that the global security order is changing: witness the ongoing rise of China, Russia's attack on Ukraine (allegedly in response to NATO expansion), and the simultaneous economic weakening of Europe and the United States. Since the end of World War II, few—if any—realignments of geopolitical influence and the balance of forces have been so serious. This era highlights the constant tension between a rules-based liberal international order and a world order characterized by economic and military weaponry power contests. By some measures, this is the most crucial change in global power since the transformation of Europe, beginning 500 years ago, from a provincial Asian peninsula into a dominant force that shaped history. But these changes to the global order have a special effect on Asia today. Each author in this work has provided new evidence for the hypothesis that we are in an epoch of global change that affects Asia in particular ways.

Part I showed that the rise of China merits an in-depth discussion because it is inherently a security consideration on its own. China's rise poses a challenge to the neoliberal, post–Cold War order in several ways as it seeks to reshape its sphere of influence in Asia. These include power projections in Central Asia, the risk of conflict with the United States, and the potentially emerging trends of multipolarity and geoeconomics in global governance.

John Miglietta, in "Great Power Rivalry and the Politics of Central Asia," showed how the United States, China, Russia, and Iran all exert their interests through various means in different countries of Central Asia. This region has high geostrategic importance because oil and gas supplies to these powers often originate in, and are carried through, these Central Asian states. While several of these countries are NATO members, Chinese geostrategic interests in the Xinjiang province mean that many Central Asian states bordering China—and thus must consider their security through that lens.

In "China's Geoeconomic Strategy and Sri Lanka's International Commercial Dispute Resolution Centre," Lorenzo Fiorito argued that the post–Cold War era seems to have marked the rise of commercial strategy that relied on state interests to achieve security aims. Based on this geoeconomic premise, he showed that China's Port City project in Sri Lanka, and particularly its International Commercial Dispute Resolution Centre, could develop into a tool through which China projects geoeconomic influence over international commercial transactions in South Asia, creating effects for regional security.

In their "Implications of Quadrilateral Security Dialogue (QUAD) on South Asia," Rajib Timalsina and Indivar Paudel have analyzed in detail how important South Asia is to China and how important China is to South Asian countries for economic and trade and development opportunities. They stressed the need for South Asian countries to weigh the pros and cons of China's Belt and Road Initiative (BRI) project and act judiciously to take advantage of the economic and technological opportunities that can be derived from the QUAD so as not to lead to further escalation of tensions between countries in the region.

Muamer Hirkić postulated that China is poised to challenge the US's global supremacy. However, it may not be competing for sole superpower status, but may rather usher in an era of multipolarity. China seems keen to avoid the "Thucydides Trap," by which a rising power must inevitably confront a declining power militarily, with the United States. The Cold War mentality of a bipolar world would thus be outdated. China's diplomatic approach of soft power is nonetheless subject to volatile challenges, presenting a risk to its overall vision of a "peaceful rise."

Part II continued by examining the changing nature of warfare and weaponry. These realist approaches to security directly oppose the foundations of liberal order by positing national security as a zero-sum game. In warfare, due to the technological capacities that permit it, there can only be winners and losers.

In "A Profitable Enterprise: The Emergence of Private Military Companies as Stakeholders in International Security," Ushmayo Bhattacharya has shown that private military companies (PMCs) have changed the nature of mercenary enterprise by adopting a corporate structure. The state, which in modern times took on the monopoly of violence, now increasingly "outsources" significant parts of that monopoly since the Gulf War. Incorporation, Bhattacharya argues, allows PMCS to circumvent the liberal controls that international law places over mercenaries.

This realist challenge to liberal conceptions of order reappears in Ghazala Yasmin Jalil's "The New Nuclear Arms Race: Implications for Global Security." Jalil demonstrated that nuclear proliferation appears to be on the rise, for although fewer nuclear weapons exist now than in the past, more countries possess them. Particularly between Russia and the United States, this promises to present challenges to peace. However, every country that possesses nuclear weapons must consider its nuclear-armed neighbors a threat. The existential threat that this situation poses is very real.

In "A Perilous Nexus: Military Drones, Power, Risk-Taking," Hafssa Fakher Elabiari examined the use of drone technology by Turkey and the United Arab Emirates in Libya. Not only do drones create an increased threat perception for the countries that use them, but they also permit wars to last longer than they otherwise would. The ratio of their cost, compared to their ability to kill, makes them an attractive option for armies. Yet, using drones creates a risk of overconfidence in their accuracy and effectiveness.

Michael Larrick, in his "US-Da Afghanistan Bank Sanctions: An Inelegant Solution to a Self-Imposed Problem," argued that the US President's Executive Order 14064-Protecting Certain Property of Da Afghanistan Bank for the Benefit of the People of Afghanistan was not accidental but rather a long-term effort to expand the power of the "Executive Order." He maintained that the Order is pivotal for understanding Washington's evolving approach of using global finance as a tool to advance their notion of global security, and at the same time raises serious concerns about the legality, and as a consequence legitimacy, of domestic and international financial and security institutions. The implications of this act reach beyond United States–Afghan relations or regional security concerns. It further legitimizes using financial means to influence other States for national security reasons and obfuscates the impact on people.

In his "US Withdrawal from Afghanistan and Its Impact on War on Terror and Peace and Stability in South Asia," Aslam Khan argued that the UDS's withdrawal from Afghanistan had severe implications for the war against terror and global order. Mentioning that the withdrawal of the United States is considered a great victory by the jihadist elements around the world, and this has inspired them, he has presented his argument that the withdrawal of the United States has weakened the position of the United States in the global order. He also explained how the regional powers' nonacceptance of the Taliban as a legitimized government in Afghanistan would pose a threat to the peace and security of the South Asian region.

Part III presented some sociological approaches to conflicts and security. People-centered cooperation and collaboration could reduce security risks and thus promote greater harmony (at least, in regional terms). These perspectives have special implications for Asia, both the largest world region and one that has been subject to near-constant power projections from without and within. Asian states thus share one of the greatest interests in appreciating such perspectives within their political approaches.

Iqbal Shailo's chapter, "Exploring the Organic Regional Security Model (ORSM) to Construct a Transborder Security Integration in the South Asian

Region," proposed an "organic" approach to security in South Asia. While South Asian countries have not, to date, shown interest in a regional trade agreement, a free-trade zone could provide an economic foundation for common security. Human development and attention to the environment could eliminate root causes of insecurity by providing a foundation for marginalized populations to secure greater rights and interact with one another while also mitigating risk factors like climate change and flooding. Reduction of nuclear armaments in the region would reduce the chances of the most destructive forms of warfare.

Siavash Chavoshi and Mohammad Reza Saeidabadi, authors of "Trauma, Ontological Insecurity, and States Conflictual Behaviors: The Case of Iran and the West," draw on the Hegelian dialectic of recognition in the conflict between master and slave. The Hegelian perspective here shows the role of trauma and desire in states' pursuit of their objectives. Ultimately, the state aims to universalize its own self-concept, to make this the way that the rest of the world sees it. This approach to overcoming collective trauma—ultimately, to transcend past wounds by overcoming the fear of death—explains Iran's seemingly "irrational" approach to gaining recognition from the West as a whole, and the United States in particular. This notion of recognition is a cultural condition of "ontological security," which may indeed be the ultimate form of security.

In "Socioeconomic Dynamics Fostering Antidemocratic Regimes in the Middle East and North Africa (MENA) Region: Ongoing Wars, Contemporary Issues, and Humanitarian Crises," Mehmet Babacan showed that the MENA region's current instability could be traced back to the collapse of the Ottoman Empire and the experience of Western colonization. In each country that experienced an "Arab Spring," religion and social structure have contributed to instability and actors articulating deeply felt grievances as problems to solve.

Part IV examined the role of nationalism, culture, and nontraditional threats in international relations.

Jean Yves Ndzana Ndzana, in "Coercion in International Affairs: Nature, Instruments, and Conditions of Effectiveness," gave a discursive analysis of the concept of coercion. The political isolation of the target state from the international community serves to create responses that otherwise would not have emerged; similarly, so does economic coercion. Assassinating key political figures is another means of changing state behavior. Weakening or incapacitating the target state's infrastructure and institutions can also become coercive mechanisms. The US's approach to Iran's government provides a case study for each form of political discourse.

In "Does International Relations Theory Fully Understand Culture?," Tamta Tskhovrebadze looks at Huntington's "Clash of Civilizations" thesis through the lens of cooperation. After all, to posit the existence of civilizations is to accept that there is internal cooperation within these units. Cooperation can be instituted through imperialist means such as the spread of cultural norms, language, entertainment, and political marketing. Counterculture can be interpreted as intra-civilizational forms of resistance to these forms of imperialism.

Adriano Mortada, in his chapter "Key Issues of Water Security in International Relations," showed that several factors promise to turn water scarcity into a security issue. As the human population rises, competition for a finite natural resource creates conflicts in some areas and increases the risk of conflict in others. The authors provide evidence that the use of industrialized irrigation links water security with food security. Climate change also means that traditionally available freshwater sources, such as glaciers, disappear. Water is thus becoming an increasingly scarce commodity, even as rising sea levels threaten human habitation of coastal areas.

Part V closed the book by examining the effects of responses to the COVID-19 pandemic on international order. The global spread of an airborne disease elicited cooperation and conflict, illuminating underlying contradictions that were refracted through many unforeseen lenses.

In "Mask Diplomacy on the New Silk Road: The Implications of the COVID-19 Pandemic for China's Quest for Global Leadership," Paulina Kanarek showed that China's approach to vaccines and other pandemic responses brought its underlying security interests to light in regions like Europe and Latin America. Countries participating in the Belt and Road system were more likely to get Chinese assistance, while many others received the benefits of China's "charm offensive." Nevertheless, this belied a contradicting trend toward "Wolf Warrior diplomacy"—a new, more assertive tone in diplomats' communications.

Maheen Farhat Raza and Muhammad Ali Raza, in "The Rise and Fall of Militant Wings in the Wake of COVID-19," showed that COVID-19 oversaw a dip in the fortunes of most militant organizations. Nevertheless, far-right terrorist groups shot to prominence in their activities. These latter organizations used social media platforms to decry the failure of democratic governance and promote agendas of hatred. In the wake of COVID-19, the conspiracy wing of the far right is now a credible threat to Western security, eliciting a measure of popular support. Even rather esoteric conspiracy theories, like QAnon, now pose a credible domestic terror threat within the United States. Russia is marked by becoming the first hypothesized state backer of a white supremacist terror group in the United States.

Each contribution to this book—from various categories, perspectives, and regions of Asia—reinforced its hypothesis. As the global order changes, liberalism is under challenge. This is particularly true in Asia's many, multifaceted, sometimes turbulent regions. Asian states—particularly, though not exclusively, China—attempt to impose their own visions of the global order, and of themselves, upon their spheres of influence and beyond. Some challenges to liberalism come from a realist perspective, others from a wish to externalize an internal self-perception, and yet others from the threat of far-right domestic terrorism. While soft-power approaches seem to become more aggressive as they interact with security dynamics, nuclear proliferation remains a growing concern. The COVID-19 pandemic accelerated nearly every single one of these trends.

If there is a constant to history, change is inevitable. State and civil society actors must prepare for this constant, rather than trying to resist it, if they wish to survive. This adaptability is, arguably, the strength that the most successful actors on the global stage have adopted throughout human history: and when they have failed to do so, such actors have also failed. In the context of economic globalization as a great equalizer, the rise of Asia is one such fact to adapt to.

Tendencies against liberalism are not necessarily so inevitable. Even attempting to withdraw from the liberal order will not turn back the geopolitical tide: a global rebalancing of power. Then, too, liberal political values, like strivings for democracy and equality, are separable from the negative effects of economic liberalism. For many countries, the downsides of this model have provoked a backlash from without and from within. To survive, global liberalism must adapt in the face of these challenges (perhaps, without compromising its core).

If rising Asia and its values are allowed to work changes within a liberal global order, this could yield a new order that sees fewer conflicts, permits greater economic integration, and oversees higher levels of equality between states and within societies. These are all trends that post–Cold War liberalism set into motion.

The chapters of this book have covered the spectrum of perspectives that might allow such a world to emerge: if decision-makers, in Asia and elsewhere, can implement them with diplomacy, accumulated wisdom—and ultimately, with courage.

NOTES

1. L. Fiorito. Centre for Media, Human Rights, and Peacebuilding, London, UK. Email: Lorenzo.fio@protonmail.com

2. S. Selvarajah. Centre for Media, Human Rights, and Peacebuilding, London, UK. Email: senthan.selvarajah@cmhrp.org

3. N. Kenar. Sakarya University, Sakarya, Turkey. Email: nkenar@sakarya.edu.tr

Index

About the Editors and Contributors

EDITORS

Lorenzo Fiorito (LLM) is a legal editor in London, and a researcher at the Centre for Media, Human Rights and Peacebuilding, UK. In addition to academic publications, Lorenzo has contributed to community and NGO media in Canada, several countries across Europe, India, and Sri Lanka. Combining practical and academic experience with the UN, WTO, and the World Bank, Lorenzo's research centers on shared interests between victims of human-rights violations, and economic and political stakeholders in the international trade and investment legal systems.

Dr. Nesrin Kenar is an associate professor at Sakarya University, Faculty of Political Sciences, Turkey. She also serves as co-director of The Centre for Media, Human Rights and Peacebuilding (CMHRP). She was the former Vice Dean of the Faculty of Political Sciences at Sakarya University and Institutional Coordinator of European Union projects and exchange programs at Sakarya University between 2006 and 2018. Nesrin served as Secretary General of the International Peace Research Association (IPRA) between 2012 and 2016 and President of the European Peace Research Association between 2008 and 2012. She is the author of several books, including *Yugoslavia: The National and International Dimension of Yugoslavia Question* and several book chapters and journal articles on globalization, religion and politics, ethnic conflicts, Yugoslavia conflicts, the Bosnia-Herzegovina civil war, international and foreign policy strategies of states, and the Israel-Palestinian question. She was also the coordinator of several EU and internationally-funded projects, including "Xenophobia in the Media" funded by the US Department of State Grants.

Dr. Senthan Selvarajah is co-director at the Centre for Media, Human Rights and Peacebuilding, UK, CEO at the Gate Foundation, UK, and an academic tutor and PhD supervisor for Unicaf University. Previously he worked as a Research and Publications Officer at the Centre for the Study of Human Rights, University of Colombo, Sri Lanka. He has over twenty years of experience as a Journalist, Researcher, Consultant, and Academic. He is an established scholar in media and communication, although his research and publications span multiple disciplines, including international relations, political science, and conflict resolution. He has published several books and edited volumes, including Human Rights Journalism and its Nexus to Responsibility to Protect (2021) and numerous book chapters and journal articles and presented at numerous conferences. He has served as both Executive Committee Member (2016–2018) and Governing Council Member (2014–2018) for the International Peace Research Association (IPRA). He serves as the Convener of the Media, Conflicts, and Journalism Commission of IPRA.

CONTRIBUTORS

Mehmet Babacan was born in Gaziantep, Turkey, in 1986 and completed his bachelor's (International Relations) and Master's (Public Administration) degrees. He gained work experience in public and private sector organisations in various roles. He is a PhD student at the Department of International Relations (IR)/Uludag University in Turkey, and at the same time, working as a project assistant. Babacan has published many articles in various national and international journals about *Turkish foreign policy, Middle East studies, and international relations.*

Ushmayo Bhattacharya is a tactical intelligence analyst working for a corporate risk analysis firm specializing in emerging conflict situations. A motivated researcher with two master's degrees in International Relations and Political Science, his specific areas of interest include African conflict situations with a focus on the Sahel region, security privatization, and Private Military and Security firms. He has experience working for multiple think tanks across India and abroad; and is an early career professional in security intelligence.

Dr. Siavash Chavoshi is a visiting scholar and a teaching assistant at the University of Tehran. Chavoshi is interested in examining the role of shared ideas and norms in shaping states' behavior. In particular, he surveys the correlation between rising states' need for recognition and ontological security and states' conflict-seeking behavior from a Hegelian perspective.

Hafssa Fakher Elabiari is an independent researcher and consultant. Her main research fields are armed conflict, civilians in armed conflict, strategy, and vulnerable populations. Hafssa Fakher Elabiari holds a BA in International Studies from Al Akhawayn University and an MSc in Political Science from Leiden University. She is the founder and host of Decrypted, a weekly podcast that covers various topics in politics and history with simplicity and nuance. She tweets @hafssafakher.

Muamer Hirkić holds an MA in International Relations and Diplomacy from the Faculty of Political Science, University of Sarajevo. He also holds a BA degree in English Language and Literature from the Faculty of Philosophy. Currently, he works as a Researcher at the Faculty of Political Science, University of Sarajevo, and in previous years, he participated in many domestic and international conferences, seminars and workshops dealing with international politics, conflict resolution and peace studies. His research interests include the role of China in the Balkans, soft power politics and great powers competition, as well as radicalization and violent extremism among youth in Bosnia and Herzegovina.

Ms. Ghazala Yasmin Jalil is a Research Fellow at Arms Control and Disarmament Center, Institute of Strategic Studies, Islamabad. She has nearly two decades of experience working on arms control and disarmament issues. She has an extensive number of national and international publications. She has also written chapters in books. Her recent works focus on recent trends in arms control, hypersonic missiles, Tactical nuclear weapons, Indian ballistic missile defense system, missile developments and dynamics of nuclear arms race in South Asia. She holds an MSc in Defence and Strategic Studies and an MPhil in International Relations from Quaid-I-Azam University, Islamabad.

Paulina Kanarek is a career diplomat and a sinologist specializing in China's foreign policy and political economy. She is a Chinese Studies and Economics graduate at the University of Oxford and the University of London (School of Oriental and African Studies). She also received a Yenching Academy scholarship at Peking University. Paulina has several years of experience interacting with China and Latin America across business, diplomacy and education. She also cooperated with the University of Warsaw as a lecturer. Her research interests include the Belt and Road Initiative, Chinese diplomacy and foreign investments in Europe and South America.

Dr. Aslam Khan is Associate Professor in Department of Gandhian and Peace Studies, Mahatma Gandhi Central University, Bihar, India. Prior to this, he served as Professor of International Relations and Dean of the Faculty of Social and Management Sciences Yobe State University, Nigeria. He also served as Associate Professor in the Department of Political Science and International Studies at Bahir Dar University, Ethiopia, Yobe State University, Nigeria, Aligarh Muslim University, Aligarh-INDIA University of Maiduguri, Nigeria and Amhara Leadership Academy, Ethiopia. Dr. Khan has actively engaged in his research pursuits concerning African Politics, the US and South Asia, Indo-Pacific, Peace and Conflict Studies, and Nuclear Issues. His more recent publications include a book titled *Great Game in Indo-Pacific: Rediscovering India's Pragmatism and Paradoxes*, published by Taylor and Francis and three chapters titled "Disarmament Policies," "Institutionalization of Nonviolence," and "Military Deterrence and Statecraft" in "Encyclopaedia of Violence, Peace & Conflict" edited by Lester Kurtz and published by Elsevier.

Michael Larrick is a US lawyer and qualified solicitor in England and Wales. He holds a Juris Doctorate from the University of Denver Sturm College of Law, an LLM with distinction in International and European Business Law from Universidad Pontificia Comillas ICADE, and an LLM with distinction in International Alternative Dispute Resolution from Queen Mary University of London, CCLS. His current practice of law includes international sanctions navigation.

John Miglietta received his BA in Political Science from Fordham University Bronx, NY, and his MA and PhD in Politics from New York University. He is a Professor of Political Science at Tennessee State University in Nashville, Tennessee, USA. His research and teaching interests are international relations with an emphasis on security issues focusing on alliances and arms transfers, American foreign relations, as well as Middle East, and Central Asian politics. He is the author of American Alliance Policy in the Middle East, 1945–1992 (Lexington Books, 2002), editor of Introduction to Political Science: An Anthology (Cognella Publishers, 2021), and Hitler's Allies: The Ramifications of Nazi Alliance Politics in World War II (Routledge, 2022). He has also presented papers at various international, national, and regional academic conferences. He also was a Fulbright Scholar to Tajikistan in academic year 2021–2022 teaching at the University of Central Asia, Khorog Campus.

Adriano Mortada is driven by a perpetual quest for knowledge and growth. With a diverse range of interests and a thirst for exploration, he has always embraced new opportunities. Adriano Mirada thrives on challenges and believes in the power of continuous self-improvement. As an accomplished professional, Adriano Mortada has demonstrated expertise in various fields, including completing the Master's thesis on the Human Right to water and developing business opportunities in renewable energy. Beyond their professional pursuits, Adriano Mortada is avid at reading different scientific magazines, astronomy, and political analysis. Driven by curiosity and a passion for lifelong learning, Adriano Mortada continues to push boundaries and strives for excellence in all endeavors they undertake.

Jean Yves Ndzana Ndzana is an external PhD candidate at Leiden University, Institute of Security and Global Affairs. His research focuses on WMD issues, notably nuclear proliferation. More specifically, he is interested in the role played by coercive diplomacy in leading (potential) proliferators toward nuclear reversal. Thereof, out of three case studies (Iran, Libya, and South Africa), his PhD project investigates under which the US coercive diplomacy could compel a State to abandon its nuclear (weapons) program. Furthermore, Jean Yves Ndzana is interested in Arms Control, Chemical and Biological weapons issues, multilateral negotiations in disarmament and the militarization of outer space. He has also published on multilateral nuclear negotiations, anti-nuclear activism in Africa, using force in international politics and arms control.

Indivar Paudel is an international affairs expert who is currently a faculty member at the Department of International Relations and Diplomacy at Tribhuvan University, Kathmandu. Mr. Paudel holds a postgraduate degree in International Relations and Diplomacy from Tribhuvan University and served as a Senior Research Fellow at the Institute of South Asian Studies, Sichuan University in 2018. He has extensively researched on Iranian political economy and the Iran Nuclear Deal. His expertise includes international political economy, US foreign policy and energy security. His latest research works are titled *Clean Energy Revolution: Why China Owns this Revolution?* and *The Political Economy of the Iran Nuclear Deal: Why Iran agreed to this deal?* Mr. Paudel teaches Foreign Policy Analysis and Politics of Climate Change and Security at Tribhuvan University.

Maheen Farhat Raza is a Visiting Faculty at National Defence University, Islamabad, Pakistan and Military College of Signals, Rawalpindi Cantt, (Affiliated with NUST). She researches on changing dynamics of global politics and issues related to international security, terrorism and counterterrorism. Her research is frequently presented at international conferences.

Muhammad Ali Raza is serving as a Lecturer at Air University, Islamabad. Muhammad Ali is an expert of data analysis tools. He is currently working on meta-materials and metasurfaces. He has supervised a number of projects of national and international repute at Air University, Islamabad Pakistan.

Dr. Mohammad Reza Saeidabadi is an associate professor at Faculty of World Studies at University of Tehran. Throughout his paper, book chapter, and book review, he has regularly sought to reflect on the role of time (historical narratives) and space (territory) in shaping the state's collective identity. In addition, His academic and research record includes more than ten books and many scholarly papers that enabled him to be a well-known academic in Middle East/Iranian politics and media studies.

Dr. Iqbal Shailo, an interdisciplinary scholar and geopolitical scientist, currently works for the Federal Government of Canada. Prior to this position, he worked as a Policy Advisor for the Department of National Defence (DND) Headquarters, Ottawa, for almost four years. He holds a PhD in Critical Geopolitics from Carleton University in Ottawa, Canada. He obtained MA in Public Policy and Public Administration and a Postgraduate Diploma in Journalism from Concordia University in Montreal, Canada. He earned his second MA in English Literature from the University of Dhaka in Bangladesh. In addition, he has three postgraduate diplomas (equivalent to triple MAs), including Arabic Literature, Interpretation, and Speeches. He has also taught at Carleton University for a couple of years. He speaks six languages fluently. Iqbal has recently co-edited *Global Studies* (2022), Vol. 10 published by IJOPEC, UK. He was considered the youngest English development journal editor in the South Asia region. He has presented several papers at numerous academic and policy forums and has numerous international publications.

Rajib Timalsina is Assistant Professor of Conflict, Peace and Development Studies at Tribhuvan University Kathmandu Nepal. He is an Advisory Council Member at People's Action for Learning (PAL Network) and serves the International Peace Research Association (IPRA) as a governing council member. Mr. Timalsina is leading Mobile Arts for Peace Research in Nepal as coinvestigator, and he is also involved with several peace education, culture of peace in schools, arts-based teaching methods and citizen-led assessments in Nepal. Mr. Timalsina leads Annual Status of Education Report (ASER Nepal) research and learning assessment related activities in Nepal. ASER Nepal is a member of Peoples Action for Learning Network (PAL Network). Rajib Timalsina serves various international organizations in different capacities. He is Coinvestigator of AHRC (UK) funded Mobile Arts for Peace (MAP) international research at University of Lincoln (UK).

Tamta Tskhovrebadze is an Associate Professor of International Relations, sharing her expertise in Contemporary and Comparative Politics, Imperialism and Cultural Politics, Conflict and Security, Negotiations and Conflict Resolution. Her research interests include the fragile security architecture of post-Soviet space, Georgia at the crossroads of empires, cultural imperialism, international security issues, and contemporary politics and has contributed to numerous scientific projects, conferences and events, including published articles and books. She holds a Doctoral Degree in Political Science, a Master's Degree in International Relations and Politics and Bachelor's Degree in International Economic Relations. She is a successful Visegrad School of Political Studies graduate with a strong commitment to facilitating "Drivers for Change" and making young leaders rethink their contribution to development. In 2022, she was selected as the Youth Ambassador for the Right to Peace for Georgia in the Global Coalition.

Milton Keynes UK
Ingram Content Group UK Ltd.
UKHW041815231123
433135UK00005B/47

9 781666 949131